Designing Context–Rich Learning by Extending Reality

Jason Braun
Western Governors University, USA

Goran Trajkovski
Western Governors University, USA

A volume in the Advances in Educational
Technologies and Instructional Design (AETID)
Book Series

Published in the United States of America by
IGI Global
Information Science Reference (an imprint of IGI Global)
701 E. Chocolate Avenue
Hershey PA, USA 17033
Tel: 717-533-8845
Fax: 717-533-8661
E-mail: cust@igi-global.com
Web site: http://www.igi-global.com

Library of Congress Cataloging-in-Publication Data

Names: Braun, Jason, 1978- editor. | Trajkovski, Goran, 1972- editor.
Title: Designing context-rich learning by extending reality / edited by
   Jason Braun, Goran Trajkovski.
Description: Hershey, PA : Information Science Reference, [2023] | Includes
   bibliographical references and index. | Summary: "This publication is a
   collection of research and readings on the context-rich learning
   approach that examines the aspects of design, delivery, and assessments.
   The variety of methods and pedagogical frameworks here should building
   speak to educators producing courses and learningware across the
   disciplines. The delivery method, the medium, will change with the times
   and as it best fits the skill studied. It is the richness of the context
   that can allow for learning engagement, the mastery of skills, and
   learning transfer in apprenticeships or in augmented reality"-- Provided
   by publisher.
Identifiers: LCCN 2023002196 (print) | LCCN 2023002197 (ebook) | ISBN
   9781668476444 (h/c) | ISBN 9781668476482 (s/c) | ISBN 9781668476451
   (ebook)
Subjects: LCSH: Inquiry-based learning. | Interdisciplinary approach in
   education. | Interdisciplinary approach to knowledge. |
   Computer-assisted instruction. | Virtual reality.
Classification: LCC LB1027.23 .C663 2023 (print) | LCC LB1027.23 (ebook)
   | DDC 371.33/468--dc23/eng/20230216
LC record available at https://lccn.loc.gov/2023002196
LC ebook record available at https://lccn.loc.gov/2023002197

This book is published in the IGI Global book series Advances in Educational Technologies and Instructional Design (AE-
TID) (ISSN: 2326-8905; eISSN: 2326-8913)

British Cataloguing in Publication Data
A Cataloguing in Publication record for this book is available from the British Library.

For electronic access to this publication, please contact: eresources@igi-global.com.

Advances in Educational Technologies and Instructional Design (AETID) Book Series

Lawrence A. Tomei
Robert Morris University, USA

ISSN:2326-8905
EISSN:2326-8913

MISSION

Education has undergone, and continues to undergo, immense changes in the way it is enacted and distributed to both child and adult learners. In modern education, the traditional classroom learning experience has evolved to include technological resources and to provide online classroom opportunities to students of all ages regardless of their geographical locations. From distance education, Massive-Open-Online-Courses (MOOCs), and electronic tablets in the classroom, technology is now an integral part of learning and is also affecting the way educators communicate information to students.

The **Advances in Educational Technologies & Instructional Design (AETID) Book Series** explores new research and theories for facilitating learning and improving educational performance utilizing technological processes and resources. The series examines technologies that can be integrated into K-12 classrooms to improve skills and learning abilities in all subjects including STEM education and language learning. Additionally, it studies the emergence of fully online classrooms for young and adult learners alike, and the communication and accountability challenges that can arise. Trending topics that are covered include adaptive learning, game-based learning, virtual school environments, and social media effects. School administrators, educators, academicians, researchers, and students will find this series to be an excellent resource for the effective design and implementation of learning technologies in their classes.

COVERAGE

- Social Media Effects on Education
- E-Learning
- Virtual School Environments
- Curriculum Development
- Instructional Design
- Adaptive Learning
- K-12 Educational Technologies
- Instructional Design Models
- Hybrid Learning
- Bring-Your-Own-Device

IGI Global is currently accepting manuscripts for publication within this series. To submit a proposal for a volume in this series, please contact our Acquisition Editors at Acquisitions@igi-global.com or visit: http://www.igi-global.com/publish/.

Titles in this Series

IGI Global
PUBLISHER of TIMELY KNOWLEDGE

701 East Chocolate Avenue, Hershey, PA 17033, USA
Tel: 717-533-8845 x100 • Fax: 717-533-8661
E-Mail: cust@igi-global.com • www.igi-global.com

Table of Contents

Detailed Table of Contents

Section 1
Context-Rich Learning Pedagogy and Instructional Design

Chapter 1
Goran Trajkovski, Western Governors University, USA
Jason Braun, Western Governors University, USA

The purpose of this chapter is to provide a comprehensive overview of context-rich learning, including its theoretical foundations, alignment with various instructional practices, and potential benefits and limitations. The chapter begins with a discussion of the theoretical underpinnings of context-rich learning, exploring its connections to constructivism, experiential learning, problem-based learning, and situated learning. Each section provides specific examples of how context-rich learning aligns with these theories and highlights the benefits of incorporating authentic, real-world experiences into the learning process.

Chapter 2
Lucas Marshall, Western Illinois University, USA
David Rawson, Independent Researcher, USA

In this chapter, we propose using Writing-About-Writing (WAW) principles, first introduced by Elizabeth Wardle and Doug Downs, in community college and vocational school settings—this pedagogical framework, we posit, can better prepare students to navigate diverse writing situations across academic disciplines and professional settings.

Chapter 3
Adam al-Sirgany, 1-Week Critique, USA

This essay explores "context-rich learning" in the arts, cases of its practice, and the virtues and limits thereof. Nevertheless, much of the essay is dedicated to articulating the contexts themselves in which art as a whole and knowledge of the human kind are rooted. The essay explores five examples of context-rich learning that may be applied to different goals under the umbrella of arts education: the Suzuki Method, a musical training method focused on craft skills and learner engagement; the Montessori method, a general education program particularly applicable to the intersection of goal-based learning and individuated student learning styles; the Critical Response Process, a technique of artist-directed critique applicable across artforms and dialogic classrooms; Multiliteracies pedagogies, an academic framework developed by the New London Group and focused on differentiated student (co-learner) experiences; and 1-Week Critique, a nonprofit organization focused on open-access literary education utilizing diversified strategies for writers across circumstances and skillsets.

Chapter 4

Jessica Mannisi, Foundry Art Centre, USA

The educational press and scholarly journals today are swooning over the latest technology, such as virtual reality (VR) or augmented reality (AR), as such tools that have the potential to immerse students into a context-rich environment designed to help them learn by exploring. This chapter will examine how exhibitions and museum engagement help visitors to better relate with the world around them and explore and understand a wide variety of concepts, issues, events, and phenomena. By interacting with the works on display, and with the help of gallery guides and educational programming, visitors learn through in-person, dynamic, and hands-on approaches. The authors will review the literature on the learning theories and the research on the most successful approaches.

Chapter 5

Travis J. Smith, Western Governors University, USA

To make the most context-rich experiences possible and avoid a myriad of problems, designers must keep a user-centric focus. By viewing our educational products through the perspective of the user, we can devise more accessible, diverse, meaningful, and above all enjoyable experiences. Using simple tools such as problem statements, personas, user maps, story boarding, wireframes, low-definition prototypes, and high-definition prototypes, we can consult users first in design to inform us on how to proceed with decisions. Using the simple outlined in the Design Thinking process of empathizing, defining, ideating, prototyping, and testing, we can deliver the most user centric experience possible. The author will show how Design Thinking couples so well with User Experience (UX), walk through what a user study is, what to do with the feedback you get from users, and how to keep the user in mind from inception to launch. In this chapter, the author will discuss the basic framework of UX, where to apply the tools within the framework and why these tools are important when developing context-rich experiences.

Section 2
Assessments and Evaluations for Learning Outcomes

Chapter 6

Heather Hayes, Western Governors University, USA
Goran Trajkovski, Western Governors University, USA
Marylee Demeter, Western Governors University, USA

Assessments, even summative, are part of the learning journey not just for the student, but for the instructors as well. In competency-based education, performance assessments (PAs) are regarded as a highly authentic method of measurement, but their complexity makes them vulnerable to construct-irrelevant variance such as group bias. A differential item functioning (DIF) study was conducted to detect potential bias in a series of information technology PA tasks in which task scenarios were identified (by SMEs) as neutral or potentially controversial, where the latter was hypothesized as more likely to trigger DIF for certain demographics. Given the variety of DIF methods available and their relative strengths and weaknesses, three common statistical methods – Mantel-Haenszel (MH), logistic regression (LR), and Lord's chi-square (LC) - were used followed by a substantive review of DIF items. Hypotheses were largely supported by the analysis and review. Discussion centers on the implication of findings for assessment strategies in education.

Chapter 7

Marylee Demeter, Western Governors University, USA

Diversity, equity, and inclusion (DEI) has become a major focus in higher education in recent years. With increasing attention on equity and fairness, institutions of higher learning are implementing approaches to reviewing and revising curricula and assessments to ensure all students are equally prepared to succeed in their programs of study. The purpose of this chapter is to describe a mixed- methods exploratory approach to identify sources of inequities in a selection of objective and performance assessments as part of a larger project focused on reviewing a selection of courses for issues related to (DEI) attainment. Procedures and results are presented for assessments in four courses across four disciplines (general education, information technology, business, and health professions) along with recommended solutions to even the playing field for all students. A discussion of limitations and next steps to create access to equitable education and assessment opportunities closes this chapter.

Chapter 8

    Sean P. Gyll, Western Governors University, USA
    Karen K. Shader, Western Governors University, USA
    Paul Zikas, ORamaVR, Switzerland
    George Papagiannakis, University of Crete, Greece

Virtual reality (VR) simulations as an assessment tool represent a much-needed effort to move beyond the shortcomings of today's forms-based measures. Within VR, we assess for competency and problem-solving skills versus the content memorization typically supported by multiple-choice assessments. This chapter reviews the development process for the behavioral healthcare coordination VR assessment deployed at Western Governors University. It follows three patients undergoing behavioral health care treatment and highlights essential design, technology, and measurement considerations in developing a VR assessment. For any assessment program, construct validity is the chief validity component. This means that standards-based principles must be maintained to support the inferences drawn from test scores. However, without a framework for developing and maintaining those standards, assessment developers are left to their own devices to determine which practices are most likely to be effective. This chapter provides practical examples to aid assessment professionals in maintaining those standards.

Section 3
Technology and Innovation in Education

Chapter 9

    Zia Nizami, Independent Researcher, USA
    Megan Hudgins, Southern Illinois University, Edwardsville, USA
    Nate Fisher, University of Idaho, USA

The role of technology in education has become salient due to the COVID-19 pandemic. As in-person instruction halted to mitigate the spread of the virus, online classes helped students continue their education. While the benefits of technology in education are clear, is it possible that institutions have gone too far? The dominant forms of new media and technology—radio, television, video cassette recorders, and more recently, the internet—have all been heralded as great boons to pedagogy. Have students and educators benefited from these advances in technology? Why do students from lower socioeconomic groups continue to fail out of the system? Will nascent technologies like virtual and augmented reality change the future of education?

Chapter 10

Canan Koçak Altundağ, Hacettepe University, Turkey
Muhammed Yunus Koçer, Hacettepe University, Turkey

The research aims to design and develop innovative materials supported by Web 2.0 tools to offer solutions to the problems of science and technology teachers in science education based on a context-based learning approach. For this purpose, the design and development research method were used to test this informative material's design, development, and validity. In the design, students and teachers are considered a common user group. Aside from the literature review, Web 2.0 tool design methods were used in the design process, and the resulting designs were presented. It is considered that innovative materials supported by Web 2.0 tools in science education based on context-based learning practices will enrich science teaching environments and support much more meaningful learning. Innovative technology applications were attempted to be presented to our teachers and students in Science and Technology Teaching using the designs realized within the scope of the research.

Chapter 11

Ambika N., St. Francis College, India

Training is a significant part of every medical services framework. Patients should be trained in their arranged methodology. The medical services experts should be prepared for their separate callings. The patient schooling and the preparation of medical care experts are face-to-face, which requires assets and is bound to specific environments. The previous methodology parts the perception plan into four levels. The issue portrayal and deliberation depend on the planned concentrate on approach, which carries us to the main level of the settled model. Diverse works are within the accompanying watchword blends connecting with the study. The framework has various pictures. The patient lies in a warped place, and a revision of their position is done. The gantry moves to its underlying location. The gantry gadget moves back to its unique position. The table dives so the patient can get up and leave the room. VIPER was furnished with sound. The term of the entire data movement was 2:45 min.

Chapter 12

Meeta Singh, Manav Rachna International Institute of Research and Studies, India
Poonam Nandal, Manav Rachna International Institute of Research and Studies, India
Deepa Bura, Manav Rachna International Institute of Research and Studies, India

In the area of virtual reality, there are some critical issues that need to deal with accessing, managing, and sharing the wide amount of information which is increasing day by day. The information produced is not in a form that machines can easily process. So, there is a need to develop and design techniques which can easily process the information and can be embedded with the techniques used for virtual reality. This chapter gives an insight into the various applications of virtual reality, and a comparative analysis of the global healthcare of virtual reality systems market by geography in the existing market scenario.

Section 4
Case Studies and Applications of Context-Rich Learning

Chapter 13

Implementing a Comprehensive Leadership Development Program at Byte Brigade: A Case Study 247
Jill Walker, Coding Dojo, USA

This chapter presents the case study of the leadership development program of a fictitious company Byte Brigade, designed to identify and nurture high-potential employees within the organization. Outlines of the evaluation and assessment methods used to measure the effectiveness of the program, including the use of Kirkpatrick's model and a focus on both qualitative and quantitative metrics are presented, as well as the initial feedback on the program's success and potential impact on the organization's success. The chapter also explores the use of the case study of Byte Brigade's leadership development program in various learning experiences. The case study is used as a tool to help participants understand the importance of leadership development programs, promote diversity and inclusion in leadership, practice effective communication and collaboration, and apply problem-solving skills to real-world situations. It emphasizes the practical nature of using case studies in learning experiences and highlights the potential for participants to apply their learning to their own work contexts.

Chapter 14

Training for Better Transfer in an Online Competency-Based Higher Education Program:
Technology's Role in Preparing the Next Generation Workforce.. 273
Sean P. Gyll, Western Governors University, USA
Karen K. Shader, Western Governors University, USA
Paul Zikas, ORamaVR, Switzerland
George Papagiannakis, University of Crete, Greece

Virtual reality simulations represent a much-needed effort to move beyond the shortcomings of traditional form-based assessments. Within VR, we assess competency and problem-solving skills versus the content memorization typically supported by conventional measures. This chapter explores an innovative VR simulation recently deployed at Western Governors University. The authors explored the utility of a VR simulation as an assessment tool when students engaged in more inclusive, immersive, and interactive experiences compared to conventional methods. The authors investigated students' summative assessment scores across a 2D (desktop) and 3D VR (headset) version and how additional factors like motion sickness, cognitive workload, and system usability impacted their scores. The results showed that students in the Desktop version outperformed those in the VR version on the summative assessment while feeling equally immersed in the simulation. Implications for future research are discussed, especially for optimizing learning experiences in an online competency-based higher education program.

Environmental sustainability is one of the major global topics of the 21st century. In order to effectively include the concept of sustainability in the topic of environmental education, educators are responsible for incorporating the concept into the existing curriculum. However, it may not always be possible to conduct field studies based on environmental education due to economic, transport, and time constraints, while certain situations and conditions may be particularly difficult to replicate. One recent solution to this problem is the application of Virtual Reality technology, which has been shown in various recent studies. VR is a computer-generated three-dimensional environment that allows the user to perceive content more realistically. In the process of teaching sustainability issues such as climate change, waste management, food consumption, air and water pollution, and deforestation, the present study has revealed that cooperation between different fields of expertise, including science education and computer and instructional technologies, plays an important role.

Preface

DESIGNING CONTEXT-RICH LEARNING BY EXTENDING REALITY

When the first human on the African savanna decided to climb up a tree to avoid a lion and lived, others copied her. That was the first apprenticeship; the first internship. When these humans sat around the campfire and asked each other what they would have done in that situation, that was the first case study. This context-rich learning was how humans survived and transmitted culture for millennia. It wasn't until the widespread adoption of literacy driven by Gutenberg's printing press that education started to become more abstract.

The case study approach inspires the exploration of essential questions contextualized in real-world environments, allowing for an in-depth appreciation of issues, events, and phenomena as they interact with the individual, group, organization, or community. Narratives are often the most effective way to illustrate how a concept is applied in an authentic environment in business, law, medical schools, and the social sciences for problem-solving, analysis, decision-making, and coping with uncertainties of a situation. In this way, we can see case studies as the original simulation.

Simulations, games, and real or virtual apprenticeships are the kinds of context-rich learning environments that leverage the power of episodic memory, boost student motivation, and create the conditions which make learning transfer more likely. Context-rich learning embodies the answer to the question "why do we need to learn this?" Many students, especially those who have dyslexia or otherwise neurodivergent brains, require the kind of context that is lacking in education.

This publication is a collection of research and readings on the context-rich learning approach that examines the aspects of design, delivery, and assessments. The variety of methods and pedagogical frameworks here should building speak to educators producing courses and learningware across the disciplines. The delivery method, the medium, will change with the times and as it best fits the skill studied. It is the richness of the context that can allow for learning engagement, the mastery of skills, and learning transfer in apprenticeships or in augmented reality.

Apprenticeships, case studies, labs, field trips, games, and simulations are routinely used in some disciplines, at some levels, and less in others. All these methods provide a context for discussions and analyses, attempting to bring the real world into the classroom. Some disciplines use them far more often than others, though this appears as much due to habit as opposed to any pedagogical rationale.

While generally seen to support learning and development of competencies, studies of context-rich learning, its implementation, and assessment, efforts for systematically designing context-rich learning are sparse. Emerging technologies open new avenues for research in scenario- and problem-based learning, and the gamification of learning. The book aims to propose novel approaches to designing and delivering context-rich learning across all disciplines and to become a valuable reference and source of inspiration to learning and training facilitators.

The abstracted, the contextless, and the disconnected courses and learning materials have already been created. However, instructional designers, educators, and training facilitators can add tremendous value by creating context-rich learning.

Relevance

The topic of context-rich learning is becoming increasingly relevant in the world today due to the need for education to prepare individuals for complex, real-world problems. As society becomes more interconnected and globalized, students need to develop skills such as critical thinking, problem-solving, and collaboration that can only be learned through context-rich learning experiences. With the rapid development of technology, virtual and augmented reality simulations are becoming more accessible and can provide students with immersive learning experiences that were previously impossible. There is a growing emphasis on diversity, equity, and inclusion in education, and context-rich learning can help ensure that all students have access to equitable and engaging learning experiences. As such, the topic of context-rich learning is vital for educators, instructional designers, and training facilitators looking to create effective and engaging learning experiences in today's world.

This book explores the concept of context-rich learning to improve the effectiveness of education and training. The authors argue that traditional, abstract approaches to learning lack the real-world context that helps students understand why they are learning what they are learning. The book presents a collection of research and readings on the topic, examining aspects of design, delivery, and assessment of context-rich learning in various disciplines. The authors suggest that a variety of methods and pedagogical frameworks, including apprenticeships, case studies, labs, field trips, games, and simulations, can be used to create context-rich learning experiences. They also discuss the use of emerging technologies, such as virtual and augmented reality, to enhance context-rich learning. The book aims to provide instructional designers, educators, and training facilitators with novel approaches to designing and delivering context-rich learning across all disciplines, becoming a valuable reference and source of inspiration for those seeking to create more effective learning experiences.

Audience

The target audience for the book "Context-Rich Learning: Designing for Authentic Inquiry" is diverse and includes instructional designers, educators, and training facilitators from various disciplines who want to create context-rich learning experiences for their learners. The book is also relevant for researchers who are interested in exploring the various aspects of context-rich learning, including design, delivery, and assessment. This book can be a valuable resource for students who want to understand the importance of context-rich learning and its relevance in real-world situations.

The volume is also relevant for organizations that are interested in implementing context-rich learning approaches in their employee training and development programs. It provides a framework for designing effective context-rich learning experiences that enhance employee engagement and improve the transfer of learning to the workplace.

The book is also relevant for policymakers who are interested in improving the quality of education and training in their countries. Context-rich learning approaches have the potential to improve student outcomes and enhance the development of competencies needed in the workforce. The book provides policymakers with a comprehensive understanding of the benefits of context-rich learning and practical examples of how to design and implement context-rich learning experiences.

SECTION 1: CONTEXT-RICH LEARNING PEDAGOGY AND INSTRUCTIONAL DESIGN

Section 1 of this book, "Context-Rich Learning Pedagogy and Instructional Design," sets the stage for exploring innovative and effective approaches to teaching and learning in the 21st century. The chapters in this section examine the theoretical foundations of context-rich learning and demonstrate how it can be applied in a variety of settings, including community colleges, the arts, and technology-enhanced learning environments.

Context-rich learning is a pedagogical approach that emphasizes the importance of connecting learning experiences to real-world situations and contexts. By doing so, students are better able to understand and apply what they are learning, as well as develop critical thinking and problem-solving skills. This approach is particularly relevant in today's rapidly changing world, where students need to be prepared to navigate complex and diverse contexts in their personal and professional lives.

The chapters in this section provide a comprehensive overview of context-rich learning and its theoretical foundations, as well as practical applications and strategies for designing and assessing context-rich learning experiences. From designing a Writing-About-Writing curriculum for community colleges to using UX design principles in creating context-rich learning experiences, the chapters in this section offer a range of perspectives and insights into the potential benefits and challenges of context-rich learning. This section provides a strong foundation for exploring the topic of innovative teaching and learning in the 21st century, highlighting the importance of connecting learning to real-world contexts and experiences. As such, it sets the stage for the remainder of the book, which explores other key themes and issues related to technology-enhanced learning, assessments and evaluations, and case studies and applications of context-rich learning.

Chapter 1: Defining the Context-Rich Learning Framework

Goran Trajkovski, Jason Braun

Chapter 1, authored by Goran Trajkovski and Jason Braun, offers a detailed explanation of the Context-Rich Learning Framework. The chapter aims to provide readers with a comprehensive understanding of context-rich learning by examining its theoretical foundations and exploring its alignment with various instructional practices. The authors also discuss the potential benefits and limitations of using context-rich learning in educational settings.

The chapter begins with a discussion of the theoretical underpinnings of context-rich learning, which include constructivism, experiential learning, problem-based learning, and situated learning. The authors provide specific examples of how context-rich learning aligns with each of these theories and how it can be used to support learning outcomes. The chapter further highlights the benefits of incorporating authentic, real-world experiences into the learning process, such as increased student engagement, improved problem-solving skills, and enhanced transfer of learning to real-life situations. However, the authors also acknowledge that there are potential limitations to using context-rich learning, such as the difficulty of designing and implementing such learning experiences, and the potential for cognitive overload if the context is too complex. Chapter 1 serves as an introduction to the topic of context-rich learning, providing readers with a strong foundation for understanding the framework and its potential applications in educational settings.

Chapter 2: Context-Rich Design and Designing a WAW Curriculum for Community Colleges

Lucas Marshall, David Rawson

Chapter 2, "Context-Rich Design and Designing a WAW Curriculum for Community Colleges," authored by Lucas Marshall and David Rawson, focuses on developing a Writing-About-Writing (WAW) curriculum for community college students from diverse backgrounds. The authors propose this pedagogical framework to better serve students and foster their academic and vocational success. The chapter begins by discussing the challenges faced by community colleges in meeting the diverse educational and career aspirations of their students. The WAW approach emphasizes the importance of teaching writing as a tool that mediates various activities, each with its own rhetorical needs. This approach equips students with essential analytical skills and threshold concepts, enabling them to navigate diverse writing situations across academic disciplines and professional settings. The chapter draws on the works of Anne Beaufort, Elizabeth Wardle, Doug Downs, and Linda Adler-Kassner to provide a theoretical foundation for the WAW approach and to demonstrate its potential benefits.

The authors provide a detailed account of how they designed a WAW curriculum for their own community college students, including the development of specific assignments and assessments. They also discuss the challenges they encountered during the design process and provide recommendations for others seeking to adopt a WAW approach. Overall, the chapter provides a valuable resource for instructors seeking to design a writing curriculum that is both context-rich and responsive to the diverse needs of community college students.

Chapter 3: The Pedagogy of Progress(ion): On Context-Rich Learning in the Arts

Adam al-Sirgany

Chapter 3 of the book explores the concept of context-rich learning in the arts and its potential benefits and limitations. The chapter begins by discussing the importance of understanding the contexts in which art and human knowledge are rooted. The author then goes on to explore five examples of context-rich learning that can be applied in arts education. The Suzuki Method, a musical training method that focuses on craft skills and learner engagement, is discussed. Next, the Montessori method, a general education program particularly applicable to the intersection of goal-based learning and individuated student learning styles, is explored. The chapter also discusses the Critical Response Process, a technique of artist-directed critique applicable across art forms and dialogic classrooms. The author then delves into Multiliteracies pedagogies, an academic framework developed by the New London Group that focuses on differentiated student co-learner experiences. Finally, the chapter explores 1-Week Critique, a nonprofit organization that provides open-access literary education utilizing diversified strategies for writers across circumstances and skillsets.

Throughout the chapter, the author highlights the benefits of context-rich learning in the arts, particularly in providing students with diverse and engaging learning experiences. The chapter also addresses the potential limitations of this approach and offers insights into how it can be effectively implemented in arts education.

Chapter 4: Temple of the Muses: The Power and Potential of Museums and Galleries for Context-Rich Learning

Jessica Mannisi

In Chapter 4, Mannisi discusses the importance of field trips as a form of context-rich learning and provides examples of how they can be utilized in different educational contexts, such as high school art classes and college Earth science courses. The chapter highlights the benefits of field trips, including the opportunity to apply classroom learning to real-world situations, develop observational and analytical skills, and foster a deeper understanding of the subject matter. Some challenges and limitations associated with field trips are discussed, and suggestions for how educators can overcome these challenges are offered.

Chapter 5: Using UX Design Principles When Designing Context Rich Learning Experiences

Travis Smith

Chapter 5 of the book delves into the topic of using user experience (UX) design principles when creating context-rich learning experiences. The author, Travis Smith, emphasizes the importance of taking a user-centric approach when designing educational products to ensure they are accessible, meaningful, and enjoyable for the end-user. Smith explains that by viewing educational products through the perspective of the user, designers can create more effective and engaging learning experiences. The chapter outlines various UX design tools, including problem statements, personas, user maps, storyboarding, wireframing, and low- and high-definition prototypes. These tools can be used to gather feedback from users throughout the design process and inform design decisions. The author highlights the importance of the Design Thinking process in creating user-centric learning experiences. This process involves empathizing with the user, defining the problem, ideating potential solutions, prototyping and testing those solutions, and iterating until a final product is developed. Smith discusses how UX design and Design Thinking can be used together to create a framework for creating effective and meaningful context-rich learning experiences.

SECTION 2: ASSESSMENTS AND EVALUATIONS FOR LEARNING OUTCOMES

Section 2 of this book focuses on Assessments and Evaluations for Learning Outcomes where researchers explore different approaches to assessing student learning and progress, including how to design effective assessments, address potential biases in assessments, and promote equity and inclusion in assessment practices.

Assessment and evaluation are crucial components of any educational system. They provide feedback to students and instructors about what has been learned and what needs to be improved. Effective assessments can help students identify areas for improvement and adjust their study habits, while instructors can use assessment results to adjust their teaching methods and curriculum. However, poorly designed, or biased assessments can lead to inaccurate results and hinder the learning process.

The section discusses Differential Item Functioning (DIF) studies, which are used to detect potential bias in assessments. The authors explore different statistical methods for identifying potential bias and provide recommendations for addressing bias in assessments. The section also emphasizes the promotion of equity and inclusion in assessments, by presenting a mixed-methods approach to identifying sources of inequities in assessments and provides recommendations for addressing these inequities. Next, the section explores the unique opportunities and challenges that come with using VR as an assessment tool. The authors highlight the importance of maintaining construct validity in VR assessments and provide practical examples for maintaining assessment standards. These chapters offer a comprehensive exploration of assessment and evaluation practices in education. They highlight the importance of effective assessment design, address potential biases in assessment practices, and promote equity and inclusion in assessment. By exploring innovative assessment tools such as virtual reality, these chapters also demonstrate how assessment practices are evolving in response to new technologies and changing educational landscapes. Section 2 contributes to the broader goal of promoting effective and equitable learning outcomes for all students.

Chapter 6: It's All About Context: Differential Item Functioning in IT Performance Assessments

Heather Hayes, Goran Trajkovski, Marylee Demeter

Chapter 6, written by Heather Hayes, Goran Trajkovski, and Marylee Demeter, explores the potential for bias in performance assessments (PAs) in Information Technology education. PAs are regarded as a highly authentic method of measurement, but their complexity makes them vulnerable to construct-irrelevant variance such as group bias. In order to detect potential bias in a series of Information Technology PA tasks, the authors conducted a Differential Item Functioning (DIF) study. The study aimed to identify task scenarios that were neutral or potentially controversial, where the latter was hypothesized as more likely to trigger DIF for certain demographics. The chapter discusses the variety of DIF methods available and their relative strengths and weaknesses. Three common statistical methods - Mantel-Haenszel (MH), logistic regression (LR), and Lord's Chi-square (LC) - were used, followed by a substantive review of DIF items. The hypotheses were largely supported by the analysis and review, and the discussion centers on the implications of the findings for assessment strategies in education.

This chapter emphasizes the importance of context in performance assessments, as the potential for bias can be greatly influenced by the specific task scenarios and demographics involved. The authors suggest that incorporating a DIF analysis can provide valuable insight into the fairness and validity of performance assessments, allowing for the identification and correction of potential biases. The chapter serves as a valuable resource for educators and assessment professionals in Information Technology education, highlighting the importance of considering context when designing and evaluating performance assessments.

Chapter 7: Diversity, Equity, and Inclusion: An Exploratory Approach to Reviewing and Improving Assessments for Equity

Marylee Demeter

Chapter 7 of the book explores the topic of Diversity, Equity, and Inclusion (DEI) in the context of assessments in higher education. Authored by Marylee Demeter, the chapter presents a mixed-methods exploratory approach to identify potential sources of inequities in objective and performance assessments in a selection of courses. The chapter begins with an overview of the importance of DEI in higher education, particularly in the context of assessments. The author highlights the role of assessments in ensuring all students are equally prepared to succeed in their programs of study. The chapter then goes on to describe the research methods used to identify sources of inequity in assessments. The study focuses on four courses across four disciplines - general education, information technology, business, and health professions - and analyzes objective and performance assessments in each of these courses. The findings of the study are presented, along with recommended solutions to ensure all students have equal opportunities to succeed in assessments.

The chapter concludes with a discussion of the limitations of the study and potential next steps to create equitable education and assessment opportunities. The author emphasizes the need for ongoing efforts to promote diversity, equity, and inclusion in higher education, particularly in the design and implementation of assessments. The chapter provides a valuable contribution to the literature on DEI in higher education and offers practical recommendations for instructors and institutions to promote equity in assessments.

Chapter 8: Design, Technology, and Measurement Considerations in Virtual-Reality Assessment

Sean Gyll, Karen Shader, Paul Zikas, George Papagiannakis

Chapter 8 of the book, written by Sean Gyll, Karen Shader, Paul Zikas, and George Papagiannakis, provides an in-depth overview of the development process for the Behavioral Healthcare Coordination VR assessment deployed at Western Governors University. The authors discuss the importance of using virtual reality simulations as an assessment tool to move beyond the limitations of today's forms-based measures. In VR, assessment is conducted for competency and problem-solving skills, which is more effective than content memorization typically supported by multiple-choice assessments. The authors also highlight essential design, technology, and measurement considerations that need to be taken into account when developing a VR assessment.

For any assessment program, construct validity is the chief validity component, which means that standards-based principles must be maintained to support the inferences drawn from test scores. Without a framework for developing and maintaining those standards, assessment developers are left to their own devices to determine which practices are most likely to be effective. The chapter provides practical examples to aid assessment professionals in maintaining those standards. It emphasizes the importance of using virtual reality simulations in assessment to provide a more authentic and engaging experience for learners. It also highlights the need for a framework to maintain standards and ensure the validity of assessments.

SECTION 3: TECHNOLOGY AND INNOVATION IN EDUCATION

Section 3 of this book, "Technology and Innovation in Education," explores the role of technology in enhancing and transforming educational experiences. The integration of technology in education has been a growing trend in recent years, and this section aims to provide insight into the various applications and benefits of technology in education. The chapters in this section cover a range of topics, including the use of Web 2.0 tools in science education, augmented reality in medical training, the application of virtual reality in education for sustainable development, and a comparison analysis of the global healthcare virtual reality systems market. These chapters highlight the diverse ways in which technology is being utilized and evaluated to improve education and training in various fields. As technology continues to advance, its potential to enhance and transform education becomes increasingly apparent. This section emphasizes the importance of incorporating technology in education to prepare students for the digital age and equip them with the skills and knowledge needed to succeed in their chosen fields. It also recognizes the challenges and limitations of technology integration in education and provides valuable insights into how these challenges can be overcome.

This section provides a comprehensive overview of the role of technology in education and its potential to enhance and transform the learning experience. It emphasizes the importance of staying up to date with technological advancements, and evaluating and integrating them into educational practices to ensure that students are prepared for the demands of the modern world.

Chapter 9: Assessing (Educational) Technology: Separating the Context-Rich Learning Applications From the Mere Spectacle

Zia Nzami, Megan Hudgins, Nate Fisher

Chapter 9 delves into educational multimedia content research, outlining key areas of investigation, emerging trends, and potential challenges. It begins by discussing how different multimedia formats and designs influence cognitive processes in learners, posing several research questions in this area. It explores the impact of emerging technologies on multimedia learning and the need to investigate their educational applications, presenting several research questions. Sections of the chapter focus on evaluating the effectiveness of multimedia learning interventions and stresses the importance of assessing their impact in broader contexts, and discusses the role of culture, equity, and inclusion in multimedia learning, highlighting the need to design content that reflects and respects diverse backgrounds and experiences. Several research questions related to this area are presented.

Authors investigate the long-term impact of multimedia learning experiences and how they contribute to the development of lifelong learning skills, retention and transfer of knowledge, and educational and career trajectories, and offer research questions to guide future investigations and insights into designing, implementing, and evaluating multimedia learning experiences to support student success.

As a comprehensive overview of educational multimedia content research, the chapter highlights key areas of investigation, emerging trends, and potential challenges.

Chapter 10: Web 2 Tools Supported Innovative Applications in Science Education Based on the Context-Based Learning Approach: The Context-Based Learning Approach

Canan Altundağ, Muhammed Koçer

Chapter 10 of the book explores the use of Web 2.0 tools to support innovative applications in science education based on the context-based learning approach. The authors, Canan Altundağ and Muhammed Koçer, discuss the increasing interest and need for Web 2.0 applications in education due to the rapid development of technology. They highlight the features of innovative materials supported by Web 2.0 tools, such as facilitating understanding and remembering, providing reinforcement, improving experimentation skills, and making the learning process exciting and enjoyable. The authors present a design and development research method to create and test informative materials designed to offer solutions to the problems faced by science and technology teachers in science education. The materials are based on a context-based learning approach, which aims to enable students to keep up with the rapidly developing and changing world and grow up as well-equipped individuals. The study's significance lies in its potential to guide students towards becoming successful and adaptable individuals, keeping up with the ever-changing world.

The chapter also discusses the validity of the developed materials, emphasizing the importance of maintaining the standards required for effective assessments. This chapter provides valuable insights into the use of Web 2.0 tools to support innovative applications in science education, offering practical solutions to improve the learning process and help students succeed.

Chapter 11: Augmented Reality Enabling Better Education

Ambika N.

Chapter 11, "Augmented Reality Enabling Better Education," provides an introduction to augmented reality (AR) and its potential applications in music therapy. AR combines real and virtual objects, is interactive, and can be registered in three dimensions. The chapter emphasizes the importance of accurately aligning the virtual world with the real one and discusses various methods for achieving this. The chapter also discusses the potential benefits of music therapy and how AR technology can be used in conjunction with music therapy to create novel therapeutic interventions. Two projects that use music therapy to help cancer patients and individuals with cerebral palsy are described. The chapter concludes by discussing the potential of AR technology to improve a user's understanding of and engagement with the real world.

Chapter 12: Comparison Analysis of Global Healthcare of Virtual Reality Systems Market by Geography in Existing Market Scenario

Meeta Singh, Poonam Nandal, Deepa Bura

Chapter 12 focuses on the analysis of the global healthcare market for virtual reality systems by geography in the existing market scenario. The authors, Meeta Singh, Poonam Nandal, and Deepa Bura, explore the critical issues in the area of Virtual Reality, such as accessing, managing, and sharing large amounts of information. They emphasize the need to develop and design techniques that can easily process information and can be embedded with the techniques used for Virtual Reality. The chapter provides an analysis of the global healthcare market for virtual reality systems, highlighting the various applications of Virtual Reality. The authors compare the market trends and demand for virtual reality systems in different regions and countries, identifying the strengths and weaknesses of each market. They also examine the challenges that companies face in the healthcare market, such as the lack of awareness and the high cost of VR systems, and suggest ways to overcome these challenges.

The authors utilize data and statistical analysis to provide a detailed understanding of the virtual reality systems market, including market size, growth rate, and competitive landscape. They also explore the various applications of VR systems in healthcare, such as surgical training, therapy, and rehabilitation, and the benefits they offer to patients and healthcare providers. The chapter provides valuable insights into the global healthcare market for virtual reality systems and its potential for growth and innovation. The authors' analysis and recommendations can help companies and healthcare providers make informed decisions regarding the adoption and implementation of virtual reality systems in their practices.

SECTION 4: CASE STUDIES AND APPLICATIONS OF CONTEXT-RICH LEARNING

Section 4 of this book focuses on case studies and applications of context-rich learning, providing real-world examples of how this approach can be implemented across different fields and disciplines. The case studies in this section demonstrate how context-rich learning can be used to enhance learning outcomes, engage students, and promote critical thinking and problem-solving skills.

The section starts with a case study of Byte Brigade's Leadership Development Program. The chapter explores how the program was designed to identify and nurture high-potential employees within the organization and assesses the program's effectiveness. This case study demonstrates how context-rich learning can be used to develop leadership skills and promote diversity and inclusion in leadership. Next, this section examines the role of technology in preparing the next generation's workforce. It presents a case study of a virtual reality simulation exploring the utility of VR as an assessment tool for competency and problem-solving skills. This case study showcases the potential of technology to enhance learning outcomes and create more inclusive and immersive learning experiences. The section further explores the use of virtual reality in education for sustainable development. It presents examples of how VR can be used to teach sustainability issues such as climate change, waste management, and deforestation. This case study highlights the potential of technology to create more engaging and impactful learning experiences, particularly in areas where field studies may be difficult or impossible to conduct. Section 4 showcases the versatility and effectiveness of context-rich learning in various contexts and disciplines.

It demonstrates how this pedagogical approach can be adapted to meet the needs of different learners and promote critical thinking, problem-solving, and real-world application of knowledge.

Chapter 13: Implementing a Comprehensive Leadership Development Program at Byte Brigade: A Case Study

Jill Walker

Chapter 13 of the book explores the case study of Byte Brigade's Leadership Development Program, which is designed to identify and nurture high-potential employees within the organization. The chapter provides an in-depth understanding of the program, its goals, and its effectiveness in achieving its objectives. The program's evaluation and assessment methods are outlined, including the use of Kirkpatrick's model, which is used to measure the program's effectiveness in terms of qualitative and quantitative metrics. The feedback on the program's success is also presented, providing insights into the potential impact of the program on the organization's success. The chapter also discusses the use of the Byte Brigade's Leadership Development Program as a case study in various learning experiences. The case study serves as a tool to help participants understand the importance of leadership development programs, promote diversity and inclusion in leadership, practice effective communication and collaboration, and apply problem-solving skills to real-world situations. It emphasizes the practical nature of using case studies in learning experiences and highlights the potential for participants to apply their learning to their own work contexts.

The chapter presents insights into the significance of leadership development programs and their potential impact on organizational success and highlights the role of case studies in learning experiences, demonstrating how they can help participants understand complex topics and apply their learning to real-world situations. It provides insights for educators, trainers, and leaders who seek to design effective leadership development programs and leverage case studies to enhance learning experiences.

Chapter 14: Training for Better Transfer in an Online Competency-Based Higher Education Program: Technology's Role in Preparing the Next Generations Workforce

Sean Gyll, Karen Shader, Paul Zikas, George Papagiannakis

In the chapter "Training for Better Transfer in an Online Competency-Based Higher Education Program: Technology's Role in Preparing the Next Generations Workforce," authors Sean Gyll, Karen Shader, Paul Zikas, and George Papagiannakis explore the use of virtual reality (VR) simulations as an assessment tool in online competency-based higher education programs. The authors present an innovative VR simulation developed and deployed at Western Governors University, and investigate the utility of the simulation in assessing students' competencies and problem-solving skills. The chapter discusses the differences in student performance and experience between a 2D (desktop) and 3D VR (headset) version of the simulation, and explores how additional factors such as motion sickness, cognitive workload, and system usability impacted student scores. The authors present their findings and discuss the implications for future research and optimization of online learning experiences in higher education programs.

The use of VR simulations as an assessment tool represents a promising approach to move beyond the limitations of traditional forms-based assessments and to provide students with more inclusive, immersive, and interactive learning experiences. This chapter highlights the importance of technology in preparing the next generation workforce and demonstrates the potential of VR simulations in assessing competencies and problem-solving skills in online competency-based higher education programs.

Chapter 15: The Use of Virtual Reality in Education for Sustainable Development

Raziye Sancar, Deniz Atal, Hüseyin Ateş

In Chapter 15, "The Use of Virtual Reality in Education for Sustainable Development," Raziye Sancar, Deniz Atal, and Hüseyin Ateş explore the use of Virtual Reality (VR) technology in teaching sustainability issues such as climate change, waste management, food consumption, air and water pollution, and deforestation. The authors highlight the challenges of incorporating sustainability concepts into existing curricula due to constraints such as economic, transportation, and time limitations. They suggest that VR can provide a solution by allowing students to experience three-dimensional simulations of environmental issues and interact with them in a more realistic way. The chapter delves into the benefits of using VR technology in teaching environmental education, including the ability to provide a safe and controlled environment for students to learn about potentially hazardous situations, as well as the ability to replicate difficult or dangerous scenarios that may not be possible in real life. The authors also discuss the importance of collaboration between different fields of expertise, including science education and computer and instructional technologies, in the successful implementation of VR technology in sustainable development education.

This chapter provides insights into the potential of VR technology in environmental education, highlighting its benefits in providing realistic, engaging, and interactive learning experiences for students. The authors emphasize the need for continued collaboration and innovation in the field of sustainability education to prepare future generations for the challenges of a rapidly changing world.

IMPACT ON THE FIELD

The book *Context-Rich Learning: Principles and Applications* provides in-depth exploration of the context-rich learning approach, examining various aspects of its design, delivery, and assessments. By highlighting the importance of incorporating authentic environments and experiences into the learning process, the book serves as a valuable resource for educators, instructional designers, and training facilitators across all disciplines.

The book's emphasis on context-rich learning provides a contribution to the field of education and training, particularly in the use of apprenticeships, case studies, labs, field trips, games, and simulations to create a more engaging and effective learning environment. It also offers a range of pedagogical frameworks and methodologies that can be used to design and deliver context-rich learning experiences in a variety of settings.

This volume proposes novel approaches to designing and delivering context-rich learning, particularly through the use of emerging technologies such as scenario- and problem-based learning and the gamification of learning. By doing so, it provides new avenues for research and development in the field of education and training.

Jason Braun
Western Governors University, USA

Goran Trajkovski
Western Governors University, USA

Section 1
Context–Rich Learning Pedagogy and Instructional Design

Chapter 1
Defining the Context–Rich Learning Framework

Goran Trajkovski

https://orcid.org/0000-0002-3745-3009
Western Governors University, USA

Jason Braun
Western Governors University, USA

ABSTRACT

The purpose of this chapter is to provide a comprehensive overview of context-rich learning, including its theoretical foundations, alignment with various instructional practices, and potential benefits and limitations. The chapter begins with a discussion of the theoretical underpinnings of context-rich learning, exploring its connections to constructivism, experiential learning, problem-based learning, and situated learning. Each section provides specific examples of how context-rich learning aligns with these theories and highlights the benefits of incorporating authentic, real-world experiences into the learning process.

INTRODUCTION

Although the term "context-rich learning" (CRL) is increasingly mentioned in passing in relation to methods like scenario-based learning, we are looking to expand the conversation and clearly define what we will be considering an umbrella term that gives space to the emergence of key moments across vastly different pedagogies and instructional practices. We can find situations where CRL is happening, at least occasionally, in nearly every discipline and at nearly every level of expertise. Often without invoking precise language, CRL is just as likely to happen in a carpenter's workshop with apprentices as it is to happen in a pilot training program with all the computational power behind the flight simulators. We hope that in looking closer at how we categorize and foster these moments as educators and researchers, we will help others who will do further research in this area and will encourage people across disciplines to confidently enter the CRL conversation and engage in the planning and play that breathes life into our lessons and positively impacts student engagement, motivation, and growth.

DOI: 10.4018/978-1-6684-7644-4.ch001

The heart of this pedagogy is a "student-focused approach." This is a great and necessary ideal, and perhaps there has never been a more apt time in our history to explore what that specifically looks like. For those interested in growing in these areas, it may seem intimidating when there is no one way into a student-focused space. What worked with one class, with one student, may not work in another. Sometimes, we as educators create meticulous lesson plans that look good on paper but do not execute effectively. Sometimes, the most engagement we have in a class period may come from something we ourselves had not intended or expected to gloss over. Teaching can be improv. It can be magic. After witnessing the COVID-19 pandemic, one thing is abundantly clear: student engagement is falling to new lows, and many school districts struggle with how to uphold high expectations and expand the depth of knowledge while also filling in fundamental gaps in scaffolding. We have middle schoolers who learned algebra via Zoom (Donham et al., 2022). We have kindergarteners whose first experience in a "classroom" was being expected to sit for hours in front of a screen in their own homes. We lost teacher-student interaction, student-student interaction, and teacher-teacher interaction. We have high school freshmen who spent middle school online and, from no fault of their own, simply do not have both the soft skills and academic skills not just to survive but excel and grow.

CRL might be the way to regain some of that lost terrain. While CRL will not diminish the progress that already successful students are making, underserved student populations, such as those that are neurodivergent or first-generation college students, are likely to make the greatest academic gains when and where CRL is implemented.

DEFINING CONTEXT-RICH LEARNING

Like the idea of justice that Aristotle puts forth in the *Nicomachean Ethics*, CRL is most easily noticed in its absence. The rote memorization, standardized testing, and other one size fits all approach to education only contains context for students who already enjoy school or who attach their self-worth to pleasing their teachers and parents. For those that worry about that student population, fear not, all of that flavor of instruction has already been created. Furthermore, those students who "know how to do school" will not be harmed by CRL.

CRL looks like a fourth-grade class raising monarch butterflies from eggs during a semester-long unit that teaches them about biology, geography, and even Spanish. CRL looks like a student reading aloud and revising a personal narrative in a one-on-one conference with their professor. CRL looks like a pilot practicing regaining control of an airplane after a malfunction while in the safe confines of a simulation. CRL emphasizes collaboration between students and educators, rather than the traditional model of a teacher imparting knowledge from on high. Even though fundamental concepts like Depth of Knowledge and I Do / You Do / We Do remain important, CRL allows for a more personalized evaluation of each student's starting point as they begin a new unit. By giving students a voice in the process, CRL allows them to contribute their own understanding of what they know and what they hope to achieve on formative and summative assessments. For student engagement to be effective, students need to trust that the work being asked of them is purposeful and designed to teach them key concepts but is also designed for them as people, as students, as specific individuals. CRL enables students to connect their real-world experiences with classroom teachings. It emphasizes the importance of critical thinking and problem solving as well as how to use resources effectively to make sense of the world around them.

Context learning seeks to foster a deeper understanding of content by helping learners make connections between what they know and what they do not know.

Every student needs to find an open door into a subject if they are going to learn. That doorway can be opened by nearly anyone. For some children-often the affluent, neurotypical children-it is their parents and guardians who demonstrate and explain to them what reading, learning, and school is for, and why it matters, and how it can be enjoyable. For others it can be a coach or a Sensei. Nearly every teacher and professor we have met is well-meaning and intends to open this door. Class size, standards, the quick sands of time, other forces, and machinations of our culture(s) all too frequently make those intentions dissolve into mere wishes or apparitions.

When it comes to learning, context is everything. By connecting our knowledge to real-world situations and experiences, we can make learning more meaningful and effective. This idea, known as CRL, aligns with several pedagogical theories, including constructivism, experiential learning, problem-based learning, and situated learning. These approaches all recognize the importance of active engagement and real-world application in the learning process. By embracing CRL, we can unlock the full potential of education and make a lasting impact.

CRL and Key Learning Theories and Pedagogies

CRL refers to the idea that learning is more meaningful and effective when it is connected to real-world situations or experiences, and when learners have the opportunity to apply their knowledge and skills in authentic contexts. This approach to learning is closely related to several pedagogical theories, including:

- **Constructivism**: This theory suggests that learners construct their own understanding of the world through their experiences and interactions with their environment. In a CRL environment, students have the opportunity to construct their own understanding of concepts by applying them to real-world situations.
- **Experiential learning:** This theory proposes that learning is most effective when it is based on firsthand experiences and when learners are actively involved in the learning process. CRL provides learners with opportunities to engage in hands-on, experiential learning activities that allow them to apply their knowledge and skills in authentic contexts.
- **Problem-based learning**: This approach to teaching involves presenting learners with real-world problems or challenges that they must solve using their knowledge and skills. CRL environments often include problem-based learning activities that allow students to apply their knowledge and skills to solve real-world problems.
- **Situated learning:** This theory suggests that learning is most effective when it is situated within a specific context or community. CRL environments provide learners with the opportunity to learn within authentic contexts, allowing them to gain a deeper understanding of the material and how it is relevant to their lives.

Whitehead

"The Aims of Education" by Alfred North Whitehead (1928) argues that true education involves both culture and expert knowledge. Ideas should be related to one another and able to be employed in any order and with any reiteration. Overall, education should be useful and relevant to the insistent present;

much is said of ethos, pathos, and logos, but much less is explicitly said about kairos, the timeliness of a topic, lesson, assignment, assessment.

Whitehead believes that education should guard against the mental dry rot of inert ideas by teaching a few important ideas thoroughly and giving children the joy of discovery. During COVID, many districts re-evaluated which state standards would be emphasized, and many have continued that practice in person as we continue to fill in the gaps from during COVID. Considering how this applies to CRL, this means that education should be focused on developing the ability to use knowledge and skills in real-world situations. This involves learning in authentic contexts that are meaningful to students and emphasizing the application of knowledge to solve problems and address real-world issues. The scientific side of education, according to Whitehead, should involve the proof and appreciation of ideas, which can be achieved through experiential and project-based learning that encourages students to actively engage with concepts and ideas in a meaningful way. This also implies that for a teacher to effectively do this, they must have time to be familiar with the standards and unit maps, the formative and summative assessments, and with their own students. CRL is effective when teachers know their students, their struggles, their successes, their past, their hopes for the future. CRL takes time to build relationships and to outline and plan. A district conversation about CRL should include an idea of a teacher's prep time. Administrations can support teachers by thinking of unique ways to foster the building of community and for teachers to do invisible labor that cannot be done in the moment while teaching. In summary, Whitehead's views on education align with the principles of CRL, which emphasizes the importance of authentic learning experiences and the application of knowledge to real-world situations.

Freire

Paulo Freire's most influential work, *Pedagogy of the Oppressed* (1970), describes a dystopian classroom created in the image of the bank. This was what was going on in the classrooms of the United States, Europe, and Freire's native Brazil in the late sixties when he published this work. Freire describes this banking model of education as students being like empty accounts that the teacher deposits knowledge into. This disregards whatever knowledge the student might have before meeting the teacher, as well as limits the amount of learning that a student can achieve to that of the teacher. In focusing on the information as something that must be transferred intact, the student is seen as the vessel. This can put a lot of stress on teachers and students while also resulting in outcomes that allow for passivity. When a teacher is working with new students, they may feel pressure to cover basic information at Depth of Knowledge level 1 (DOK 1), which students are then expected to repeat back as a demonstration of their "understanding." In contrast to this banking model, Freire proposes a "problem-posing educational" approach. In chapter two he grounds his theory not just in philosophic terms, but also nails down its physics: "In problem-posing education, people develop their power to perceive critically *the way they exist* in the world *with which* and *in which* they find themselves; they come to see the world not as a static reality, but as a reality in process, in transformation."

Instead of focusing on the student's adaptation to the learning environment and content, we could focus on ways to adapt the environment and content for the students. The banking model can be described as passive learning in a fixed reality of universals, designed for children, with out of context coursework, as a solitary experience. In contrast the problem-posing model of Freire is one of active learning with an understanding that reality is in flux, designed for adults, with coursework that has meaningful context and features at least some work done in a team or partnership either with peers or with an instructor acting as a peer. There can be many roles for both teacher and student in a learning environment. Freire's problem-posing pedagogy is a student-centered approach to education that emphasizes the importance of the learner's context in the learning process. In this approach, the teacher is not seen as the sole source of knowledge, but rather as a facilitator who helps students discover knowledge through critical dialogue and inquiry. If one of the goals of education is to prepare students for the world they will live, work, and socialize in, then we can turn the classroom into something that more closely resembles the world in which the students will implement what they have learned.

Central to the problem-posing approach is the idea that education should start from the students' own lived experiences and contexts. Freire argues that students should not be passive recipients of information but active participants in the learning process, who bring their own knowledge, experiences, and perspectives to the classroom.

In problem-posing pedagogy, the teacher presents a problem or challenge to the students, and together they explore possible solutions, drawing on the students' own experiences and knowledge. This process involves a dialogue between the teacher and the students, in which both parties learn from each other.

Through this approach, students become critical thinkers who can analyze and question their own experiences and the world around them. They become active agents of their own learning, able to apply their knowledge and skills to real-world situations. In this way, Freire's problem-posing pedagogy centers around students bringing their own context to learning and using that context as a starting point for critical inquiry and dialogue.

Rose

Mike Rose's *Lives on the Boundary* (1990) provides a unique lens for thinking about the context or lack of context students bring with them to college. In the first chapter, Rose explains that his book is an "autobiography, case study, commentary" describing not only *his* educational journey, but that of his students. *Lives on the Boundary* dramatizes the kinds of ways that students fall through the cracks at many universities. He also unearths various models of how a student-focused university might do it differently. Many institutions have commitments to research, athletics, and the bottom line that would make such changes difficult.

Rose notes that professors have a boatload of implicit expectations that are frequently unknown to their students. Professors and teachers often do not explain the history or even the current application of what they are teaching in their discipline. Moreover, they know precisely how they want a student to perform a given assignment but do not tell them. While this method, full of assumptions, may be good enough for the homogeneous groups of students that were going to universities before the 1950s, it does not work today. One example of the hidden disciplinary motives that Rose uses comes from his own experience as a graduate student studying literature: "The unstated agenda was that we should come up with an original interpretation, argue that what seems fairly simple is really complex, that traditional readings miss the point, that yet another reading is possible. We would examine a poem, then with great care and cleverness—scrutinizing sentences patterns, meter, images, and alternate meanings of words to support our argument." This "unstated agenda" is something that his professors did not clearly explain to him.

Rose argues that students, especially first-generation college students, veterans, and working parents, need mentors who understand their backgrounds and see the significant challenges for what they are and not dismiss them as mere excuses. Rose refers to "models" that will help provide context for the instruction. He explains that the typical professor-student relationship falls short in such situations: "To live your early life on the streets of South L.A… or any of the hundreds of other depressed communities –and to journey up through the top levels of the American educational system will call for support and guidance at many, many points along the way. You'll need people to guide you into conversations that seem foreign and threatening. You'll need models, lots of them, to show you how to get at what you don't know…You'll need people to watch out for you."

From the signage directing students on move-in day to the way most libraries are structured, this is a world designed for professors, administration, and possibly alumni. They have the context necessary to navigate the university, and much of this context is unspoken. Many first- year writing teachers at colleges and universities have said something like the following: "We will not be focusing on grammar as that should have been covered in high school." Except maybe it was not. Maybe it was in some sense. But when students are asked about their concerns as writers, they often go back to grammar. They have been taught a way to write an essay, and they are trying very hard to communicate, and we cannot dismiss gaps with *shoulds*. We meet our students where they are, not where we feel they should be, especially not on arbitrary expectations about an education that came before.

Effective implementation of CRL may mean a reassessment of how we view success in both students and teachers. Rose responds to the critics who will point to an excellence in teaching award here or there in defense of the faculty-centric model (1990): "Regardless of what the university publicist says, faculty are promoted and given tenure and further promoted for the research they publish, not for the extent of their involvement in undergraduate, especially introductory-level, teaching."

Even when it is clear why students should learn a particular subject or lesson, the way it is presented is so watered-down, so far removed from the actual context that motivation stalls. In the exceptional cases when motivation persists, by force of will, the carrot or the stick, or particularly strong coffee, then what is learned might be shallow, fragile, and not able to be applied to the targeted practice. In such cases learning transfer would be very unlikely.

This is what happened with the proliferation of "remedial English" courses at colleges in the 1980s. Rose wrote about how the lessons, worksheets, activities, homework, and assessments were all about grammar and correctness in an abstract, idealized way. His work led the way to reform more than the title of these programs from "Remedial English" to titles like "Foundational English," and the curriculum moved to center the act of students' own writing and thinking in the course.

Rose's provocation and example changed the way his discipline (or disciplines) was practiced. He was fighting against the sort of idea that students would be harmed by slopy practice. The idea that one must practice with perfect form is not only a fiction (who ever could do such a thing?), but wrong in terms of the neuroscience as explained by the work in *Make it Stick* and elsewhere. They cite studies of high school students dislike taking no-stakes quizzes on topics they have yet to study and college baseball players who preferred batting practice where the pitchers or coaches made it clear what kinds of pitches were coming over practices where the pitcher threw random types of pitches. In both cases the desire for perfection or idealization of a perfect practice runs counter to real life, or a real game. Furthermore, both the students and the players improved their performance drastically and were not harmed by making the kinds of mistakes one makes when predicting and learning.

The mistakes and errors in learning and practicing add authenticity, effort, and context for tremendous rewards. This nearly approximates the Japanese concept of Kintsugi where broken pottery is fixed, the parts being rejoined with a lacquer made of gold or other precious metals: "As a philosophical practice, kintsugi implies that the authentic is that which displays and values its true, dynamic relation to history" (p15).

Some educators believe certain students are not ready to know the *why* when they are learning this, or not ready to apply the rudimentary skills as they are developing them. They do not want to read papers full of comma splices, homophone errors or incorrect word choices, and claimless attempts at thesis statements. They say the student is not ready to write an academic paper, so why let them try. We will do worksheets, until they have proved they are ready. The elitism and paternalism here is obvious.

Gagne's Nine Events of Instruction

While all of Gagne's events of instruction (1970) would likely be present in CRL, the first one "gain attention of the students" is the most crucial. In many classrooms, gaining such attention is either assumed or ignored. And yet a student may be looking at a teacher and be daydreaming in a world all their own. Here we argue it is because they do not know or do not believe that the instruction has anything to do with them.

Much of the educational theory and writing about instructional practice does not attend to students who have a self-concept that is anti-intellectual or academically interferent. This is a tragedy as many of the straight A students would learn to master the required material no matter how they are taught.

There are a lot of students who consider themselves not "good at school," who do not have many books in their house, who do not have a reliable internet connection or computer, whose parents have not gone to college, who are financially struggling, of a minority, or have various brain differences. Students like these can see school as a kind of punishment or purgatory. They are quizzed over words and concepts they have never seen or heard before. They are awash in unwritten rules which they do not understand. They consistently fail to intuit the implicit instructions in assignments. But most of all, when they see assignments, lessons, classes, school, and education in general as being entirely disconnected to their everyday life, they tune out.

When the only thing unifying much of the instruction is the standardized test they will take, students who do not have their identity tangled up in pleasing their teachers and parents-or ideally, who have not somehow fell in love with learning for its own sake- it will be a terrible challenge to spark students' interest in a subject.

Bloom's Taxonomy

Bloom's Taxonomy of the Cognitive Domains (1956) suggests that learning should scaffold up in the following sequence: knowledge, comprehension, application, analysis, synthesis, and evaluation. Here we argue that application and comprehension should come first, at least in part, in order to create the kind of CRL environment that can entice a learner to participate when they do not already have a positive relationship with the subject, the teacher, or education at large.

Bloom's Taxonomy of the Cognitive Domains can be seen as a roadmap for learning, suggesting that knowledge and comprehension should come first in order to foster a positive relationship between student and subject. However, we believe that application and comprehension must come first in order to create an engaging learning environment. This type of CRL offers students the opportunity to explore their interests in ways that traditional schooling often does not, encouraging them to take ownership of their own education.

By applying Bloom's Taxonomy of the Cognitive Domains in this way, educators can provide learners with meaningful content that is tailored to their individual needs. It creates an atmosphere where students are encouraged to think critically about topics, ask questions, and explore their curiosities. Bloom's Taxonomy of the Cognitive Domains can be an incredibly powerful tool in helping students master the content and develop a lifelong passion for learning.

Whether it is for personal or professional development, Bloom's Taxonomy of the Cognitive Domains is an invaluable tool that can help anyone learn more effectively. By emphasizing application and comprehension first, teachers are able to create engaging learning environments that foster curiosity, exploration, and critical thinking skills. This kind of scaffolding will not only lead to better educational outcomes but also provide learners with a newfound sense of ownership over their education. Bloom's Taxonomy of the Cognitive Domains can be a great way to encourage lifelong learning.

Rossett

In Rossett's article "Needs assessment" in *Instructional technology* (1995) she distills student motivation down to this equation: "Value X Confidence = Motivation" (p. 187). While certain academics will argue this is vastly oversimplified, we challenge them to come up with a better explanation that could be written by hand on the inside of a matchbook. Until that happens, we will hold this equation as cornerstone with which we build contest-rich learning around. Besides the conciseness of this idea, it is, unlike many educational propositions, actionable. She spells it out like this: "If you want to increase student motivation, build value and/or confidence" (p. 187).

When students are provided with a rich and engaging learning environment that is relevant to their interests and experiences, they are more likely to see the value and importance of what they are learning. For example, if a history lesson is taught through a hands-on, immersive experience, such as a reenactment or field trip to a historical site, students are more likely to appreciate the relevance of history and be motivated to learn more.

When students are given opportunities to explore and engage with content in meaningful ways, they are more likely to develop a deeper understanding and greater confidence in the subject matter. For example, if students are given the chance to work collaboratively on a project that requires them to apply their understanding of a concept, they are more likely to feel confident in their abilities and motivated to continue learning. Rossett adds that "If they aren't confident that they can handle it, you may have to build their confidence through training that provides successful models and provides early experiences with success" (p. 187).

The New Motivation Equation

We would like to build upon Rossett's equation in the following way:

Motivation= (Value×Confidence)^{CRL}

The equation captures the impact of CRL (CRL) on motivation levels. Specifically, a student's perceived value of a task and their confidence in their ability to complete it are multiplied together, and the result is raised to the power of the CRL factor. The CRL exponent represents the degree to which CRL experiences enhance or diminish motivation levels. When the CRL factor is greater than one, it amplifies motivation levels. Conversely, when the CRL factor is less than one, it diminishes motivation levels. The closer the CRL factor is to zero, the more significant the decline in motivation. This equation underscores the potential of CRL to profoundly impact motivation levels, depending on the effectiveness of the learning environment and the degree to which the learning experiences align with students' interests and needs.

OPTIMIZING BRAIN RESOURCES AND LEARNING STRATEGIES

Inclusive education acknowledges the diverse learning needs of all students, striving to establish an environment where everyone, including those with unique learning styles and abilities, can flourish. A fundamental aspect of realizing this objective is understanding the brain's processing and allocation of resources for various learning tasks.

Brain Resource Allocation

Inclusive education aims to cater to the diverse learning needs of all students, taking into account the brain's resource allocation for different tasks. Barrett (2020) likens this process to a budget, where the brain makes economic decisions about when to spend or save resources like glucose and energy. Understanding this aspect is crucial for creating teaching strategies that optimize learning outcomes for students with diverse learning styles and abilities.

Barrett emphasizes that the concept of a brain network is not a metaphor, but the best scientific description of the brain. Recognizing the brain as a complex network can help educators appreciate the intricate learning processes and adapt their teaching methods accordingly. Notably, the brain's primary function is not thinking, but managing a complex body. This understanding can guide educators to develop more inclusive and effective teaching strategies, incorporating movement and sensory experiences that engage both the brain and body.

By considering the brain's resource allocation and primary function, educators can create more effective, engaging learning experiences that cater to the unique needs of all students. This approach promotes an inclusive educational environment, fostering success and well-being for students with diverse learning styles and abilities.

Retrieval Practice

A critical aspect of effective learning is retrieval practice, which involves recalling facts, concepts, or events from memory (Brown, Roediger, & McDaniel, 2014). This strategy, more effective than simple review or rereading, can enhance learning and retention. For example, using flashcards or taking quizzes after reading or listening to lectures yields better results. However, a misconception in education is the belief in "errorless learning" (p. 90-94), which can hinder students from applying learning sooner. Embracing imperfections in the learning process allows for more effective skill development.

Brown et al. (2014) highlight the importance of spacing, interleaving, and variability in learning experiences, emphasizing reflection as a form of retrieval practice that requires thinking about past actions and considering improvements for the future (p. 66).

Educators should create inclusive learning environments by understanding the brain's resource allocation, employing effective learning strategies like retrieval practice, embracing failure, and promoting reflection. These approaches cater to diverse learning styles and abilities, fostering a more inclusive and successful educational experience.

The WHOLISTIC Approach

Susan Winebrenner (2018) emphasizes the importance of using a WHOLISTIC (Whole, Holistic, Organized, Logical, Integrative, Systematic, Thinking, Instruction, and Learning) approach to teaching global thinkers, which involves presenting the "whole" before exploring its individual components. As Winebrenner states, "Whole to parts means we always make available a model of the 'whole' before expecting global thinkers to make sense of its specified parts. We can do this by 'surveying' the entire content before actually starting instruction or by using videos and/or graphic organizers that makes the material more visual" (p. 128-129).

Traditional teaching methods often present content section by section, which can create a distinct disadvantage for global learners who may become confused without continuous visual access to the whole. Winebrenner further explains that "seeking patterns and connections applies to the work on Advance Organizers by David Ausubel that describes the power of helping the brain connect new learning to something it already knows" (p. 129). This connection between new and prior knowledge is essential for fostering deeper understanding and retention of information.

She also advocates for integrating skills into content, which "moves students beyond learning facts to using that data in more than one learning context" (p. 130). Global learners can better remember required content once visual and experiential connections have been made. Furthermore, she encourages the transition from concrete to abstract thinking and recommends hands-on learning activities, especially in subjects that may not typically incorporate such methods at the secondary grade level. These hands-on activities "are also helpful in showing the connections between various subject areas and between subjects and the real world. Social Studies school service catalogues, virtual reality tours of museums and other locations, and interaction with primary documents also improve student understanding of abstract ideas" (p. 130-131). By employing these WHOLISTIC teaching practices, educators can create a more inclusive and effective learning environment that caters to the unique needs of global thinkers.

Exceptionalities

Multiple exceptionalism (ME) refers to individuals who possess two or more exceptionalities or unique abilities and challenges that coexist. It recognizes that individuals can be gifted or talented in one or more areas, while also having a learning difference, a physical or sensory disability, or a mental health condition that impacts their functioning (Kaufmann, 2018; Yates and Boddison, 2020). ME can include a wide range of combinations of abilities and challenges, including giftedness and autism, or intellectual disability and artistic talent.

One specific form of multiple exceptionalisms is twice-exceptionalism (2e), which refers to individuals who are both gifted or talented and have a learning or developmental difference (Trail, 2022), such as ADHD (Attention-Deficit/Hyperactivity Disorder) (Wilens and Spencer, 2010), dyslexia (Wolf and Bowers, 1999), or autism (Kanner, 1943). These individuals may have significant strengths in certain areas, such as mathematics, music, or creative writing, while also experiencing challenges with executive functioning, social interaction, or attention regulation. Twice exceptional students can be difficult to identify and support in traditional educational settings, as their exceptionalities can mask or exacerbate each other, and their needs may not be fully understood or addressed.

Multiple exceptionalism challenges traditional notions of intelligence and ability and require a flexible and individualized approach to education and support. Recognizing and valuing the unique strengths and challenges of ME individuals can help to foster their development, increase their academic and social success, and promote their well-being.

Understanding the unique challenges faced by students with learning differences is crucial for designing teaching strategies that cater to their specific needs. Brock L. Eide and Fernette F. Edie's book, *The Dyslexic Advantage: Unlocking the Hidden Potential of the Dyslexic Brain* (2011), sheds light on the struggles faced by dyslexic students in traditional classrooms. Eide and Edie assert that dyslexic students, who tend to be "big picture, top-down learners," often find themselves ill-suited to typical classrooms, where "bottom-up teaching approaches predominate" (p. 99). These students struggle when schools demand memorization of new information before providing explanations of its meaning or significance. This teaching approach overlooks the strengths of dyslexic students, who are better equipped to comprehend and retain information when presented with the overall context and connections. To support the learning of dyslexic students, educators must consider alternative teaching methods that take into account their global thinking style. One such method involves presenting the overarching context and concepts before delving into specific details. This approach enables dyslexic students to establish connections between the broader ideas and individual elements, enhancing their comprehension and retention of the subject matter. Incorporating visual aids, such as graphic organizers, mind maps, and videos, can facilitate learning for dyslexic students. These tools allow students to visually represent the relationships between ideas, making it easier for them to grasp abstract concepts and see the "big picture."

IMMERSION AND ENGAGEMENT

The classrooms and course today have context designed, if not consciously, then by default. Computer Science classrooms decorated with stereotypical "tech bro" science fiction memorabilia, RTFM hacker ethos, and energy drinks sends a signal that is welcoming to some and off-putting to others as noted in a recent *Scientific American* (Cheryan et al., 2022). Loving S*tar Trek*, wearing a hoodie, and being overcaffeinated has little to no relationship to how well one can learn to program a computer. Though it might have a lot of correlation with who is currently programing them. If we create classrooms, online collaborative coding platforms, and courses where all feel welcome and we show how programing can be used to solve a wider variety of problems beyond the next ride sharing or dating app, the future will be much brighter.

Virtual and Augmented Reality

Virtual and augmented reality (VR/AR) technologies offer new possibilities for CRL that can enhance inclusion and engagement in the classroom. As Greengard (2019) notes, the internet has already changed education in remarkable ways, enabling distance learning and introducing new ways to view and explore data and information. However, online learning still struggles to provide a dynamic and immersive experience that truly engages students.

VR and AR offer a solution to this challenge by providing students with a sense of presence and immersion in a virtual environment that mimics the familiarity of a real-world school without the need to travel to a campus or set foot in a physical classroom (Greengard, 2019). This technology can help create a more inclusive learning experience by providing students with different learning styles and abilities the opportunity to engage with content in new and exciting ways.

Research conducted at the University of Saskatchewan in Canada found that the use of VR improved learning accuracy by about 20 percent for medical students studying spatial relationships (Greengard, 2019). The study found that those who learned through virtual reality scored higher than those who used textbooks even when tested five to nine days after undergoing instruction. This suggests that VR technology can enhance learning outcomes and help create a more engaging and effective context for learning.

It is important to note that VR and AR are not a panacea for all educational challenges. As Greengard (2019) points out, the technology is still in its early stages and requires careful design and implementation to ensure that it is accessible, equitable, and effective for all learners. In addition, while VR and AR can create a more immersive and engaging learning experience, it is important to balance this with other pedagogical strategies and not rely solely on technology to deliver content.

Artificial Intelligence and CRL

The future development of Artificial Intelligence (AI) has the potential to fulfill the promises that people have been making about adaptive learning for the past decade. As the capabilities of AI continue to advance, it is poised to revolutionize the field of education and technology, offering students unprecedented access to personalized learning experiences.

The potential of AI to function as a world-class tutor lies in its ability to adapt to the individual needs, interests, and learning styles of students. By harnessing large data sets and powerful algorithms, AI can analyze student performance, interests, and learning preferences, allowing it to create tailored learning experiences that seamlessly connect the required material with students' own hobbies and subjects they have already mastered. This CRL environment can enhance students' engagement, motivation, and retention of the material, leading to improved educational outcomes.

We can expect AI-powered adaptive learning systems to become widely accessible soon, as the cost of computing approaches zero and AI becomes increasingly sophisticated. These systems will democratize access to world-class tutoring, enabling students from all walks of life to benefit from personalized learning experiences that were once reserved for the elite.

However, as AI surpasses the capabilities of systems like ChatGPT-4, it raises important questions about the potential limitations of human learning. While AI can facilitate personalized learning experiences, the human capacity for knowledge absorption, retention, and application remains a critical factor. Cognitive limitations, such as working memory capacity and the ability to transfer knowledge across domains, may pose constraints on how much a person can learn. Moreover, the pace of learning and the amount of knowledge one can acquire will still be influenced by factors such as time, dedication, and motivation.

The future development of AI holds immense promise in fulfilling the visions of adaptive learning that have been envisioned for the past decade. As the cost of computing approaches zero and AI technology continues to advance, a new era of CRL will emerge, offering students unparalleled access to personalized educational experiences. Nevertheless, it is important to remain cognizant of the limitations of human learning and the ethical considerations that come with the widespread adoption of AI in education. By thoughtfully addressing these challenges, we can harness the power of AI to transform education and empower learners to reach their full potential.

Limitations of CRL

Added financial costs of lab actives, field trips, virtual and augmented reality program development and equipment, smaller teacher to student ratios or additional tutors can be prohibitive. Added time to develop novel and niche approaches to introduce new lessons, lack of ease and choices for off the shelf learning resources can limit the implementation of CRL.

If we do not take care to match the individual students interests, we could create context that pushes them away from the subject. This could appear to be CRL but does not fulfill the promise of it if students do not have a choice. We have seen this in practice like when our peers teach English 101 with a *The Matrix* movie theme. The film provides many useful points of intersection with ideas about epistemology, rhetoric, thought experiments, self-reflection, critical thinking, and so forth. Yet, many students might want to spend sixteen weeks watching Keanu learn kung fu. They might wish they could just see the montage. This is an example of what could be a potentially great CRL environment for certain individual learners being forced upon a whole class. Some percentage of students in courses like that would surely feel this context does not apply to them, feel resentment, and have additional barriers to learning in front of them. If the students know what they are signing up for that is fine. But if they do not know the whole 16-week course is based around a theme, we are removing agency and all the positive consequences that come along with choice and self-selection.

CONCLUSION

So, how do we define Context-Rich learning? CRL is a powerful educational approach that seeks to integrate real-world experiences and relevant contexts into the learning process. It goes beyond rote memorization and standardized testing to promote a deeper understanding of the subject matter and encourage students to apply their knowledge in meaningful ways. By providing learners with a diverse range of experiences and opportunities to engage with content, it creates a more immersive, engaging, and dynamic learning environment that can significantly enhance motivation, retention, and learning outcomes. CRL recognizes that students come to the classroom with diverse backgrounds, experiences, and interests. It seeks to leverage this diversity by creating learning experiences that are relevant and meaningful to each student. This approach provides learners with a sense of ownership over their education and encourages them to take an active role in the learning process. By promoting critical thinking, creativity, and problem-solving skills, CRL equips students with the tools they need to succeed both in and outside of the classroom. Appendices A and B provide CRL taxonomies and examples.

The benefits of CRL are not limited to the classroom. By integrating real-world experiences and relevant contexts into the learning process, CRL prepares students for the challenges and opportunities of the 21st century. It equips them with the skills and knowledge they need to navigate complex systems, think critically about complex issues, and communicate effectively with diverse audiences. These skills are essential for success in a rapidly changing world where innovation, adaptability, and collaboration are increasingly critical.

CRL also recognizes the importance of creating a supportive learning environment that is conducive to student success. It seeks to provide learners with the guidance, support, and mentorship they need to overcome challenges and reach their full potential. This approach recognizes that students come to the classroom with diverse backgrounds and experiences and seeks to meet each student where they are. By providing learners with the tools and resources they need to succeed, CRL empowers them to achieve their goals and fulfill their potential.

The implementation of CRL requires a fundamental shift in the way we think about education. It requires educators to move beyond the traditional "sage on the stage" model of instruction and embrace a more student-centered approach. This approach requires a willingness to experiment, take risks, and challenge traditional assumptions about teaching and learning. It also requires a commitment to ongoing professional development, collaboration, and the continuous improvement of teaching practices.

In this chapter, we have examined various learning theories and pedagogies that emphasize the importance of CRL, experiential education, and problem-solving in fostering deeper understanding and engagement among students. To further illustrate the practical application of these theories, we present three lesson plans that incorporate hands-on activities, real-world connections, and collaborative problem-solving to facilitate learning in diverse subject areas. These lesson plans serve as exemplars, demonstrating how the integration of CRL experiences can effectively support the acquisition and application of knowledge in fields such as genetics, biology, and digital humanities, ultimately enhancing student outcomes and promoting the development of critical thinking and problem-solving skills.

REFERENCES

Aristotle. Ross, W. D. 1., & Brown, L. (2009). The Nicomachean ethics. Oxford; New York, Oxford University Press.

Barrett, L. F. (2020). *Seven and a half lessons about the brain*. Houghton Mifflin.

Bloom, B. (1956). *Taxonomy of Educational Objectives*. Longmans.

Brown, P. C., Roediger, H. L. III, & McDaniel, M. A. (2014). *Make it stick: The science of successful learning*. Harvard University Press.

Cheryan, S., Master, A., & Meltzoff, A. (2022). There Are Too Few Women in Computer Science and Engineering. *Scientific American*, (July), 27.

Donham, C., Pohan, C., Menke, E., & Kranzfelder, P. (2022). Increasing student engagement through course attributes, community, and classroom technology: Lessons from the pandemic. *Journal of Microbiology & Biology Education*, 23(1), e00268-21. doi:10.1128/jmbe.00268-21 PMID:35496700

Eide, B. L., & Eide, F. F. (2011). *The Dyslexic Advantage: Unlocking the Hidden Potential of the Dyslexic Brain*. Hudson Street Press.

Freire, P. (1986). *Pedagogy of the Oppressed*. Continuum.

Gagne, R. M. (1970). *The conditions of learning*. Holt, Rinehart and Winston.

Greengard, S. (2018). *Virtual Reality*. The MIT Press.

Kanner, L. (1943). Autistic disturbances of affective contact. *Nervous Child: Journal of Psychopathology, Psychotherapy, Mental Hygiene, and Guidance of the Child*, 2, 217–250.

Kaufman, S. B. (Ed.). (2018). *Twice exceptional: supporting and educating bright and creative students with learning difficulties*. Oxford University Press. doi:10.1093/oso/9780190645472.001.0001

Rose, M. (1990). *Lives on the Boundary*. Penguin Books.

Rossett, A. (1995). Needs assessment. *Instructional technology: Past, present, and future*, 183-196.

Trail, B. A. (2022). *Twice-Exceptional Gifted Children: Understanding, Teaching, and Counseling Gifted Students* (2nd ed.). Routledge., doi:10.4324/9781003261216

Whitehead, A. N. (1929). *The aims of education & other essays*. Macmillan.

Wilens, T. E., & Spencer, T. J. (2010, September). Understanding attention-deficit/hyperactivity disorder from childhood to adulthood. *Postgraduate Medicine*, *122*(5), 97–109. https://doi.com/10.3810/pgm.2010.09.2206. doi:10.3810/pgm.2010.09.2206 PMID:20861593

Winebrenner, S. (2018). How we can recognize and teach twice- or multi-exceptional students. In Oxford Scholarship Online. doi:10.1093/oso/9780190645472.003.0007

Wolf, M., & Bowers, P. (1999). The double-deficit hypothesis for the developmental dyslexia. *Journal of Educational Psychology*, *91*(3), 415–438. doi:10.1037/0022-0663.91.3.415

Yates, D., & Boddison, A. (2020). *The School Handbook for Dual and Multiple Exceptionality: High Learning Potential with Special Educational Needs or Disabilities*. Routledge. doi:10.4324/9780429352041

APPENDIX A: CRL MODALITIES

Table 1 outlines diverse CRL methods, including hands-on projects, internships, field experiences, problem-based learning, service learning, and online courses. These methods engage students in real-world scenarios, providing practical experience and skill development opportunities in specific fields. These approaches are valuable for students seeking hands-on experience and educators aiming to create engaging learning experiences.

Table 1. Example CRL Methods

Method	Description
Action research	Researching real-world problems and using results for positive impact.
Apprenticeships	Working with a mentor in a specific field to gain hands-on experience.
Capstone projects	Culmination of learning in a specific subject or program.
Case studies	Analyzing real-world problems based on data or documents.
Collaborative projects	Group projects with other students, schools, or organizations.
Community-based learning	Learning experiences connected to local community needs.
Co-op programs	Work experiences related to the field of study.
Entrepreneurial projects	Developing and implementing business or entrepreneurial ideas.
Experiential learning	Learning through direct, hands-on experiences.
Field experiences	Students observe, collect data, or interact in real-world situations.
Field trips	Visiting real-world locations for immersive learning.
Flipped classrooms	Watching lectures online, engaging in hands-on activities in class.
Game-based learning	Learning through playing games or simulations.
Gamification	Incorporates game elements to make learning engaging, developing problem solving and critical thinking.
Hands-on projects	Real-world projects involving design, research, or marketing.
Independent study	Self-directed learning on a specific topic with a mentor.
Inquiry-based learning	Asking questions and seeking answers to develop critical thinking skills.
Internships	Real-world work experience in a business or organization.
Learning communities	Participating in groups to support and share knowledge.
Mobile learning	Using mobile devices for flexible and personalized learning.
Peer mentoring	Providing mentorship and support to peers.
Peer review	Reviewing peers' work to improve quality and develop critical thinking skills.
Peer teaching	Teaching peers to develop leadership and communication skills.
Problem-based learning	Solving real-world problems using learned knowledge and skills.
Project-based learning	Real-world projects to develop skills and knowledge.
Role-playing	Acting out roles/scenarios in group activities.
Service learning	Participating in service projects related to the field of study.
Service-learning courses	Courses with a service-learning component to apply concepts to real-world problems.
Simulation	Participating in simulated real-world experiences.
Study abroad programs	Participating in learning programs in other countries.
Team-based learning	Small group work on real-world tasks to develop collaboration skills.
Team-based projects	Group work on real-world tasks to develop collaboration skills.
Webinars	Participating in online seminars to gain practical knowledge.
Work-based learning	Work experience or programs related to the field of study.

Key Dimensions of CRL Approaches

Table 2 presents several key dimensions that can help educators and instructional designers evaluate and compare various approaches to CRL. Each dimension is characterized by specific aspects of the learning experience, such as the level of immersion or the degree of interaction. By considering these dimensions, educators can make informed decisions when selecting and designing learning experiences that best align with their objectives and the needs of their students.

Table 2. Key CRL approaches - dimensions

Key Dimension	Explanation
Accountability Level	Degree to which students are held accountable for their learning progress and performance
Assessment Level	Extent to which students are formally assessed on their learning progress and performance
Authenticity Level	Degree to which the learning experience is based on real-world problems or issues
Challenge Level	Degree to which the learning experience is designed to be challenging or demanding for students
Collaboration Level	Degree of encouragement for students to work together during learning
Engagement Level	Level of motivation and interest students have in the learning experience
Feedback Level	Degree to which students receive feedback on their learning progress and performance
Flexibility Level	Degree to which students can customize the learning experience to meet their needs
Guidance Amount	Amount of support provided to students during the learning process
Immersion Level	Extent of integration between the learning experience and the real world
Interaction Degree	Degree to which students actively participate in the learning process
Personalization Level	How well the learning experience is tailored to individual students' needs and preferences
Realism Level	How closely the learning experience reflects real-world situations
Reflection Level	Extent to which students are encouraged to reflect on their learning progress and experience
Scaffolding Level	Extent to which the learning experience is structured to support and guide students to success
Support Level	Level of resources and support provided to help students succeed in the learning experience
Transferability Level	Degree to which the skills and knowledge acquired can be applied to other contexts or situations

APPENDIX B. CRL EXAMPLE LESSON PLANS

Lesson Plan: Fly Fishing and "Match the Hatch"

In this lesson plan, seventh-grade students investigate key concepts of biology through the context of fly fishing and the strategy of "matching the hatch." By connecting scientific concepts to a real-world activity, students gain a deeper understanding of ecosystems, food chains, and species adaptation. The lesson plan features a mix of student presentations, group discussions, and problem-solving activities, encouraging students to apply their knowledge to practical scenarios and fostering a sense of relevance and engagement in learning.

Objective: By the end of this lesson, students will be able to:
- Understand and explain the concept of "match the hatch" in fly fishing.
- Identify and explain key concepts of biology, such as ecosystems, food chains, and species adaptation.
- Apply their understanding of these biological concepts to real-world scenarios and problem-solving activities.

Materials:
- Fly fishing equipment (rod, reel, flies)
- Pictures or videos of various insects at different life stages
- Poster paper
- Markers or colored pencils
- Internet access or relevant textbooks
- Handout on key biology concepts

Session 1: Introduction to Fly Fishing and "Match the Hatch"

1. Introduction (5 minutes)
   - Introduce the concept of fly fishing and its connection to biology.
   - Explain the objective of the lesson plan and what students can expect to learn.
2. Fly Fishing Basics (10 minutes)
   - Show students the fly fishing equipment and briefly explain its use.
   - Describe the art of fly fishing and the role of the fly in attracting fish.
3. "Match the Hatch" Concept (15 minutes)
   - Explain the concept of "match the hatch" as it relates to fly fishing.
   - Discuss the importance of imitating insects at various life stages to attract fish.
   - Show pictures or videos of various insects and their life stages.
4. Introduction to Key Biology Concepts (15 minutes)
   - Hand out the biology concept sheet.
   - Discuss ecosystems, food chains, species adaptation, and other relevant concepts.
   - Relate these concepts to the "match the hatch" strategy in fly fishing.
5. Wrap-up and Homework (5 minutes)
   - Assign students to research a specific insect species and its life stages, as well as its role in the ecosystem.
   - Instruct students to prepare a short presentation on their findings for the next class session.

Session 2: Insect Life Stages and Ecosystems

1. Student Presentations (25 minutes)
   - Have each student present their research on their chosen insect species.
   - Discuss the insects' life stages, roles in the ecosystem, and how they relate to the "match the hatch" concept.

2. Group Discussion (10 minutes)
   - Discuss the importance of understanding insect life stages and their roles in ecosystems for successful fly fishing.
   - Talk about the implications of human activities on ecosystems and how they can affect fly fishing success.
3. Group Activity: Building a Food Chain (15 minutes)
   - Divide students into groups of 3-4.
   - Assign each group a specific ecosystem (e.g., river, lake, or stream).
   - Have groups create a food chain poster, including their chosen insects and other organisms in their assigned ecosystems.

Session 3: Species Adaptation and Problem Solving

1. Review and Discussion (10 minutes)
   - Review the key biology concepts covered in the previous sessions.
   - Discuss species adaptation and its relevance to the "match the hatch" concept.
2. Problem-Solving Activity (25 minutes)
   - Present students with a hypothetical fly fishing scenario, where they need to determine the best fly to use based on the insect life stages and ecosystem.
   - In small groups, have students analyze the scenario and apply their knowledge of ecosystems, food chains, and species adaptation to make their decision.
3. Group Presentations (10 minutes)
   - Have each group present their decision and reasoning to the class.
4. Conclusion and Reflection (5 minutes)
   - Review the key concepts covered in the lesson.
   - Encourage students to reflect on the importance of understanding biology concepts in their daily lives and future careers.

Lesson Plan: Extracting DNA From a Strawberry

This lesson plan explores CRL by engaging third-grade students in a hands-on lab activity, extracting DNA from a strawberry, to introduce fundamental concepts in genetics, the scientific method, and clean room practices. The lesson plan emphasizes experiential learning, combining collaborative group work, student presentations, and guided discussions to help students understand the real-world applications of scientific concepts and promote critical thinking and problem-solving skills.

Objective: Understand basic concepts of genetics and DNA, the steps of the scientific method, the concept of a "clean room" and the importance of preventing cross-contamination in scientific experiments, and to conduct a hands-on lab activity to extract DNA from a strawberry

Materials for the lab activity include fresh strawberries, Ziplock bags, dish soap, table salt, meat tenderizer, cold isopropyl alcohol, plastic cups, coffee filters, plastic pipettes or droppers, wooden sticks or toothpicks, gloves, paper towels, a handout on key science concepts, chart paper, and markers.

Session 1: Introduction to Genetics, Scientific Method, and Clean Room Practices

1. Introduction (5 minutes)
    ◦   Introduce the lesson plan objective and what students can expect to learn.
    ◦   Introduce the lab activity of extracting DNA from a strawberry.
2. Genetics and DNA Basics (10 minutes)
    ◦   Outline basic genetics concepts and what DNA is.
    ◦   Discuss the role of DNA in living organisms and its importance in inheritance.
3. The Scientific Method (10 minutes)
    ◦   Explain lab activity as an example to illustrate the steps.
4. Clean Room Practices and Cross-Contamination (10 minutes)
    ◦   Discuss the concept of a "clean room" in scientific research.
    ◦   Explain the importance of preventing cross-contamination in experiments.
    ◦   Demonstrate proper glove use, workspace cleanliness, and handling of materials.
5. Preparation for Lab Activity (15 minutes)
    ◦   Instruct students to create a hypothesis about the lab activity.
    ◦   Discuss and review the materials needed for the lab.
    ◦   Assign roles for each student during the lab (e.g., materials manager, recorder, etc.).
    ◦   Ensure students understand the importance of following directions and safety rules.

Session 2: Conducting the Lab Activity

1. Review and Setup (5 minutes)
    ◦   Review the key concepts and lab safety rules from the previous session.
    ◦   Set up the materials and workspace for the lab activity.
2. Lab Activity: Extracting DNA from a Strawberry (30 minutes)
    ◦   Step 1: Place a strawberry in a ziplock bag and gently crush it for 2 minutes.
    ◦   Step 2: In a plastic cup, mix a small amount of dish soap, a pinch of table salt, and a pinch of meat tenderizer.
    ◦   Step 3: Pour the mixture into the ziplock bag with the crushed strawberry and gently mix for 1 minute.
    ◦   Step 4: Place a coffee filter over a new plastic cup and pour the strawberry mixture into the filter. Let the liquid drain into the cup.
    ◦   Step 5: Use a pipette or dropper to add cold isopropyl alcohol to the filtered liquid in the cup. Be careful not to mix the alcohol and liquid.
    ◦   Step 6: Observe the DNA precipitating at the interface between the alcohol and the strawberry liquid.
    ◦   Step 7: Use a wooden stick or toothpick to carefully collect the DNA strands.
3. Observation and Recording (10 minutes)
    ◦   Have students observe the DNA strands they collected and record their observations in their science notebooks.
    ◦   Encourage students to discuss their observations with their peers.

4. Discussion and Reflection (5 minutes)
    ◦   As a class, discuss the results of the lab activity and compare them to the students' initial hypotheses.
    ◦   Talk about the importance of the scientific method, genetics, and clean room practices in conducting successful experiments.
5. Wrap-up (5 minutes)
    ◦   Review the key concepts covered in the lesson.
    ◦   Encourage students to reflect on the importance of understanding genetics, the scientific method, and clean room practices in their daily lives and future careers.
    ◦   Assign students to write a short reflection on their experience with the lab activity and what they learned about genetics, the scientific method, and clean room practices.

Lesson Plan: Introduction to Digital Humanities - Literary Research on Shakespeare's Work

This lesson uses problem-based learning approach to introduce literary research on Shakespeare's work, focusing on the development and application of computational thinking, algorithms, concordances, and data literacy in an online Introduction to Digital Humanities course.

Objective: Describe computational thinking, research methods before computers and the internet, and define algorithm, concordance, and data literacy.

Materials: access to an online platform and discussion boards, relevant articles or texts on Shakespeare's work and related topics, a problem-based learning activity handout, and online collaboration tools such as Google Docs or Padlet.

Procedure:

*   Introduction (10 min): Welcome and review learning objectives. Introduce literary research on Shakespeare and its connection to digital humanities.
*   Pre-Activity Discussion (15 min): Lead discussion on computational thinking in digital humanities, using Shakespeare as an example. Define key terms: algorithm, concordance, data literacy.
*   Problem-Based Learning Activity (40 min): Divide students into small groups. Distribute activity handout. Instruct groups to develop a solution that incorporates computational thinking, algorithms, concordances, and data literacy. Encourage online collaboration.
*   Group Presentations (15 min): Each group presents solution. Encourage questions and feedback.
*   Post-Activity Discussion (5 min): Lead discussion on solutions and emphasize importance of computational thinking, algorithms, concordances, and data literacy in digital humanities research.
*   Wrap-up and Homework Assignment (5 min): Assign reflection on activity and encourage exploration of additional resources.

Note: To adapt this lesson plan for a fully online course, consider using a combination of asynchronous and synchronous tools. Discussion boards, recorded lectures, or readings can be used to introduce the learning objectives and key terms asynchronously. Synchronous video conferencing tools can be used to facilitate the problem-based learning activity and group presentations in real-time.

Chapter 2
Context–Rich Design and Designing a WAW Curriculum for Community Colleges

Lucas Marshall
Western Illinois University, USA

David Rawson
Independent Researcher, USA

ABSTRACT

In this chapter, we propose using Writing-About-Writing (WAW) principles, first introduced by Elizabeth Wardle and Doug Downs, in community college and vocational school settings—this pedagogical framework, we posit, can better prepare students to navigate diverse writing situations across academic disciplines and professional settings.

INTRODUCTION

The community college landscape is replete with students from diverse backgrounds, each with unique educational and career aspirations. In order to better serve these students and foster their academic and vocational success, we propose a writing curriculum based on the Writing-About-Writing (WAW) approach. This pedagogical framework, first introduced by Elizabeth Wardle and Doug Downs in their 2007 article "Teaching about Writing, Righting Misconceptions," emphasizes the importance of teaching writing as a tool that mediates various activities, each with its own rhetorical needs. Drawing on the works of Anne Beaufort, Wardle, and Linda Adler-Kassner, the WAW approach equips students with essential analytical skills and threshold concepts, enabling them to navigate diverse writing situations across academic disciplines and professional settings.

Community colleges stand to benefit significantly from adopting a WAW-based curriculum. By teaching students the intricacies of discourse communities, rhetoric, genre, and research, the WAW approach primes them to tackle unpredictable writing situations they may encounter in various fields.

DOI: 10.4018/978-1-6684-7644-4.ch002

Moreover, this curriculum is well-suited for community college students seeking transfer to four-year institutions, as it ensures they are equipped with the necessary analytical skills to adapt to new writing contexts at their destination schools.

One of the major strengths of a WAW curriculum is its flexibility. Instead of prescribing rigid syllabi, WAW serves as a set of curricular guideposts that accommodate and complement the unique expertise of experienced community college instructors. Thematic approaches, such as those popularized during the cultural studies era, can be integrated into a WAW curriculum, provided they focus on introducing students to rhetorical concepts applicable across contexts.

Implementing a WAW curriculum involves incorporating assignments that address key knowledge domains, such as discourse community knowledge, rhetorical knowledge, genre knowledge, critical thinking and research knowledge, and metacognition. By embedding these domains in the curriculum, students will be better prepared to transfer their writing skills to various academic and non-academic settings. In sum, a context-rich writing curriculum, grounded in the WAW approach, holds significant potential for enhancing the educational experience and outcomes of community college students.

LITERATURE REVIEW

The Community College

The inception of America's first community college took place in 1901 at Joliet Junior College in Illinois. The purpose of these early institutions was to provide a general liberal arts-based curriculum, a mechanism through which all citizens could gain access to higher education. However, the perception of these institutions by higher education leaders was not one of mutual respect but one of patronization: the general liberal arts-based curriculum was meant to introduce citizens to higher education while maintaining the elitism of the university (Brint & Karabel, 1989). That is, only the most capable of community college students would move on to university studies. Furthermore, the negative perception of community colleges as less academic and more vocational grew as they began offering job-training programs in response to widespread unemployment caused by the Great Depression. This perception continued to grow as, following World War II, soldiers returning home were enabled through the GI bill to use community colleges as a way to learn the skills needed for joining the workforce (Weisberger, 2005). Today, community colleges consistently offer financial benefits, though the academic risks that surround community colleges' poor perception have been enough to detract many prospective students (Bowen, Chingos, & McPherson, 2009).

At the community college, writing programs have historically been in large part indefinable in comparison to writing programs at the 4-year college. Helon Howell Raines (1990), in a survey of some 236 two-year colleges, found no pattern between how community colleges across the nation structure their writing programs. Tim N. Taylor (2009) sought to replicate Raines and found similar results. Albeit constrained by collecting fewer results than Raines, he confirmed the "de-centered" nature of the community college writing program. Joseph Janangelo and Jeffrey Klausman (2012) conclude that the "very concept of 'writing program' --and by extension how writing courses ought to fit together or not--continues to be in-flux at two-year colleges" (p. 134-5). They also conclude, "Our sense, in looking at the responses to these questions as a whole, is that our sample respondents did not see a consistent underlying theoretical frame in any of their institutions" (p. 135). The haphazard nature of community college writing programs, and their theoretically indistinct frameworks, is grounds for some concern.

Furthermore, while community colleges continue to offer vocational associate's degrees and self-purporting transfer programs to 4-year colleges and universities, whether these programs can offer seamless transfer is questionable. The efficacy of the process of remediation at community colleges is also up for debate. Some studies have investigated the extent to which community colleges in fact hinder baccalaureate attainment (Bowen, Chingos, & McPherson, 2009; Melguiza, Kienzel, & Alfonso, 2011; Roksa & Calcagno, 2010), some finding this indeed to be the case (Bowen, Chingos, & McPherson, 2009; Roksa & Calcagno, 2010). Another study, by contrast, found that former community college students' rate of baccalaureate attainment was comparable to that of 4-year college rising juniors—albeit still slightly worse—but reported that these findings did not take into account the number of remediation classes taken at the community college level (Melguiza, Kienzel, & Alfonso, 2011). One study in fact showed that of those students enrolling in community colleges, a significant 42% of students were obliged to take one or more remedial courses before enrolling in college-level courses, in effect causing a costly and time-consuming process, should these students remain in college (Melguiza, Serra Hagerdorn, & Cypers, 2008). Hence, while it is uncertain whether supposed university equivalent courses, provided at community colleges, are satisfactory, it is somewhat clear that many students entering at this level will be required to take uncredited classes that could slow down their progress toward the baccalaureate degree.

This literature review is intended to assist prospective teachers of writing at the community college level to understand the various approaches to teaching writing while focusing on writing-about-writing as a particularly fruitful approach to teaching writing at the community college. As we will argue, Anne Beaufort's discussion (2007) about writing situations being mediated by genres with rhetorical ends for specific discourse communities can be a helpful guiding post to designing an audience/context-specific curriculum for the community college, where these issues are high stakes. In order to teach at the community college, it is important to acknowledge the distinct institutional factors that are present at community colleges. As scholars such as Patrick Sullivan and David Nielson (2013) have noted, community colleges' open-admission policies attract financially burdened and systemically marginalized students. These students, Greg Shafer (2007) argues, possess unique dialects, a supposed "'substandard' English," (p. 169) over which they become self-conscious and apprehensive. Furthermore, 21st century students bring their own technologically mediated language to the classroom (Daemmrich, 2007; Relles & Tierney, 2013).

Teaching at the community college, then, involves realizing cultural and socioeconomic factors present at community colleges. While the culture of the community college isn't necessarily dissimilar to diverse public 4-year colleges, the way community colleges view and employ remediation is different to 4-year colleges. Writing students at the community college face deeper remediation than at public 4-year universities, and training in developmental writing is thus necessary for community college writing instructors (Gleason, 2006). If community colleges consciously employ instructors with experience implementing a developmental writing curriculum, they will ensure that community college students don't fall through the cracks or become dissuaded from their higher education aspirations because of their remedial writing courses (Riley-Bahr, 2011). Howard Tinberg (2011) takes issue with the feedback overloaded community college instructors provide their students, which becomes impersonal and vague. Beth Gulley (2012), similarly, finds that community college developmental writing students' papers improved upon receiving teacher feedback and ultimately encourages us to provide substantive, not purely grammatical, feedback. However, doing this can be challenging amid the heavy teaching loads assigned to community college instructors (Lee, 2009), especially when the developmental curriculum focuses on grammar instruction.

Kenneth Levinson (2005) has found success in approaching the teaching of basic writers through guided exploration of sociolinguistics. Furthermore, Ingrid Daemmrich (2007) and Stefani Relles and William Tierney (2013) have recommended approaching the developmental academic writer through media more familiar to them. Oliver Breary (2015) implores us to reconsider how we teach Comp II, and encourages us to avoid conflating the two-part composition sequence as merely freshman composition. He urges us to rethink Comp II and promote the preparation for writing-across-the-curriculum contexts students will encounter in other community college classes as well as in upper-division classes taken at the university. To best prepare for teaching at the community college level, I propose to examine an existing community college's writing curriculum with the goal of revising that curriculum. This will help us understand what pedagogical priorities the department has, if any, and provide a starting place for developing a new curriculum using WAW and research on transfer and threshold concepts. We are interested, furthermore, in seeing how WAW might be useful at a community college, particularly one that feeds students to a 4-year university that employs WAW itself.

Writing About Writing

In 4-year universities, recent writing scholars have championed "Writing about Writing" (WAW) as an effective method through which to approach the teaching of writing. Proponents of this approach to teaching writing posit that teaching how genre functions is important so that students might become aware of how writing changes from one context to another. Anne Beaufort (2007) finds that teaching "general writing" causes struggles for students moving from one writing context to another. She ultimately concludes that writing instructors should abandon futile attempts at teaching a general academic discourse for a systematic approach of preparing students to respond to contextual factors that new writing situations demand. Elizabeth Wardle (2009) has found that instructors who are unaware of genre theory in effect facilitate the production of "mutt genres" by students, writing divorced from clear genre and purpose. Since there is no way to teach every particular genre of writing a student might encounter in a neat and perfected way, Wardle contends that the best way to teach writing is to teach about writing. Teaching students how to analyze genres, she believes, will allow them to note the patterns between new and old genres and transfer knowledge from one writing context to another. In addition to champions of WAW, "threshold concepts" have been argued as an integral part of writing studies. Scholars such as Linda Adler-Kassner, John Majewski, and Damien Koshnick (2012) believe that concepts such as genre, purpose, audience, and situated practice are necessary threshold or baseline concepts for all students to understand in the writing classroom.

Threshold Concepts

In their 2015 book, Naming What We Know: Threshold Concepts of Writing Studies, Linda Adler-Kassner and Elizabeth Wardle define threshold concepts as "concepts critical for continued learning and participation in an area or within a community of practice" (2). In keeping with Wardle's and Doug Downs's claims (2007) that FYC should offer an introduction to the field of writing studies rather than a reductive skills boot camp in writing for college, Naming What We Know outlines 37 threshold concepts pedagogically tied to FYC.

Writing about Writing and Threshold Concepts, more than courses that teach college writing as a skill that can be attained and generalized to all writing in college, teach about critical thinking insofar as, for example, they demand students to consider the ways in which writing "works in the world and how the 'tool' of writing is used to mediate various activities" (Downs and Wardle 558).

Although skills-based writing courses purport to offer transferable skills, they do so in a reductive way that misleads students into thinking about writing as a one size fits all type of task--once mastered, one should succeed in all future tasks. Doug Downs and Elizabeth Wardle (2007) contend that the umbrella term "academic writing," often used to characterize writing taught in FYC, fails to acknowledge the mediation of the "various activities within higher education"; they go on to suggest that such a narrow scope doesn't specify what content, genre, activity, context, and audience each writing situation calls for, which is necessary due to writing's complexity (p. 556).

Transfer Theory

In their book, Writing Across Contexts: Transfer, Composition, and Sites of Writing (2014), Kathleen Blake Yancey, Liane Robertson, and Kara Taczak discuss an approach to teaching writing called "Teaching for Transfer (TFT)" from which their "interest in transfer" centers on "two main areas--content and transfer, and reflection of transfer" (p. 63). They believe that a "specific kind of reflection, one that [is] interwoven into the course as a regular, systematic, and knowledge-producing practice" is critical to the transfer of knowledge in a given course (p. 63). Using a portfolio assignment in FYC, they find, helps them examine "multiple texts inside one portfolio... [and] learn from the student," how "he or she has made a successful transition," and how to "support such a transition" (p. 2). They also find reflection as a "systematic theory and practice keyed to creating a theory of writing" (p. 34). They suggest employing curricular goals that value "incorporating a set of key terms as conceptual anchors for a composition content" as well as "threading throughout the course a specific, reiterative, reflective practice linked to course goals, which themselves take transfer of knowledge and practice as a first priority" (p. 42).

In their article, "The Value of Troublesome Knowledge: Transfer and Threshold Concepts in Writing and History," (2012) Linda Adler-Kassner, John Majewski, and Damian Koshnick discuss the implication of threshold concepts shared among history and writing courses and suggest the interrelation between threshold concepts and writing transfer. Adler-Kassner, Majewski, and Koshnick's exploration of the inherent nature of threshold concepts for writing success suggests an important and valuable framework for teaching writing in the community college, where issues of transferring coursework between colleges is so predominant.

Writing About Writing, Threshold Concepts, Transfer Theory, and the Community College

While a threefold approach to teaching writing--which draws upon writing about writing, threshold concepts, and transfer theory--we believe this framework would be useful to the community college, a level at which transfer is considerably important. The community college's inherent obligation to prepare for transfer is perhaps even more high stakes than at 4-year universities due to transfer concerns being more immediate than at universities--whereas at 4-year universities transfer perhaps most immediately refers to writing-across-the-curriculum, community colleges must prepare for cross-institution transfer (in the case of community college-to-university transfer) as well as for the workforce (for those enrolled in occupational programs). While there is no one right way to approach the teaching of writing at community colleges, a writing program that familiarizes students first and foremost with discourse community knowledge seems justifiable as well as useful to occupationally oriented students who may be skeptical about the worth of their general education courses.

The community college is an ideal location to adapt and adopt a curriculum that intersects writing about writing, threshold concepts, and transfer theory found at work in various R-1 institutions. Community colleges first and foremost, perhaps even more so than at universities, find themselves in a position in which teaching for transfer is an implicit necessity. Two-year colleges instruct introductory students enrolled in transfer programs who seek admission into major programs at 4-year universities and therefore require transferable knowledge. Two-year colleges also instruct students preparing for the workforce whose programs must teach transferable skills lest facing one's accreditation revoked. A curriculum that draws upon these curricular objectives might better prepare students with diverse educational and occupational goals to reach them.

College Composition in the Community College

Holly Hassel and Joanne Baird Giordano (2009) have noted how students enrolling in first- and second-year composition have had trouble transferring knowledge between classes. Mark Blaauw-Hara (2014) discusses how transfer theory and threshold concepts provide a healthy response to the struggles of making general education writing courses "relevant to students and connected to the college at large" (p. 357). The community college seems like an ideal location to transplant a curriculum that intersects writing about writing, threshold concepts, and transfer theory found at work in various R-1 institutions; for community colleges first and foremost, perhaps even more so than at universities, find themselves in a position in which teaching for transfer is an implicit necessity. Two-year colleges instruct introductory students enrolled in transfer programs who seek admission into major programs at 4-year universities and therefore require transferable knowledge. Two-year colleges also instruct students preparing for the workforce whose programs must teach transferable skills or risk having one's accreditation revoked. Discourse community, genre, and rhetorical awareness seem appropriate for students who either plan to enter the workforce upon earning their associate's degree or plan on transferring into a university to declare a major with which they might otherwise be unfamiliar.

Basic/Developmental Writing in the Community College

As seen in Sara Webb-Sunderhaus and Stevens Amidon (2011), remedial writing courses have begun to move out of the university, with community colleges bearing the brunt of these responsibilities. Basic writing theory, as argued by such seminal figures as Mia P. Shaughnessy (1977), David Bartholomae (1980), and Mike Rose (1983), has suggested basic writing instruction should move toward error analysis as opposed to a one size fits all approach to grammar instruction with ineffective grammar workbook style exercises. From the looks of it, many community colleges have retained the old ways of teaching basic and developmental writing. Webb-Saunderhaus and Amidon (2011) suggest that students leaving BW courses should possess knowledge of rhetoric; critical thinking, reading, and writing; writing process; and knowledge of conventions "including the ability to follow common formats for different kinds of genres; to practice appropriate means of documenting one's work; to control such surface features as syntax, grammar, punctuation, and spelling" (p. 7). Bruce Horner and Min-Zahn Lu (1999) have called for a redefining of Shaughnessey to best map the future of basic writing pedagogy. Horner suggests engaging students in the "negotiations with readers and error in their writing and in theorizing about error" (p. 157). "Teaching the history of the negotiation of particular conventions as 'correct,'" he posits, "can have value to the extent that it encourages students to take active roles in continuing such negotiations in their own writing" (157). An alternative to the skill-and-drill approach to teaching basic and developmental writing might, then, be one that empowers student writing, embeds writing process knowledge and allows for one-on-one instructor-student sessions and multiple revisions. A basic/developmental writing course that intersects writing about writing, threshold concepts, and transfer theory is valuable insofar as its curricular inclination is to facilitate students' realization of how community impacts writing.

Writing Program Administration in the University

In the university, the Writing Program Administrator is what Diane George (1999) refers to as both a plate twirler and a troubadour because of the many different hats he or she must wear. Shirley K. Rose and Irwin Weiser (1999; 2002) recommend that writing program administrators consider themselves both researchers and theorists, respectively; that they be aware of the institutional stakeholders that necessitate writing program fluidity; and that they be attuned to how necessary program assessment is to the overall development and sustainment of the writing program. Eli Goldblatt, in his 2007 book, Because We Live Here: Sponsoring Literacy Beyond the College Curriculum, demonstrates and advocates for literacy partnerships across institutions and many different levels. Several scholars, too, featured in Rita Malenczyk's 2013 book, A Rhetoric for Writing Program Administrators, note the importance of writing program administrators acknowledging how much students from diverse backgrounds--ESL students, basic and developmental writers, transfer students, etc.--must inform and shape program goals.

Writing Program Administration in the Community College

Heather Ostman (2013) discusses the imperative need to revitalize community college writing departments in the wake of President Obama's 2009 address, which called for an increase of college graduates and a heavier utility of America's community colleges. She emphasizes curriculum reform that moves away from workbook style exercises and toward a writing-across-context design to introduce students to college-level reading, writing, and critical thinking. As previously discussed, Holly Hassel and Joanne Baird Giordano, in their Teaching English in the Two-Year College article (2009), stress the level of difficulty underprepared writers--who are found so frequently at the community college--face in transferring knowledge between first and second-semester writing courses. Speaking from a community college setting, Mark Blaauw-Hara (2014) outlines how transfer theory and threshold concepts could be applied to a general-education writing course. Elizabeth A Nist and Helon H. Raines, (1995) and Jeffrey Klausman (2008; 2013), discuss the importance of a strong writing program administrator at the community college who acknowledges diversity of the community college as well as the need for instruction that takes into account various occupational and educational objectives sought out by students enrolling at community colleges. They note how English faculty at community colleges often necessarily "emphasize classroom practice and applied learning over theorizing about writing" (p. 63) in their instructional design. They also discuss the need for better collaboration between two- and four-year colleges--one such collaboration being internships for graduate students considering community college teaching careers in which experienced community college instructors oversee and provide guidance to these student-teachers in order to better prepare them for a more seamless entrance into the workforce (p. 69). Such steps, they suggest, could better facilitate instruction that is appropriate for both kinds of institutions as well as awareness of cross-institutional instruction without entirely forcing uniformity between institutions whose demographic makeup might not call for it.

Implementing a writing-about-writing curriculum as a writing program administrator is beneficial from a community college perspective in allowing departmentally to advertise a program that keeps writing transfer as its main priority while also providing leniency for current instructors to operate within an agile and resilient writing curriculum.

"Changing How Writing is Taught"

Steve Graham's "Changing How Writing is Taught" assesses the progress we have made in the last few years and also maps out a clear vision of what still needs to be done, which areas are lacking, and who needs to be involved for there to be more progress. Graham begins with the given that "if students are to be successful in school, at work, and in their personal lives, they must learn to write. This requires that they receive adequate practice and instruction in writing, as this complex skill does not develop naturally." Now 85% of the world can write, and schools are meeting the needs and teaching writing skills to many students, but still not all. In the United States, roughly two thirds of students in 8th to 12th grade scored at or below basic level on the most recent (as of the original publication of this research) Writing Test administered by the National Assessment of Educational Progress National Center for Educational Statistics, 2012, "denoting only partial mastery of grade level writing skills. Based on previous scores and this more recent score, the National Commission on Writing (NCOW, 2003) labeled writing a "neglected skill in American schools" (p. 278).

Graham then pivots to questioning what our data for judging success in writing actually is: "most of what we know about how writing is currently taught in school settings comes from surveys asking teachers about their instructional practices in writing" (p. 278). To get a bigger picture, his research reflects on 28 survey, observation, and mixed method studies "involving the writing practices of more than 7,000 teachers" (p. 278). One main result from this research is that "some teachers provide students with a solid writing program, and in some classrooms this instruction is exemplary," but that in general, these results are not typical for all students. Some of the classrooms that were successful were applying evidence-based practices: in elementary grades, this looked like "writing for different purposes, teaching strategies for carrying out writing processes such as planning and revising, conducting formative assessments to guide writing instruction, and teaching students foundational writing skills" plus skills like "handwriting, spelling, and sentence construction" (p. 279). Secondary level focused on these same skills, except handwriting, spelling, and sentence construction scaffolding received less of an emphasis. While it is important to celebrate successes and to look at what successful classrooms are doing, meeting the needs of all students means exploring in detail what was less successful. In one study (Parr & Jesson, 2016), teachers under-emphasized persuasive and expository writing" while another study (Cutler & Graham, 2008) overemphasized grammar and handwriting while underemphasizing teaching students how to plan and revise. Much of the writing from these 28 studies revealed a large amount of "writing without composing" in not just composition classes but also in secondary level content classes. This looks like "filling in blanks on a work sheet, note taking, and one-sentence responses to questions" (p 280).

The second major finding from Graham's research is that students in a typical class are not writing frequently enough, and that the teaching procedures for evaluating this writing was happening too infrequently:

While teachers commonly assigned a variety of different types of writing over the course of a year, students engaged in most of these activities no more than once or twice during the year (e.g., Brindle et al., 2016; Kiuhara et al., 2009; Koko, 2016). The writing activities most commonly assigned to students involved very little extended writing, as students were seldom asked to write text that was a paragraph or longer (e.g., Gilbert & Graham, 2010). [Another] indicator of insufficient writing instruction involved the use of teaching procedures. While the typical teacher applied a variety of different instructional practices (e.g., McCarthy & Ro, 2011; Tse & Hu, 2016) and made many different instructional adaptations over the course of the school year (e.g., Troia & Graham, 2017), most of these teaching procedures were applied infrequently, often less than once a month (e.g., Graham et al., 2014; Graham, Harris, MacArthur, & FinkChorzempa, 2003; Hertzberg & Roe, 2016). This included teachers' use of evidence-based practices for teaching writing (e.g., Drew et al., 2017; Gilbert & Graham, Graham: Changing Writing Instruction 281 2010). Undoubtedly, how frequently teachers applied specific instructional practices, made particular instructional adaptations, or assigned different types of writing was related to the time they devoted to teaching writing (p. 281).

Other major takeaways from Graham's research are that the primary audience for students' writing is still the teacher, not much writing involved collaboration among students, too much times spent in repairing for "high-stakes writing tests," classrooms do not have enough resources for effectively teaching writing, formative assessments are infrequent, student motivation for writing outside of wanting to pass the class was ignored, and "the writing needs of students with a disability or who were learning a second language were not sufficiently addressed." It stands to reason that individual passionate teachers are operating outside the confines of this particular study and are finding success in a variety of writing assignments that require more planning, synthesis, and feedback, but "nevertheless, the typical teacher does not devote enough time to writing and writing instruction. Students do not write often enough, and they are seldom asked to write longer papers that involve analysis and interpretation" (p. 281).

Based on these findings, Graham argues that for real, lasting, systemic improvement, writing and writing instruction must be valued, and every stakeholder needs to "acquire specific know-how, which includes knowledge about writing, a vision for teaching writing, and professional commitment." Teachers need "knowledge, vision, and commitment" to "become masterful, efficacious, and motivated writing teachers." Teachers must be able to devote more time to teaching writing. Policymakers, district personnel, and principals need to "acquire specific know-how about writing in order to make writing instruction an educational priority so that teachers' efforts are valued and supported." Graham also argues that society itself needs to "view writing as valuable" for effective, lasting results (p. 283).

Strong writing comes from practice: "some forms of writing take many years to master, and writing growth is a consequence of writing and deliberate practice," and everyone involved in the success of the student should be on the same page about the importance of the role of writing in the student's success and should have a clear image of what effective teaching of writing looks like and what is involved to make it happen (p. 286).

Writing is an amalgamation of many skills, and if students do not have confidence in one of those areas, it may impact the entire writing process for that student, so knowing that every stakeholder in this education understands what writing success looks like and agrees about its significance in success, the student may be more likely to embrace the idea that failure is a marker of progress and that risk is needed for growth in the skills that make up writing. Writing development includes" learning as a consequence of action. Students acquire knowledge and beliefs about the cognitive and physical actions they use when writing by evaluating the effectiveness of these operations. It involves learning by expansion" (p. 286). Students learn by observing others and how their writing is perceived and accepted. In the community college classroom, many students may be speaking English as a foreign language and may also have started their education later in life. An English 1 comp class is their introduction into "academic writing," and the student should trust that their teacher's models for writing will not just apply to this present class but their entire college careers.

For this reason, models are very important and may ease anxieties about "what it's supposed to look like" and open up a space for application, effort, creativity, risk, and exploration. This is an area where the teacher's role can be one of passing on knowledge from "multiple rodeos." The teacher may have a system where they ask for volunteers for students to have their papers read anonymously in future classes. Students can discuss as a group and with the person who is grading their own writing what is and is not working in a model essay. They can talk about what grade they would give the paper and then ask at the end what grade the teacher did / would give this paper. Students can then hear in the teacher's response there in the moment with a model in front of them what the teacher would consider and how they would weigh the product based on the rubric, as well as any other specific criteria. The actual product may be written alone, and that product may be graded alone, but that does not mean that the writing and grading processes are lone processes. In the moments when the student is staring at a blank screen and trying to remember something their teacher said about the writing process in class, the student will hopefully feel the sturdiness of the architecture of the writing program and know they are supported as writers.

CONCLUSION AND FURTHER RESEARCH

In conclusion, the implementation of a Writing-About-Writing (WAW) approach in community college writing curricula holds great promise for addressing the diverse needs of students and preparing them for success in both academic and professional contexts. By emphasizing the role of writing as a tool that mediates various activities and rhetorical situations, the WAW approach equips students with the analytical skills and threshold concepts necessary for navigating the complex landscape of writing in the 21st century.

The flexibility inherent in the WAW approach allows for the incorporation of a variety of thematic approaches and pedagogical techniques, thus making it adaptable to the unique expertise of community college instructors. By embracing a context-rich writing curriculum, educators can address key knowledge domains and provide students with opportunities to apply their learning in diverse situations. This, in turn, prepares them to transfer their writing skills to various academic and non-academic settings, supporting their educational and vocational aspirations.

Despite the promising implications of the WAW approach for community college writing curricula, further research is needed to address several critical questions. First, how can community college educators best tailor WAW-based curricula to meet the specific needs of their diverse student populations? In particular, research should focus on identifying instructional strategies and resources that facilitate the learning of non-native English speakers and students from underrepresented backgrounds.

Second, as community college students often face unique challenges in terms of time constraints and competing responsibilities, it is crucial to investigate how the WAW approach can be adapted to maximize efficiency and effectiveness in these contexts. This includes identifying optimal course structures, delivery methods, and support systems that promote student engagement and success while minimizing the burden on students and instructors.

Third, there is a need for empirical studies that assess the long-term impact of WAW-based curricula on students' writing development and transfer of skills across disciplines and professional settings. Such research should employ rigorous methodologies, such as longitudinal designs and control-group comparisons, to establish causal relationships between WAW-based instruction and student outcomes.

Finally, as the WAW approach continues to gain traction in community college settings, it is essential to explore best practices for faculty development and support. This includes identifying effective strategies for training and mentoring instructors in the WAW approach, as well as developing resources and networks that facilitate collaboration and the sharing of knowledge among educators.

In summary, the WAW approach represents a powerful tool for enhancing the writing instruction and support provided to community college students. By embracing this context-rich curriculum, educators can better serve the diverse needs of their students and empower them to achieve their academic and vocational goals. However, to fully realize the potential of this approach, further research is necessary to address the critical questions outlined above. Through rigorous investigation and collaboration, the community college landscape can continue to evolve, ensuring that all students have the opportunity to develop the writing skills they need to thrive in an increasingly interconnected world.

REFERENCES

Adler-Kassner, L. (2015). *Naming what we know: Threshold concepts of writing studies*. Utah State University Press.

Adler-Kassner, L., Majewski, J., & Koshnick, D. (2012). The value of troublesome knowledge: Transfer and threshold concepts in writing and history. *Composition Forum, 26.* https://www.compositionforum.com/issue/26/troublesome-knowledge-threshold.php

Adler-Kassner, L., & Wardle, E. (2015). *Naming what we know: Threshold concepts of writing studies*. Utah State University Press.

Bartholomae, D. (1980). The study of error. *College Composition and Communication, 31*(3), 254–269. doi:10.2307/356486

Beaufort, A. (2007). *College writing and beyond*. Utah State University Press.

Beaufort, A. (2007). *College writing and beyond: A new framework for university writing instruction*. Utah State University Press.

Blaauw-Hara, M. (2014). Transfer theory, threshold concepts, and first-year composition: Connecting writing courses to the rest of college. *Teaching English in the Two-Year College, 41*(4), 354–365.

Bowen, W. G., Chingos, M. M., & McPherson, M. S. (2009). *Crossing the finish line: Completing college at America's public universities*. Princeton University Press. doi:10.1515/9781400831463

Brearey, O. (2015). Understanding the relationship between first- and second-semester college writing courses. *Teaching English in the Two-Year College, 42*(3), 244–263.

Brint, S., & Karabel, J. (1989). *The Diverted Dream, Community Colleges and the Promise of Educational Opportunity in America, 1900-1985*. Oxford University Press. doi:10.1093/oso/9780195048155.001.0001

Daemmrich, I. (2007). Novices encounter a novice literature: Introducing digital literature in a first-year college writing class. *Teaching English in the Two-Year College, 34*(4), 420–433.

Dougherty, K. J. (1995). *The contradictory college: The conflicting origins, impacts, and future of the community college*. SUNY Press.

Downs, D., & Wardle, E. (2007). Teaching about writing, righting misconceptions: (Re)envisioning 'first year composition' as 'introduction to writing studies. *College Composition Composition and Communication, 58*(4), 552–584.

George, D. (1999). *Kitchen cooks, plate twirlers, & troubadours*. Boyton/Cook.

Gleason, B. (2006). Reasoning the need: Graduate education and basic writing. *Journal of Basic Writing, 25*(2), 49–75. doi:10.37514/JBW-J.2006.25.2.04

Goldblatt, E. (2007). *Because they live here: Sponsoring literacy beyond the college curriculum*. Hampton Press.

Graham, S. (2019). Changing how writing is taught. *Review of Research in Education, 43*(1), 277–303. doi:10.3102/0091732X18821125

Gully, B. (2012). Feedback on developmental students' first drafts. *Journal of Developmental Education, 36*(1), 17–36.

Hassel, H., & Baird Giordano, J. (2009). Transfer institutions, transfer of knowledge: The development of rhetorical adaptability and underprepared writers. *Teaching English in the Two-Year College, 37*(1), 24–40.

Horner, B., & Lu, M. Z. (1999). *Representing the "other": Basic writers and the teaching of basic writing*. NCTE.

Janangelo, J., & Klausman, J. (2012). Rendering the idea of a writing program: A look at six two-year colleges. *Teaching English in the Two-Year College, 40*(2), 131–144.

Klausman, J. (2008). Mapping the terrain: The two-year college writing program administrator. *Teaching English in the Two-Year College, 35*(3), 238–251.

Klausman, J. (2013). Toward a definition of a writing program at a two-year college: You say you want a revolution? *Teaching English in the Two-Year College, 40*(3), 257–273.

Lee, M. (2009). Rhetorical roulette: Does writing-faculty overload disable effective response to student writing? *Teaching English in the Two-Year College, 37*(2), 165–177.

Malenczyk, R. (2013). *A rhetoric for writing program administrators*. Parlor Press.

Melguizo, T., Kienzl, G. S., & Alfonso, M. (2011). Comparing the educational attainment of community college transfer students and four-year college rising juniors using propensity score matching methods. *The Journal of Higher Education, 82*(3), 265–291. doi:10.1353/jhe.2011.0013

Michaud, M. (2011). The "reverse commute": Adult students and the transition from professional to academic literacy. *Teaching English in the Two-Year College, 38*(3), 244–260.

Nist, E. A., & Raines, H. H. (1995). Two-year colleges: Explaining and claiming our majority. In *Resituating writing: Constructing and administrating writing programs*. Boynton/Cook.

Ostman, H. (2013). *Writing program administration and the two-year college*. Parlor Press.

Howell Raines, Helon. (1990). Is there a writing program in this college? Six-hundred and thirty-six two-year schools respond. *College Composition and Communication 42*(2), 151-165.

Relles, S., & Tierney, G. (2013). Understanding the writing habits of tomorrow's students: Technology and college readiness. *The Journal of Higher Education, 84*(4), 477–505.

Roksa, J., & Carlos Calcagno, J. (2010). Catching up in community colleges: Academic preparation and transfer to four-year institutions. *Teachers College Record, 112*(1), 261–288. doi:10.1177/016146811011200103

Rose, M. (1983). Remedial writing courses: A critique and a proposal. *College English, 45*(2), 109–128. doi:10.2307/377219

Rose, S. K., & Weiser, I. (1999). *The writing program administrator as researcher*. Boynton/Cook.

Rose, S. K., & Weiser, I. (2002). *The writing program administrator as theorist*. Boynton/Cook.

Shafer, G. (2007). Dialects, gender, and the writing class. *Teaching English in the Two-Year College, 35*(2), 169–178.

Shaughnessy, M. P. (1977). *Errors and expectations: A guide for the teacher of basic writing*. Oxford University Press.

Sullivan, P., & Nielson, D. (2013). "Ability to benefit": Making forward-looking decisions about our most underprepared students. *College English, 75*(3), 319–343.

Taylor, T. (2009). Writing program administration at the two-year college: Ghosts in the machine. *WPA. Writing Program Administration, 32*(3), 120–139.

Tinberg, H. B. (1997). *Border talk: Writing and knowing in the two-year college*. National Council of Teachers of English.

Wardle, E. (2009). "Mutt genres" and the goal of FYC: Can we help students write the genres of the university? *College Composition and Communication, 60*(4), 765–789.

Wardle, E., & Downs, D. (2007). Teaching about writing, righting misconceptions: (Re)envisioning "first-year composition" as "introduction to writing studies.". *College Composition and Communication, 58*(4), 552–584.

Wardle, E., & Downs, D. (2014). *Writing about writing: A college reader*. Bedford/St. Martin's.

Webb-Sunderhaus, S., & Amidon, S. (2011). "The *kairotic* moment: Pragmatic revision of basic writing instruction at Indiana University-Purdue University Fort Wayne." *Composition Forum 23*, https://www.compositionforum.com/issue/23/ipfw-revision.php

Weisberger, R. (2005). Community colleges and class: A short history. *Teaching English in the Two-Year College, 33*(2), 127–141.

Yancey, K., Robertson, L., & Taczak, K. (2014). *Writing across contexts: Transfer, composition, and sites of writing*. Utah State University Press. doi:10.2307/j.ctt6wrr95

APPENDIX

Transfer Theory and Transfer Institutions: A Practical Guide for Using Writing-About-Writing Principles in the Community College

What is Writing-About-Writing?

In their 2007 *College Composition and Communication* article, "Teaching about Writing, Righting Misconceptions: (Re)envisioning 'First-Year Composition' as 'Introduction to Writing Studies,'" Elizabeth Wardle and Doug Downs compel college writing instructors to consider the impracticality of teaching academic writing in two semesters. They urge instructors to "resist conventional but inaccurate models of writing" (p. 557), considering a more robust approach would teach writing as a tool that mediates various activities, each with its own separate rhetorical needs. In her 2007 book, *College Writing and Beyond: A New Framework for University Writing Instruction*, Anne Beaufort considers subject matter knowledge integral to successful writing performance but puts more specific emphasis on intersecting broad concepts of discourse community, genre, and rhetorical tools in order to empower student writers with the tools to "analyze similarities and differences among writing situations they encounter" (p. 149). In 2015, Wardle and Linda Adler-Kassner released a book titled *Naming What We Know: Threshold Concepts of Writing Studies* in which they further reiterate the importance of students comprehending a given discipline's "threshold concepts" in order to effectively succeed as a participatory member of that discipline, naming 37 threshold concepts of writing studies, including the rhetorical and social nature of writing.

WAW advocates keep issues of writing transfer as a foremost pedagogical priority by embedding analytical practices in the curriculum so that students are not solely prepared to write for other writing classes but prepared to enter new, unfamiliar writing situations, such as vocational ones. What's more, a writing-about-writing curriculum does not require a rigid, unyielding syllabus that all faculty must abide by exhaustively; rather, a WAW curriculum can be used as pedagogical guideposts that allow for seasoned instructors to draw upon their own pedagogical areas of expertise so long as these areas are contextualized for students within programmatic objectives.

Why Community Colleges Could Benefit from Writing-About-Writing

Many WAW advocates agree that WAW principles offer a robust approach to teaching writing; students are taught concepts such as discourse community, rhetoric, genre, and research, and are implored to consider writing as a genre-mediated response to the rhetorical needs of different discourse communities. In learning these concepts, students are primed to approach the various, sometimes unpredictable, writing situations they may encounter in various fields by drawing upon analytical skills learned in a WAW curriculum. A WAW curriculum can provide students at the community college, who come from diverse backgrounds and hold diverse career and educational plans, with a robust, transfer-motivated writing education. Students, on leaving a WAW classroom, will both understand the concepts informing the field of writing studies and be prepared to enter various writing contexts equipped to analyze each context for its audience's rhetorical needs and genre expectations. A WAW curriculum is particularly useful for the community college whose transfer programs are sought by students intending to transfer seamlessly to four-year institutions. While catering to individual academic programs at different colleges nationwide is a difficult and unfeasible goal for one community college, offering a writing-about-writing curriculum within a writing program is one way to ensure students are, to the best of the program's abilities, equipped with the necessary analytical skills to approach new writing situations as they occur in unique academic and non-academic settings.

Writing-About-Writing Course Design: How to Implement a Writing-About-Writing Curriculum

One major benefit to implementing a WAW curriculum in the community college is that WAW allows flexibility for experienced community college instructors. WAW advocates do not propose to prescribe rigid syllabi that all faculty are bound by. Rest assured that experienced instructors' unique areas of expertise will only be complemented by a WAW curriculum; WAW advocates like Anne Beaufort (2007) propose WAW as a set of curricular guideposts that uses "broad concepts (discourse community, genre, rhetorical tools, etc.)" to empower students to analyze "similarities and differences among writing situations they encounter" (149).

Instructors working within a WAW curriculum are given great flexibility in how they introduce students to these broad concepts. For example, thematic approaches made popular during the cultural studies era can accommodate WAW approaches as long as the focus of the class remains on introducing students to rhetorical concepts that allow them to employ writing knowledge across contexts.

There is no one necessary syllabus for WAW, but many advocates of the WAW approach agree on the kinds of assignments instructors might draw upon. Many WAW advocates agree that assignments that embed the following knowledge domains will best prepare students for transfer:

- Discourse Community Knowledge: Using assignments that introduce writing as a tool employed by specific discourse communities to facilitate communication between members will aid in students' understanding of writing as context- and audience-specific.
- Rhetorical Knowledge: Using assignments that introduce students to the elements of the rhetorical situation (exigence, audience, and context), which they can apply while composing their own texts, will aid in students' understanding of writing as a tool that can achieve rhetorical ends.
- Genre Knowledge: Using assignments that teach how genre functions as a typified response to recurring situations among discourse communities will aid in students' understanding of writing as a context- and audience-specific practice that seeks to respond to rhetorical ends through the use of audience-specific genres.
- Critical Thinking and Research Knowledge: Using assignments that encourage students to think critically about real-world problems, and that embed research strategies, will facilitate students' understanding of how to participate in ongoing academic and non-academic conversations.
- Metacognition: Using assignments that encourage students to reflect on their writing will help foster awareness of writing knowledge and thus prime students to transfer writing knowledge into other situations.

Chapter 3
The Pedagogy of Progress(ion):
On Context–Rich Learning in the Arts

Adam al-Sirgany
1-Week Critique, USA

ABSTRACT

This essay explores "context-rich learning" in the arts, cases of its practice, and the virtues and limits thereof. Nevertheless, much of the essay is dedicated to articulating the contexts themselves in which art as a whole and knowledge of the human kind are rooted. The essay explores five examples of context-rich learning that may be applied to different goals under the umbrella of arts education: the Suzuki Method, a musical training method focused on craft skills and learner engagement; the Montessori method, a general education program particularly applicable to the intersection of goal-based learning and individuated student learning styles; the Critical Response Process, a technique of artist-directed critique applicable across artforms and dialogic classrooms; Multiliteracies pedagogies, an academic framework developed by the New London Group and focused on differentiated student (co-learner) experiences; and 1-Week Critique, a nonprofit organization focused on open-access literary education utilizing diversified strategies for writers across circumstances and skillsets.

It is the objective of this essay to describe "context-rich learning" in the arts, cases of its practice, and the virtues and limits thereof. Nevertheless, a portion of the essay is dedicated to articulating the contexts themselves in which art as a whole and knowledge of the humankind are rooted.

It is necessary to explore these contexts—cursorily—in order to dispel fundamental misconceptions about art, art-purposes, and art-capacities before speaking to "tried" practices in the pedagogy of the arts, or rather approaching a pedagogy situated in more richly-comprehended pluralities of art contexts. This necessity emerges from the fact that, in most practices, the contexts of that which is taught and the context(s) in which its lessons are taught differ. Context-rich learning is, simply put, a twining of the two.

Art, however, as a practice, the end results of which are always unassured—in this sense art differs notionally from craft, the intentional shaping of media into repeated objects of purpose—, has always required a pedagogy that interacts with the past in of the present to contribute to formulations of futures, the results of which neither "students" nor their mentors will ever fully see. Thus, with regard to art

DOI: 10.4018/978-1-6684-7644-4.ch003

pedagogy more broadly, this text will not discuss "best" practices—which in the instance of art may reference predefined impacts on observers and predefined, assessable goals of the artist, and which treat the art object as a mere tool for the crosspieces of the two. Rather, it will look at certain approaches being undertaken by pedagogues interested in crafting context-rich learning environments, the experiences and inspirations from which such practices have been derived, some of what may be learned from those practices, and what fundamental belief systems underpin the angles of pedagogy we utilize in our own work towards the limited but worthy ends we as artists and "teachers" may ever hope to achieve.

Despite the often-vaunted consistencies and stabilities of mathematics, those of us who have never lived outside the post-Enlightenment age sometimes forget the contexts in which numbers were reified to begin with: those in which it was perceived useful by some human beings to distinguish object units within sets of form and to demonstrate relationships between those units. Though not a mathematician, I begin here in order to articulate the belief that all human knowledge, even the most stable, demonstrable, translatable knowledge, is functional knowledge, and that the function of such knowledge exists in the perceptions of the humans utilizing, upholding, and altering its taxonomies, measurements, tools and meanings. These perceptions are subject to change within context and form.

Art is qualitative, and even to speak this binary conception is antithetical to the means by which arts—of any kind—act on human beings in their experiences of living. Questions of measurable success in artistic pedagogy are always ineffectual. This is not because arts are inherently unteachable but because what can be taught of the arts are the craft strategies used by our predecessors to achieve particular effects as we (a given community) understand and experience them in the present, while the objective of art is to engage an individual or a community in as yet unexplored aspects of sensory, narrative and intellectual potentials.

What separates us (many present-day humans) from true art-encounters (as contrasted with acquirable, listable art experiences, such as are described when one says, "I have seen the works of Picasso in Barcelona" or "so-and-so's CV lists that his sculpture has been shown at MoMA in such-and-such a show") begins in a systemic and linguistic detachment from the media of art crafted by, among other pre- and post-cursor powers, Capitalist acquisition. Relatively few educational techniques encourage actual learning (the development of awarenesses that allow individuals to interact with and adapt to their circumstances across contexts)—as opposed to the practice of craft techniques towards rote capability (i.e. to write a sentence that has, minimally, a subject and a predicate, or even to write a succession of such sentences in variegated rhythmic patterns). Most align with what Brazilian educator Paulo Freire calls "the banking model of education." Friere's "pedagogy of the oppressed" actively opposes such models and instead focuses on putting learners at the center of their own education and liberation. It does so through problem posing, dialogue and democratic inquiry, rather than more authoritarian strategies such as memorization, lectures, moralization and the like (Freire, 2020).

There is an essential difference between 1) an education designed for a nearly ethic-less marketplace controlled by "growth" and growth principles—these objectives have limited and mindless ambitions, their sole aim being abstract increase to which even the human "instincts" of power and control become secondary, thus driving forward, with little regard to consequences, incitable animal desires and anxieties—and 2) an education developed out of the root impulses of life, the tools of interacting with such impulses, and allowing from those interactive encounters the yet-undefined actions which—rather than unformulated progress, conservative maintenance, or instinctual survival—constitute the basis for the narrative potentials of the human-animal. The need to articulate these distinctions becomes critical if we are to take seriously a "pedagogy of art" and concomitantly of "art appreciation," the latter being the basis for a "market" of art, regardless of whether that market is Capitalist or otherwise delimited. In short, one must know a song well before singing it. In sum, we cannot teach what we cannot know.

A pedagogy of art must begin with what art is. And because what art is is experiential, transitive, and transitory, any effectual pedagogy of art must be one of collaborative experience and change with ourselves, with our "students" (I prefer co-practitioners, co-learners, co-laborators) and with the media with which we reify objects of artistic encounter for those outside the processes of their creation.

So, what is this art to begin with that must be known before we can begin? When we refer to art, we are speaking to one or any number of permutations of the following:

1) the interactions between artist-hopeful and media-in-potentia (art as work),
2) the interactions between a "completed" art-object and its receivers (art as embodied Other),
3) the historical and politically defined and codified objects viewed as "artful" by a given community (art as objects of culture),
4) the individuated encounters with senses, ideations, objects that for the artist-hopeful constitute a starting place for further explorations with media (art as lineage, or personal narrative formation).

Even if we don't speak to them specifically, all four are at work in active, real-world conceptions of art. All four must thus be integrated into art pedagogy if it is to be effectual in engaging the chimeric tulpa that art is.

For the individual observer, art is the intellectual framework used to distinguish, among craft productions, those which have particular emotive hold and sensory magnetism for them. Many of us can recall witnessing someone caught in the wordless rapture of encountering a work of significance (to them) for the first time. Such an event is not coequal with the passing shock and fascination aroused by what Guy Debord has labeled "spectacle" (Debord, 2012).

In conversation with Frankfurt School theorists such as Herbert Marcuse and artist communities such as the Dadaists, as well as alluding to Homer's complaint to the Maecenas (Speriani, 2017), Debord, a founding member of the Situationist International, believed capitalism, in its perpetual need for production, replaced meaningful encounter and thus human truth with the consumption of commodities. Even at the time Debord's work was first published, 1967, capitalism had well-instituted systems of thought and action that allowed individuals to replace experience with acquisition: a percentage of income due an engagement band in evidence of love, and the like. In art, acquisition becomes a similar problem. To own a print of "Starry Night" becomes a myth of one's artistic inclinations. To purchase a ticket to stand in line to stand in front of "Starry Night" establishes the "truth" of commitment to these inclinations. And luckily enough, Bank of America has arranged tax breaks for itself by giving cardholders free general admission access "to more than 225 cultural institutions"—so the real ones deposit with them (Bank of America, 2023).

For Debord, the spectacle is both an event and the self-replicating system-structure that promotes such events. And because it is so hard to see outside this cycle, he warns "[i]n societies where modern conditions of production prevail, life is presented as an immense accumulation of spectacles. Everything that was directly lived has receded into a representation" (Debord, 2012).

This is of import as, for social units, art is an application of personal frameworks to create and secure bonds across individuals and communities. The idea of the Western World, for instance, is at least partially held together by the always-tangled marionette strings of an art history that perceives Roman mosaics and Duchamp's "Fountain" to be in the same conversation. Which invites those of us privileged to hold even passing familiarity with one or both to lay intellectual claim to an imagined (but consequential) community gifted us simply by being born with a "known," public past behind us. Accessing such privileges, however, even oppositionally and by individual consent, also commits us to the system(s) of acquisition we have accessed. Each system is one present basis by which we assess art. None is one and the same with a person becoming enraptured by a piece independently.

Individual taste is the basis for art appreciation, and organic mutual appreciation is the basis for a community of art derived from distinct, created objects. By organic, we mean grown from existing (as opposed to—anyone's—utopianly or dystopianly imagined) conditions. The intentional, forced, enforced application of these connectivities sometimes uses the term "art" or "Art" to substantiate itself. Force is not art, nor is it related to art. Rather, such forceful applications bind and dilute genuine, individual art-experiences and thus deteriorate occasions for social apparatuses that are created through art-experiences as points of connection. Art pedagogy must therefore resist force and enforcement—or become the authoritarian tool of its own conceptual dismantling.

In one of his most famous essays, the philosopher and "Father of the Harlem Renaissance," Alain LeRoy Locke states, "My chief objection to propaganda, apart from its besetting sin of monotony and disproportion, is that it perpetuates the position of group inferiority even in crying out against it" (Locke, 1928, p. 1-2).

This recognition of Locke's—that, given wholly to political or social upending, art becomes a mere facet of counterculture (situated in relation to a dominant culture itself) is key to understanding what art may do politically and makes a case for art's perpetuation independent of definable social outcomes and stated objectives. Speaking out of a position of externally-perceived social inferiority (to a white over-class) and to a community of which he was a part (Black artists), Locke suggests a recognition of necessary (that is factual) predecessors and conditions, while purporting that "free and purely artistic expression" may be one of the ways in which this (perhaps any) self-identified community may actualize and (re)formulate relatively independent identities (here, cultures) and their meanings. "Our espousal of art thus becomes no mere idle acceptance of 'art for art's sake,' or cultivation of the last decadences of the over-civilized, but rather a deep realization of the fundamental purpose of art and of its function as a tap root of vigorous, flourishing living," writes Locke (Locke, 1928, pp. 1-2).

Art as potentiality of craft and form may have more to do with alternative (thus far socially underappreciated, unaccepted and unacceptable frameworks). As Ovid is quoted, *Barbarus hic ego sum, quia non intelligor illis.* In his *First Discourse* 18th Century philosopher Jean-Jacques Rousseau, explores the question of whether "the restoration of the sciences and arts [has] contributed to the refining of moral practices" and famously asserts that they not only haven't but have been a moral detriment. "Before art fashioned out manners and taught our passions to speak an affected language, our habits were rustic but natural, and differences in behaviour announced at first glance differences in character" (Rousseau, 2009).

While much of Rousseau's theory is loose and dated to an Enlightenment-era, "state of nature" mindset that itself uses reason to form an artificial conception of what humankind is and should be, Rousseau's famous discourse asserts that art creates and then acts against morality, and this holds true because morality is normative. The conditions of art have more to do with a Gilliganian ethics of care—an ethical, feminist framework formulated by psychologist Carol Gilligan focusing on interpersonal relationships, rather than "rational"-decision making—than with an Enlightenment era fixation on Reason, more to do with a Freirian liberation than a neoliberal marketplace, not because art is feminine or because it is inherently bound to, say, leftist politics of some particular definition. Art is by its condition nonnormative until it has been historicized by curation and enshrinement into a political sphere. It then upends itself again with new outliers and abnormativities.

Understanding the depths of art, even as a function within Western ideologies, inevitably includes grasping that happiness, the good, the beautiful, truth are plastic ideas distinguished from the plastic idea of art itself. There is some, but not necessary, crossover in these conceptions. Those crossovers resemble Pollock's spatters more than either a Venn diagram or a genealogical chart where one births or is the objective correlative of any of the others. When John Keats' Grecian urn claims, "Beauty is truth, truth beauty," it does so through the poetic speaker's voice. For most of us to lay the same claim outside a temporary moment of profound encounter would likely seem ridiculous. Though, the end of art is such moments and the stories we form (with ourselves and our communities) from them, and these cannot be actualized simply by insisting, *It is true that this is beautiful and beautiful that this is true.*

The truth of the beauty must be believed by its receivers, or it becomes a platitude. To quote John Dewey, "When artistic objects are separated from both conditions of origin and operation in experience, a wall is built around them that renders almost opaque their general significance, with which esthetic theory deals. Art is remitted to a separate realm, where it is cut off from that association with the materials and aims of every other form of human effort, undergoing, and achievement. A primary task is thus imposed upon one who undertakes to write upon the philosophy of the fine arts. This task is to restore continuity between the refined and intensified forms of experience that are works of art and the everyday events, doings, and sufferings that are universally recognized to constitute experience" (Dewey, 1934).

A valid and sustainable pedagogy of art is achieved by assisting art-crafters in developing their craft with an eye beyond re-creation. Effectual art pedagogy—that is, educational strategies which pursue the ends of art qua art rather than art synonymous with craft, social objects, propaganda, or imitative decoration; pedagogy that distinguishes art as a study of distinct substance and concern—meaningful art pedagogy as such must aid the art-practitioner in seeing the art-object and its likely initial receivers, as well as in helping potential art-receivers better witness the attention and nuance of created works in general so that encounters-with-art may arise for them, so they (the receivers) may better connect with artworks of meaning for them, and with communities who have like experiences with art of similar aesthetics.

In the arts, this has almost always been done via exercises of context-rich learning (CRL). "Context-rich learning…" according to the editors of this book, Braun and Trajkovski, "embodies the answer to the question '[W]hy do we need to learn this?'" It does so by developing learning and mentorship spaces that recreate or actively participate in the real-world scenarios wherein a skillset is used towards a desired end" (Braun and Trajkovski, 2023).

If art is, to use a limited shorthand, craftwork made in such a manner as to hold special significance (to someone or a collective of someones), then CRL in the arts is a pedagogical practice of consciously shaping educational spaces that develop craft knowledge and skills while cultivating and protecting co-practitioners' capacities for individuated encounter and exploration.

The pursuit of authentic—I prefer the term "effectual"—learning is not new. Audrey C. Rule points out that the concern for meaningful pedagogy has been an issue for decades. Rule goes on to define authentic learning using four key factors: "real-world problems that engage learners in the work of professionals; inquiry activities that practice thinking skills and metacognition; discourse among a community of learners; and student empowerment through choice" (Rule, 2006). What's especially useful about these criteria is that they emphasize the obligation of the pedagogue to present the subject in context for a student who can experience and think critically about that context and its applications and who can make independent decisions to and how to enact their labors.

With regard to craft skills in the arts this may refer to any number of pedagogical strategies already in use in studios and classrooms. Concerning music, for example, there is great and well-actualized potential in the Suzuki method of instrument instruction. According to the school's website, the practice's namesake, "violinist Shinichi Suzuki realized the implications of the fact that children the world over learn to speak their native language with ease. He began to apply the basic principles of language acquisition to the learning of music and called his method the mother-tongue approach. The ideas of parent responsibility, loving encouragement, constant repetition, etc., are some of the special features of the Suzuki approach."

Using a combination of listening skills development and practice that focuses on increasingly-complete, ear-trained performance (as opposed to the repetition of scales, for instance), the Suzuki method trains students to interact directly with music, with their instruments, and with their peers, as well as with the ideally supportive and long-standing audiences of their work.

As the memorization of verb tenses tends to be simple for the purposes of grading—correct or incorrect—but less effective than language immersion for the purposes of the most common use of language—that is to speak and communicate with others in the world—the memorization and development of intermediary, conceptual skills that create familiarity with the tools of, but not the actions or enmeshments with, art (i.e. platonic concepts of pianos in general, viols in general; reading notes; scales; and theories of composition) are not ineffectual, they are simply unessential conceptual barriers between the artist-in-craftskills-development (or art-encounterer) and the creation of craft/art and/or its appreciation. These barriers shape conditions wherein the practitioner's mind is not trained to respond—hand-to-tool—with world-facing sincerity, spontaneity or meaning-in-the-moment. Instead, they are trained to search for the answer most appropriate to a situation defined by educators in the bounded timeframes of teaching and confined for the student by what is covered and correct, rather than by what is presently occurring. The student may overcome this by practice in the world and may have greater context and knowledge for that endeavor. Yet what sense is there in restraining education to the abstract as a go-to approach when guided context-rich strategies are available to us as learners and pedagogues-in-learning?

Here's a practical exercise to demonstrate the point. Read a two- or three- year-old a short, favorite book every night for five or six days. Preferably, find a non-linear, non-narrative (story-less) text. ABC books and readers for learning colors work perfectly. Read the book as often as the child wants you to. Several days in, begin skipping pages to get to the end faster. It's not uncommon for children to insist that something is wrong, to ask where the duck went, to announce that something is wrong. Contrast this against any attempt to ask an older child, even of seven or eight, to memorize the same book for the purposes of being tested. You're likely, in the latter case, to find that the anxiety of potential, personal failure contributes to the difficulties they have with this request.

Suzuki, not surprisingly and akin to sibling-approaches in the gen eds, relies heavily on structure, especially in the early years of ear-training and performance. Communal student development depends on a common student repertoire, as a theater troupe requires common plays and actors well-versed enough in all or several parts to guarantee distribution of the necessary players. Two Ophelias won't do. But an actor ready to adapt to Hamlet at a moment's notice is attuned pluralistically to the emerging possibilities of their environment.

If the Suzuki method is one fine guide for craft-skills development in the arts, Montessori, among general education courses and the liberal arts, especially those focused on early-childhood education may be a corollary for those aspects of pedagogy emphasizing art as an exploratory approach to skill-based craftwork and as the framing of experiences of directed discovery. Montessori, originally conceived by

Dr. Maria Montessori out of a response to her work with developmentally delayed children, emphasizes educational circumstances that are designed around the needs of the children learning, their independent interests and abilities. While the approach has never been trademarked and has consequently, with expanded popularity, taken on many forms, there are several key—and fairly universal—Montessori practices particularly relevant to context-rich learning (Benyamin, 2021).

Montessori utilizes "freedom within limits," a concept expressly bound to Rousseau's *Emile* and perhaps best articulated by Dr. Montessori herself:

Let us consider the attitude of the teacher in the light of another example. Picture to yourself one of our botanists or zoologists experienced in the technique of observation and experimentation; one who has travelled in order to study "certain fungi" in their native environment. This scientist has made his observations in open country and, then, by the aid of his microscope and of all his laboratory appliances, has carried on the later research work in the most minute way possible. He is, in fact, a scientist who understands what it is to study nature, and who is conversant with all the means which modern experimental science offers for this study.

Now let us imagine such a man appointed, by reason of the original work he has done, to a chair of science in some university, with the task before him of doing further original research work with hymenoptera. Let us suppose that, arrived at his post, he is shown a glass-covered case containing a number of beautiful butterflies, mounted by means of pins, their outspread wings motionless. The student will say that this is some child's play, not material for scientific study, that these specimens in the box are more fitly a part of the game which the little boys play, chasing butterflies and catching them in a net. With such material as this the experimental scientist can do nothing.

The situation would be very much the same if we should place a teacher who, according to our conception of the term, is scientifically prepared, in one of the public schools where the children are repressed in the spontaneous expression of their personality till they are almost like dead beings. In such a school the children, like butterflies mounted on pins, are fastened each to his place, the desk, spreading the useless wings of barren and meaningless knowledge which they have acquired.

It is not enough, then, to prepare in our Masters the scientific spirit. We must also make ready the school for their observation. The school must permit the free, natural manifestations of the child if in the school scientific pedagogy is to be born. This is the essential reform (Montessori, 2012, pp. 26-27).

None of this suggests that Montessori method learning is purely wandering about or that it is without goals and objectives. On the contrary, Montessori educators, commonly called directresses, directors, or guides, facilitate exploration in a structured environment meant to be easily interacted with and navigated through at most children's proportions.

These environs typically include limited but significant materials, called works: blocks to be arranged in numerical order, color-differentiated sound cylinders children must shake in order to identify matching tones, metal inserts that assist in the training of pencil grip and present connections to shapes that will eventually be utilized in writing, etc. Crucial to the Montessori approach, each work is simple and has a specified learning objective. Each objective is presented to a child by a guide, and the objectives generally utilize "isolation of difficulty," offering children opportunities to master skills that compound and coordinate. Still, the works are to be chosen by the child and explored with curiosity, so that the child can, though by their own development, discover the processes of a work's architecture and purpose.

With guides overseeing these interactions, children are encouraged to expand their curiosity and approaches to the works available to them. In Montessori, as in art, the individual mind guides basic learning, but a common and interactive language develops from the works and the spaces of common relationship.

The "natural" world is critical to this conception, being the space out of which and upon all conceptions of artifice and their manifest creations become. Montessori education thus actively encourages students to "work"—the methodological term for children's activities in this realm—outside and to recognize connections between the natural environment and the environment within.

The virtue of this approach is manyfold, not least of which is that it encourages pedagogues to witness children in their uniquenesses. Even where work is uniform and demands the accomplishment of essentially uniform goals, Montessori guides thus, at their best, circumnavigate the educational—engagement—attrition common to schools and employment institutions that insist work be done as prescribed rather than done well—to say nothing of with joy, commitment, ingenuity, or élan.

To create such classrooms for artists, to offer artists-in-development apt tools to achieve skill sets in their crafts and imaginative ends in their actions, it is necessary to conceptualize a meaning of art, to escape the grand-scale, top-down, and typically abstract assertions that allow authoritarian forces to impose aesthetic values on individuals—the function of which is never more nuanced than power gain or power maintenance. That's all hating has ever been. The effectiveness of its niggling, bullying, and dismissal (refusal to see the Other) is a Machiavellian case for its use, but like all Machiavellian proposals, the fact that something can or has worked towards some limited end is not the same as saying it's fulfilling to achieve that end in such a manner. Burning a house to the ground to avoid doing the dishes works, reasonably, well. But…

For some, the academic art studio and workshop have taken on this character, accrediting students without significant job prospects, editing them without substantially providing them skill sets for editing, critiquing them without supporting their work or substantiating their support of the work of others, proposing for them problems in the marketplace while leaving them relatively ignorant of market functions (i.e. the processes and logics of agenting, curation, pricing, distribution, etc.) and of how these functions have historically related to art at any pin in the hermeneutic circle of its coming into being (Myers, 2006).

There is variance across institutions here. The access to and accessibility of market systems and "networking" connections differs between schools, educators, and individual student-teacher connections, the effects of which are, as often as not, constant striving by practitioners to be "seen" by magic helpers in the forms of teachers, professors, better-published and recognized peers, agents, editors, publishers, curators, etc. And reciprocally encourages the (for the arts) delusional belief of decorated academics and artists that they have "established" themselves, a market and social situation occasionally true but incompatible with the mercurial, antinormative natures of art as itself.

Liz Lerman's Critical Response Process (CRP) is a pedagogical strategy particularly useful for navigating this set of circumstances, as it offers every practitioner the opportunity to present work on terms they've established, as well as gifting co-learners opportunities to see and interact with work on practitioner-established terms.

CRP was originally developed by Lerman, a former ballerina and active choreographer, for the purposes of group feedback on dance, as a means for helping dancers constructively discuss revisions to their peers' works. But CRP can and has been widely applied across the arts and other arenas. The practice divides a workshop into three roles: the artist, the responders, and the facilitator. The artist(s) share works-in-progress with responders who then offer "statements of meaning" about their experiences—what the work evoked, what was exciting or compelling about the work they've just been introduced to. The artist then asks questions about the work, after which responders share thoughts relevant to each specific question. When artist questions have concluded, responders may ask "neutral questions." These questions may be about choice but should not be innately critical. ("What motivated or inspired this work?" may be a neutral question. Whereas "Why would anyone make this?" or "Don't we have enough stories about 'coming out?'" are not.) Finally, responders may share opinions, though these opinions may only be shared if a responder has asked to share, offered what their opinion is about (i.e. "I have an opinion about the use of food language in this poem, would you like to hear it?"), and the artist has affirmed their desire to explore the topic (Lerman, 1993).

While Lerman's CRP may seem unlike the real worlds of art-in-practice Context-Rich Learning promotes (at least for those who conceptualize "real worlds" as full of dehumanizing criticism, cut-throat dealings, and limited winners), CRP, in fact, mimics very closely the positive efforts exercised by contemporary publishers, curators, editors, etc.—in conjunction with artists—to bring artworks into a dynamic public realm. We live in globalized and "digitized" communities, whose communicative styles and art experiences differ vastly. There is a cap here, and anywhere, on $100 million paintings and $30 million book deals, but these anomalies have rarely had much to do with art qua art, or have generally had to do with the practice of art preservation incorporated into non-art markets seeking the abstract "value" (i.e. social capital, tax shelter) some artworks can offer. Yet, CRP provides art-practitioners tools for developing and asserting what marketers often call "their brand," opportunities for discovering those communities that comprehend and might wish to market such a brand, and these while providing practitioners chances to explore and deepen ideas about their works-in-progress so they may edit and adapt work to their aims and intentions rather than toward the intentions of a singular market hypothesized and created by the minds of their particular co-practitioners or teachers. In this sense of seeking coordination between product/work and lens CRP mirrors much of the work done by editors and publishers, curators and directors, as they prepare an already strong piece for a wider public.

Moreover, while during an initial presentation, a CRP facilitator may act primarily as a responder and moderator (whose role is to assure commitment to the method and its intentions), an active, thoughtful facilitator will also foster the potential for connections, offering platforms for extended "subject matter discussion" and sometimes overseeing the "labbing" of a piece. This is necessary to the actualization of real-world work, the foundations of which are experimental (research and development, R&D).

While CRP is arguably most attuned to practitioners of some development in their crafts, it also recognizes that art-in-practice—like all subject fields—is only about skillset execution where it is about repetition and automation. Defined progress, including childhood development models, always maps to a normative and averaged set of learners as defined by a given community at a static moment. Innovation in art—or in the workflow of a logistics firm, for that matter—requires understanding how an end goal is brought to bear, as well as comprehending the useful, forward-looking questions that might assist in producing an outcome if it is worth producing for the art-practitioner and their communities. It is the role of the CRP facilitator to help bring these possibilities to being.

Ultimately art is, to quote Simone Weil, "an attempt to transport into a limited quantity of matter, modeled by man, an image of the infinite beauty of the entire universe" (Weil, 1951, pp. 168). For Weil, such an attempt reveals itself to all when successful, and success requires attention in order to be actualized for its receiver (Weil, 1951). Art is art then when it is crafted with a loving welcoming of beauty as it may be. Art becomes art for us as receivers when we can practice the negative effort necessary to witness art as itself. Open to encounter and learning from others, we are open to more art, perhaps at the cost of what is called growth (in economic terms) and what is experienced as fame and in the interest of the developments of humanity as it could be but hasn't been yet.

For the past thirty years or so, the New London Group's (NLG) "Multiliteracies" approach has been a framework for understanding the "metalanguages" educators may seek in order to better actualize platforms for objective-based learning (Oozeerally, et al, 2020). Multiliteracies models of pedagogy are, simply put, educational strategies recognizing the manyfold differences in those experiences that lead us (at any age) to the education we are presently pursuing, and which build their approaches in real time and in response to the diversity of our potentials. They are of significant appeal to us, as, like Lerman's Critical Method these models begin with the language experiences of co-learners and practitioners in their contexts, as well as with adaptive learning objectives (adaptive to the emerging needs of the real world as well, as to the functional needs of the co-learner).

Multiliteracies pedagogies recognize that the "traditional" form of mandated, rote school learning has not been historically dominant in human history, and that enforced learning as such, has tended to create gaps between students and encourage the "success" of a limited few who match (even in advance of schoolwork itself) that traditional model's expectations, standards and grammars. The lines between the successful and supposedly unsuccessful tend to grow thicker with time and are not merely drawn between races, genders and sexual orientations, but as well between languages, socioeconomic circumstances, parental and familial education, whether or not a learner has eaten at any time of the day before their classes, etc.

In the Multiliteracies viewpoint, all learning has objectives and an adept pedagogue sees and responds to the learners in front of them, in large part by integrating student experiences into the curricula of coursework. Thus, even if pursuing an unchanging or unalterable course goal—say, introducing a given method of completing a type of math equation or a certain technique often practiced in screen printing shops—the pedagogue works with the students who are working with them, as opposed to with presupposed tabula rasas, the most legible slates of which are those most advantaged by genetic and social lotteries present learners may (to some degree be obliged to but may) not wish to or be equally prepared to partake in.

There are many exercises in empathy and communication that have emerged from Multiliteracies models and adjacent approaches, but the NLG began its work in contexts of "literacy," that is comprehending communication (often written communication perceived as being most fully actualized in works of "great" literature, but in fact a much broader concept). The NLG originally laid out several domains of literacy that work in tandem to make communication possible: linguistic, gestural and spatial, as well as the ever-increasingly important audio and audio-visual aspects of literacy (New London Group, 1996). The work of these academics, and others, has continued to explore these domains, their adaptation to real-world (rather than academically conceived and codified notions of "proper") use. This includes the rise of multimodal media—that is, not the technology of our contemporary fascination but the manners in which, through digital spaces and not, we have increasingly come to interact with media that requires multisensory literacy to comprehend multimodal means of communicating.

Herein is an approach that attends to three primary questions for CRL pedagogies and education more broadly: what ends do the skillsets we teach serve; what do we perceive the world to be like wherein we believe these ends should be served; attending to the perceptions of Others, should our perceptions, approaches and/or goals change?

Typically multiliteracies pedagogues find that the final answer is yes, and that the changes to our goals as educators should be toward the recognition of our real-world linguistic, economic, cultural, social, bodily experiences, experiences which are diverse, overlapping and contrary to the idea of a "right way" of writing, speaking, articulating color, form, haptics and sound, and which, when witnessed, may open the door to more nuanced communication and better-defined goals for even the stodgiest "reasonable" professor in tweed and elbow patches.

To provide such mentorship necessitates interacting with individual learners, observing them specifically and pursing classroom and course design that suits their needs through the methods by which they communicate—as well as recognizing the coordination between the needs of any given learner and those other learners in a classroom or studio. Kuby and Gutshall Rucker's work investigating children's "literacy desiring" is particularly compelling here. "Our intent with literacy desiring," they write, "is to focus on the intra-actions of people- with-materials, -movements, and -surprises while creating, not necessarily a future end product" Kuby and. Gutshall Rucker, 2016, p. 314). Their exploration of a single child's (Neil's) interactions with multimodal media (his communications about a pop-up book) demonstrate not only methods of co-learner recognition but the rewards of seeking such recognition: among them, better achieving our own goals as pedagogues by better understanding our co-learners (their speech, their intents, their meaning and its forms...). In turn, we are better able to comprehend how we, ourselves, might translate our own intentions, not trapping our co-learners outside the veil of "learning" but rather using the veil as part of how we understand course design.

Because defining course goals means committing to an integral process of discovery between (sometimes several) individuals, the ideal structure of a context-rich art classroom is an adaptive form. Inspiration for such a classroom, a more or less permanent one, can certainly be taken from the likes of 826 Valencia (now 826 National). In its co-founder Dave Eggers' telling 826 emerged from listening to teacher friends who saw a need for more one-on-one mentorship in writing. Eggers, who is also a co-founder of *McSweeney's Quarterly*, worked with his collaborators on the publication to find connection points between the press and the tutoring center with which it shared office space. They then began redesigning their own time and space—decking it out in pirate-themed decorations, for example—to allow more fluid interactions between themselves, as professional publishers, and the kids with whom they were hoping to develop literary skills (Eggers, 2009).

I'd like, towards conclusion, to offer one final example, that of some of my own work as an arts advocate and pedagogue with 1-Week Critique (1WC). Begun in 2020, 1WC intends to provide and partake in an intimate experience of editing with writers, editors, co-learners, pedagogues-in-learning, and their work, taking what's most engaging from creative writing workshop models and making these processes active and adaptive to differential learning tendencies and experiences.

As professional editors, ghostwriters and academics, each of us involved in the organization's origins had and continued to, actively or from time-to-time, teach. We recognized challenges and gaps in the academic marketplace—particularly the supply-demand issue of producing (through MAs, MFAs, PhDs, various forms of community workshops and writers' groups, etc.) relatively large numbers of self-identifying poets and writers, whose primary goal was to produce works of entertainment or literature, and whose professional credentials—if any— were suited for an academic market which produces academically-credentialed writers.

The incidental pyramid-scheme elements of these circumstances are not one and the same with literary or artistic encounters themselves being a scheme (Myers, 2006). Rather, we reflected that canonized, historicized art (however newly so) in a mass culture is an object of purpose for that culture, and a culture that proliferates artists en masse inevitably fractures its aegises. This is only upsetting to their conservators.

Art requires connection, witness, memory. Who connects, who witnesses and where, who remembers and when—these answers don't make art greater, more or less. Our concern was that literary artworks typically require slow, intimate engagement, and while it is the nature of any art community to produce more work of merit than can be engaged by any one individual in it, especially in a community that continues to pursue the curation of historical works, the systems we ourselves benefited from were likely to have diminishing returns for future writers.

We started as a primarily web-based project offering highly personalized but fairly rapid feedback—hence our name—but, since, our goals have expanded. At that time and now, writers who submit work to us receive a response discussing the craft of their piece, what stands out to the editor engaging the work, what experiments and alterations may emphasize the writer's apparent goals, as well as reading recommendations for the editorial process. In many ways, though alleviating writers of the burdens of cost and locational commitments that are barriers between some writers and university coursework, our original model was a modified rendition of that space.

Traditional university workshops often focus on dictating what is wrong, not on the crafts or art of editing, alone or collaboratively. This is the inherent consequence of reading and shaping work during the course of a confined timeframe, such as a 16-week university term, and the practice, in that timeframe, of emphasizing the outcome of publishing in a market workshoppers typically have little experience with, having only seen the end products of magazines or books. The problems with this model are several fold and include that not all writers wish to publish in these venues—or at all—, that the world of the literary arts is large and our exposures to and understandings of venues of publication and their aesthetics differ widely, and that both for the purposes of art and market, what exists is only a baseline for what we hope to achieve next.

As an organization, we've increasingly taken an interest in framing what we offer writers around the needs and aims of those writers we encounter. This has come in the form of several projects whose goal is to provide our co-learners tools for self- or group-directed inquiry into ways of reading and editing. Our roundtable podcast, *StoryTalk*, for instance, examines a single short story at a time. The stories themselves are chosen by podcast participants and, as a result, are often thematically interconnected across discussions but reflect the individual experiences and tastes of the participants, both in choice and in response. Similarly, our web series *Appreciations*, welcomes literary magazine editors to share poems they value that have been published by other literary magazines.

More to the exploration of editing itself, *The Interview Series*, a podcast/web series, invites authors to share early or "draft" forms of a work that was later published, providing context for the editorial choices and approaches they used. We explicitly encourage the writers who engage with *The Interview Series* to experiment with those choices that work for them in their own writing and always remind co-learners they may freely access and download the comparative materials on our website. Anyone may likewise download *Teaching Takeaways*, short assessments of poems by a single author that include analysis of a poem's language, some of the functions of that language, and craft prompts reflecting a given way of reading the work.

Though we began, as a pandemic-era website and primarily develop editorial resources for writers of some familiarity with their craft, we've grown into a small, 501(c)(3) nonprofit, and this is one means by which we've connected with other organizations and been gifted opportunities to collaborate with them. Most relevant to the topic at hand, our collaboration with the Iowa City Public Library's Teen

Space and its preexisting writing club has given us the chance to provide weekly, hands-on workshops for local kids, ages 13-18. The intimacy and consistency of these workshops, which typically include 4-10 co-learners, allows our volunteers the opportunity to meet and learn about the children with whom they work and, most importantly, to devise exercises that suit the children's particular interests and skills.

While we come to the Teen Space with craft goals—developing forms of musicality, for example—we have been able to shape interactive exercises around the awareness that, for instance, a consistently attending teen co-learner is a cellist, who, though shy, enjoys sharing her knowledge of rhythm and articulation. Given encouragement by volunteers, she has offered us examples from her performance groups—patterns and transitions from Bach and Suzuki workbooks—that have helped our volunteers articulate connections between language and sound and have contributed to her and her co-learners diversifying the means by which they connect sounds in poetry and expanding beyond the sometimes iambic- and end rhyme-heavy lines her particular group of co-learners previously leaned into.

The more we listen, the better able we find ourselves to meet the children where they are at and to provide questions of significance to them, which they listen to in return. This isn't true of children alone, but of all the writers we have the pleasure of working with. None of these approaches is unique in itself. They are offerings we at 1WC have been able to provide and experiment with in our own attempts to explore and structure an inclusive community of creation.

It is through nuanced understandings of what art is that we can come to something like what Halberstam calls "low theory," appreciating the strangeness of localized talent and wisdom by welcoming the diversity of glorious failures at ground level (Halberstam, 2011). Or, alternatively, that those of us who find it helpful can accept that art may be a grandiose concept inappropriate to our low and "low" intentions, ourselves, our social spheres, our political systems. After all, of the many things art might assuredly be called, good is not one of them.

Articulating a conflict between University-professionalized critics and those they call "The Undercommons," a conflict where ideological boundaries are maintained through the process of privileging action-less critique, Fred Moten and Stefano Harney, assert "The sovereign's army of academic antihumanism will pursue this negative community into the Undercommons, seeking to conscript it, needing to conscript it. But as seductive as this critique may be, as provoked as it may be, in the Undercommons they know it is not love…When the critical academic who lives by fiat (of others) gets no answer, no commitment, from the Undercommons, well then certainly the conclusion will come: they are not practical, not serious about change, not rigorous, not productive."

I have outlined, here, not the only or the best methodologies for a pedagogy of art, but rather a swift sample of frameworks in whose nascent loam is the seed of possible love. I have not argued, but rather have shared that the work of art pedagogy is an intermingling of rigorous craft practice with the uncompromising freedom necessary for the discovery inherent in the actualization of art as divergence.

In this sense, a pedagogy of art is suicidal by its nature. To succeed in mentorship is to be upended by our co-learners. To create new frameworks for living that become the common is to de-identify ourselves and our work. We are therefore reliant on each other in art, as elsewhere, for loving support in the perpetual processes of un-becoming.

We learn through listening first. We practice the attention necessary to encounter rather than merely judge a practitioner's work. We explore together. We never fail: the work of reifying art, like the work of true science, is to hypothesize. We don't dictate outcomes or resent those outcomes. We learn from them, and from them develop more nuanced and newly directed hypotheses towards our next pursuits. Of all the aforementioned, we try and are not always as successful as we would like to be.

The term experimental art is a redundancy. All art is born in a failure of the normative. Thus, as pedagogues seeking to prepare our co-learners for the real "art world," we pursue bounded structures in which normativity collapses but out of which our co-learners may grow.

REFERENCES

Bank of America. (2023). *About.* Bank of America. https://about.bankofamerica.com/en/making-an-impact/museums-on-us-partners.

Benyamin, C. (2022). Montessori: An effective learning approach or a matter of faith? *The Perspective.* https://www.theperspective.com/amp/debates/1321/montessori-universally-effective-learning-approach-simple-matter-faith.html

Braun, J. & Trajkovski, (2023). *Designing Context Rich Learning.* IGI Global. https://www.igi-global.com/book/designing-context-rich-learning-extending/309084

Debord, G. (2012). *Society of the Spectacle.* Bread and Circuses Publishing.

Dewey, J. (1934). *Art as experience.* GP Putnam's Sons.

Eggers, D. (2009). *Dave Eggers TED prize 4 minute talk.* [Video]. TED. https://youtu.be/l3QbzvT6vko

Freire, P. (2020). *Pedagogy of the oppressed.* UCSC. https://envs.ucsc.edu/internships/internship-readings/freire-pedagogy-of-the-oppressed.pdf

Gilligan, C. (2014). Moral injury and the ethic of care: Reframing the conversation about differences. *Journal of Social Philosophy, 45*(1), 89–106. doi:10.1111/josp.12050

Halberstam, J. (2011). *The queer art of failure.* Duke University Press.

Keats, J. (2023). *Ode on a Grecian urn.* Poetry Foundation. https://www.poetryfoundation.org/poems/44477/ode-on-a-grecian-urn

Kuby, C. R., & Gutshall Rucker, T. L. (2015, May). Everyone has a Neil: Possibilities of literacy desiring in Writers' Studio. *Language Arts, 92*(5), 314–327.

Lerman, L. (1993). Toward a process for critical response. *High Performance, 16*(4), 46–49.

Locke, A. (1928, November). Art or Propaganda? In *Harlem: A Forum of Negro Life, 1*(1), 1-2. https://www.vonsteuben.org/ourpages/auto/2015/5/8/45168339/lockeartorpropaganda.pdf

Montessori, M. (2004). *The discovery of the child.* Aakar books.

Montessori, M. & George, A. (2012). *The Montessori Method: Scientific Pedagogy as applied to child education in 'the children's houses' with additions and revisions by the author.* Project Gutenberg. https://archive.org/details/TheMontessoriMeathod/mode/2up?q=%22Let+us+consider+the+attitude+of+the+teacher+in+the+light+of+another+example.%22

Myers, D. G. (2006). *The Elephants Teach: Creative Writing since 1880.* University of Chicago Press. https://eric.ed.gov/?id=ED525636 .

New London Group. (1996, Spring). *Harvard Educational Review*, 66(1).

Oozeerally, S., Ramma, Y., & Bholoa, A. (2020). *Science Education in Theory and Practice: An Introductory Guide to Learning Theory*, 323-342. Multiliteracies—New London Group.

Rousseau, J. J. (2009). *Discourse on the Arts and Sciences*. University of Adelaide Library. https://www.academia.edu/download/61519660/5018_Rousseau_Discourse_on_the_Arts_and_Sciences20191215-95479-hstkne.pdf

Rule, A. C. (2006). *The components of authentic learning*. Digital Library. https://digitallibrary.oswego.edu/SUOS000026/00001

Weil, S. (1951). *Waiting for God*. Fontana Books.

Chapter 4
Temple of the Muses:
The Power and Potential of Museums and Galleries for Context-Rich Learning

Jessica Mannisi

Foundry Art Centre, USA

ABSTRACT

The educational press and scholarly journals today are swooning over the latest technology, such as virtual reality (VR) or augmented reality (AR), as such tools that have the potential to immerse students into a context-rich environment designed to help them learn by exploring. This chapter will examine how exhibitions and museum engagement help visitors to better relate with the world around them and explore and understand a wide variety of concepts, issues, events, and phenomena. By interacting with the works on display, and with the help of gallery guides and educational programming, visitors learn through in-person, dynamic, and hands-on approaches. The authors will review the literature on the learning theories and the research on the most successful approaches.

INTRODUCTION

The educational press and scholarly journals are swooning today over the latest technology such as virtual reality (VR) or augmented reality (AR), as such tools have the potential to immerse students into a context-rich environment designed to help them learn by exploring. While much of that praise may be warranted, the authors of this chapter argue that museums and galleries should not be overlooked or diminished merely because they are not always getting headlines. "Museum" comes from the word for "temple of the muses," and as such, they have been creating these kinds of context-rich learning experiences for hundreds of years.

   This chapter will examine how exhibitions and museum engagement help visitors to better relate with the world around them and explore and understand a wide variety of concepts, issues, events, and phenomena. By interacting with the works on display, and with the help of gallery guides and educational

DOI: 10.4018/978-1-6684-7644-4.ch004

programming, visitors learn through in-person, dynamic, and hands-on approaches. We will review the literature on the learning theories and the research on the most successful approaches.

THE HISTORY OF MUSEUMS AND GALLERIES AS CENTERS FOR EDUCATION

Museums and galleries have a rich history as centers for education, curating and preserving human knowledge, culture, and history. Although the concept of museums has evolved significantly over time, their essential mission to educate and inspire curiosity has remained constant. In an interview with NPR, Ford Bell, the head of the American Association of Museums talked about how they are often overlooked in terms of the value they provide in terms of learning: "People don't think about museums as being a critical piece in our educational infrastructure in this country." The journey of museums and galleries from early collections to modern-day institutions sheds light on their enduring role in promoting education and understanding.

The origins of museums can be traced back to ancient civilizations, where rulers and scholars established collections of artifacts, art, and natural specimens as symbols of power and knowledge. The term "museum" is derived from the Greek word "mouseion," which means "temple of the muses." The ancient Greeks revered the Muses, the goddesses of inspiration in literature, science, and the arts, and built temples in their honor, like the Mouseion at Alexandria, where scholars gathered to study and share ideas. This reverence is echoed in what the former Metropolitan Museum of Art director, Philippe de Montebello, told NPR, "A museum is the memory of mankind."

During the Renaissance, the concept of museums as centers for education began to take shape. Wealthy patrons, scholars, and artists established private "cabinets of curiosities," which housed collections of art, antiquities, and natural specimens. These cabinets served as precursors to modern museums, fostering an atmosphere of learning and curiosity among their visitors. The Age of Enlightenment in the 18th century further fueled the development of museums as public institutions, with a focus on education and the dissemination of knowledge. This period saw the establishment of some of the world's most renowned museums, including the British Museum in London, the Louvre in Paris, and the Uffizi Gallery in Florence.

Throughout the 19th and early 20th centuries, museums continued to evolve as educational institutions, reflecting the societal and cultural changes of the time. The emergence of the industrial revolution and advances in science led to the creation of specialized museums, such as natural history museums, science museums, and technology museums. These institutions aimed to educate the public about the natural world and the rapid advancements in science and industry. During this period, museums also began to focus on educational programming and interpretation, employing professional curators, educators, and interpreters to develop exhibitions and facilitate learning experiences for visitors.

The mid-to-late 20th century saw a significant shift in the role of museums and galleries as educational institutions. The rise of the "new museology" movement emphasized the importance of audience engagement, participation, and accessibility, challenging traditional museum practices and encouraging institutions to adopt more inclusive and diverse approaches to education. This period also witnessed the development of museum education as a distinct field of study, with scholars and practitioners exploring the unique learning opportunities offered by museums and galleries, and devising strategies to enhance visitor engagement and learning outcomes.

In recent decades, museums and galleries have continued to adapt and innovate in response to the ever-changing educational landscape. Digital technologies have revolutionized the way museums share and present information, with many institutions embracing virtual reality (VR), augmented reality (AR), and interactive displays to create immersive and engaging learning experiences. The rise of the internet and social media has also enabled museums to extend their educational reach beyond their physical walls, connecting with audiences around the world through online collections, virtual exhibitions, and educational resources.

Moreover, contemporary museums and galleries are increasingly focused on fostering cross-disciplinary and interdisciplinary learning, collaborating with experts from diverse fields to create exhibitions that challenge traditional boundaries and promote critical thinking and problem-solving skills. This approach reflects the growing recognition that real-world problems and issues often require multifaceted and interdisciplinary solutions, and that museums and galleries can play a vital role in cultivating the necessary skills and mindsets.

The history of museums and galleries as centers for education is a testament to their enduring power to inspire curiosity, foster understanding, and facilitate the exchange of ideas. From their ancient origins as temples of the muses to their modern-day incarnations as dynamic, accessible, and technologically advanced institutions, museums and galleries have consistently evolved to meet the educational needs of their visitors. As they continue to innovate and adapt, they remain crucial spaces for context-rich learning experiences, where individuals can engage with the world around them, explore diverse concepts, issues, events, and phenomena, and develop the critical thinking and problem-solving skills necessary for navigating the complexities of the 21st century.

As we move further into the digital age, museums and galleries will continue to face new challenges and opportunities in their mission to educate and inspire. Many, like Kratz and Merritt (2011) are calling for more federal resources: "The U.S. needs to scale up the educational resources and skills provided by its museums via online access, better indexing of online resources, physically incorporating museums into schools and schools into museums, and making museums central points for teacher training. This will ensure museums can provide equitable access to their unique resources and fulfill their potential in the new educational landscape" (p.1). The ongoing integration of digital technologies, the increasing emphasis on inclusivity and accessibility, and the importance of fostering cross-disciplinary and inter-disciplinary learning will shape the future of museum education. However, the core principles that have guided museums and galleries throughout their history – the celebration of human knowledge, culture, and history, and the commitment to fostering curiosity and understanding – will undoubtedly continue to define their role as centers for education.

The history of museums and galleries demonstrates their resilience and adaptability, as well as their unique ability to connect individuals with the world around them in meaningful and lasting ways. By examining this history and reflecting on the lessons it offers, we can better understand the power and potential of museums and galleries for context-rich learning, and envision a future in which these institutions continue to thrive, innovate, and inspire generations of learners to come.

LEARNING THEORIES IN THE CONTEXT OF MUSEUMS

Museums and galleries are unique educational environments, offering visitors the opportunity to explore, discover, and learn through a variety of experiences. Several learning theories underpin the educational strategies employed by museums, each emphasizing different aspects of the learning process. This section will delve into three prominent learning theories—constructivism, experiential learning, and informal learning—that support the efficacy of museums and galleries as educational spaces.

Constructivism posits that learning is an active, constructive process where individuals build their understanding based on personal experiences and interactions with the world around them. Museums and galleries embody the principles of constructivist learning, as they encourage visitors to engage with exhibits, artifacts, and artworks, stimulating their curiosity and prompting them to ask questions, make connections, and form their interpretations. Interactive displays, hands-on activities, and opportunities for dialogue with museum educators further support the constructivist learning process by fostering critical thinking, problem-solving, and reflection.

Experiential learning, as formulated by David Kolb, emphasizes the importance of learning through direct experience and reflection. This theory posits that effective learning occurs in a cycle consisting of concrete experience, reflective observation, abstract conceptualization, and active experimentation. Museums and galleries provide an ideal setting for experiential learning, allowing visitors to engage with exhibits and objects in a tangible, multisensory manner. By examining artifacts, artworks, and historical materials firsthand, visitors gain a deeper understanding of the subjects they are exploring. Museum educators and interpretive materials can facilitate the reflective observation and abstract conceptualization phases of the experiential learning cycle, guiding visitors in making sense of their experiences and applying their newfound knowledge to other contexts.

Informal learning refers to the acquisition of knowledge, skills, and attitudes outside of traditional educational settings, such as schools and universities. This type of learning is often self-directed, voluntary, and driven by personal interests and motivations. Museums and galleries serve as vital spaces for informal learning, offering visitors the freedom to explore their interests, set their learning pace, and engage with exhibits and programs in ways that resonate with their individual needs and preferences. For example, Kratz and Merritt cite San Francisco's Exploratorium as leading the way by "*Using a transdisciplinary approach to explore the connections between science, art and human perception, topics include everything from astronomy to nanotechnology. During school trips and teacher seminars, museum educators use an inquiry-based process to relate science topics to the world around their students*" (p.4).

Moreover, research such as the work that Kratz and Merritt refer to has shown that informal learning experiences can enhance formal education by fostering curiosity, promoting the development of lifelong learning skills, and cultivating positive attitudes toward learning.

Each of these learning theories—constructivism, experiential learning, and informal learning—emphasizes different aspects of the learning process, but all underscore the value of museums and galleries as effective educational environments. By designing exhibitions and programs that align with these theories, museums can create rich, engaging, and meaningful learning experiences that cater to a diverse range of visitors and support their cognitive, emotional, and social development.

THE ROLE OF MUSEUM CURATORS, EDUCATORS, AND INTERPRETERS

Museum curators, educators, and interpreters play a pivotal role in shaping the educational experiences of visitors to museums and galleries. Tran argues that "*research on the effective use of field trips and museums as school resources has been predominantly conducted from the perspective of teachers and students, despite the fact that there are museum staff, both paid and unpaid, who have responsibilities to design, organize, and implement educational experiences for visiting school groups and who have been there since the inception of museums*" (p. 279). Their expertise, creativity, and passion for their subject matter contribute to the development of exhibitions and programs that engage, inspire, and inform. Tran underlines the importance of the staff when she writes, "*such individuals have a significant role in shaping the nature of the educational experiences afforded by their museums*" (p. 279). This section will discuss the roles and responsibilities of these professionals in facilitating learning within museums and galleries.

Curators are responsible for the research, acquisition, and interpretation of the objects and materials within a museum's collection. They work closely with other museum professionals, such as conservators, designers, and educators, to develop exhibitions that showcase the collection in ways that are informative, accessible, and engaging. Curators ensure that the objects on display are presented within their historical, cultural, and artistic contexts, providing visitors with the necessary background information to appreciate and understand the significance of the exhibits.

Museum educators play a crucial role in designing and implementing educational programs, workshops, and activities that complement the museum's exhibitions and align with the learning needs and interests of its visitors. They collaborate with curators, designers, and other stakeholders to create interpretive materials, such as exhibit labels, audio guides, and multimedia installations, that help visitors connect with the content and make meaning from their experiences. Museum educators are also responsible for designing and facilitating workshops, lectures, guided tours, and other programs that engage diverse audiences, including children, families, school groups, and adults.

Interpreters serve as the bridge between the exhibits and the visitors, employing various techniques to communicate complex ideas and concepts in an accessible and engaging manner. They may be museum staff, volunteers, or even digital platforms that provide information and context to help visitors navigate and understand the exhibitions. Interpreters often use storytelling, demonstrations, and hands-on activities to bring exhibits to life, fostering a sense of connection and empathy with the subject matter. In addition, interpreters are skilled at facilitating dialogue and encouraging visitors to share their thoughts, questions, and perspectives, creating a dynamic and inclusive learning environment.

The collaborative efforts of curators, educators, and interpreters are essential for creating meaningful, engaging, and context-rich learning experiences in museums and galleries. Their combined expertise and passion ensure that visitors have the opportunity to explore, discover, and learn in ways that are personally relevant and resonate with their interests, backgrounds, and experiences.

THE IMPACT OF ENVIRONMENT AND EXHIBITION DESIGN ON LEARNING

The physical environment and exhibition design of museums and galleries can have a significant impact on the learning experiences of visitors. Factors such as layout, lighting, and display techniques can facilitate or hinder learning, as well as affect visitors' overall perception and enjoyment of the museum. This section will explore the role of environment and exhibition design in promoting effective and engaging learning experiences in museums and galleries.

Layout plays a crucial role in shaping the visitor experience, as it influences the ease with which visitors navigate the museum, access information, and engage with the exhibits. An effective layout balances the need for clear pathways and logical flow with opportunities for exploration, discovery, and serendipitous encounters. Well-designed spaces also consider the needs of diverse audiences, incorporating elements such as ramps, wide corridors, and ample seating to ensure accessibility for visitors with disabilities, families with strollers, and elderly guests.

Lighting is another key aspect of museum design, as it affects the visibility, legibility, and aesthetic appeal of exhibits. Strategic lighting can highlight specific objects or features, create mood and atmosphere, and guide visitors' attention through the exhibition. However, lighting must also be carefully balanced with conservation concerns, as excessive light can cause damage to delicate artworks, artifacts, and specimens.

Display techniques and materials, such as exhibit cases, mounts, and labels, are essential for presenting objects and information in ways that are visually engaging and informative. Innovative display techniques, such as immersive installations, multimedia presentations, and interactive elements, can enhance the learning experience by offering visitors multiple entry points and opportunities for hands-on exploration. However, it is crucial that these techniques are employed judiciously and in service of the exhibit's educational goals, rather than as mere gimmicks or distractions.

The environment and exhibition design of museums and galleries play a vital role in shaping the learning experiences of visitors. By creating spaces that are inviting, accessible, and conducive to exploration and discovery, museums and galleries can promote effective and engaging learning experiences, enabling visitors to connect with the exhibits, artifacts, and artworks on display and develop a deeper understanding of the world around them.

ENGAGING DIVERSE AUDIENCES THROUGH INCLUSIVE EXHIBITIONS AND PROGRAMS

Museums and galleries have a responsibility to serve and engage diverse audiences, including people from various cultural, socioeconomic, and age backgrounds, as well as those with disabilities. Inclusive exhibitions and programs play a crucial role in ensuring that all visitors feel welcome, valued, and represented within the museum space. This section will discuss strategies for creating inclusive exhibitions and programs that cater to the needs and interests of diverse audiences.

One key strategy for engaging diverse audiences is to adopt a visitor-centered approach to exhibition and program design. This involves conducting audience research to gain insights into the needs, interests, and preferences of different visitor groups, and using these insights to inform the development of exhibitions and programs that resonate with and cater to their specific needs. For example, a museum might develop a program that explores the experiences and contributions of immigrant communities within a local area or create an exhibition that highlights the work of underrepresented artists or marginalized groups.

Another important aspect of inclusivity is ensuring that exhibitions and programs are accessible to visitors with disabilities. This includes making physical modifications to the museum environment, such as installing ramps, elevators, and wider doorways, as well as incorporating accessibility features into exhibition design, such as tactile exhibits, audio descriptions, and large-print labels. In addition, museums and galleries can offer specialized programs and resources, such as sensory-friendly events, sign language tours, and social stories, to accommodate the unique needs and preferences of visitors with disabilities. Further, in a post-Covid world, museums and galleries have become aware of the needs of those who cannot physically visit and experience the exhibitions. Virtual exhibitions and online resources have become another important tool for museums and galleries to engage and accommodate their "visitors."

Cultural sensitivity is another crucial component of inclusive museum practice. This involves recognizing and valuing the diverse cultural perspectives, experiences, and knowledge systems that visitors bring with them to the museum and ensuring that these perspectives are represented and respected within the exhibition and program content. Cultural sensitivity can be achieved by collaborating with community members, cultural advisors, and other stakeholders in the development of exhibitions and programs, as well as by providing opportunities for visitors to engage in dialogue and share their own experiences and perspectives.

Finally, engaging diverse audiences requires a commitment to ongoing evaluation and improvement. Museums and galleries should regularly assess the effectiveness of their exhibitions and programs in meeting the needs and expectations of diverse audiences and use this feedback to inform future practice. This might involve conducting visitor surveys, focus groups, or observational studies, as well as engaging in dialogue with community members and other stakeholders to gain insights into the impact and relevance of the museum's offerings.

COMMUNITY COLLABORATION AND PARTNERSHIPS

Museums and galleries can amplify their educational impact and reach by collaborating with community organizations, educational institutions, and other partners. These collaborations can take many forms, including joint programming, resource sharing, and knowledge exchange, and can benefit both the museum and its partners by fostering innovation, building capacity, and increasing public engagement. Kratz and Merritt highlight one innovated program called "Urban Advantage" which is a collaboration between the Denver Museum of Nature and Science, the Denver Zoo, the Denver Botanic Gardens and three local school districts" (p.6). This section will explore the value of community collaboration and partnerships in enhancing the educational role of museums and galleries.

One key benefit of community collaboration and partnerships is the potential for shared learning and knowledge exchange. By working with external organizations, museums and galleries can gain insights into new approaches, techniques, and perspectives that can inform their practice and improve the quality and relevance of their exhibitions and programs. For example, a museum might collaborate with a local university to develop a research project exploring the impact of an exhibition on visitor learning, or partner with a community organization to develop a program that engages marginalized youth in arts and culture.

Another advantage of collaboration and partnerships is the potential for resource sharing and capacity building. This might involve sharing expertise, facilities, or financial resources, which can help museums and galleries achieve their educational goals more efficiently and effectively. For example, a museum might partner with a local school to provide professional development opportunities for teachers or collaborate with a community group to co-facilitate a workshop or event.

Collaboration and partnerships can also help museums and galleries increase their public visibility and reach, by tapping into the networks and resources of partner organizations. This can lead to increased visitor numbers, greater community awareness and engagement, and a more diverse audience base. For example, a museum might partner with a local festival or event to host a pop-up exhibition or collaborate with a community radio station to promote its programs and events.

Furthermore, community collaboration and partnerships can foster social cohesion and contribute to the cultural vitality of a community. By working together, museums, galleries, and partner organizations can address shared challenges, celebrate local heritage, and promote understanding and appreciation of diverse cultures and perspectives. This can lead to stronger relationships and a greater sense of community pride and identity.

Community collaboration and partnerships offer significant benefits for museums and galleries in their educational endeavors. By engaging in mutually beneficial relationships with external organizations, museums and galleries can enhance their capacity, reach, and impact, while also contributing to the social and cultural well-being of their communities.

THE FUTURE OF MUSEUM EDUCATION: EMBRACING DIGITAL TECHNOLOGIES AND NEW APPROACHES

As we move further into the digital age, museums and galleries must continue to adapt and innovate in order to remain relevant and effective as educational spaces. This will involve embracing new technologies, approaches, and methodologies that enhance the visitor experience, facilitate learning, and help museums and galleries engage with diverse audiences in new and meaningful ways. This section will explore some of the emerging trends and opportunities shaping the future of museum education.

Digital technologies offer exciting opportunities for museums and galleries to enhance their exhibitions, programs, and visitor engagement strategies. For example, VR and AR technologies can be used to create immersive, interactive experiences that transport visitors to different times, places, and perspectives. Mobile apps and digital guides can provide personalized, on-demand information and resources tailored to individual visitors' interests and learning needs. Social media and online platforms can also be used to extend the reach of museums and galleries, enabling them to connect with audiences who may be unable to visit in person.

Another trend shaping the future of museum education is the increasing emphasis on interdisciplinary and cross-disciplinary learning (see Kratz and Merritt). This involves exploring the connections between different disciplines, such as art, science, history, and technology, and encouraging visitors to think critically and creatively about the complex, interrelated issues facing the world today. Museums and galleries can support interdisciplinary learning by developing exhibitions and programs that explore multiple perspectives and themes, and by collaborating with external partners from different sectors to develop innovative educational initiatives.

Finally, the future of museum education will be shaped by the ongoing quest for inclusivity, accessibility, and social justice. This will involve not only creating exhibitions and programs that cater to the needs and interests of diverse audiences, but also rethinking the ways in which museums and galleries collect, interpret, and display cultural heritage, in order to challenge dominant narratives and promote greater understanding and empathy. The future of museum education will be characterized by innovation, adaptation, and a continued commitment to fostering curiosity, understanding, and engagement among diverse audiences. By embracing new technologies and approaches, and by continually reflecting on and refining their practice, museums and galleries can ensure that they remain at the forefront of educational innovation and continue to inspire generations of learners to come.

PROMOTING LIFELONG LEARNING THROUGH MUSEUMS AND GALLERIES

Museums and galleries have the potential to support and nurture lifelong learning by providing stimulating, engaging, and accessible learning experiences for visitors of all ages and backgrounds. By offering a wide range of exhibitions, programs, and resources, museums and galleries can foster curiosity, creativity, and critical thinking, and inspire visitors to continue learning throughout their lives. Kratz and Merritt forecast *"that the next era may be driven by life-long learners drawing on a variety of resources, traditional and non-traditional, and based on diverse methods of sharing, collaboration and use of educational resources"* (p.1). This section will discuss the role of museums and galleries in promoting lifelong learning and the strategies they can employ to encourage and support learning at every stage of life.

One key strategy for promoting lifelong learning is to offer a diverse range of exhibitions and programs that cater to different interests, learning styles, and age groups. This might involve providing hands-on, interactive exhibits for young children, in-depth interpretive materials for adults, and intergenerational programs that bring together people of all ages to learn and create together. By offering a variety of experiences that cater to the unique needs and preferences of different audiences, museums and galleries can encourage visitors to engage with their offerings and develop a lifelong love of learning.

Another important aspect of promoting lifelong learning is fostering a culture of curiosity and inquiry within the museum environment. This involves creating spaces and opportunities for visitors to ask questions, explore ideas, and engage in dialogue with others. Museum educators and interpreters can play a crucial role in fostering this culture by facilitating discussions, prompting critical thinking, and encouraging visitors to make connections between their own experiences and the content on display.

Museums and galleries can also support lifelong learning by providing resources and tools that help visitors extend their learning beyond the museum walls. This might involve offering educational materials such as lesson plans, activity sheets, and online resources that can be used by educators and learners in their homes, schools, or communities. In addition, museums and galleries can engage with audiences through social media, blogs, and other digital platforms, providing ongoing opportunities for learning and dialogue.

Finally, museums and galleries can promote lifelong learning by partnering with other educational institutions and organizations to develop joint programs and initiatives. This might involve collaborating with schools, libraries, or community centers to develop educational resources or co-host events, or partnering with universities to offer internships, research opportunities, or professional development opportunities for museum professionals.

THE ROLE OF MUSEUM VOLUNTEERS IN SUPPORTING EDUCATIONAL GOALS

Museum volunteers play a crucial role in supporting the educational goals of museums and galleries. They contribute their time, skills, and passion to help create engaging and meaningful experiences for visitors and ensure the smooth operation of the museum's educational programs and services. This section will discuss the role of museum volunteers in supporting educational goals and the strategies museums and galleries can employ to recruit, train, and retain effective and committed volunteers.

Volunteers can contribute to the educational goals of museums and galleries in a variety of ways. They may serve as gallery guides, leading tours and sharing their knowledge of the museum's collections with visitors. They may also assist with educational programs and events, helping to facilitate workshops, demonstrations, and other activities. Volunteers may provide support for museum educators and curators by conducting research, preparing materials, or assisting with the development of new exhibitions and programs.

Recruiting and retaining effective museum volunteers requires a strategic approach that involves identifying the skills and interests of potential volunteers, providing appropriate training and support, and recognizing and rewarding their contributions. Museums and galleries should develop clear volunteer position descriptions and expectations and should conduct interviews and background checks to ensure that volunteers are a good fit for the organization.

Training is a crucial component of a successful museum volunteer program, as it helps to ensure that volunteers are well-prepared to contribute to the museum's educational goals. Training should be ongoing and should cover topics such as museum policies and procedures, customer service, and the museum's collections and exhibitions. In addition, training should also include opportunities for volunteers to develop their communication, interpretation, and facilitation skills, as these are essential for engaging with visitors and supporting their learning experiences.

Recognizing and rewarding the contributions of museum volunteers is essential for maintaining their motivation and commitment to the organization. This might involve organizing volunteer appreciation events, providing opportunities for professional development and growth, or offering tangible rewards such as discounts or exclusive access to museum events and programs.

Ultimately, museum volunteers play a vital role in supporting the educational goals of museums and galleries. By investing in the recruitment, training, and retention of dedicated and skilled volunteers, museums and galleries can enhance their capacity to deliver engaging and meaningful learning experiences for their visitors.

EVALUATING THE IMPACT OF MUSEUM EDUCATION: METHODS, CHALLENGES, AND OPPORTUNITIES

Understanding the impact of museum education is essential for museums and galleries to demonstrate their value to stakeholders, inform their practice, and guide future development. However, evaluating the impact of museum education can be a complex and challenging task, due to the diverse nature of learning experiences, the varying needs and preferences of visitors, and the often-intangible nature of learning outcomes. This section will discuss the methods, challenges, and opportunities associated with evaluating the impact of museum education.

Several methods can be employed to evaluate the impact of museum education, ranging from quantitative measures such as visitor numbers and survey data to qualitative approaches such as interviews, focus groups, and observational studies. Each method has its advantages and limitations and may be more or less suited to evaluating different aspects of museum education.

Quantitative measures, such as visitor numbers, demographic data, and survey responses, can provide valuable insights into the reach and accessibility of museum education programs and the satisfaction of visitors. However, these measures may not capture the full depth and complexity of the learning experiences that take place within museums and galleries.

Qualitative approaches, such as interviews, focus groups, and observational studies, can provide richer, more nuanced insights into the ways in which visitors engage with museum education programs and the learning outcomes they achieve. These methods can help to illuminate the processes, experiences, and contexts that shape visitor learning and can be particularly valuable for exploring the impact of museum education on intangible outcomes such as critical thinking, creativity, and empathy.

Despite the benefits of these evaluation methods, there are several challenges associated with evaluating the impact of museum education. One key challenge is the need to balance the demands of evaluation with the resources and capacity available to museums and galleries, particularly smaller institutions with limited staff and funding. Another challenge is the difficulty of attributing specific learning outcomes to museum education programs, given the complex and multifaceted nature of the learning process.

To address those challenges, museums and galleries can employ a range of strategies, such as collaborating with external partners to conduct evaluations, using a mix of methods to capture different aspects of the learning experience, and developing evaluation frameworks that align with their specific goals and objectives.

Evaluating the impact of museum education is a complex but essential task for museums and galleries. By employing a range of methods and strategies, and by embracing the challenges and opportunities associated with evaluation, museums and galleries can deepen their understanding of the ways in which they contribute to the learning and development of their visitors and can use this knowledge to inform and improve their practice.

POTENTIAL LIMITATIONS OF CONTEXT-RICH LEARNING IN MUSEUMS AND GALLERIES

While museums and galleries offer significant opportunities for context-rich learning, there are certain limitations that must be acknowledged. We will explore some of the key challenges and limitations associated with context-rich learning in these settings, including issues related to accessibility, inclusivity, funding, biases, and the ephemeral nature of certain learning experiences.

1. **Accessibility**: One of the primary limitations of museum and gallery education is that it is often limited by physical accessibility. Visitors must be able to visit the institution in person to fully benefit from the context-rich learning experiences offered. This poses a challenge for those who live in remote areas, have limited mobility, or face financial constraints that hinder their ability to travel. Although some museums and galleries have sought to address this issue through online exhibitions and virtual tours, these digital offerings may not fully replicate the immersive, hands-on experience of an in-person visit.

2. **Inclusivity**: Museums and galleries have historically been perceived as elitist institutions, catering primarily to the interests and preferences of a specific demographic. As a result, some visitors may feel alienated or unwelcome, limiting their ability to engage with and benefit from the context-rich learning experiences on offer. In response, many museums and galleries have made concerted efforts to become more inclusive and diverse in their programming, exhibitions, and audience engagement strategies. However, there is still much work to be done to ensure that these institutions are truly representative of and accessible to the diverse communities they serve.

3. **Funding**: The financial constraints faced by many museums and galleries can limit their ability to offer context-rich learning experiences. Budget cuts, shrinking endowments, and a growing reliance on commercial revenue streams can result in a reduction of educational programming, staff

layoffs, and the closure of certain galleries or facilities. This can have a significant impact on the quality and range of context-rich learning opportunities available to visitors.

4. **Biases and Misrepresentation**: The content and narratives presented in museums and galleries are often shaped by the biases and perspectives of curators, institutions, and funding bodies. This can result in the misrepresentation or omission of certain stories, cultures, or viewpoints, limiting the scope of context-rich learning experiences available to visitors. To address this issue, some museums and galleries have begun to actively engage with diverse communities, scholars, and artists to ensure that their exhibitions and programs are more inclusive and representative of a wider range of perspectives.

5. **Ephemeral Learning Experiences**: While museums and galleries offer a wealth of context-rich learning opportunities, some of these experiences may be ephemeral or difficult to measure. For example, the emotional impact of an artwork or the sense of awe inspired by a historical artifact may be deeply meaningful to a visitor but challenging to quantify or evaluate. As a result, the full value and impact of context-rich learning in museums and galleries may not always be apparent or easily demonstrable.

6. **Overwhelming Information:** Museums and galleries often present vast amounts of information, which can be overwhelming for visitors. This can make it challenging for them to engage with and absorb the context-rich learning experiences on offer. To address this issue, museums and galleries must carefully consider the design and presentation of their exhibitions, ensuring that they are engaging, accessible, and digestible for a diverse range of visitors.

7. **Reliance on Trained Staff:** The quality of context-rich learning experiences in museums and galleries often relies heavily on the expertise and skill of museum educators, interpreters, and volunteers. However, these professionals may not always be available, and the quality of their training and support can vary significantly between institutions. This can limit the effectiveness of context-rich learning experiences, particularly in smaller or underfunded museums and galleries.

8. **Limitations of Physical Space**: The physical layout and design of museums and galleries can also limit the effectiveness of context-rich learning experiences. In some cases, the available space may not be sufficient to accommodate large groups or to allow for the display of all relevant artifacts and information. Additionally, the design of exhibition spaces may not always be conducive to fostering interaction, exploration, or engagement. To address these challenges, museums and galleries must invest in the thoughtful design and renovation of their spaces, taking into account the needs and preferences of their visitors.

9. **Overemphasis on Traditional Learning Approaches**: While many museums and galleries have embraced innovative, hands-on, and interactive learning experiences, some institutions may still rely heavily on traditional didactic methods, such as static displays, labels, and lecturing. These approaches may not always be effective in engaging visitors or facilitating context-rich learning. To overcome this limitation, museums and galleries must continue to experiment with and adopt new educational strategies, tools, and technologies that better align with contemporary learning theories and visitor expectations.

10. **Competition with Digital Media:** The proliferation of digital media and online resources has created new opportunities for context-rich learning, but it has also introduced new challenges for museums and galleries. In some cases, visitors may be more inclined to engage with digital content on their devices than to fully immerse themselves in the museum or gallery environment. This can detract from the context-rich learning experiences offered by these institutions. To remain relevant

and competitive, museums and galleries must find ways to integrate digital technologies into their offerings, while also emphasizing the unique value of in-person learning experiences that cannot be replicated online.

Museums and galleries offer valuable context-rich learning opportunities, but they also face a variety of limitations and challenges that must be addressed to ensure that these experiences are accessible, inclusive, and effective. By acknowledging and addressing these issues, museums and galleries can continue to evolve and adapt, providing engaging and meaningful learning experiences that inspire and educate visitors from all walks of life. Embracing new technologies, fostering inclusivity, and investing in the ongoing development of staff, exhibitions, and programming are essential steps in overcoming the limitations and unlocking the full potential of context-rich learning in museums and galleries.

THE FOUNDRY ART CENTRE: CASE STUDIES IN CONTEXT-RICH LEARNING

The Foundry Art Centre in St. Charles, Missouri, just 30 miles outside of St. Louis, resides in what was once a train car factory - a 1920s structure formerly owned by American Car & Foundry. Rather than demolish the 36,800 square foot building, the community of St. Charles worked tirelessly to complete a $2.2 million renovation and opened the region's premiere, interactive, interdisciplinary art center in 2004. As a vibrant home to the arts, the Foundry Art Centre raises awareness and appreciation of the arts throughout the St. Louis-St. Charles region. The center's programming reinforces the importance of the arts and helps ensure that arts and culture remain vital. The public's active participation continues to make the Foundry successful in its mission to connect people with the arts through exhibitions, studio artists, performances, and education. The exhibitions and programming teams explore and implement context-rich learning through many programs, events, tours, classes, and workshops.

1. **Art in Mind** is a free, interactive, multi-faceted program created in 2021 as a partnership between the Foundry Art Centre's programming and exhibitions departments and the Bev Roy Hope Foundation, whose mission is to offer support, build connection, and provide hope for those living with Alzheimer's disease and other forms of dementia and their caregivers. This twice-monthly program engages participants through a series of interactive art activities, gallery tours, physical activities, and artist relationships. Art therapy is at the core of this program, providing meaningful art-centered activities that create positive emotional and cognitive experiences, enhance verbal and non-verbal communication, reduce isolation, and build community.

A typical session begins with a guided tour through the main galleries, which feature rotating exhibitions by regional, national, and international artists and touch upon a variety of themes, concepts, and points of view. Guided by a docent, Art in Mind participants are introduced to particular artworks and overall themes of the exhibition. From there, participants are asked questions that allow for meaningful interaction and cognitive exercise. Questions, discussion points, and even games can include, "Create a story about this painting," "What do you think this subject is thinking?", "What moods are expressed through the use of color in the artwork?", and "What does this painting remind you of?" These gallery tours are light-hearted and fun, with participants creating stories around the artworks.

Foundry director Hilda Andres also notes: "*When the caregiver and patient go into the galleries and are prompted by questions, it is difficult to distinguish the caregiver from the person with dementia. Something magical happens when they are looking at art together and engaging in conversation.*"

Following the tour of the galleries, participants are invited to create artwork related to the exhibitions, however loosely. Fine and gross motor skills are utilized, an important component of dementia therapy and connection with caregivers and community members. This activity is often led by a resident or visiting artist, assisted by Foundry staff.

Physical therapists are often invited to lead a physical exercise - chair yoga and dancing, games, and music. Art in Mind serves as a safe, comfortable, and enriching space in which participants can connect and socialize.

Shelly Roy, the founder and president of the Bev Roy Hope Foundation, has been incredibly enthusiastic with the level of engagement and therapeutic assistance this program has garnered since its inception. "*The one quote that is near and dear to my heart and that I have used many times in describing the impact this program has had with our participants is by Georgia O'Keefe, 'I found I could say things with color and shape that I couldn't say any other way - things I had no words for.'*" Though cognition becomes increasingly difficult with participants as the disease progresses, art is able to tap into and access those elements of the mind, helping them communicate more eloquently through art than they can with words.

2.   **Field trips** provide a rewarding and engaging way to learn outside the classroom. At the Foundry Art Centre, student groups are given an in-depth tour of the current exhibitions. Invited to sit on the floor in a relaxed environment that is friendly, nonthreatening, and lively, the docent typically begins by asking questions related to observation and storytelling. What is the artist thinking? How did the artist feel when creating the work? What story is the artist trying to communicate?

These questions and discussion points often break the ice and help the students engage with the work and ask questions that they often feel too reserved to ask. Many first-time museum goers are intimidated by their initial experience in a gallery. Museums are, after all, the mouseion - a temple. But through these opening interactions, students learn that there's no need to be silent and serious in museums and galleries.

Once the students have warmed up and learn that there are no wrong answers or questions, the docent dives deeper into the background of the artists and the artist's intent. The students have the chance through this exchange to learn about the elements of art: color, form, line, shape, space, texture, and value, along with important cross-disciplinary concepts such as current events, history, art history, science, math, and social studies, to name just a few. Students are able to relate these ideas to modern concepts and current events. An environmental exhibition can allow the students to discuss climate change, renewable resources, and ecology.

A recent installation by St. Louis-based artist, Sarah Knight, titled *Crystal Queer*, in which the artist reimagined the definition of queering as a disorientation of visual and conceptual cohesion, opened the door for students to discuss social issues surrounding the queer community and how the meaning and definitions of words can be open for reinterpretation. Several students came up to the curator to open up about their own journeys with identity and how the exhibition helped them feel seen.

An exhibition of portraiture can assist students in discussing emotional well-being and have insightful conversations about identity, cultural history, and political history. Paintings and mixed media works by artist Rachel Lebo led to lively discussions with grade school-aged students during their time in the gallery. Creating "short stories" through a body of work, Lebo's artwork includes paintings of friends in mundane settings such as bathrooms and basement rec rooms, and large-scale sculptures of laundry baskets and cowboy boots. Students enjoyed figuring out what story Lebo was trying to tell through these works.

Following the gallery tours, the students are led upstairs, where resident artists have studios and create artwork. This allows students to see that artists aren't just from the past (often what is learned in school), but are living, breathing, people of the NOW. They may look like them, have similar interests, and live in their community. Artists demonstrate how they make their work, creating connections between the artwork students may learn about or create in school and the similarities to what professional artists do.

The field trips typically end with an art activity tied to the exhibitions, an important learning component tying in emotional learning, gross and fine motor skills, problem solving, and critical thinking.

3. **There's no need for art to be a static object**. The Foundry Art Centre hosts an annual steamroller printing event, the Block Party, each summer. The largest steamroller printing event in the Midwest and entering its third year, this interactive and demonstrative community event focuses on all things related to printmaking. The Foundry's Block Party centers on a unique and over-the-top method of printmaking, using a STEAMROLLER! Large-scale images created by regional artists are carved on large woodblocks. St. Louis print house Grafik House USA's team of inkers roll ink onto these blocks, canvas is laid on top, and then the whole thing is run over with a steam roller – squishing the ink from the woodblock to the sheet. These fantastic prints will be taken into the Foundry's Grand Hall to dry on display.

In addition to the steamroller prints, the Block Party includes woodcut, linocut, and screen-printing demonstrations, along with print-related art activities for all ages.

Through these demonstrations and hands-on activities, visitors learn about the basics of a variety of printmaking techniques and can experience printmaking in a real-world setting.

With this engagement, the community learns how art is not just a static image on a wall or pedestal; art is a process.

Liz Hermanson, one of the head printmakers at Grafik House USA, with whom the Foundry partners for this event, is enthusiastic about the mission of Block Party. "Our goal is to educate and share traditional printmaking both locally and globally. It's exciting to work with the Foundry to host this event and always look forward to getting inky and making art with the community!"

4. **Museums and galleries** can offer professional development for the university-aged student, as well. Through partnerships with college art professors and galleries and museums, students have access to a wide variety of professional development tools.

Gallery directors and curators are typically happy to meet with college art majors for portfolio reviews, as well as discuss the typical process for how they choose the artists they show or represent. Some gallery professionals are also more than willing to impart advice on what the students are doing well, what they need to work on, and how to proceed moving in the direction of their chosen careers. Personal experiences are often shared - educational backgrounds, best ways to market themselves, other connections they should make, and more "tips of the trade" give invaluable feedback and insight into the professional realm of the arts and museum and gallery work.

Internship opportunities can provide in-depth training and knowledge of the field the students are considering after graduation. By providing a behind the scenes, "how the sausage is made"-style experience about the plethora of career paths within the art world, students can put into practice what they've learned in the classroom. They can help hone the direction they want to go in for a career (education, visitor services, exhibition, conservation, fundraising, among others). By working one on one with professionals, they gain valuable insight and training that would never be possible in the classroom. Even much needed connections are made with regional artists, organizations, and other professionals.

CONCLUSION

In conclusion, museums and galleries have immense potential as spaces for context-rich learning, capable of fostering curiosity, understanding, and engagement among diverse audiences. While the advent of digital technologies, such as virtual reality (VR) and augmented reality (AR), has revolutionized the way we learn and interact with the world around us, the unique, immersive, and hands-on experiences offered by museums and galleries remain vital to the learning process.

Throughout this article, we have explored several key aspects of museum education, including the role of exhibitions and museum engagement in helping visitors better relate to the world around them; the importance of visitor-centered approaches in creating inclusive, accessible, and engaging learning experiences; and the significance of interdisciplinary learning in fostering critical thinking and creativity. Additionally, we have discussed the benefits of community collaboration and partnerships, the incorporation of digital technologies and new approaches in museum education, and the promotion of lifelong learning through museum and gallery programs.

Museum volunteers play a critical role in supporting the educational goals of museums and galleries, with their passion and commitment being essential for the success of these institutions. Furthermore, evaluating the impact of museum education is a complex but necessary task that allows museums and galleries to demonstrate their value, inform their practice, and guide future development.

As we look to the future of museum education, museums and galleries must continue to adapt and innovate, embracing new technologies, approaches, and methodologies that enhance the visitor experience and facilitate learning. This will involve not only creating exhibitions and programs that cater to the needs and interests of diverse audiences, but also rethinking the ways in which museums and galleries collect, interpret, and display cultural heritage, in order to challenge dominant narratives and promote greater understanding and empathy.

At the heart of museum education lies the belief that museums and galleries can serve as powerful agents of change, capable of inspiring, informing, and transforming the lives of their visitors. By investing in the development and implementation of innovative, visitor-centered, and context-rich learning experiences, museums and galleries can continue to fulfill their educational mission and ensure that they remain at the forefront of educational innovation.

The power and potential of museums and galleries for context-rich learning is undeniable. As "temples of the muses," they have been creating immersive and engaging learning experiences for centuries. By harnessing the power of their collections, the expertise of their staff, and the creativity of their programs, museums and galleries can continue to inspire generations of learners to come, promoting curiosity, understanding, and engagement with the world around them. As we move further into the digital age, it is vital that museums and galleries continue to evolve, adapt, and embrace the opportunities presented by new technologies and approaches, ensuring that they remain relevant, accessible, and inspiring for all.

REFERENCES

Jones, J. (2022, June 3). Foundry Art Centre's Block Party Steamrolls its Way into St. Charles. *Riverfront Times*.

Mastro, M. (2022, May 11th). Meet the six local art businesses that call St. Charles' Foundry Arts Centre home. *St. Louis Magazine*.

Modello, B. A history of museums, 'The memory of mankind'. NPR. (2008, November 24). Kratz, S., & Merritt, E. (2011). Museums and the future of education. *On the Horizon*.

Tran, L. U. (2007). Teaching science in museums: The pedagogy and goals of museum educators. *Science education*, *91*(2), 278–297. doi:10.1002ce.20193

APPENDIX A

Field trips to museums and galleries provide valuable learning opportunities for students, allowing them to engage with and explore new ideas, artifacts, and experiences outside the traditional classroom setting. However, to maximize the educational impact of these excursions, teachers must carefully plan and prepare activities before, during, and after the field trip. Based on educational research, the following guidelines should be considered when creating lesson plans for each stage of the field trip process:

1.   Preparing for the Field Trip (Day Prior)
   a.   **Establish clear objectives:** Define the specific learning goals and objectives for the field trip. Consider how the trip aligns with the curriculum and what students are expected to learn or achieve during the visit. Communicate these objectives to students, so they understand the purpose and focus of the field trip.
   b.   **Build background knowledge:** Provide students with background information and context about the museum or gallery and its exhibitions. This may include historical context, artistic or cultural significance, and information about the artists or curators. This will help students build a foundation of understanding and make connections during the field trip.
   c.   **Develop pre-visit activities:** Engage students in activities that pique their interest and curiosity about the field trip. This could include research projects, discussions, or creative tasks related to the museum or gallery's theme or content. These activities help students make connections between their prior knowledge and the upcoming field trip experience.
   d.   **Foster collaboration and inquiry:** Encourage students to work together in small groups to develop questions or topics they would like to explore during the field trip. This promotes collaboration, critical thinking, and inquiry-based learning.
   e.   Coordinate logistics: Ensure that students are aware of the logistical details of the field trip, including the schedule, transportation, and any necessary materials or supplies. This will help the day run smoothly and reduce any potential confusion or anxiety.
2.   During the Field Trip
   a.   **Active engagement:** Encourage students to actively engage with the exhibits and activities at the museum or gallery. This may include asking questions, discussing ideas, and making connections between the exhibits and their prior knowledge or experiences.
   b.   **Structured learning activities:** Provide students with structured activities or assignments to complete during the field trip. These may include scavenger hunts, guided tours, or worksheets designed to help students focus their attention and explore specific themes or concepts related to the museum or gallery.
   c.   **Encourage reflection**: Throughout the field trip, encourage students to reflect on their experiences and consider how they relate to the learning objectives established before the visit. This may involve periodic check-ins, discussions, or journal entries.
   d.   **Facilitate group collaboration**: Organize students into small groups and assign tasks or roles that promote collaboration, communication, and problem-solving. This will help students engage with the content more deeply and foster teamwork.
   e.   **Capture the experience:** Encourage students to document their experiences through photos, sketches, or notes. This will provide valuable material for post-visit activities and reflections.

3. Post-Field Trip (Day After)
   a. **Debrief and reflect**: Begin the post-field trip lesson by providing students with an opportunity to debrief and reflect on their experiences. This may include discussions, journal entries, or presentations in which students share their thoughts, insights, and observations from the field trip.
   b. **Analyze and synthesize:** Engage students in activities that require them to analyze and synthesize the information they gathered during the field trip. This could involve comparing and contrasting different exhibits, discussing themes or patterns, or connecting the field trip experience to broader course concepts.
   c. **Creative expression**: Encourage students to express their learning and experiences creatively through projects such as writing, art, or multimedia presentations. This allows students to process their experiences in a personal and meaningful way.
   d. **Assess learning outcomes:** Assess students' understanding and achievement of the learning objectives established before the field trip. This may involve quizzes, tests, or project-based assessments that evaluate students' knowledge, skills, and abilities related to the museum or gallery visit.
   e. **Extend the learning:** Create opportunities for students to extend their learning beyond the field trip experience. This could include further research, community engagement, or connections to other curriculum areas. Encourage students to explore related topics, issues, or ideas that were sparked by the field trip.
   f. **Provide feedback**: Provide students with feedback on their performance during the field trip and their post-visit activities. Acknowledge their achievements and identify areas for improvement. Encourage students to reflect on their learning and consider how they can apply the knowledge and skills they gained during the field trip to other areas of their education and life.
   g. **Communicate with the museum or gallery**: Share your students' experiences and feedback with the museum or gallery staff. This can help the institution improve its educational offerings and provide valuable insights into the impact of the field trip on your students' learning.

Planning and preparing for a field trip to a museum or gallery involves a series of thoughtful, research-based steps that aim to maximize the educational impact of the experience. By designing engaging and relevant activities before, during, and after the field trip, teachers can help students make meaningful connections, develop critical thinking skills, and foster a lifelong love of learning. With careful planning and execution, museum and gallery field trips can become transformative experiences that enrich and expand students' understanding of the world around them.

LESSON PLAN: FIELD TRIP TO THE ST. LOUIS ART MUSEUM

Lesson 1: The Day Before the Visit - Preparing for the Field Trip

Here's a context-rich lesson plan for a high school freshmen art class based around a field trip to the St. Louis Art Museum, including three separate lessons: one for the day before the visit, one for the visit itself, and one for the day after the visit.

Objectives:

- ° Introduce students to the St. Louis Art Museum and its collections
- ° Encourage students to think about the exhibits they will be viewing and to generate questions based off current curriculum for further exploration
- ° Provide students with an opportunity to discuss their expectations and goals for the field trip.

Materials:

- ° St. Louis Art Museum website
- ° Worksheets with guiding questions

Procedure:

- ° Introduce the St. Louis Art Museum to students, providing information about its history and collections.
- ° Give students a graphic organizer with guiding questions about the museum and ask them to explore the museum's website.
- ° Allow students to work in pairs or small groups to discuss the exhibits they are most interested in viewing and to generate specific questions they would like to explore further.
- ° Have students share their questions with the class and facilitate a class discussion about their expectations and goals for the field trip.

Assessment:

- ° Students will complete a written reflection outlining their expectations and goals for the field trip based on their graphic organizer and class discussion.

Lesson 2: The Visit - Exploring the Museum

Objectives:

- Engage students in the museum experience and encourage them to observe and critically analyze the exhibits they are viewing
- Encourage students to think critically and ask questions about the artwork or collection
- Provide students with an opportunity to reflect on their experiences and discuss their observations with their peers

Materials:
- Museum map and brochures
- Guiding questions worksheet

Procedure:
- Provide students with a museum map and brochures, highlighting the exhibits they will be viewing during the visit.
- Give students a worksheet with guiding questions to prompt them to analyze and interpret the chosen exhibits.
- Allow students to explore the exhibits in small groups or pairs, encouraging them to discuss their observations and ask questions.
- Facilitate a class discussion in which students share their observations and reflect on their experiences.

Assessment:

- Students will complete a written reflection about their experience at the museum, detailing their observations and discussing what they learned from the exhibits and experience.

Lesson 3: The Day After the Visit - Reflection and Extension

Objectives:

- Encourage students to reflect on their experiences and connect what they learned to their own lives and work
- Encourage students to extend their learning beyond the field trip by exploring the museum's on-line resources with the goal of adding to the knowledge obtained during the in person visit.
  Materials:
- Internet access
- Reflection worksheet
  Procedure:
- Provide students with a reflection organizer and/or rubric, instructing them to reflect on what they learned and how they can apply relevance to their own lives.
- Allow students to explore the museum's online resources, such as virtual exhibits, videos, and articles to expand the knowledge they gained from their in-person experience.
- Have students work in pairs or small groups to interview each other, facilitating a discussion on what they learned and how they can continue their exploration of the museum's collections.
- Further facilitate a whole class discussion in which students share their reflections and discuss their plans for further exploration.
  Assessment:
- Students will complete a written reflection about their plans for further exploration and how they can apply relevance to what they learned to their own lives.
- By following this lesson plan, high school freshmen art students will have a meaningful and en-riching experience during their field trip to the St. Louis Art Museum and continue their learning beyond the trip.

LESSON PLAN: FIELD TRIP TO THE NATURAL HISTORY MUSEUM OF UTAH

Here's a context-rich lesson plan for a college Earth Science class based around a field trip to the Natural History Museum of Utah:

Objectives:

- Introduce students to the geological and ecological history of Utah and the surrounding regions
- Provide students with an opportunity to apply what they have learned in class to real-world examples
- Encourage students to develop their observation and data analysis skills

○ Encourage students to consider the implications of their findings for current and future environmental issues

Materials:

○ Natural History Museum of Utah website
○ Guiding questions worksheet
○ Note-taking materials
○ Camera or smartphone for taking pictures

Procedure:

○ Introduce the Natural History Museum of Utah to students, providing information about its exhibits and collections.
○ Provide students with a worksheet with guiding questions to prompt them to analyze and interpret the exhibits.
○ Allow students to explore the exhibits in small groups or pairs, encouraging them to take notes and pictures to document their observations.
○ Facilitate a class discussion in which students share their observations and discuss their findings, with a focus on the geological and ecological history of Utah and the surrounding regions.
○ Provide students with an opportunity to apply what they have learned in class to the exhibits they have observed, with a focus on how the exhibits illustrate concepts such as plate tectonics, erosion, and climate change.
○ Encourage students to consider the implications of their findings for current and future environmental issues, such as the effects of human activity on natural systems.

Assessment:

○ Students will complete a written reflection about their experience at the museum, discussing their observations and what they learned from the exhibits.
○ Students will present their findings to the class, including their analysis of the geological and ecological history of Utah and the surrounding regions and their implications for current and future environmental issues.

Extension:

○ Have students conduct independent research on a topic related to the exhibits they observed, such as the effects of climate change on Utah's ecosystems or the geological history of the Great Salt Lake Basin.
○ Have students create a multimedia presentation, such as a video or podcast, summarizing their research and presenting their findings to the class.

By following this lesson plan, college Earth Science students will have a meaningful and enriching experience during their field trip to the Natural History Museum of Utah and will be able to apply what they have learned in class to real-world examples.

Chapter 5
Using UX Design Principles When Designing Context–Rich Learning Experiences

Travis J. Smith
Western Governors University, USA

ABSTRACT

To make the most context-rich experiences possible and avoid a myriad of problems, designers must keep a user-centric focus. By viewing our educational products through the perspective of the user, we can devise more accessible, diverse, meaningful, and above all enjoyable experiences. Using simple tools such as problem statements, personas, user maps, story boarding, wireframes, low-definition prototypes, and high-definition prototypes, we can consult users first in design to inform us on how to proceed with decisions. Using the simple outlined in the Design Thinking process of empathizing, defining, ideating, prototyping, and testing, we can deliver the most user centric experience possible. The author will show how Design Thinking couples so well with User Experience (UX), walk through what a user study is, what to do with the feedback you get from users, and how to keep the user in mind from inception to launch. In this chapter, the author will discuss the basic framework of UX, where to apply the tools within the framework and why these tools are important when developing context-rich experiences.

INTRODUCTION

"Good design is actually a lot harder to notice than poor design, in part because good designs fit our needs so well that the design is invisible." (Norman, 1988) When designers create context rich learning experiences for learners, research shows that creating a learning experience that is intrinsically motivating for the learner, that the learner feels a connection to that learning experience gets better pass rates, more engagement and provides for long lasting indelible experience for the learner. One way to achieve this connection is through **User Experience Design** (UX design). UX design is the process of putting the user at the center of a product. In this case the user would be the learner and the product would be the context rich learning experience. UX design coupled with **Design Thinking** can help solve a myriad

DOI: 10.4018/978-1-6684-7644-4.ch005

of issues, such as issues with accessibility, diversity, equity, context relevance, content alignment, and learning engagement. Design thinking is a set of strategic and practical procedures that help designers define problems and solutions to those problems while creating the learning experience. This chapter will go through the process of using design thinking and UX design to create more user centric experiences for learners to create a deeper connection for the learner. It will walk through each stage of the process and provide both best practices and helpful tools that help produce the best results.

Design Thinking

Design thinking is the process designers follow to implement a learning experience or a solution to a learning experience that is already available to learners. Design thinking follows a six-stage model which is empathize, define, ideate, prototype, test and implement. Each stage produces an artifact that helps inform the next stages. Within each of these stages there are helpful tools that help designers make decisions for their learning experience to make them user centric. This section will break down each of these stages, discuss the tools that help designers create context rich experiences, and what artifacts should be produce within the stage.

Stage 1: Empathize

In the first stage of design thinking designers will empathize with their learners. "Design is really an act of communication, which means having a deep understanding of the person with whom the designer is communicating" (Norman, 1988). They will find out who their learners are and what the learner needs from the experience to accomplish the giving objective for the learning experience. For example, an information technology instructor is creating a course on a basic software coding language. They are not sure if the course needs a lab component to the curriculum to help the learner to complete the assessment, which in this case the artifact produced by the learner is to write working code within the coding framework. The decision to have a lab should be made on who the learners and what they need are in the course. Knowing this will guide the instructor to the decision that needs to be made. If the learners are all novice in coding, they will need a lab to practice in. However, if the learners are already in the industry with experience in the coding language and are taking the course get a certificate to show that they are knowledgeable in the language, they most likely wouldn't need a lab to pass the assessment. If the instructor finds it is a mixture of both novice and expert learners in the class, they may want to have a lab that isn't required in the curriculum but is still there for the novice learners.

As shown in the example above, who the students are can inform many aspects of creating a learning experience. The best way to find out who the learners might be for a learning experience is through research. On way to find learner data is if there is data from past experiences such as a course can have data like, learner demographic, pass rates, and end of experience surveys can tell designers who the typical learner by giving designers information like age and experience range. One of the most powerful tools a designers can research is user surveys of the learning experience if the learning experience has already been experienced, such as student surveys. If the learning experience is brand new with no data available, the designer can look at what other experiences are available, to see if there is any information that can be gleaned from those experiences called a **competitive audit**. A competitive audit looks like any experience that is similar to the experience, this could be course in school setting, or a learning experience provided by a company. The designer looks for such data as their target audience age range and level of difficulty of the experience. If none of these options exist, designers can set a target audience for their learning experience and validate that information through **learner surveys**. Learner surveys can be done may ways, such as interviews, online surveys, or learner questioners. For example, if the information technology instructor has no data on potential students for their course, they can interview potential learners to validate the target audience. It is always best practice to get a diverse cross section of learners to make sure the entire learner populations is included.

User Personas

"You have to know why people behave as they do—and design around their foibles and limitations, rather than some ideal" (Kuang & Fabricant, 2019). Once the data guides the designer to validation of the target audience. The designer can create **User Personas** to guide them through the rest of the design process this is a very powerful tool. User personas are based on what the data tells the designer, it informs who will be the most likely learners of the experience. The designer will create a few personas based on what the data says about their learners. For example, if the information technology instructor learns that the learners will be taking the course are going to be learners, age 18-25 and novice learners. The designer will want to create at least two personas based on this information. These two personas should be diverse in nature for example two persons with different genders, race, and age. This will help make more diverse design decisions. Depending on the problem of the learning experience the information from the personas' data fields needed can vary. For example, for the information technology instructor it would be good to know if the learners are full time learners or have jobs, but the income level wouldn't be relevant. In a different scenario the opposite might be true though. Once the designer has defined the target audience fields, they can create the personas such as creating a learning experience for a company that is targeting executive leadership. Designers usually create two or more personas to avoid designing for only one type of learner. This helps give designers make have a better understanding of how to solve problems for a varying target audience. In the example above if the learners happen to be learners aged 18-40 which includes novice and expert learners the designer will want to have both represented.

It is also good to have varying genders, race, and accessibility levels within personas, to address both diversity, equity, and inclusion and accessibility issues that may come up. For example, the information technology instructor would want to make one of the personas a female to make sure the experience is seen through the lens of diversity, equity, and inclusion to help remove any gender bias. They also might want to include a person where the learner needs an assistive technology to help remove accessibility issues of learners.

Stage 2: Define

"A brilliant solution to the wrong problem can be worse than no solution at all: solve the correct problem" (Norman, 20119). Once designers have a clear picture of who their learners will be, they need to define "what problem they are trying to solve for their learners". This what the define stage does. In the define stage it is important to come up with the problem statements the designer wants to solve for the learner. To help articulate what issues the context rich content will solve for the learns a helpful tool is to use the **Six Ws** approach. The Six Ws are six questions that the designer asks from the perspective of the created personas these questions make up the problem statement.

Problem statements consist of six questions:

- Who – The who refers to the learner experiencing the problem.
- What – The what refers to the pain points the research showed the learner is experiencing.
- Where – The where refers to where the learner is using the learning experince.
- When – The when refers to when the learner experiences the pain point occurs within the learning experience.
- Why –The why is refers to why the problem is important.
- How – The how refers to how the context rich content will help the learner finish the learning experience

Personas become immensely helpful in helping to define these problems. For example, a curriculum designer for a demonstrative teaching program is looking to expand their clinical hour opportunities for their learners. They have learned through the empathize phase that their learners are mainly learners who work while most schools are open in the area, so the learners cannot fulfill all the requirements to finish the program. The designer has made a persona named Lia, based on the research they conducted that shows the learner must work during the day, due to this conflict the learner cannot complete their clinicals. The problem statement for this scenario would be "Lia is a working learner who needs more options to compete clinical hours, because they have to work during the day when the school is open." This problem statement clearly articulates what the problem is. The designer can now ideate a solution to address the problem statement.

Once the problem statement is defined, the designer can now articulate a **hypothesis statement** on what they believe the solution will solve. The hypothesis statement is an educated guess about what the solution might be. For example, for the clinical hours issue above the hypothesis statement would be "If Lia has a online substitution for her in person clinical hours, then she will be able to pass the program on time." This allows the designer to align the problem statement with a proposed solution. The designer still does not know how the solution will be implemented, but they have an educated guess on what the solution is based on the data from the research.

As each stage builds on the previous stage such as how the define stage builds on the empathize stage it is important to make sure the designer align the learners that they define with their personas making sure to get a cross section of diverse learners within the learner's spectrum. Doing this will help designers avoid any issues with diversity, equity and inclusion and accessibility. This is very important to do since all decisions are informed by the user persons in the following stages. The decisions that are made in the define stage are based off the personas created from data in the first stage if they are not diverse, they could not solve the need for all the learners represented in the data. The designer will then run into issues in the testing stage when the learners

Stage 3: Ideate

Once the designer has their hypothesis statement, they can start to ideate solutions for the solution of the problem. The Ideate stage is about generating as many solutions as possible. The quality of the solution doesn't matter at this point. After the solutions are generated, the designer can decern which ones are the best for the problem statement. Designers use many techniques to generalate as many solutions as they can this section will touch upon some of the most common techniques.

One of the most powerful tools designers can use is a **competitive audit**. "Users spend most of their time on other sites, and they prefer your site to work in the same way as all the other sites they already know" (Yablonski, 2020). This is similar to the competitive audit that is done in stage one, the difference between the two is what the designer is looking at. In the first stage the designer looks at what kind of learners' other organizations are addressing. During a competitive audit a designer looks at how others have addressed the issue they are looking at for their learners. This can be another learning experience that is similar such as another course or program. It be a single aspect of an experience that is different, but addresses a similar problem. For example, Stacy a learning experience designer for a nursing school could look at how another course in nursing that delt with the same problem they are running into. The learning experience designer might not find a solution in any similar courses, but she finds that a college of business has successfully addressed the problem. A competitive audit is all about seeing what is out there in the field and what aspects the designer can incorporate into their designs.

Designers should try to get a cross section of competition from both educational and corporate institutions. This way they see what a breadth of designers have done in addressing the issue. When looking at other context rich learning experiences designers take notes of what they like about the experience and what they don't. Designers want to bring over the best aspects of a design if possible and remove any weaknesses from the experience they can. A good rule of thumb is for designers to look at five originations during their competitive audit this helps to get a good view of what is in the field.

There will be times when designers do not find any solutions through a competitive audit. However, the competitive audit is still a helpful exercise for the designer to do, since the designer has taken notes on what they have seen out in the industry, they know what won't work for their learning experience. Weather the designer found solutions or not during the competitive audit the designer02 will still need to ideate other solutions to make sure they have explored all solutions thoroughly.

One of the most common exercises to generate ideas is the **"How might we" (HMW) exercise**. In this exercise the designer asks, "how might we address the problem statement". For example, Stacy the learning experience designer for the earlier example has a problem that learners must get more experience noting vital signs on a chart, Stacy is exploring building a context rich learning scenario to place into one of the foundational courses for the program. Stacy might ask "how may we address getting charting into the course. Stacy can insert prompts into the how might we statement to generate ideas.

Some common prompts to add to the how might we statement are:

- Amp up the good - this prompt looks at how you can amplify positives about the problem.
- Break the point of view into pieces - this prompt breaks the problem into different viewpoints of people that are in the interaction with the problem such as the learner and instructor.
- Question an assumption - this prompt questions an assumption that the designer might have such as the learner only will perform a task one way.
- Go after the adjective – this prompt looks to take any negative adjectives and turn them into a positive.
- Create and analogy using a established context. – this prompt has designers build an analogy based on a real-world context such as a video game.
- Identify unexpected resources that can aid competitive audit – the prompt looks at how the designer could look at outside the box resources that could assist with the problem, such as a chat bot.

There are numerous prompts that can be inserted within the exercise framework available on the internet. Designers write as many as their time allows and discern the best ones.

Another excersie the designers employ is **Crazy Eights**. Crazy eights are another way to ideate solutions for a problem quickly. Crazy eights require the designer to fold a piece of paper together until the paper has eight squares. The designer then times themselves for eight minutes with a timer. The goal is to write or draw a solution within each square of the piece of paper. Each square should take one minute to complete. This helps designers generate eight solutions quickly. The designer then discerns the best generated solutions. The benefit of using crazy eights is the designer has to quickly produce ideas that can help remove any metal block that the designer may be experiencing.

Most designers us all three exercises to generate solutions for their problem. Designers also will tap into the other designers they know to see if they have missed something in their solutions. These designers maybe coworkers, fellow designers in the field or a trusted manager or mentor.

Stage 4: Prototype

"Rule of thumb: if you think something is clever and sophisticated beware-it is probably self-indulgence" (Norman, 1988). Once the designers have generated a lot of ideas, they can us their problem statement and personas to discern which solution will meet the need of the problem. In some cases, the designer will use aspects of one solution with the aspects of another solution. Combining ideated solutions is one of the biggest benefits to exploring as many ideas as possible during the previous stage.

Once the solution has been finalized it is best practice to create a **goal statement**. A goal statement gives the designer and anybody else working on the project clarity of what the outcome should be for the learning experience. The goal statement should include the specific action that the learner will be allowed to do after using the learning experince. Who will the action affect? What positive impact this will have on the learner. Lastly the outlined measurable terms of success. For example, a goal statement for a new interactive lab in a chemistry course would be "The lab will let learners practice interacting with the various chemicals which will affect learners by reinforcing the readings on various chemicals within the unit. We will measure effectiveness by looking at the pass rate of the learners interacting with the lab versus the learners who are not."

Once the goal statement is created, the designer creates a learner path. A learner path is a high-level path the learner will take to get through the learning experience. It will include the topics that will be included, what sequence the topics should be in, and any decisions the learners should make such as any interactions needed to advance through the learning experience. These interactions could be an assessment, or in the example of chemistry lab above an interaction would be the learner selecting chemicals to use. The user journey could be a visual representation of what that flow looks like or it could be as a simple as a numbered list of topics with interactions noted where appropriate. The most important action is to map the sequence for the learner in a logical way.

After the learner flow is created, the designer can flush out the design more thoroughly with a **storyboard**. A storyboard can be a visual representation of the learning experience with a narrative, or it could be a more flushed version of a numbered outline that breaks down topics into subtopics with learning objectives. The most import aspect of the story board should be able to tell the flow the learning experience and what should be flushed out in the next step.

Once the storyboard has been created it is time to flush out the learning experience in a wire frame. A wire frame could be a static visual representation of the experience which includes the layout of the experience, or it could be a word document that will be a template for all the content to be flushed out later. For example, it makes sense to make a static representation of a interactive chemistry lab to show

how the lab will be laid out for learners, however it makes more sense to make an outlined manuscript if the designer is creating the whole unit of chemistry that the interactive lab will be housed.

After the wire frame is in place the designer will start the low fidelity prototype. The low fidelity prototype is the first draft of the learning experience. Depending on the level of expertise of the designer and the subject, the designer may flush out all aspects of the learning experience with the guidance of a subject matter expert. For example, if the designer is a chemistry instructor, they may flush all the content themselves. However, if the designer is creating the chemistry module with very little knowledge the subject it is always best to consult an expert.

Once the content is flushed out it can be authored in whatever platform the learning experience will be in. This can take shape in many forms for example in the chemistry lab above if the lab is the only experience being produced the low fidelity prototype would be the functional version of the learning experience created in a software platform. If the designer created a manuscript for the unit the lab will be housed in then the designer, will need to transfer that manuscript into the authoring platform. The designer wants this to be a functional as it can be to do testing in the next stage.

Stage 5: Test

"The most important problems to solve were those that weren't being expressed. The most important questions to ask were those that people never thought to ask themselves" (Kuang & Fabricant, 2019). After the low fidelity has been authored the designer will want to make sure that everything functions correctly, any assessment is aligned to the content, and provides a satisfactory overall learning experience. The best way to accomplish this is to get learner feedback on the learning experience.

During this stage the designer will create research plan. A research plan outlines a brief introduction to the learning experience background. Research questions that should be answered during the study. Key performance indicators which are critical measures of a progress toward the end goal. They could include:

- Time on Task – measures how long a learner spends on a learning experience task for example how long it takes the learner to finish a lab.
- User Error Rates – indicates the parts of a design that may make a learner make an error such as misalignment in curriculum and the assessment or a assessment question that is poorly written.
- Drop Rates – this indicates how many learners abandoned the learning experience.
- Conversion rates – this indicator is the inverse of drop rate how many people complete the learning experience.
- System usability Scale – is a questionnaire that asks learners their opinions about the learning experience. The questions focus on the usability of the learning experience. The questionnaire is on a scale of strongly disagree to strongly disagree.

The next piece of the research proposal is methodology. Methodology is how the research will take place. Usability studies are useful methodology when looking at learners going through a learning experience for the first time. Usability studies are a primary research method. the research is done by the designer. Because usability studies are on a scale of one to five, they can be counted a quantified, this means they are also quantitative research. These qualities are helpful to make sure the learning experience aligns to what the designer wants for final learning experience.

After the methodology is chosen, the designer needs to describe the participants, they attend to use in the study. For example, for a five-learner usability study would look like "learners aged 19-25, two male, two females, one non binary learner, and one learner that has an assistive technology device." As a best practice designers should try to make the group of learners be as diverse as possible for the study. This ensures the best perspective and data. Designers should have participants from different genders, race, and ages if possible. It is also helpful to get a learner who has an assistive technology device need to see if there are accessibility issues with the design.

The final component of the research proposal is the script. The script is the steps that the designer wants the learner to take during the testing. For a usability study the script consists of two parts prompts and questions. Prompts are declarative statements. For example, "complete the following reading and answer the questions after the reading" would be a prompt. The question would be a follow up to the prompt such as "How confusing did you find the questions that followed the reading?" The learner would use the one to five scale to rate how confusing they found the questions. The designer will also ask the learner if they would like to elaborate anymore on the question. This is to flush out as much feedback as possible about that particular part of the learning experience.

Once the designer has the research proposal flushed out, they can do the study. The designer will proceed to test their learning experience with learners. The first way to conduct the test is to do it in person in given in the same room as the learner. Designers will follow their script and as questions. It is best practice for the designer to keep the tone of their voice and the overall test warm but neutral. The designer wants to get the learner to open up about their experience, so the designer should speak in a conversational tone, but they should stay neutral to what the learner expresses. This is to ensure that the designer is not leading the learner in their responses. Designers want to make sure their tone is neither positive nor negative when a learner responds. It is important to keep body language neutral as well, designers should try not to frown or cross their arms during a negative answer, nor should they nod and smile during a positive answer. This keeps the designers biases out of the study. It is important for the designer to watch what they say as well, designers should not follow up questions with words such as "good" or "awesome. Designers don't want to show praise to a question in case learners are trying to please the designers asking them questions and not portraying the learners' true feelings. The Second way of conducting a usability study is holding the interviews remotely. The designer creates a slideshow with each prompt and with the question that follow on the next slide. The interview participant records their responses through a screenshare explaining their thought process as they go through the learning experience. They then answer the question. The designer watches the videos and take notes later just like they would if interviewing the participants in person.

There are pros and cons for conducting the useability study in these two ways. A few of the in person study's pros are the designer can ask participants to elaborate on their answers and if the participant needs further clarification on a prompt. Some of the cons for in person studies are bias can be injected by the designer's language and body language and scheduling can be more difficult to get all participants to a location for the study. As previously discussed, the best way to counteract injecting the designers bias into a useability study is to keep neutral language and body language with all participants. Pros for remote useability studies include not injecting bias in from the designer conducting the research and scheduling is easier due to participants being able to do the interview at their convince. Cons for remote usability studies include lack of ability to ask participants to elaborate and participants cannot ask to follow up questions if they don't understand a prompt. To counteract some of these pros and cons designers try to write their scripts as clear as they can when creating both prompts and questions.

It is best practice to keep a spreadsheet of notes taken during the usability study. This helps the designer organize the data later. Each question and prompt should have its own column for notes along with a place to put the **task completion scale number**. The task completion is a scale from one to three one being "completed with no difficulty" two being "completed with difficulty" and three being "participant didn't complete task". Some other items that designers may include are click path, and an observation field where notes on body language would go. The click path is the path the learner try to finish the prompt, this can help designers figure out if one part of the design is confusing to navigate. For example, "The learner clicked on home, the reading, clicked on the assessment item, and clicked submit." Would be a click path for a prompt. While designers take notes during the usability studies, it can be difficult to note everything. A best practice to counteract this issue is for the designers to record the interviews even when in person. This allows the designers to go back and review both question answers and any body language that needs to be noted. It is important to get consent before recording an interview.

After the usability study is finished the designer will look at all the data collected, such as task completion rate, error rate, questions to prompts, and any other relevant data. The designer can synthesize this data to look for **patterns** in the data. Patterns are any issue that show up multiple times within the study. These patterns will then inform the **themes** from the research. Themes are like item of issues. For example, a usability study shows that four out of the five learners didn't get one of the questions correct in the learning experience. The pattern here would be "the question is difficult". The designer then takes all the patterns they see and creates themes to encapsulate the patterns. For example, if the reason the question in the above example is because of a misalignment in the learning experience to the assessment the theme would be "misalignment of content and assessment". Any other misalignment patterns the designer sees in the patterns of data would fall under this theme. After all themes are found and patterns sorted the designer creates the **insights. Insights** are articulations of the themes that will turn into action items that need to be taken during the next stage. For example, the theme "misalignment of content and assessment" would be turned into the insight "Learners need better alignment in the curriculum to the assessment in regards to these specific areas". Doing this helps designer articulate the revisions that need to be made for the high-fidelity prototype given the data taken from the study for everyone working on the learning experience.

One poplar way to sort the data into patterns and themes is through an affinity board. An affinity board is a board that sticky notes go on. Designers first put each observation from the useability study on a sticky note. Once all the observations are on a sticky note the designer puts the liked items together the clusters that come from these observations are a pattern. After all the patterns are sorted out the designer moves the liked clusters together. For example, if there is a missed alignment with multiple assessment items the misalignment for question five would be clustered next to misalignment for question eight. After all the patterns are clustered the designer uses the commonalities of the patterns to create the theme. For example, misalignment of the assessment would be a theme for the misalignment in question five and eight of the previous example. There usually will be some miscellaneous observations that won't fit into any patterns or themes. It is up to the designer to review the outliers and determine if they need action as well. Affinty boards can be done on paper or using a software platform.

If designers do not have time to make all revisions before the initial release of the learning experience the designer will go through the themes and us a **revision priority scale** to make sure the most perinate revisions are done first. A revision priority scale is a three-level scale, level one is the most important that have to be done before launch, and level three is the least important. An example, of a level one revision would be a misalignment in assessment or a gap in content. A level two would be revisions that need to be done first after the final learning experience is first released. An example of a level two priority would be a learner requested image that would help explain a concept better, but is already explained in the learning experience. Level three would encompass any revisions that are purely style based such a different color on pie graph. It would also include any themes that could be added in a future state of the learning experience such as a simulation within the learning experience that learners would like, but the time frame doesn't accommodate to be built. These revisions are not time pressing. so the designer will wait until version two of the learning experience is launched or when time allows to add them to the original learning experience later.

Once all revisions are done to the learning experience the designer will go through the prototype do a quality assurance check. The designer makes sure all content is fully flushed out, all web links go to where they need to, and all interactions work correctly. An interaction is anything that the learnier will engage with, this could be a button, a checkbox or an assessment question that needs to be submitted. Once all these items have been checked the designer now has the high-fidelity prototype of the learning experience. If time allows the designer should run another usability study with a new set of participants. This time there should be very little to have to revise in the prototype. Once all revisions are done from the second usability study the designer would release the beta version of the learning experience. If the timeline does not incorporate time to do the usability study the designer would release the beta version of the learning experience at this time but would want to monitor the data closely for the initial launch.

Stage 6: Implement

Now that the learning experience is ready to implement the designer may have to hand off the learning experience to other stakeholders to build the final version of the course. This will depend on the organization and the responsibilities of the designer. Whatever this launch looks like the designer will than monitor data while the learning experience is in beta with learners. This time frame will vary depending on organization usually the time frame is the first few months.

The data the designer looks at is based on the proposed goals that were set in stage 3. Any revisions at this point should be based on what the data is showing. An example of this would be an assessment item that was misaligned but was missed during learner testing. The data would show this in pass rate of the item, then the designer would find a solution to this issue. The designer shouldn't be making revisions unless the data shows an issue that needs revision. The reason for this is the data could be skewed if any changes are made without a rationale. If changes are made it is always best to release them in a new version to keep the data from the original revision intact.

Once the designer has finished the monitoring phase. The learning experience will periodically be reviewed for performance to see if there is a need for a new version. In context rich learning experiences there may be a need versioning more than other learning experiences. This is due to he context changing quickly for the learning experience. For example, a nursing course may need new revisions every year based on new guidelines from the Department of Health. In this example the reason for revisions was not based on the performance of the experience but based on changes in context.

Data informing revisions is one of the most important aspects of user design. The data that is gathered after launch will inform the next version the learning experience starting the design process all over again. The data from the launch and beyond will inform the empathize phase the next time the designer has to revise the learning experience or create another version of the experience. This ensures that learning experiences are always informed by the learners.

Benefits of User Design

In the next view sections of the chapter will touch upon the benefits of user design. These include:

- Diversity, Equity, and Inclusion
- Accessibility
- Data Driven Decisions

Diversity, Equity, and Inclusion in User Design

User design is all about putting users first in the design. In learning experience design this is the learners. The best way to make sure the learners feel like they are at the center of the design is through diversity, equity, and inclusion practices. This chapter has touched upon some of these practices. Such as interviewing the most diverse cross section of learners during the empathy phase, creating diverse personas to get varied views of an issue during the solution phase, and including divers learning for the usability testing. The common denominator to all these practices is to get the most diverse cross section of viewpoints that the designer can. This allows to point out weakness in the design that probably wouldn't be surfaced with one viewpoint.

Representation is a great tool for the designer to implement. When designers are creating learning experience components such as written scenarios, videos, images of people, and assessment items it is always best to pick a divers set of names and representation of people. For example, designers should us diverse names when writing a scenario. They should also use a variety of races and genders in the media assets. This helps all learners identify better with the learning experience, this allows for better learning.

Accessibility

Designing for the one can help the many. This is a phrase that is good to keep in mind when designing accessible learning experiences. Including alt text for images, adding captions and transcripts for videos, using high contrast text and images, and using screen reader friendly html for math equations are all tools' designers can use to make their learning experiences more accessible. Not only does accessibility help learners who rely on these practices to succeed, but they also make the experience better for all learners. For example, transcripts for videos help learners with a hearing impairment, but other learners might prefer to read the transcript rather than watch the video as well.

User design helps address accessibility the same way it addresses diversity, equity, and inclusion by bringing in a diverse learner population, some with assistive technology needs designers are able to design for the one to benefit the many. Designers should always give great weight to accessible designs. For example, if a designer is testing a lab that has images with alt text tags, with high contrast colors, but a learner with a visual impairment needs to have the images bigger than they can be housed, the designer should find a solution to this issue. In this case it might be best for the designer to find platform that allows for this capability when experience is built and launched. The designer could include a link to a larger version of the image underneath the image to resolve this issue as well.

Data Driven Decisions

Beyond the benefit of creating leaner centric experiences. One of the biggest benefits of using UX principles when designing experiences is the data created throughout the UX process. From the very beginning of the process designers are gathering data from learners to inform the final learning experience. This is a very important tool not only to make learner centric designs, but to support these designs and the decisions behind those designs.

Designers usually have to explain their decisions to someone weather that be a superior, accreditation, or another designer on their team. Having data helps provides evidence for these to help explain the design. For example when a testing a learning experience if the data shows the four of the five users are confused by one of the more popular aspects of a design, it is easier for a designer to remove this from the learning experience even if it was popular with the design team.

From collecting learner information in the empathize stage to looking at learner data after launch, the learner data is at the forefront of user design. Making it easier for designers truly know what is best for the leaner this makes decision making easier. By looking at the data and patterns it directs the designer to go with a certain aspect of their design. It also reduces designer bias if a designer thinks something is best for a design, but the learner data says it is not, it is easier for the designer to remove it. One of the most powerful aspects of the learner data is having a base line for future revisions after launching the learning experience. This allows for the designer to revisit their learning experiences when it is time to update the experience. Thus, designer can take the initial data driven from the testing phase and compare the data gathered after to launch and see how it is performing. Data is also helpful to decide when a experience should be revisited. For example, if the designer has set a certain pass rate for the learning experience and the pass rate starts to either drop or never reaches the initial number it may be time to revise the experience to improve the pass rate performance.

SUMMARY

This chapter introduced what user design is, how it incorporates design thinking into user design to make the most user centric learning experiences. It provides the basic framework of design thinking and how to take a design through the process from concept to launch. The chapter walked through the empathize stage where designers empathize with learners, the define stage where designers define the problem, the ideate stage where designers generate solutions for the problem, the prototype stage where designers prototype the solution, the test stage where designers test the prototype with learners, and the implement stage where designers launch and monitor the learning experience. The chapter touch upon the benefits of user design such as creating learner centric designs, user design aiding in counteracting diversity, equity, and inclusion issue, addressing accessibility issues, and making data driven design solutions. Using this design frame will allow learning experience that are not only context rich, but user centric that is very beneficial to learners.

REFERENCES

Bamberger, M., & Segone, M. (n.d.). *How to design and manage equity-focused evaluations.* UNICEF.https://evalpartners.org/sites/default/files/EWP5_Equity_focused_evaluations.pdf

Bobier, J. F., Merey, T., Robnett, S., Grebe, M., Feng, J., Rehberg, B., & Hazan, J. (2022). *The Corporate Hitchhiker's guide to the metaverse.* Boston Consulting Group.

Costa, R. (2019, April 4). Information architecture: A UX designer's guide. *Justinmind.* https://www.justinmind.com/blog/information-architecture-ux-guide/

Harley, A. (2017). *Ideation for Everyday Design Challenges.* Nielsen Norman Group. https://www.nngroup.com/articles/ux-ideation/

Holladay, M. (2018, November 16). The eight principles of information architecture. *Medium.* https://medium.com/@hollabit/the-eight-principles-of-information-architecture-6feff11f907a

Isaacson, W. (2011). *Steve Jobs.* Simon & Schuster.

Kane, L. (2019, June 30). *The attention economy.* Nielsen Norman Group. https://www.nngroup.com/articles/attention-economy/

Kuang, C., & Fabricant, R. (2019). *User friendly: How the hidden rules of design are changing the way we live, work & play.* Random House.

Liedtka, J., Salzman, R., & Azer, D. (2017). *Design Thinking for the Greater Good.* Columbia Business School Publishing. doi:10.7312/lied17952

M, R. (2018, March 19). *Psychology + design: Gestalt principles you can use as design solutions.* UX Collective. https://uxdesign.cc/psychology-design-4-gestalt-principles-to-use-as-your-next-design-solution-fcdec423a6bf

Moran, K. (2019, December 1). *Usability testing 101.* Nielsen Norman Group. https://www.nngroup.com/articles/usability-testing-101/

Norman, D. A. (1988). *The design of everyday things.* Basic books.

Sapio, D. (2020, March 2).*10 principles for ethical UX designs.* UX Collective.https://uxdesign.cc/10-principles-for-ethical-ux-designs-21faf5ab243d

Sheppard, B. (2018). *The Business Value of Design.* McKinsey & Company. https://www.mckinsey.com/capabilities/mckinsey-design/our-insights/the-business-value-of-design

Tubik. (2017, May 25). *Information architecture. Basics for designers.* UX Planet. https://uxplanet.org/information-architecture-basics-for-designers-b5d43df62e20

Vaidya, M. (2020, September 5). *Accessibility: Guidelines for information architecture, UX design, and visual design.* IBM Design.https://medium.com/design-ibm/accessibility-guidelines-for-information-architecture-ux-design-and-visual-design-5ae33ed1d52d

Waldron, C. (2020). Design Products for the End User, Not the Stakeholders. *Medium.* uxdesign.cc/design-products-for-the-end-user-not-the-stakeholders-6171695b6c78.

Yablonski, J. (2020). *Laws of UX: Using psychology to design better products & services.* O'Reilly Media.

Section 2
Assessments and Evaluations
for Learning Outcomes

Chapter 6
It's All About Context:
Differential Item Functioning in IT Performance Assessments

Heather Hayes
Western Governors University, USA

Goran Trajkovski
https://orcid.org/0000-0002-3745-3009
Western Governors University, USA

Marylee Demeter
Western Governors University, USA

ABSTRACT

Assessments, even summative, are part of the learning journey not just for the student, but for the instructors as well. In competency-based education, performance assessments (PAs) are regarded as a highly authentic method of measurement, but their complexity makes them vulnerable to construct-irrelevant variance such as group bias. A differential item functioning (DIF) study was conducted to detect potential bias in a series of information technology PA tasks in which task scenarios were identified (by SMEs) as neutral or potentially controversial, where the latter was hypothesized as more likely to trigger DIF for certain demographics. Given the variety of DIF methods available and their relative strengths and weaknesses, three common statistical methods – Mantel-Haenszel (MH), logistic regression (LR), and Lord's chi-square (LC) - were used followed by a substantive review of DIF items. Hypotheses were largely supported by the analysis and review. Discussion centers on the implication of findings for assessment strategies in education.

DOI: 10.4018/978-1-6684-7644-4.ch006

INTRODUCTION

Student assessment is an integral part of the education process. Educational assessments can serve multiple purposes such as the case with assessment of learning versus assessment for learning (William, 2011; Padmanabha, 2021). Assessment of learning typically refers to summative assessments, in which the assessment outcome represents the culmination of a student's work and degree of success in learning a particular set of knowledge, skills, and abilities (KSAs) related to course objectives. In competency-based education, the summative assessment outcome reflects whether the student is competent or not yet competent in a set of course-related KSAs and, if competent, he or she passes the course and moves on to more advanced courses in the program. Thus, there is a sense of finality to summative assessments. Assessment for learning is more often associated with formative assessments that are taken during the course, where the goal is to estimate a student's progress toward achieving competency. Formative assessments are crucial to learning through the feedback it provides to the extent that this feedback is useful – i.e., specific, detailed, and actionable. When useful feedback is given to the student regarding assessment performance (such as with a coaching report), it increases the likelihood of KSA attainment through adjustments in self-regulation and learning strategies. Assessment performance feedback is also helpful to course instructors in terms of modifying their teaching strategy to be more conducive to student learning, which includes personalization of methods to students at different levels of achievement and academic needs (William, 2011).

It can be argued that the dichotomy between formative and summative assessment is an oversimplification (Bennett, 2009). For example, formative assessment outcomes can be used as evidence of learning at various points throughout the course, and summative assessment outcomes can be used to provide feedback on key performance indicators related to the quality of the program and institution (Bresciani Ludvik, 2019; McClarty & Gaertner, 2015; Rubin, 2016; Zlatkin-Troitschanskaia & Pant, 2016). Moreover, feedback on assessment quality is useful for continuous quality improvement of the assessment, itself, particularly for large-scale, standardized educational assessments including those in competency-based education (Hayes, Gyll, Ragland, & Meyers, 2021; McClarty & Gaertner, 2015). Regardless of whether a course assessment is formative or summative, outcomes theoretically measure achievement of the same course-based competency or skill set, and they both require evidence of validity for assessment outcomes to be useful.

Validity, Fairness, and DIF in Educational Assessments

Validity refers to the degree to which inferences made from assessment outcomes are appropriate given their purpose (AERA, APA, & NCME, 2014). For example, if the purpose of an assessment is to predict an individual's level of success on a job, then you should evaluate that claim by correlating assessment scores with scores from on-the-job performance via performance evaluations, longevity, or promotion. If there is no relationship, then validity is lacking, meaning the results cannot be trusted because interpretations are unclear, and any feedback you might hope to gain will not be useful. In competency-based education, an assessment outcome (pass/fail) is useful if a student who is competent in the course-relevant KSAs passes but a student who is not yet competent fails. Threats to validity occur when assessment scores contain construct-irrelevant variance; namely, when assessment scores are impacted by factors unrelated to the competency or skill we intend to measure (Embretson, 1983; Messick, 1989). Construct-irrelevant variance in assessment scores may contribute to a lack of measurement invariance, violating a critical assumption in modern test theory (Embretson & Reise, 2000). Measurement non-invariance occurs when a statistical parameter of the assessment (e.g., mean scores) or item (e.g., item difficulty) vary by some characteristics of the test-taker, such as gender or ethnicity. When there is a lack of measurement invariance, the interpretation of assessment outcomes differs according to group membership (Raju & Ellis, 2002).

Fairness in assessment is a validity issue that has received an increasing amount of attention within academia and assessment industry circles in recent years, being elevated to one of the foundational pillars of assessment quality (next to reliability and validity) as per the 2014 Standards for Educational and Psychological Testing. Fairness in assessment refers to the extent to which students have equal opportunity to demonstrate knowledge and skills regardless of age, gender, ethnicity, socioeconomic status, disabilities, and various other personal characteristics unrelated to the KSAs. One goal of standardized testing is to limit construct-irrelevant variance, achieve measurement invariance, and make testing conditions fair and equitable by homogenizing test material, test conditions, and test scoring for all students. Unfortunately, students are not homogenous in how they best demonstrate knowledge or how they respond to certain testing conditions, and as a result, there remains potential for construct-irrelevant variance in scores due to personal characteristics of the test-taker (Sireci, 2020).

Although changes have been effectively made in terms of flexibility of test accommodations, these changes have only been legally and widely implemented for students with disabilities and English language learners (Faulkner-Bond & Soland, 2020; Sireci, Banda, & Wells, 2018; Sireci & O'Riordan, 2020). Characteristics such as gender and ethnicity are often over-looked, despite evidence of bias in the literature. For example, research has shown that test anxiety negatively impacts test performance in STEM (Science, Technology, Engineering, and Mathematics) courses but for females only (Cotner, Jeno, Walker, Jorgensen, & Vandvik, 2020). Moreover, students of different ethnic groups often have quite different experiences in terms of quality of education and exposure to learning materials leading up to assessment. For example, students who are African American, Latino, and Native American often attend schools that are underfunded and have lower quality instructors than Caucasian students (Darling-Hammond, 2004; Lankford, Loeb, & Wyckoff, 2002; Peske & Haycock, 2006). These groups also tend to have lower standardized test scores (Jencks & Phillips, 2011), suggesting that a lack of equity in instruction and resources is a precursor to, and an explanation of, different performance levels.

The research just described pertains to impact, where test parameters such as test score means or pass rates vary between groups despite the assessment being psychometrically sound and composed of items whose scores achieve measurement invariance (Holland & Thayer, 1988). However, the latter assumption should only be made when there is evidence of assessment validity. A key step in validity testing is addressing measurement invariance at the item level to eliminate any bias or unfairness in the assessment and prevent impact (unless impact reflects true group differences in KSAs). Differential Item Functioning (DIF) is a statistical method for evaluating the degree to which members of one group (the focal group) are less likely to answer an item correctly than members of another group (the reference group) despite having the same ability level (e.g., Dorans & Holland, 1993; Swaminathan & Rogers, 1990). Differences in ability between groups are controlled for using a matching variable such the summed test score. DIF can be applied to any item parameter of interest, the most common being item difficulty and discrimination. In Classical Test Theory, the difficulty of the item is measured as the proportion of respondents in a sample who answered the item correctly, whereas item discrimination refers to the level of measurement precision in an item and is calculated as the correlation between an item score and the overall, summed score.

Depending on which item parameters are of interest in the analysis, there is a useful, further distinction between uniform and non-uniform DIF (Roussos & Stout, 1996). The presence of uniform DIF implies that the item is more difficult for one group than another for all ability levels, whereas non-uniform DIF indicates that the difference in item difficulty is specific to a particular ability level or range. In other words, there is an interaction between group membership and ability level when predicting item difficulty. For example, the item may be more difficult for females if they are also on the high end of the ability spectrum, whereas the item is more difficult for males at low ability levels. Non-uniform DIF also indicates that the item score discriminates better among members of one group compared to other (i.e., the ability levels of one group's members is more precisely measured than the ability levels of another group's members). Hence, non-uniform DIF provides greater specificity in where the measurement invariance lies.

It is important to keep in mind that the presence of DIF does not necessarily indicate bias; it is merely an indication of potential bias that requires further investigation (AERA, APA, & NCME, 2014; Penfield & Camilli, 2007) into what is called "substantive DIF" (Roussos & Stout, 1996). The latter process typically involves further review of item content and an attempt to determine what construct-irrelevant (or relevant) factors are responsible for DIF. For example, one cause of DIF may be the wording of the item stem or response options (e.g., slang; non-inclusive content, awkward or obscure phrases or vocabulary) which may offend or confuse the student during the response process. However, false positives (i.e., Type I error rates) are common and can result in unnecessary loss of items and confusion over the source of DIF (Roussos & Stout, 1996). Thus, statistical DIF analysis is the first step in the evaluation of item bias, and item bias needs to be confirmed or rejected in step two via an extensive item review by subject matter experts (SMEs) prior to discarding and/or modifying items on live assessments.

Performance Assessments: Authenticity, Fairness, and DIF

Performance or task-based assessments (PAs) grew in popularity in the 1990s for at least two reasons. First, the initial thinking was that PAs are fairer and more inclusive than multiple choice assessments (Chen, Liu, & Zumbo, 2018; Hambleton & Murphy, 1992), given their constructed response formats which are naturally less constrictive than a multiple-choice format in which the response to a question is selected from a set of options. Second, PAs have been regarded as more authentic measures of learning because they have the potential to tap into higher levels of cognitive complexity and levels of knowledge by requiring the student to demonstrate how they use knowledge by performing a task (Darling-Hammond, 2017; Struyven et al., 2006). Multiple choice assessments, on the other hand, are viewed as more appropriate for measuring knowledge that is low in cognitive complexity such as recall or recognition and limited application (see Hancock, 1994). As a result, PAs are highly recommended for competency-based higher education and certification tests that are supposed to prepare students for on-the-job performance (Gallardo, 2020). PAs can take on many forms – short or long essays, research papers, e-portfolios, individual or group projects, oral or video presentations, and conducting laboratory investigations. Thus, PAs are theoretically more conducive to students who best demonstrate their competency in non-standardized conditions.

Unfortunately, the less constrictive and more complex nature of PAs and PA scoring methods increase its vulnerability to new sources of construct-irrelevant variance in scores, thus threatening the validity of PA outcomes (Leighton, 2019). For example, scoring inconsistencies or inaccuracies among evaluators can undermine the reliability and validity of assessment outcomes. If the PA involves a video or oral presentation, there is potential for group or identity bias in evaluator scores. For example, a female evaluator may grade males more harshly than females, and vice-versa. Differential access to technology may affect the quality and fairness of portfolio scores. Thus, despite its allure regarding authenticity and fairness, DIF research has become highly active amongst PAs (Chen et al., 2018; Penfield & Lam, 2000; Zwick, Donogue, & Grima, 1993). There have been challenges, however, in finding the most appropriate method for detecting DIF in PAs for two reasons. One, the tasks in PAs are typically not dichotomously scored, so the most common DIF methods (e.g., Mantel Haenszel statistic; Holland & Thayer, 1988) are not considered. Second, it is difficult to find a matching variable to represent overall ability because the summed PA score is often based on only a few tasks, and scores are typically given at the task level (i.e., tasks are items; there are no "items" within a task).

The purpose of the current study is to test for DIF in a series of summative course PAs in an IT data analytics master's degree (MSDA) program at an online competency-based higher education (OCBHE) institute. PAs in the MSDA program typically consist of at least one task in which a scenario is given along with instructions and several prompts. Each prompt is a brief instruction or question regarding an aspect of the task such as data analysis, demonstration of results via graphs or screen shots, interpretation of results, and making predictions or recommendations for solving problems. Thus, these PAs can best be described as case studies or research reports. Although the task prompts are like test items, and it is possible that the wording of the task prompts may contribute to DIF, the primary research question in this study is, to what extent does the nature of the task scenario or context contribute to DIF?

Based on a review of the PAs in the MSDA program by SMEs with a combined total of 50 years of experience in education and item writing, a sample of PAs was chosen in which the scenarios were categorized as neutral or controversial in nature, where the latter is defined as being more likely to emotionally trigger certain individuals or group, be divisive based on group differences in beliefs related to elements or the theme of the scenario, or in some other way affect the item response differently for members of one group versus those of another. Two PAs that contain one task (each) with controversial scenarios were chosen, and two single-task PAs with neutral task scenarios were chosen for the current study. In the first PA ("Controversial PA 1"), the task scenario revolves around police activity and funding. It is hypothesized that this scenario is more likely to result in DIF for ethnicity (Hypothesis 1a). For example, minorities may be more negatively impacted than Caucasians given the intense media coverage of police brutality toward African Americans (e.g., Breanna Taylor; George Floyd) and/or personal experience. The second PA task scenario ("Controversial PA 2") concerns banking and emergency loans in a downturned economy. It is hypothesized that this scenario is more likely associated with DIF for income level (Hypothesis 2a). For example, low-income students and/or students who declined to report their income level may be negatively impacted by the banking scenario due to the current unstable economic conditions and inflation, which is most detrimental and potentially stressful for those with lower incomes. The third and fourth PA task scenarios ("Neutral PA 1" and "Neutral PA 2") involve using Python to scrape census data from websites and create a data file ("Neutral PA 1") and cleaning and prepping census data to perform multiple regression and predict population growth by state ("PA Neutral 2"). It is hypothesized that these scenarios will not result in DIF for their respective PA task outcomes.

In general, it is hypothesized that the proportion of task prompts (i.e., aspects) with DIF will be greater for PA tasks with controversial or divisive scenarios than for PA tasks with neutral scenarios. Furthermore, it is expected that the interpretation and recommendation aspects of the task are more likely to exhibit DIF since there is more room for variability and subjectivity in these responses as compared to data preparation and analysis, both of which pertain to more technical skills (Hypothesis 1b and 2b for Controversial PAs 1 and 2, respectively). Finally, if the prompts are unclear or confusing in any way, this could also result in DIF; thus, a substantive DIF analysis of prompt and rubric aspect verbiage will also be performed and considered when drawing final conclusions regarding the presence of item bias in the four PAs.

There are several methods of testing DIF, each with strengths and weaknesses depending on the conditions under which they are used. These methods have differential tendencies toward Type I error or spurious DIF as well as Type II error (when items with DIF are not detected due to insufficient power) as a function of sample size, test length, differences between the two groups in ability or impact, and the proportion of the test items with DIF to name a few (e.g., Atalay Kabasakal, Arsan, Gök, & Kelecioğlu, 2014; Diaz, Brooks, & Johanson, 2021; Fidalgo, Ferreres, & Muñiz, 2004; Wiberg, 2009; Sireci & Rios, 2013). Thus, it is appealing and often recommended to use multiple DIF detection methods (e.g., Kim & Cohen, 1995; Shealy & Stout, 1993 but see Fidalgo et al., 2004). Given that the PAs selected for study do vary on some of these factors, three of the most common DIF methods were used in the current study – Mantel Haenszel (MH), logistic regression (LR), and Lord's Chi-square (LC).

The MH test is a nonparametric approach to DIF that involves comparing the odds of correctly answering an item between the focal and reference groups via a series of chi-square tests conducted at each ability level (Holland & Thayer, 1988). The weighted average across group scores is the common-odds ratio, α_{MN}, and the statistical significance of the common odds ratio can be tested with a χ^2 test with 1 degree of freedom. The effect size is measured as $\Delta_{MH} = -2.23(\ln(\alpha_{MN}))$, where positive values indicate focal group advantage, and negative values indicate reference group advantage. When MH χ^2 is not statistically significant at the $p < .05$ level or where Δ_{MH} is less than 1, DIF is classified as negligible (A). When both the MH χ^2 is statistically significant ($p<.05$) and is greater than 1.5 in absolute value, DIF is classified as large DIF (C). Intermediate DIF (B) applies to all items not classified as A or C DIF (Dorans & Holland, 1993). Finally, when the focal group is disadvantaged, a minus sign is placed after A, B, or C. A plus sign indicates that the reference group is disadvantaged. MH is the most common DIF method due to its power, conceptual simplicity, ease of use (in statistical software), provision of an effect size based on the odds-ratio, and its smaller sample size requirements (Holland & Thayer, 1988; Raju, Drasgow, & Slinde, 1993; Guilera, Gómez-Benito, Hildago, & Sánchez-Meca, 2013). However, MH can only test for uniform DIF and is prone to Type I error when sample size is large (e.g., N>3000; Guilera et al., 2013). The recommended sample size for MH is 250-500 per group (Camilli & Shepard, 1994; Muniz, Hambleton, & Xing, 2001).

The logistic regression method (Swaminathan & Rogers, 1990) is a probability-based modeling method that is conducive to testing for non-uniform DIF. It entails comparing the fit of multiple logistic regression models for each item. In the first model, overall ability is regressed onto the item score, and group membership is added as a predictor variable to create a second model. A likelihood ratio test (LRT) compares the fit of the two models – specifically, gauging the extent to which adding the group variable significantly improves the fit of the model to the data. If it does, then DIF is present. Non-uniform DIF can be further explored by adding a third model with an interaction term for group by score. If the third model fits the data better than the second model, then there is evidence of non-uniform DIF. Finally, effect size is based on the difference of R^2 values between the models (Gómez-Benito, Hidalgo, & Padilla, 2009). The effect sizes are classified as A ("negligible") for incremental R^2 values less than .035, B ("moderate") for incremental R^2 values between .035 and .070, or C ("large") for incremental R^2 values above .070 (Jodoin & Gierl, 2001). To determine the direction of DIF, a visual inspection of the logistic regression curves for each group is required. Advantages of the LR method include its conceptual simplicity and ease of use (i.e., in any statistical software), availability of effect sizes, and its ability to test for non-uniform DIF. Moreover, additional matching variables can be easily incorporated into the regression equation. Disadvantages of LR include increased Type I error when the sample size or ability distributions vary between groups (Zumbo, 1999). It is recommended that the sample size be at least 200 examinees per group (Zumbo, 1999).

The previous two methods are limited to observed scores and are based in Classical Test Theory (CTT). In contrast, the third DIF approach considered in the current study is based in Item Response Theory (IRT). The greatest advantage of IRT over CTT is greater precision in parameter estimation because item parameters are a) independent from a person's ability level and b) theoretically sample-free (Embretson & Reise, 2000; Lord & Novick, 1968). Thus, reliability and sampling error are no longer a concern. For example, an item's difficulty should be the same regardless of the ability of the test taker, and a test taker's ability should be the same regardless of the difficulty of the items on the assessment. IRT consists of mathematical models in which item parameter(s) interact with person parameters (ability) to predict the probability of a student correctly answering an item in an assessment, and this relationship can be visualized in an item characteristic curve (ICC). The independence of person and item parameters, compounded by the theory that they share the same scaling properties, indicates that they can be directly compared to one another on the same latent trait continuum (Hayes & Embretson, 2012). According to the simplest IRT models, the Rasch and 1PL (parameter logistic) models, as the difference between person and item decrease, the probability of an examinee correctly answering the item increases (Embretson & Reise, 2000).

Lord's chi-square (LC) method estimates item parameters separately for each group and then compares the difference between parameter values using a chi-square statistic (Hambleton, Swaminathan, & Rogers, 1991). The null hypothesis is that the item characteristic curves (ICCs) do not differ between groups. Depending on the IRT model chosen, uniform and non-uniform DIF can be explored (Lord, 1980). Namely, a Rasch or 1PL can only be used to detect uniform DIF. However, the 2PL model includes item discrimination as an additional parameter, and differences between groups in item discrimination results in non-uniform DIF. To determine the direction of DIF, a visual inspection of an item's characteristic curve for each group is required. An advantage of LC is that Type I error is well controlled (Kim, Cohen, & Kim, 1994). However, disadvantages include the conceptual complexity of IRT, more limitations in terms of available software, and lack of an effect size guideline. Rather, a statistical significance level is reported (e.g., $p<.05$, $p<.01$, $p<.001$, and $p<.00001$). Moreover, a large sample size is required to estimate model parameters (DeMars, 2010). In general, there should be 200 examinees per parameter per group, so simpler models such as Rasch/1 PL require at least 400 examinees total, the 2PL requires at least 800 examinees, and the 3PL (which adds a third, guessing parameter) requires 1200 examinees total (e.g., Sireci & Rios, 2013).

Finally, it is worth noting that each DIF procedure performs multiple iterations as an item purification process. Item purification involves removing items detected as having DIF from the overall ability score or matching criteria, and repeating the process until there is no change in the items identified as having DIF. The purpose of this procedure is to remove DIF from the matching criteria and reduce erroneous DIF or Type I error.

Method

Sample

The sample consisted of 4,067 graduate students enrolled in an MSDA program in the college of IT at an OCBHE institution between 2018 and 2022. Two demographic variables were included in the analysis: 1) ethnicity and 2) income. Minorities accounted for 31.4% of the overall sample. Students who reported having a low income ($35,000 per year or less) represented 12% of the sample, 65.15% of students reported middle to high income, and 22.86% of students declined to respond. However, as detailed in Table 1, these proportions vary by course PA.

Table 1. Sample size by group and assessment

Demographic	Group	Controversial PA 1	Controversial PA 2	Neutral PA 1	Neutral PA 2
Ethnicity	Minority	506 (33.4%)	213 (24.3%)	431 (32.6%)	130 (37.0%)
	Caucasian	1007 (66.6%)	665 (75.7%)	893 (67.4%)	221 (63.0%)
Income	Low	178 (11.7%)	133 (15.1%)	146 (11.0%)	33 (9.4%)
	Mid to High	984 (65.1%)	539 (61.4%)	877 (66.2%)	247 (70.4%)
	N/A	351 (23.2%)	206 (23.5%)	301 (22.7%)	71 (20.2%)
TOTAL		1513	878	1324	351

Testing Conditions

All task submissions are electronic, as well as scoring and reporting. Furthermore, it is important to note that evaluators are, as a rule, not given any information regarding the student's identity prior to or during the scoring process. Flexibility in test conditions is offered to students to increase fairness for students beyond disability and language-based accommodations at the OCBHE institute under study. Specifically, a) students can take the assessment wherever is most convenient and helpful to them, b) students schedule and make their assessment attempt at a time that is most convenient for them (within their six-month term), and c) students are allowed to pause and take breaks during testing. Cheating is prevented by using video and remote proctoring. Also, students are allowed to make multiple attempts at the PAs because the scoring is compensatory such that all aspects of the task must be passed to pass the assessment; thus, only first attempt scores were used in the current analysis.

Assessments

Controversial Scenarios

Controversial PA 1 contains the following scenario (paraphrased):

You have been recruited as a data analyst for a local police department that is interested in detecting behavior, trends, and needs of the department based on a data set that is provided. Specifically, the police chief asks you to provide a summary report of data trends regarding emergency 911 calls, the number of officers onsite per incident, and based on the data, recommend whether the department needs additional funding.

There are eleven prompts associated with the task, thus eleven aspects to be scored. Aspects include A) data set preparation (submission of a data set), B) explanation of data preparation, C) graphs and tables, D) observation summary, E) graphical representation of linear regression fit to data, F) outliers in data, G) residual plot, H) recommendation (related to funding), I) precautionary behavior when reporting results, J) use of in-text citations and references, and K) professional communication in task submission.

Controversial PA 2 contains the following scenario (paraphrased):

You are a credit analyst at a local bank in a downturn economy. The bank has received government funding to distribute emergency loans to individuals and small businesses, and an infrastructure needs to be built to support it. Specifically, you have been asked to identify gaps in the data that would impact the stability of the infrastructure and potentially result in loans being given out unfairly.

There are seven prompts associated with the task, thus seven aspects to be scored. Aspects include A) status of data governance, B) gaps in data, C) origin of data gaps, D) recommendations for improvement (agenda items for presentation), E) justification of recommendations, F) use of in-text citations and references, and G) clarity and organization of task submission.

Neutral Scenarios

Neutral PA 1 contains the following scenario (paraphrased):

As a professional data analyst, you are given a project in which you must use Python to create a data file by scraping data from a website that contains census (population) data.

There are ten prompts and aspects associated with the task. Aspects include A) Python program for extracting links; B) criteria for determining whether a link locates another HTML page; C) criteria for ensuring links are saved as URI; D) program to prevent duplicate links in file; E) Python code; F) HTML code; G) final data set (csv file); H) screenshot of successfully execute script; I) in-text citations and references; J) clarity and organization of task submission.

Neutral PA 2 contains the following scenario (paraphrased):

As a professional data analyst, you are given a U.S. census data project in which you must use R to complete a regression analysis and predict the size of your state at various points in time.

There are six prompts and aspects associated with the task. Aspects include A) Screenshot of results for 2020 estimate; B) Screenshot of data import; C) Screenshot of results summary; D) Screenshot of results for 5-year prediction; E) in-text citations and references; F) professional communication in task submission.

In terms of scoring, each response to a prompt is scored on an associated "aspect" or competency-based skill, as previously mentioned, and the aspects are reflected in the grading rubric. Since each prompt (aspect) is akin to an item, DIF will be conducted on each of the associated aspect scores within the task. Although each aspect score ranges from 0 to 2 (not competent=0, approaching competence=1, and achieved competence=2), only a score of 2 results in a "pass" outcome. Moreover, the summative PA task scores are non-compensatory, meaning that a student must pass all task aspects to pass the PA. Thus, aspect scores are treated as dichotomous in the scoring and reporting process and will remain as such in the analysis. Given that there are anywhere from five to 20 aspects in a task, a summed score is more acceptable as a matching variable here than for PAs reported in the literature, which tend to score at the task level and have only 1-2 tasks (Chen et al., 2018).

Inter-rater reliability could not be evaluated due to the institution's limited sample of evaluators relative to the large volume of PA task submissions each month. In lieu of reliability, a fairness metric is frequently used to determine the degree to which task pass rates are affected by bias (e.g., leniency versus strictness) among evaluators. This metric is based on a value-added model (VAM; Hanushek, 1971) – specifically, a hierarchical random effects logistic model in which submissions are nested within evaluators, and the likelihood of a student passing an assessment is determined by the evaluator (random effect) while controlling for other variables. In our parameterization of the model, we control for the difficulty of the task (across all students), the general ability of the student (across all assessments), and the number of attempts the student has made for the PA task (B. Kuhlman, personal communication, October 13, 2019). Usually, these results are used to individualize pass rate expectations for each evaluator. However, the impact of evaluator bias on a PA task's pass rate can also be estimated by cumulating the proportion of submissions for which there was a statistically significant effect for evaluator. For each of the four PA tasks used in this study, the evaluator effect was not statistically significant (see Table 2), and thus bias from evaluator was ruled out as a potential cause of DIF.

Table 2. Evaluator effect by PA task

PA	β Evaluator Effect
Controversial PA 1	0.09 (n.s.)
Controversial PA 2	0.10 (n.s.)
Neutral PA 1	-0.01 (n.s.)
Neutral PA 2	0.10 (n.s.)

ANALYSIS

Before proceeding with DIF analysis, all task scores were submitted to factor analysis and IRT analysis. Exploratory factor analysis was conducted to determine the degree to which scores are unidimensional and therefore, theoretically, 1) less prone to DIF Type I error rates due to multidimensionality (Yeşim &

Baştuğ, 2016) and 2) appropriate for unidimensional IRT models (Embretson & Reise, 2000) used in LC. Principle axis factoring (PAF) was conducted using mean and variance weighted least squares estimation (WSLMV). Dimensionality was assessed by evaluating the ratio of the first and second eigenvalues, where a value greater than three indicates unidimensionality (Slocum-Gori & Zumbo, 2011). Next, the degree to which a unidimensional model best fits the data was evaluated using the Comparative Fit Index (CFI) and Root Mean Square Error of Approximation (RMSEA). Unidimensionality is supported when CFI values are above .90 and values for RMSEA are below .08 (Kline, 2010).

Next, IRT analysis was performed for each PA with unidimensional scores to determine which IRT model best fits the data and should be used for LC because model misspecification can result in spurious DIF or high Type I error rates (Atalay Kabasakal, et al., 2014; Camilli & Smith, 1990; but see Paek & Guo, 2011). The sample size for Neutral PA 2 was too small for IRT analysis (n=351). The fit of the following four nested models were compared for the three remaining PAs: 1) the Rasch model, in which only difficulty varies across items and item discrimination (which weights the difference between person and item when predicting item response) is constrained to a value of 1 for all items, 2) the 1 PL model, in which item discrimination is also constrained to be equal across items, but the value can vary from 1, 3) the 2PL model which builds on the prior models by allowing discrimination to vary across items; and 4) the 3PL model which builds on the prior model by allowing for a lower asymptote greater than 0 for possible guessing or easiness of the aspect. Relative model fit was determined by comparing log-likelihood values among models, where improvement in model fit is indicated by a significant decrease in this value.

Statistical DIF was examined using three methods – MH, LR, and LC. However, LC will only be considered if a) sample size is sufficient for the best fitting model and b) scores are unidimensional. Since DIF was only expected for certain groups for each of the PAs with controversial scenarios (e.g., minorities for Controversial PA 1 and low/unreported income for Controversial PA 2), both demographic variables (ethnicity and income) were included in the analysis for each PA for comparison purposes. Namely, our hypotheses are further supported if there is DIF (or a greater magnitude of DIF) for only one of these demographic groups in each of the controversial PA tasks. In an attempt to balance control of Type I and Type II error, items flagged for DIF with the highest effect sizes (e.g., C-level) among any of the three methods were of primary focus in testing the hypotheses, and if any aspects displayed C-level DIF, the entire PA task was submitted to further review regarding "substantive" DIF. Three subject matter experts (SMEs) were given the prompts and aspects description and rubric for review without knowledge of which aspects were flagged for DIF in order to control for confirmation bias (Fidalgo et al., 2004).

RESULTS

Descriptive stats for PA first attempt pass rates for all groups are in Table 3. Although groups differed in mean pass rates for all PAs, these differences were statistically significant only for Controversial PA 1 and Neutral PA 1. Specifically, Caucasians had a significantly higher pass rate than minorities for both of these PAs.

Table 3. Mean PA score by group and assessment

Demographic	Group	Controversial PA 1	Controversial PA 2	Neutral PA 1	Neutral PA 2
Ethnicity	Minority	34.3%	64.5%	48.6%	78.3%
	Caucasian	41.4%**	68.3%	54.6%*	84.6%
Income	Low or N/A	35.9%	76.9%	51.3%	82.5%
	Mid to High	40.7%	77.4%	53.4%	82.2%
TOTAL		1513	878	1324	351

Note: Chi-square test of independence is statistically significant (*p<.05; **p<.01)

The results of the factor analysis are in Table 4. Undimensionality was supported for all PAs. Namely, all four PAs passed the ratio test of Eigenvalues 1 to 2 being over three and met the required values for CFI and RMSEA. In the IRT analysis, a 2PL provided the best fit to the data for PA Controversial 1 and 2 data as well as PA Neutral 1 data (see Table 5).

Table 4. Results of factor analysis

PA	Eigenvalue 1	Eigenvalue 2	Eigenvalue Ratio	CFI	RMSEA
Controversial PA 1	6.04	1.58	3.82	0.91	0.07
Controversial PA 2	4.12	0.96	4.29	0.94	0.05
Neutral PA 1	6.21	1.07	5.80	0.93	0.06
Neutral PA 2	3.21	0.89	3.61	0.92	0.07

Table 5. Comparison of IRT model fit

Model	Controversial PA 1	Controversial PA 2	Neutral PA 1
Rasch model	-1403.65	-722.42	-1101.87
1 PL	-1228.23*	-549.04*	-968.18*
2 PL	-1071.50*	-387.51*	-578.35*
3 PL	-1050.01	-382.11	-577.15

*$p < .01$
Note: Neutral PA 2 is not included due to low sample size

Statistical DIF Analysis

The DIF results for the two neutral PAs are presented first (Tables 6 and 7 for Neutral PA 1 and 2, respectively). Only MH detected any DIF for aspects from these two PAs, and in all cases, the magnitude of DIF was small to medium. For Neutral PAs 1 and 2, DIF was balanced for ethnicity, meaning that there are an approximately equal number of aspects that disadvantage minorities as those that disadvantage Caucasians. The same was true for income in Neutral PA 2. This is sometimes considered acceptable because the DIF cancels out, minimalizing group differences in total test score (e.g., Pae & Park, 2016; Sireci & Rios, 2013). This balanced DIF pattern also emerged for income in Neutral PA 2. Thus, in general, DIF analysis for the two neutral scenario PAs did not indicate substantial differences in item performance between focal and reference group for either ethnicity or income.

Table 6. Ethnicity and income DIF for neutral PA 1

Aspect	Ethnicity			Income		
	MH	LR	LC	MH	LR	LC
A Python-links	A+			B+		
B Link-HTML criteria	A+			A+		
C Link-URI criteria	A-			A-		
D Duplicate links	B+			A+		
E Python code	A+			B-		
F HTML code	A-			A-		
G Csv file	A+			A-		
H Screenshot of script	B-			A-		
I Citations/references	A-			A-		
J Clarity/organization	A+			A-		

Note: "-" indicates disadvantage for focal group while "+" indicates advantage for focal group
Note: "uni" indicates uniform DIF while "nu" indicates non-uniform DIF

Table 7. Ethnicity and income DIF for neutral PA 2

Aspect	Ethnicity		Income	
	MH	**LR**	**MH**	**LR**
A 2020 estimate	A-		B-	
B Data import	B-		B+	
C Results summary	B+		A-	
D 5-year prediction	B+		B-	
E Citations/references	B-		B+	
F Professionalism	A-		B-	

Note: "-" indicates disadvantage for focal group while "+" indicates advantage for focal group

Note: "uni" indicates uniform DIF while "nu" indicates non-uniform DIF

The DIF results for Controversial PA 1 are in Table 8. Results vary by method and demographic. The MH and LR methods did not detect high levels of ethnicity DIF in any of the aspects. However, LC detected C-level ethnicity DIF for aspects H and I, which reflect recommendations and interpretations of data analysis as well as describing precautionary behavior when communicating results. Moreover, DIF was non-uniform for both aspects as can be seen in the ICCs (Figures 1 and 2 for aspects H and I, respectively). Both aspects H and I are more difficult for minorities than Caucasians, especially at the high end of the ability scale, while discrimination (i.e., slope; precision of estimate) is higher for Caucasians than minorities. For income, only MH detected C-level DIF for aspect I, where low/unreported income students are advantaged relative to mid-high-income students. Thus, Hypotheses 1a and 1b are largely supported.

Table 8. Ethnicity and income DIF for controversial PA 1

Aspect	Ethnicity			Income		
	MH	LR	LC	MH	LR	LC
A Clean data	A+			A-	A+	A+(nu)
B Explain data prep	A+			B-	A+	
C Data sheets	A-			B-	A+	
D Summary statistics	A-			A-	A+	
E Linear regression	A+	A-		A+		
F Outlier Impact	A+	B-		A+		
G Residual plot	A+	B-		B+		
H Explain funding	A-		C- (nu)	A+		A+(nu)
I Precautionary behavior	A-		C- (nu)	C+	A-	B-(nu)
J Citations/references	B-	A+	B- (uni)	A+		B-(nu)
K Professionalism	A-		A- (uni)	A+		B-(nu)

Note: "-" indicates disadvantage for focal group while "+" indicates advantage for focal group

Note: "uni" indicates uniform DIF while "nu" indicates non-uniform DIF

Figure 1. Aspect H

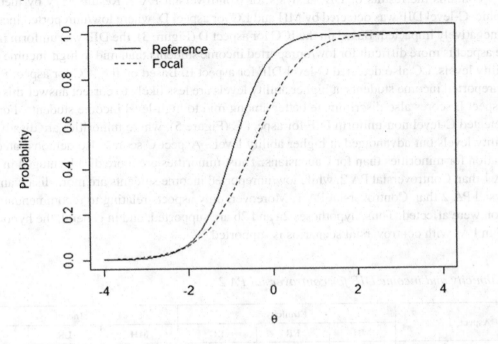

Figure 2. Aspect I

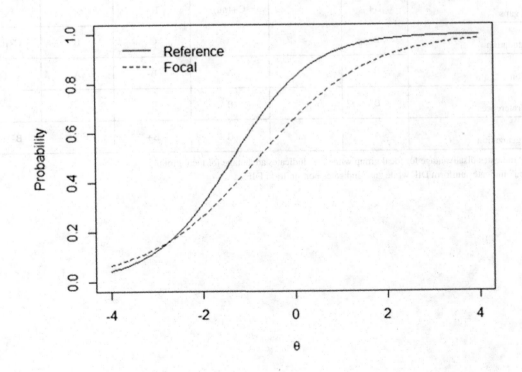

Table 9 contains the results of DIF analysis for Controversial PA 2. Results vary by method and demographic. C-level DIF was detected by MH and LC for aspect D, where low/unreported income students are negatively impacted. Based on the ICC for aspect D (Figure 3), the DIF was uniform in nature, where the aspect is more difficult for low/unreported income students than mid to high-income students for all ability levels. LC also detected C-level DIF for aspect E. Based on the ICC for aspect E (Figure 4), low/unreported income students at higher ability levels are less likely to correct answer this prompt/ aspect. Aspect E scores also discriminate better among mid to high-level income students. For ethnicity, LC detected C-level non-uniform DIF for aspect C (Figure 5), where minorities are disadvantaged at low ability levels but advantaged at higher ability levels. Aspect C scores also demonstrated higher discrimination for minorities than for Caucasians. Thus, minorities are more disadvantaged in Controversial PA 1 than Controversial PA 2, while low/unreported income students are more disadvantaged in Controversial PA 2 than Controversial PA 1. Moreover, only aspects relating to recommendations and justification were affected. Thus, hypotheses 2a and 2b are supported, and in general, the hypothesis of more DIF in PAs with controversial scenarios is supported.

Table 9. Ethnicity and income DIF for controversial PA 2

Aspect	Ethnicity			Income		
	MH	**LR**	**LC**	**MH**	**LR**	**LC**
A Status of data	B+		A	B+		
B Gaps in data	B-	A-	A	A+		
C Origin of gaps	B+		C+(nu)	B+		
D Recommendation	B-		A	C-	B	C- (uni)
E Justification	B-		A	B-	A	C- (nu)
F Citations/references	B-		B	B-		
G Clarity/organization	A-		B	B+		B- (uni)

Note: "-" indicates disadvantage for focal group while "+" indicates advantage for focal group

Note: "uni" indicates uniform DIF while "nu" indicates non-uniform DIF

Figure 3. ICC for aspect D

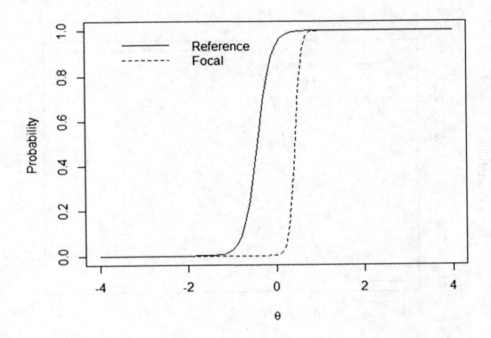

Figure 4. ICC for aspect E

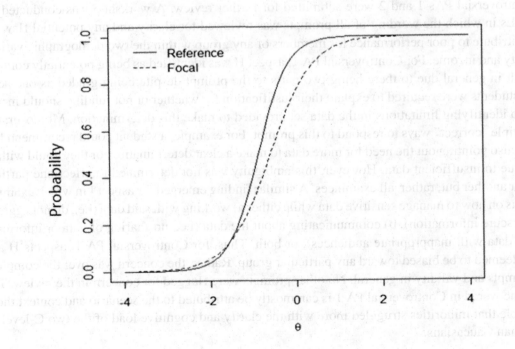

Figure 5. ICC for aspect D

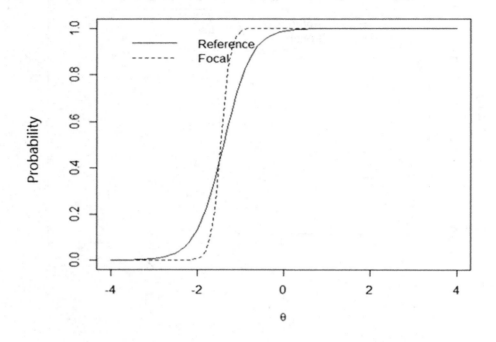

Substantive DIF Review

Only Controversial PAs 1 and 2 were submitted for further review. A workshop was conducted with three SMEs in which the wording of all prompts was reviewed for clarity and any potential flaws that might contribute to poor performance for members of any group within the two demographic variables of ethnicity and income. For Controversial PA 1, aspect H was identified as being potentially confusing or difficult in general due to there being two parts to the prompt despite being graded as one action. Namely, students were required to explain their justification for whether or not funding should increase while also identifying limitations in the data set provided to make this determination. Moreover, there were multiple "correct" ways to respond to this prompt. For example, a student could recommend funding while also pointing out the need for more data to make a clear determination, or they could withhold funding due to insufficient data. However, this ambiguity was not determined to affect one particular group over another but, rather, all examinees. A similar finding emerged for aspect I in which examinees could focus on how to manage sensitive data while either a) working with said data (i.e., do not aggregate stats to obscure information), b) communicating about the data (i.e., no sharing of data or information related to data with inappropriate audiences), or both. Thus, for Controversial PA 1, aspects H and I were not deemed to be biased toward any particular group. Rather, the concern was over the complexity of the prompts and validity in general. No other prompts were flagged for concern in the review. Thus, the DIF uncovered in Controversial PA 1 is can mostly be attributed to the scenario and context though it is possible that minorities struggled more with the clarity and cognitive load of the two C-level DIF prompts than Caucasians.

For Controversial PA 2, only aspect D was flagged for concern. Specifically, the use of "agenda item" (in reference to preparation for a meeting in the scenario) was considered potentially confusing for examinees not familiar with lingo associated with projects and meetings in the workplace. For aspect C, which favored minorities, it was determined that, if anything, the wording of the prompt and the information embedded (a bullet point list of topics to include in the response) was considered more helpful in guiding the response than interfering with or confusing the examinee in the response process. No other aspects were flagged for concern. Thus, the DIF uncovered in Controversial PA 2 can be attributed only to the nature of the scenario.

Discussion

Standardized assessment has been the cornerstone of evaluating a student's progress toward learning and readiness for further education for over a century. Although the original intention of standardization was to increase comparability of test scores among students by controlling for construct-irrelevant variance arising from test conditions and different scoring methods, it has resulted in construct-irrelevant variance of another kind – namely, variation among students in how they best demonstrate their knowledge. Put another way, standardized multiple choice assessment scores may not accurately reflect knowledge for students who more effectively demonstrate their skills in alternative forms of assessment such as PAs with a constructed response format. However, there is still room for potential bias in PA scores given added complexity of PA tasks and error in human scoring. The purpose of the current study was to investigate bias in a series of PAs via DIF and substantive reviews, where it was hypothesized that PAs with controversial scenarios would yield higher magnitudes of DIF for certain groups than PAs with more neutral scenarios. In one controversial scenario (Controversial PA 1), which revolved around police funding, it was expected that DIF was more likely to manifest for students as a function of their ethnicity, whereas in the second controversial scenario (Controversial PA 2), which focused on banking and emergency loans in a downturn economy, it was expected that students with low or unreported income would be disadvantaged. Moreover, we hypothesized that aspects involving interpretation, justification, or recommendations would be more prone to DIF than aspects involving technical, data analytic skills. The results of DIF analysis and substantive review supported these hypotheses. Therefore, we conclude that the PA scenario can have differential impact on aspect scores for students as a function of their background or demographics.

There are caveats to these conclusions including the DIF methods chosen, interpretation of DIF across the methods, the specificity of content or subject area represented in the PA scores, and other potential sources of DIF not considered. We sampled some of the most common DIF methods based on their relative strengths and weaknesses, and as expected, there were discrepancies in the results from these three methods. Given the discrepancies among methods, we chose a quasi-liberal approach when flagging aspects for DIF. A liberal approach, in which an item is interpreted as potentially biased if it is flagged by any method, is contrasted with a more conservative approach in which items are interpreted as having DIF if it is flagged by multiple DIF statistics (Hambleton & Jones, 1994; Kim & Cohen, 1995; Shealy & Stout, 1993). The downside of the liberal approach is that there is more likely to be Type I error, whereas the conservative approach is more likely to result in greater Type II error (Fidalgo et al., 2004). We sought a compromise between the two approaches by focusing on aspects with C-level DIF, as recommended by Educational Testing Services (Zwick, 2012), according to any DIF method.

Finally, the content of the PAs included in the current study was specific to data analytics, and all four PAs were formatted as case studies and research reports. A more balanced study would include a variety of content areas and domains as well as PA formats. Moreover, the scenarios varied in complexity defined as the amount of information required to complete the task as well as the cognitive complexity of the response, itself. The two controversial PAs involved more details and reading (1–2-page description of the scenario) prior to beginning the task, and the responses involved a combination of data analytics and more extensive interpretation involving recommendations and justification directed toward an organization who is trying to achieve a goal or detect errors in their process. The two neutral PAs had simpler scenarios and less additional material (e.g., supporting documents such as case studies). Ideally, the effect of scenario on DIF would be evaluated by using different scenarios for the same task to control for variance in task complexity. Furthermore, given the higher reading requirement for the controversial scenario PAs, there may be DIF due to reading ability or proficiency with the English language. We were unable to address this source of DIF due to lack of data on the primary language spoken by students. Ideally, a future study would include English as a second language and/or scores on a reading assessment as DIF variables or at least control for them when investigating primary sources of DIF.

Given how crucial assessments are in education, it is unsettling to imagine that they could be replaced with assessments that are too subjective or difficult to grade, equitably, across students. However, mounting research suggests that a one-size-fits-all standardized form of assessment is not conducive to a fair and valid assessment outcome. There needs to be some common or middle ground, where assessments are flexible enough to be fair but not so flexible that it becomes difficult to score, interpret, and compare students on knowledge obtained. A key to determining where to draw the line is the evaluation of measurement invariance and potential bias in an assessment at the item level. More importantly, the source of DIF must be determined in order to confirm or reject the presence of bias and to prevent bias in future assessments; hence the need for a subsequent substantive review to confirm that DIF is adverse rather than benign in nature. The results of the current study provide clarity into one source of DIF in PA aspects relating to interpretation of results in data analytics: the scenario or context that serves as the impetus for data analysis, interpretation, and recommendations. A data analyst must not only be able to accurately manage and statistically model data but also interpret the results and make recommendations for action based on these results. It is demonstration of the latter skill that is most clouded by the nature of scenarios which can be perceived as more controversial for members of one group than another. For example, a student with a bias toward police, responding to a scenario in which they must make recommendations for whether to increase or decrease police funding for a particular department may recommend a decrease in funding by selectively attending more to details of the data that support this recommendation, and thus make an error in their recommendation. Therefore, scenarios should be chosen carefully, although not so carefully that we sterilize content and lose diversity in scenario types (Randall & Paek, 2022; Sireci, 2020). Another recommendation would be to include multiple, equally complex scenarios as options and allow the student to choose the scenario they prefer. This approach would allow for even more personalization in assessments without sacrificing comparability of PA outcomes among students due to differences in scenario complexity or personal bias relating to the scenario.

As a final note, circling back to the use of assessments for learning versus of learning, assessments outcomes that are free of DIF and bias are more likely to provide useful feedback to the students, the instructors, the program, and the institution. When assessments lack fairness or are riddled with validity issues such as lack of clarity, then assessment outcomes will not be helpful to students in terms of gauging their progress toward attaining competency, instructors who are trying to personalize the educational journey to the student, and the program and institution who wish to evaluate the quality of education and success of students in the program. Assessments must be evaluated for validity and fairness after launch, and when concerns emerge based on the results of DIF and bias and sensitivity reviews, it is paramount that these assessments under continuous quality improvement and modifications to achieve valid, fair assessment outcomes.

REFERENCES

American Educational Research Association, American Psychological Association, & National Council on Measurement in Education. (2014). *Standards for Educational and Psychological Testing*. American Educational Research Association.

Atalay Kabasakal, K., Arsan, N., Gök, B., & Kelecioğlu, H. (2014). Comparing performances (Type I error and Power) of IRT likelihood ratio SIBTEST and Mantel-Haenszel methods in the determination of differential item functioning. *Educational Sciences: Theory and Practice, 14*(6), 2186–2193.

Bennett, R. E. (2009). A Critical Look at the Meaning and Basis of Formative Assessment. Educational Testing Service., ETS RM-09-06.

Bresciani Ludvik, M. J. (2019). *Outcomes-Based Program Review: Closing Achievement Gaps In- and Outside the Classroom with Alignment to Predictive Analytics and Performance Metrics*. Stylus Publishing, LLC: Sterling.

Camilli, G., & Shepard, L. A. (1994). *Methods for Identifying Biased Test Items*. Sage.

Camilli, G., & Smith, J. K. (1990). Comparison of the Mantel-Haenszel Test with a randomized and jackknife test for detecting biased items. *Journal of Educational and Behavioral Statistics, 15*(1), 53–67. Advance online publication. doi:10.3102/10769986015001053

Chen, M. Y., Liu, Y., & Zumbo, B. D. (2018). Testing for Differential Item Functioning in Performance Assessments [Conference presentation]. *11th conference of The International Test Commission*, Montréal, Canada.

Cotner, S., Jeno, L. M., Walker, J. D., Jordensen, C., & Vandvick, V. (2020). Gender gaps in the performance of Norwegian biology students: The roles of test anxiety and science confidence. *International Journal of STEM Education, 7*(1), 55. doi:10.118640594-020-00252-1

Darling-Hammond, L. (2004). The color line in American education: Race, resources, and student achievement. *Du Bois Review, 1*(2), 213–246. doi:10.1017/S1742058X0404202X

Darling-Hammond, L. (2017). *Developing and Measuring Higher Order Skills: Models for State Performance Assessment Systems*. Council of Chief State School Officers.

DeMars, C. (2010). *Item Response Theory: Understanding Statistics Measurement*. Oxford University Press. doi:10.1093/acprof:oso/9780195377033.001.0001

Diaz, E., Brooks, G., & Johanson, G. (2021). Detecting differential item functioning: Item Response Theory Methods versus the Mantel-Haenszel Procedure. *International Journal of Assessment Tools in Education, 8*(2), 376–393. doi:10.21449/ijate.730141

Dorans, N. J., & Holland, P. W. (1993). DIF detection and description: Mantel Haenszel and standardization. In P. W. Holland & H. Wainer (Eds.), *Differential Item Functioning* (pp. 35–66). Lawrence Erlbaum Inc.

Embretson, S. E. (1983). Construct validity: Construct representation versus nomothetic span. *Psychological Bulletin, 93*(1), 179–197. doi:10.1037/0033-2909.93.1.179

Embretson, S. E., & Reise, S. P. (2000). *Item Response Theory for Psychologists*. Lawrence Erlbaum Associates Publishers.

Faulkner-Bond, M., & Soland (2020). Comparability when assessing English learner students. In A. Berman, E. Haertel, & J. Pellegrino (Eds.) *Comparability issues in large-scale assessment* (pp. 149-175). National Academy of Education Press.

Fidalgo, A. M., Ferreres, D., & Muniz, J. (2004). Liberal and conservative differential item functioning detection using Mantel-Haenszel and SIBTEST: Implications for Type I and Type II error rates. *Journal of Experimental Education, 73*(1), 23–39. doi:10.3200/JEXE.71.1.23-40

Gallardo, K. (2020). Competency-based assessment and the use of performance-based evaluation rubrics in higher education: Challenges toward the next decade. *Problems of Higher Education in the 21st Century, 78*, 1, 61-79.

Gómez-Benito, J., Hildago, M. D., & Padilla, J. L. (2009). Efficacy of effect size measures in logistic regression: An application for detecting DIF. *Methodology, 5*(1), 18–25. doi:10.1027/1614-2241.5.1.18

Guilera, G., Gómez-Benito, J., Hildago, M. D., & Sánchez-Meca, J. (2013). *Type I error and statistical power of the Mantel-Haenszel procedure for detecting DIF: A meta-analysis*. American Psychological Association. doi:10.1037/a0034306

Hambleton, R. K., & Jones, R. W. (1994). Item parameter estimation errors and their influence on test information functions. *Applied Measurement in Education, 7*(3), 171–186. doi:10.120715324818ame0703_1

Hambleton, R. K., & Murphy, E. (1992). A psychometric perspective on authentic measurement. *Applied Measurement in Education, 5*(1), 1–16. doi:10.120715324818ame0501_1

Hambleton, R. K., Swaminathan, H., & Rogers, H. J. (1991). *Fundamentals of Item Response Theory*. Sage Publications, Inc.

Hancock, G. R. (1994). Cognitive complexity and the comparability of multiple-choice and constructed-response test formats. *Journal of Experimental Education, 62*(2), 143–158. doi:10.1080/00220973.1994.9943836

Hanushek, E. A. (1971). Teacher characteristics and gains in student achievement: Estimation using micro-data. *The American Economic Review, 61*(2), 280–288.

Hayes, H., & Embretson, S. E. (2012). Psychological measurement: Scaling and analysis. In H. Cooper, M. N. Coutanche, McMullen, L. M., & A. T. Panter (Eds.) APA Handbook of Research Methods in Psychology: Volume 1. Foundations, Planning, Measures, and Psychometrics. American Psychological Association.

Hayes, H., Gyll, S. P., Ragland, S., & Meyers, J. L. (2022). High-Stakes Assessments in Online Competency-Based Higher Education: The Assessment Development Cycle. In Handbook of Research on Future of Work and Education: Implications for Curriculum Delivery and Work Design (p. 230-252). IGI Global.

Holland, P. W., & Thayer, D. T. (1988). Differential item performance and the Mantel-Haenszel procedure. In H. Wainer & H. I. Braun (Eds.), *Test Validity* (pp. 129–145). Lawrence Erlbaum, Inc.

Jencks, C., & Phillips, M. (Eds.). (2011). *The Black-White Test Score Gap*. Brookings Institution Press.

Jodoin, M. G., & Gierl, M. J. (2001). Evaluating power and Type I error rates using an effect size with the logistic regression procedure for DIF. *Applied Measurement in Education*, *14*, 329–349. doi:10.1207/S15324818AME1404_2

Kim, S.-H., & Cohen, A. S. (1995). A comparison of Lord's chi-square, Raju's area measures, and the likelihood ratio test on detection of differential item functioning. *Applied Measurement in Education*, *8*(4), 291–312. doi:10.120715324818ame0804_2

Kline, R. B. (2010). *Principles and practice of structural equation modeling* (3rd ed.). Guilford.

Kuhlman, B. B. personal communication, October 13, 2019

Lankford, H., Loeb, S., & Wyckoff, J. (2002). Teacher sorting and the plight of urban schools: A descriptive analysis. *Educational Evaluation and Policy Analysis*, *24*(1), 37–62. doi:10.3102/01623737024001037

Lord, F. M., & Novick, M. R. (1968). *Statistical Theories of Mental Test Scores*. Addison-Wesley.

McClarty, K. L., & Gaertner, M. N. (2015). *Measuring Mastery: Best Practices for Assessment in Competency-Based Education*. AE Series on Competency-Based Higher Education.

Messick, S. (1989). Validity. In R. Linn (Ed.), *Educational Measurement* (3rd ed., pp. 13–100). American Council on Education.

Muniz, J., Hambleton, R. K., & Xing, D. (2001). Small sample studies to detect flaws in item translations. *International Journal of Testing*, *1*(2), 115–135. doi:10.1207/S15327574IJT0102_2

Padmanabha, C. H. (2021). Assessment for Learning, Assessment of Learning, Assessment as Learning: A Conceptual Framework. *i-manager's. Journal of Educational Psychology*, *14*(4), 14–21. doi:10.26634/jpsy.14.4.17681

Pae, T.-I., & Park, G.-P. (2016). Examining the relationship between differential item functioning and differential test functioning. *Language Testing*, *23*(4), 475–496. doi:10.1191/0265532206lt338oa

Paek, I., & Guo, H. (2011). Accuracy of DIF estimates and power in unbalanced designs using the Mantel-Haenszel DIF detection procedure. *Applied Psychological Measurement*, *35*(7), 518–535. doi:10.1177/0146621611420559

Penfield, R. D., & Lam, T. C. M. (2000). Assessment differential item functioning in performance assessment: Review and recommendations. *Educational Measurement: Issues and Practice*, *19*(3), 3, 5–15. doi:10.1111/j.1745-3992.2000.tb00033.x

Peske, H. G., & Haycock, K. (2006). *Teaching inequality: How poor and minority students are short-changed on teacher quality: A report and recommendations by the Education Trust*. Education Trust.

Raju, N., & Ellis, B. (2002). Differential item and test functioning. In F. Drasgow & N. Schmitt (Eds.), *Measuring and analyzing behavior in organizations* (pp. 156–188). Jossey-Bass.

Raju, N. S., Drasgow, F., & Slinde, J. A. (1993). An empirical comparison of the area methods, Lord's chi-square test, and the Mantel-Haenszel technique for assessing differential item functioning. *Educational and Psychological Measurement*, *53*(2), 301–314. doi:10.1177/0013164493053002001

Randall, J., & Paek, P. (2022, March 21-23). *Taking the BS out of Bias & Sensitivity* [Conference presentation]. ATP Innovations in Testing 2022, Orlando, FL, United States.

Roussos, L. A., & Stout, W. F. (1996). Simulation studies of the effects of small sample size and studied item parameters on SIBTEST and Mantel-Haenszel Type I error performance. *Journal of Educational Measurement*, *33*(2), 215–230. doi:10.1111/j.1745-3984.1996.tb00490.x

Rubin, B. D. (2016). *Excellence in Higher Education Guide: A Framework for the Design, Assessment, and Continuing Improvement of Institutions, Departments, and Programs* (8th ed.). Stylus Publishing.

Shealy, R., & Stout, W. (1993). A model-based standardization approach that separate true bias/DIF form group ability differences and detects test bias/DTF as well as item bias/DIF. *Psychometrika*, *58*(2), 159–194. doi:10.1007/BF02294572

Sireci, S. G. (2020). Standardization and UNDERSTANDardization in Education Assessment. *Educational Measurement: Issues and Practice*, *39*(3), 100–105. doi:10.1111/emip.12377

Sireci, S. G., Banda, E., & Wells, C. S. (2018). Promoting valid assessment of students with disabilities and English learners. In S. N. Elliott, R. J. Kettler, P. A. Beddow, & A. Kurz (Eds.), *Handbook of Accessible Instruction and Testing Practices: Issues, Innovations, and Application* (pp. 231–246). Sage. doi:10.1007/978-3-319-71126-3_15

Sireci, S. G., & O'Riordan, M. (2020). Comparability issues in assessing individuals with disabilities. In A. Berman, E. Haertel, & J. Pellegrino (Eds.), *Comparability issues in large-scale assessment* (pp. 177–204). National Academy of Education Press.

Sireci, S. G., & Rios, J. A. (2013). Decisions that make a difference in detecting differential item functioning. *Educational Research and Evaluation*, *19*(2-3), 2–3, 170–187. doi:10.1080/13803611.2013.767621

Slocum-Gori, S. L., & Zumbo, B. D. (2011). Assessing the unidimensionality of psychological scales: Using multiple criteria from factor analysis. *Social Indicators Research*, *102*(3), 443–461. doi:10.100711205-010-9682-8

Struyven, K., Dochy, F., Janssens, S., Schelfhout, W., & Gielen, S. (2006). The overall effects of end-of-course assessment on student performance: A comparison between multiple-choice testing, peer assessments, case-based assessment, and portfolio assessment. *Studies in Educational Evaluation, 32*(3), 202–222. doi:10.1016/j.stueduc.2006.08.002

Swaminathan, H., & Rogers, H. J. (1990). Detecting differential item functioning using logistic regression procedures. *Journal of Educational Measurement, 27*(4), 361–370. doi:10.1111/j.1745-3984.1990.tb00754.x

Thissen, D., Steinberg, L., & Wainer, H. (1993). Detection of differential item functioning using the parameters of item response models. In P. Holland & Wainer (Eds.), Differential Item Functioning (pp. 67-113). Hillsdale, NJ: Lawrence Erlbaum Associates.

Wiberg, M. (2009). Differential item functioning in mastery tests: A comparison of three methods using real data. *International Journal of Testing, 9*(1), 41–59. doi:10.1080/15305050902733455

William, D. (2011). Assessment for learning? [PDF in files]. *Studies in Educational Evaluation, 37*(1), 3–14. doi:10.1016/j.stueduc.2011.03.001 PMID:22114905

Yeşim, Ö., & Baştuğ, Ö. (2016). A comparison of four differential item functioning procedures in the presence of multidimensionality. *Educational Research Review, 11*(13), 1251–1261.

Zlatkin-Troitschanskaia, O., & Pant, H. A. (2016). Measurement advances and challenges in competency assessment in higher education. *Journal of Educational Measurement, 53*(3), 253–264. doi:10.1111/jedm.12118

Zumbo, B. D. (1999). A Handbook on the Theory and Methods of Differential Item Functioning (DIF): Logistic Regression Modeling as a Unitary Framework for Binary and Likert-Type (Ordinal) Item Scores. Ottawa, Canada: Directorate of Human Resources Research and Evaluation, Department of National Defense.

Zwick, R. (2012). *A review of ETS differential item functioning assessment procedures: Flagging rules, minimum sample size requirements, and criterion refinement.* Educational Testing Service.

Zwick, R., Donoghue, J. R., & Grima, A. (1993). Assessing differential item functioning in performance tests. *ETS Research Report Series, 1993*(1), i-42. doi:10.1002/j.2333-8504.1993.tb01525.x

Chapter 7
Diversity, Equity, and Inclusion:
An Exploratory Approach to Reviewing and Improving Assessments for Equity

Marylee Demeter
Western Governors University, USA

ABSTRACT

Diversity, equity, and inclusion (DEI) has become a major focus in higher education in recent years. With increasing attention on equity and fairness, institutions of higher learning are implementing approaches to reviewing and revising curricula and assessments to ensure all students are equally prepared to succeed in their programs of study. The purpose of this chapter is to describe a mixed- methods exploratory approach to identify sources of inequities in a selection of objective and performance assessments as part of a larger project focused on reviewing a selection of courses for issues related to (DEI) attainment. Procedures and results are presented for assessments in four courses across four disciplines (general education, information technology, business, and health professions) along with recommended solutions to even the playing field for all students. A discussion of limitations and next steps to create access to equitable education and assessment opportunities closes this chapter.

INTRODUCTION

Diversity, equity, and inclusion (DEI) are related concepts that refer to the ways in which people with different characteristics and experiences are treated and valued in society and within organizations. Diversity refers to the variety of characteristics and experiences that exist among individuals and groups. These can include, but are not limited to, race, ethnicity, gender, sexual orientation, age, religion, ability, and nationality. Equity refers to the fair treatment, access, and opportunity for all individuals, regardless of their background or identity. This means that everyone is provided with the resources and support they need to succeed and thrive, rather than being disadvantaged because of their identity or circumstances. Inclusion refers to the active, intentional, and ongoing engagement with diversity – creating an environment in which all individuals feel valued, respected, and supported. Inclusion involves creating a sense of belonging and ensuring that everyone is afforded the opportunity to fully participate and contribute to

DOI: 10.4018/978-1-6684-7644-4.ch007

the organization or community. Together, diversity, equity, and inclusion are about creating a society and organizations that are inclusive and equitable, and that value and respect the differences among people.

Equity attainment refers to the extent to which individuals or groups are able to achieve fair and equal opportunities, access to resources, and outcomes. It is concerned with ensuring that everyone has an equal chance to succeed and reach their full potential, regardless of their background or identity. Achieving equity often requires addressing systemic inequalities and discrimination that may have historically disadvantaged certain groups. This can involve creating policies and programs that provide targeted support and resources to those who have been historically marginalized or disadvantaged to level the playing field and create more equitable outcomes. It is important to note that equity does not necessarily mean that everyone will have the same outcomes or receive the same treatment. Rather, it involves providing the necessary resources and support to ensure that everyone has an equal chance to succeed, given their unique circumstances and needs.

This chapter will illustrate a project undertaken at Western Governors University focused on DEI attainment, including quantitative and qualitative methods used to explore potential sources of inequities in competency-based assessments, recommended improvements, and future considerations for furthering assessment practices in the DEI arena.

BACKGROUND

Context: Western Governors University

Western Governors University (WGU) is a private, nonprofit, online university that was founded in 1997 by 19 U.S. governors. WGU is headquartered in Salt Lake City, Utah, and serves students throughout the United States. WGU offers more than eighty undergraduate and over sixty graduate degree programs that are designed to be flexible and competency-based, meaning that students can progress through their studies at their own pace and demonstrate their knowledge and skills through assessments rather than credit hours. One of the key features of WGU is its focus on student success and affordability. The university has a low tuition rate and offers financial aid and scholarships to help students cover the cost of their education. Since the onset of the COVID-19 pandemic, WGU has also added emergency funding and scholarships for students facing financial barriers to completing their degrees. WGU also provides students with personalized support, including one-on-one instruction and program mentoring, to help them stay on track and achieve their goals. Overall, WGU is known for its innovative approach to higher education through its competency-based approach, distributed faculty model, and commitment to helping students succeed in their studies and careers.

WGU Student Body

The student body at WGU is comprised of 142,459 students as of January 2023 that includes a mix of traditional and non-traditional students from a wide range of backgrounds and demographics, shown in table 1. One of the unique characteristics of WGU's student body is that it is primarily made up of working adults looking to further their education to advance their careers. The median age of WGU students is 37 years old and is typically returning to school after several years in the workforce. The majority of WGU students are enrolled in a bachelor's or master's program offered through one of WGU's four colleges: the Leavitt School of Health, the College of Information Technology, the College of Business, or the Teachers College, as shown in table 2. WGU tailors its programs to the needs and demands of the workforce, providing competency-based education in fields that are in high demand in today's job.

WGU's student centered, self-paced approach to degree attainment attracts a diverse group of students, with many coming from rural and low-income areas. The online format enables students' flexibility to pursue a degree that might not be possible in a traditional college or university format. WGU has been seeing an increase in enrollment in recent years and is a testament to the quality of education and the flexibility offered by its competency-based model.

Table 1. WGU student body

Gender	Income[a]	Community	First Generation Student	Underrepresented Minority[b]	Marital Status
63.7% Female	77.2% Middle/High	81.8% Urban	22.8% Yes	27.0% Yes	53.0% Not Married
36.3% Male	27.0% Low	18.2% Rural	77.2% No	73.0% No	47.0% Married

[a]Low income is defined as a household income of $35,000 per year or less. [b] Underrepresented minority includes African Americans, Alaska Natives, Latinos, and Native Hawaiian/Pacific Islanders.

Table 2. WGU enrollment

	Teachers College	College of IT	College of Business	Leavitt School of Health	Total
Bachelors	22,699	34,094	33,275	16,583	106,651
Masters	16,565	3,939	11,811	7,803	40,118
Other	80	N/A	N/A	13	93
Total	39,344	38,033	45,086	24,399	146,862

Note: Students categorized as "other" are enrolled in Post-Baccalaureate, Post-Masters, or Teacher's preparation programs. Enrollment as of 2/22/23.

WGU's Competency Based Model

WGU employs a Competency-based education (CBE) model where students are evaluated based on their ability to demonstrate competencies comprised of specific skills and knowledge, rather than based on the traditional credit-hour rooted in amount of time spent in class. In the CBE model, students typically work through a series of learning modules or "competencies" at their own pace and demonstrate competency through objective assessments (OAs) or performance-based assessments (PAs) such as research projects, presentations, or authentic tasks. Once students demonstrate their mastery course competencies, they receive course credit and advance to the next course in their program path.

WGU's Distributed Faculty Model

WGU employs a distributed faculty model, as opposed to a traditional faculty model where one instructor assumes responsibility for course development that often includes the development of a syllabus, selection of learning resources, formative and summative assessment development, and test administration, in addition to offering student support in a group setting as well as a one-to-one basis often only for those students who choose to interact with their instructors. WGU's distributed faculty model is based on a machine learning model that consists of multiple sub-models, or "faculties," that work together to make predictions or solve problems. Each faculty is typically specialized in a specific aspect of the problem and the final output is obtained by combining the predictions of all faculties. WGU "faculties" consist of instructors who work one-on-one with students to support course completion, program mentors who work one-on-one with students to support progress through their programs. Evaluation faculty are solely responsible for assessing student PA submissions and do not interact with students. Product development faculty include assessment developers, instructional designers, and instructional technologies who bring their expertise to develop courses based on design documents provided by learning-centered design faculty in the areas of assessment strategy, educational product designers, and standards and practices.

WGU program and subsequent course development is initiated during the design phase, employing faculties from various areas who create design documents and prototypes for handoff to the development team. Course development teams consist of an assessment developer, instructional designer, instructional technologist, and internal subject matter experts in instruction and evaluation faculty roles, and often an external subject matter expert who can bring work experience particularly to the development of PAs. Development teams are also supported by Product Development Owners, Assessment Strategists, Psychometricians, and Academic Program Managers throughout the development process.

Diversity, Equity, and Inclusion Project

As WGU's enrollment increases, so does diversity among our student body. As a result, WGU acknowledges several challenges to developing and redeveloping WGU curricula and assessments that are suitable for a diverse learner population. With a lack of specific guidelines, methodologies, training, or tools to address DEI, WGU's Program Development Division initiated a project to address these issues and "provide an education to all students that will enable them to learn and be comfortable with the content they are consuming. Because education is a vehicle for social mobility, it is imperative that WGU's offerings embrace the evolving demographic profile of the U.S. population" (WGU, 2022). This initial step will enable us to begin developing guidelines, methodologies, and tools to help us meet an increasingly diverse student population with the goal of improving enrollment and completion rates for students of color as well as all students who embrace diversity, equity, and inclusion.

As part of this initiative, the DEI in Learning Design project team developed an assessment and learning framework to improve both course content and assessments that identifies our guiding principles and the learning development practices, measures of implementations, and measures of impact on students associated with each. In the fall of 2022, twenty courses were selected to be a part of WGU's Program Development DEI Attainment Project initiative. Program Development staff from the Course Quality Improvement and Early Care Team (CQI/EC) attended a kickoff meeting where principal investigators explained the purpose and goals of the DEI Attainment project. Meeting participants were then asked to volunteer to review at least one course with the requirement that each course team consist of an assessment developer, instructional technologist, and an instructional designer. Volunteer reviewers were also required to complete a series of five courses focused on equity design.

Volunteer reviewers were asked to enroll in their assigned courses and experience the course material and assessments from the student point of view. Each course team designated a leader responsible for scheduling and leading weekly meetings, tracking progress in an online tracking sheet, communicating weekly updates during DEI Attainment Project meetings with leadership, and presenting results. Course teams met on a weekly basis throughout the project to discuss procedures, findings, and identify areas for improvement. All volunteer reviewers were invited to attend PD-wide DEI Attainment Project meetings on a weekly basis to track progress across all DEI Attainment project courses.

Course teams reviewed assigned courses for approximately two months, then met with DEI Attainment Project leadership, CQI/EC Team leadership, Product Development Owners, Directors of Assessment and Curriculum for the associated colleges, and Assessment Strategists to report initial DEI findings. Leadership then collaborated to review results and follow up meetings were scheduled to determine next steps.

METHODS

Project Course Selection

Twenty courses were included for review as part of the DEI Attainment project and were selected based on course completion rates (CCR) where courses with a 7 – 10% CCR difference between reference groups (i.e., minority and low income) and focal groups (e.g., white, male, earning $35,000 or more) were chosen for inclusion, as shown in table 3.

Table 3. Course completion rates for minority and low-income students

Course Name	College	Type of Assessment	Equity Framework Guiding Principles	Minority Student* Course Completion Rate	Low-income Student* Course Completion Rate
IT Leadership Foundations	College of IT	Performance	1. Show me people like me.	88.2%	85.3%
Applied Probability and Statistics	General Education	Objective	1. Make it matter. 2. Personalize my needs	74.2%	82.5%
Healthcare Information Systems Management	Healthcare Professions	Objective	1. Make it matter 2. Remove barriers	60.1%	55.2%
Information Technology Management Essentials	College of Business	Objective	1. Make it matter 2. Remove barriers	70.1%	67.9%

Quantitative Measures

Assessment Quality Index

The assessment quality index (AQI) is a measure of the quality and reliability of an assessment or evaluation. It is used to determine the extent to which an assessment accurately and consistently measures the skills, knowledge, or abilities that it is intended to assess. There are a range of factors that can influence the AQI of an assessment, including the content and format of the assessment, the scoring criteria, the training and expertise of the assessors, and the reliability and validity of the assessment. WGU AQI values range from 20 to 80, higher AQI scores indicate an assessment is reliable, accurate, and likely to produce consistent and meaningful results. Lower AQI scores may suggest an assessment is unreliable, biased, or may not produce consistent, valid results. The AQI is an important consideration in the design and implementation of assessments, as it can impact the validity and reliability of the results and the usefulness of the assessment in making decisions or taking action.

First Attempt Pass Rate

The first attempt pass rate refers to the percentage of people who pass a test, assessment, or evaluation on their first try. It is often used as a measure of the difficulty of the assessment and the effectiveness of preparation or training for the assessment. A high first-attempt pass rate may indicate that the assessment is not too challenging or that the preparation or training provided was sufficient to help individuals pass the assessment. On the other hand, a low first-attempt pass rate may suggest that the assessment is difficult or that the preparation or training was inadequate. First-attempt pass rates are often used in educational or professional settings to evaluate the effectiveness of programs or courses, or to set standards or benchmarks for performance. It can also be used to identify areas for improvement or to provide targeted support to individuals who may be struggling.

Reliability

Reliability refers to the consistency and stability of a measurement or assessment. It is a measure of the degree to which an assessment produces the same or comparable results when administered multiple times, or when administered by different people. An assessment is considered reliable if it produces consistent results over time and across different administrations. This means that the assessment should produce equivalent results when given to the same group of people on different occasions, or when given to different groups of people. There are several factors that can impact the reliability of an assessment, including the design and content of the assessment, the scoring criteria, and the training and expertise of the assessors. Assessments that are well-designed and carefully administered are more likely to be reliable than those that are poorly designed or administered. Reliability is an important consideration in the design and use of assessments, as it is necessary for the results of an assessment to be meaningful and useful. Reliable assessments are more likely to produce valid and accurate results, which can be used to inform decisions or take action.

Discrimination

Discrimination in assessments refers to the unfair or biased treatment of individuals or groups based on their identity or characteristics, such as race, ethnicity, gender, age, religion, or sexual orientation. This can occur when an assessment is designed or administered in a way that disproportionately disadvantages or disadvantages certain groups of people, or when the results of an assessment are used unfairly to discriminate against certain individuals or groups. Discrimination in assessments can take many forms, including direct discrimination, which occurs when an assessment is designed or administered in a way that directly disadvantages a particular group of people. For example, an assessment that is only available in English may disproportionately disadvantage individuals who do not speak English as their primary language. Indirect discrimination occurs when an assessment is neutral on its face but has a disproportionate impact on certain groups of people. For example, an assessment that tests knowledge of a particular cultural context may disproportionately disadvantage individuals who are not familiar with that context.

It is important to ensure that assessments are designed and administered in a way that is fair and unbiased, and that they do not discriminate against any particular group of people. This can involve considering the diversity of the population being assessed and ensuring that the assessment is appropriate and relevant for all individuals. It can also involve providing accommodations or support for individuals who may be disadvantaged by the assessment, such as providing translated versions of the assessment or offering extra time for individuals with disabilities.

Item Analysis

Item analysis is used to evaluate the quality of test items, identify item difficulty, and improve test reliability and validity. The pass rate and point biserial coefficient are generated for each item, with the latter representing item-test correlation. The point biserial coefficient ranges between -1 and 1 where a high correlation indicates the item is a good measure of the construct it is intended to measure, as it is strongly related to overall test scores. A low point biserial coefficient may indicate that the item is not a good measure of the construct and should be revised or removed from the test. It is best practice at WGU to avoid using items that have a negative point biserial coefficient.

Differential Item Functioning

Differential item functioning (DIF) refers to the phenomenon where items on a test, such as multiple-choice questions, perform differently for different groups of test takers. DIF occurs when an item functions differently for one subgroup of test takers as compared to another subgroup, even though the test takers in both groups have the same level of knowledge or ability. For example, if an item on a math test functions differently for girls than for boys, even though both groups have the same level of math ability, that item is said to have DIF. The same applies if an item functions differently for students from different ethnic or socioeconomic backgrounds, despite the students having the same level of knowledge or ability.

There are several methods that are commonly used to detect DIF, including the Mantel-Haenszel, the logistic regression, the likelihood ratio, and the Bayes methods. These methods compare the performance of different groups on a given item and calculate a statistic to indicate the level of DIF. It is important to note that DIF does not imply bias in the test, it only indicates that a particular item (or test form, as we shall see in our results) may perform differently for different groups of test-takers. If DIF is identified, it is important to investigate the cause and make decisions about the appropriate course of action such as modifying the item or removing it from the test. DIF analysis is an important step in ensuring that tests are fair and accurate for all test takers. It allows test developers and administrators to identify any items that may be biased, and to adjust the test to ensure that it is as fair as possible for all test takers.

Courses of Focus in This Chapter

The author voluntarily selected the following four courses for review: IT Leadership Foundations (College of Information Technology), Applied Probability and Statistics (general education), Healthcare Information Systems Management (College of Health Professions), and Information Technology Management Essentials (College of Business). Three of the courses included summative OAs, and one course included a summative PA consisting of two tasks.

ANALYSIS

Objective Assessments

Courses designed to measure competencies with OAs are associated with three summative assessments: a pre-assessment students can complete in preparation for the final high stakes assessment, and two forms of the high stakes assessment. A mixed methods approach was used, where quantitative data were collected at the assessment level for all high stakes forms including the first attempt pass rate, reliability, discrimination, and assessment quality index (AQI). Item level statistics were also conducted by running item analysis which generates the item pass rate and point biserial. Each item was also analyzed and flagged for DIF, then matched to item analysis statistics to see if there was a relationship between items identified as potentially having DIF and poor performing items. Two group comparisons were considered for DIF: minorities (focal group) versus Caucasian (reference group); and low income, defined as a household income of \$35,000 per year or less (focal group), versus middle/high income defined as a household with an income above \$35,000 per year (reference group). Our qualitative analysis involved a substantive review of all high stakes items for potential bias using guidelines outlined in the WGU Item Development Handbook (2019), as it is based on psychometric principles rooted in fairness (see appendix 1). Items flagged for DIF were then compared to the results of the substantive review to see if bias was confirmed.

Pre-assessment data were not considered in this analysis, as WGU students engage in pre-assessments for several reasons and often take the pre-assessment multiple times, therefore rendering the results unreliable in terms of decision making. Nevertheless, pre-assessment items were substantively reviewed for potential bias using the WGU Style guide.

Performance Assessments

Courses measuring competencies with summative PAs do so by evaluating a task or series of tasks students must successfully complete to achieve recognition of attaining competencies. Each task includes a series of "prompts" that describe the artifact a learner needs to produce, and each prompt has a corresponding three level rubric aspect that defines the evaluation criteria for students are competent, approaching competence, and not competent as shown in table 4. PAs require students to engage in a variety of tasks including but not limited to research reports, authentic tasks, hands-on projects, presentations, and executive summaries. For example, students in the College of IT might be tasked with building a mobile application, while students in Teachers College might be required to develop lesson plans based on authentic curricula from an existing school district. All students complete at least one PA during their tenure at WGU, as each program requires successful completion of a Capstone project that includes submitting topic release and approval forms, project proposals, proposed artifacts, and project reflections. It is important to note courses with PAs do not include pre-assessments.

Table 4. WGU PA prompt and rubric example

A. Prepare a dataset from the data provided in the "Raw Data" spreadsheet, attached below. Remove any potential errors or outliers, duplicate records, or data that are not necessary. Provide a clean copy of the data in your submission.			
Aspect	**Not Evident**	**Approaching Competence**	**Competent**
A. Dataset Preparation	A dataset is not provided.	A dataset containing potential errors or outliers, duplicate records, or data that are not necessary is provided.	A clean dataset with any potential errors or outliers, duplicate records, or data that are not necessary removed. A clean copy of the data is provided.

The data collected for PAs included the total number of task submissions, task submission success rate, and difficulty (represented by the average number of submissions of a task per student). An evaluation performance summary for each aspect for each task was also generated to identify prompts with low pass rates. Individual prompts and their associated rubrics also underwent substantive reviews for potential bias using the online WGU Style Guide for performance assessments which is shared internally. DIF data were also generated by our psychometrician to identify potential bias in task prompts; prompts flagged for DIF were compared to the results of the substantive review to see if bias was confirmed.

Formative Assessments

Courses featuring both OAs and PAs offer students a variety of formative opportunities such as multiple-choice questions, online labs, and open-ended reflection questions to support students in preparing for summative assessments. However, WGU does not collect psychometric data on formative items, so the author was unable to generate quantitative formative assessment data for review. However, formative objective items existing within courses were reviewed qualitatively using the WGU Item Writing Handbook (2019) to determine the existence of possible bias.

Additional Qualitative Data

The "Voice of the Student" project consisted of a series of focus groups comprised of students who completed the twenty courses selected for the DEI Attainment Project and were categorized as belonging to a minority group or as low income, defined as a household income of $35,000 per year or less, or both. Students were asked to discuss how inclusive these courses feel to minority students, identify challenges they faced in specific courses, how they navigated those challenges, what they learned, how they were supported by faculty to gain an understanding of the overall learner experience. Students were selected to participate in the "Voice of the Student" project if they successfully completed one of the twenty courses selected for inclusion in the DEI Attainment project. In addition, students had to self-identify as belonging to a minority group, and/or be identified as low income, defined as a yearly household income of $35,000 or less.

RESULTS

Quantitative results (pass rate, reliability, discrimination, AQI) for each assessment within each course are shown in table 5. The Applied Probability and Statistics and Information Technology and Management Essentials assessments met all psychometric benchmarks at the assessment level (see appendix 2, table 6). The Healthcare Information Systems Management course did not meet the psychometric benchmark for pass rate and the AQI index is low, particularly for form A of the high stakes assessment.

Table 5. Quantitative assessment measures in selected DEI courses

Course Name	Form (OA) Task (PA)	1st Attempt Pass Rate	Reliability	Discrimination	AQI (OA) Difficulty (PA)
IT Leadership Foundations	Task 1	97.3%	-3.313	.577	1.32
	Task 2	97.4%	-0.616	.531	1.20
Applied Probability and Statistics	A	79.17%	.82	.23	80
	B	80.09%	.79	.21	80
	C	81.07%	.83	.23	80
Healthcare Information Systems Management	A	51.9%	.60	.12	20
	B	58.33%	.60	.12	43
Information Technology Management Essentials	A	80.0%	.66	.24	N/A
	B	75.3%	.68	.26	N/A

Item analysis for Applied Probability and Statistics yielded twenty-three low or poor performing items in terms of pass rate, discrimination, or both, across all three high-stakes forms of the assessment (see appendix 2, table 7), however, none of the items have negative discrimination values. Fifteen items were flagged as having DIF; five of these items also have low or poor pass rates, one had low discrimination, and three had both poor or low pass rates and low discrimination. A substantive review of the pre-assessment and all three high stakes forms determined the items flagged for DIF to be benign. Interestingly, one item flagged for DIF includes male and female proper names in the stem, which violates the WGU Style Guide. While DEI concerns related to gender and ethnicity were allayed, several issues identified are overwhelmingly related to table formatting and images, and some items included potential sensitive content.

Individual item analysis for Information Technology and Management Essentials found twenty-one low or poor performing items in terms of pass rate, and two items had low discrimination values. Unfortunately, DIF analyses are unavailable as the pre-assessment and high stakes forms are administered via a third-party vendor, whose platform does not currently have this capability. The pre-assessment substantive review resulted in minor edits for grammar on two items, while the high-stakes substantive review revealed nine items in need of revision to align with the WGU Style Guide (e.g., parallelism, learning material, redundancy). Interestingly, three of these items included proper names in the scenario which is not permitted; DIF analysis would have been helpful to determine if this is affecting groups differently based on gender.

Finally, item analysis for Healthcare Information Systems Management identified sixty-one low or poor performing items in terms of pass rate, discrimination, or both, across both forms of the high-stakes assessment with 12 of the items demonstrating negative discrimination values. Thirty-three items were flagged as having DIF, twenty-three of which were also identified as having low or poor pass rates, and discrimination values. A substantive review of the high-stakes items determined most items, including those identified as having DIF, to be benign. One item flagged as C+ for gender may be detecting adverse DIF favoring women, as they may be more knowledgeable about the topic assessed in the item. Overall, there were no potential DEI issues with language or accessibility detected in the pre-assessment or high stakes assessments.

The IT Leadership Foundations PA met all psychometric benchmarks (see appendix 1) except reliability. Considering the competencies measured in each task are different (task 1 measures professional reflection, while task 2 is focused on leadership strategies, communication, team strategies), this is not surprising. The first task prompts learners to complete an assessment of their professional strengths, then write a series of reflective responses based on their results. The second task presents learners with a video case study and authentic email illustrating an ill-defined problem with several viable solutions. The learner then responds to a series of prompts about the case, and creates an artifact aimed at remedying the problem as if they were in the situation presented. DIF analysis did not reveal any differences between groups in difficulty or number of attempts, and a substantive review of task prompts and rubric aspects did not yield any DEI concerns.

Substantive reviews of formative items across all four courses did not generate any major DEI concerns. Formative items were most often cited as violating WGU Item Writing Guidelines which could be remedied through CQI. Common issues include parallelism, clueing, and use of proper names and gendered pronouns, the latter of which could potentially be related to DEI issues related to gender.

"Voice of the Student Data" was reviewed for each course, however, none of the feedback yielded assessment concerns for Applied Probability and Statistics, Information Technology and Management Essentials, and IT Leadership Foundations. Feedback for Healthcare Information Systems Management noted the formative items within the course were not in alignment with the pre-assessment and high stakes forms. In addition, students shared the formative, pre-assessment, and high stakes forms included acronyms that were not spelled out.

CONCLUSION

This DEI project provided the opportunity to engage a wide range of course development roles in practices aimed at identifying bias and providing recommendations for improvement regarding issues related to DEI. By actively reviewing course and assessment materials, all course reviewers as a result experienced hands-on training in DEI design and development that could transfer to future development projects.

Future research is needed to determine the professional development effects resulting from engagement in this project. In addition to developing skills for DEI design and development, course reviewers were able to identify additional areas for improvement, while not directly related to the DEI framework, finding these problems will nonetheless level the playing field for all students.

For courses with OAs, it was recommended that poor performing items be reviewed by a psychometrician and assessment strategist for consideration of replacing them with well-performing items that were previously field tested. This approach could improve the assessment experience for students and may possibly increase pass rates. Item analysis should be conducted once the assessment reaches one hundred takes on each form to determine how well the items and the test overall are performing. Feedback resulting from the Applied Probability and Statistics assessment review advocated for replacing items containing sensitive content as well as those pertaining to accessibility issues (e.g., table and image formatting, alternate text) with previously field tested, well-performing items.

While the IT Leadership Foundations PA is performing well and review of the formative and summative assessments did not result in any DEI concerns, the instructional designer noted in their course review that one student submitted course feedback regarding the description of one of the characters associated with the scenario in the second task. Moreover, this feedback was cited as a concern prior to review, as course leadership was aware of the feedback. The student shared a concern that the description of one of the characters is based on gender stereotypes and should be revised. A review of the documentation confirmed the student's concern, and a draft revision of the description was provided during the initial DEI findings meetings.

Substantive reviews of formative items across all four courses did not generate any major DEI concerns. Formative items were most often cited as violating WGU Item Writing Guidelines which could be remedied through CQI. Common issues include parallelism, clueing, and use of proper names and gendered pronouns. Nonetheless, substantive reviews resulted in several recommendations aimed at improving formative and summative assessments across all four courses. While most of the recommendations were not specifically related to DEI concerns, implementing these suggestions could potentially result in resolving latent equity attainment issues. For example, several formative and summative multiple-choice items include proper names and/or gendered pronouns. Implementing suggested revisions may result in equity attainment in terms of gender, however, future research is needed to determine such effects.

Three of the four courses reviewed by the author in this chapter advanced to CQI projects. Items identified as having sensitive content in the Applied Probability and Statistics high-stakes assessment as well as poor performing items in Healthcare Information Systems Management high-stakes assessment were replaced with items developed for the corresponding evidence statements that performed well during field testing. The Information Technology and Management Essentials formative items were revised for WGU style and will undergo a SME review to determine alignment with the course content, current pre-assessment, and high-stakes OA forms, as the scope for this course includes updates to the learning resources. Formative items in the Healthcare Information Systems Management course will undergo similar revisions and review for alignment with the pre-assessment and high-stakes OA.

FUTURE RESEARCH DIRECTIONS

This chapter reports on the various approaches used by one assessment developer for DEI attainment review, twelve additional assessment developers reviewed the remaining 16 courses (in some cases assessment developers reviewed courses in pairs). Future work should investigate the approaches used across all courses in the DEI Attainment project to develop best practices for achieving equity attainment in assessment revision and redevelopment.

Course selection was determined by CCR, as were participants for the Voice of the Student Project. That is, course selection did not consider students who have attempted but not completed the course, only students who successfully completed the course were included in the Voice of the Student focus groups. Students who did not finish selected courses were not asked to participate in the Voice of the Student focus groups, therefore it is likely the sample did not include dissatisfied students. Furthermore, the results of the Voice of the Student data did not find identity to be factor in completing courses. Finally, the questions posed to focus groups were not designed to elicit information that would speak to DEI (that is, the questions were not aligned with project goals).

In terms of measures, it should be noted first attempt pass rates are not a comparable measure for PAs and OAs. There is a limit to the number of times students can take an OA, students must make an appointment in advance and take the test via online proctoring where they are observed during the entirety of the assessment. Students in courses with PAs can access the assessment at any time and are often encouraged to complete and submit to receive feedback so they can determine which areas they need to focus on to successfully pass. Courses with summative PAs do not include pre-assessments, they typically only include formative opportunities throughout the course. Therefore, students often treat their first attempt at a PA as a "pre-assessment," where OAs offer students the opportunity to engage in a pre-assessment that mirrors the conditions of the high-stakes form.

DIF analysis should also be further expanded as WGU's reporting platform only reports DIF statistics for minority and gender. While additional group analyses based on characteristics such as socio-economic status, community (urban, rural), and first-generation student status are available upon request to the psychometrics department, it was not feasible to request such analyses for a large number of courses. Future initiatives should plan for generating DIF analysis for targeted groups prior to review.

While the DEI Attainment Project did not result in discovering major issues related to DEI in these assessments, the substantive reviews resulting in CQI projects may ultimately have a positive effect on DEI. The WGU Item Development Handbook outlines psychometric guidelines for item writing, they are not just "rules." The guidelines presented are rooted in fairness; one such guideline stresses avoiding the use of gendered pronouns; substantive item reviews found several instances where proper names were used, which may inadvertently contribute to latent DEI issues for students based on gender. More research is needed in this area to determine if there is an association between items using gendered names and pronouns and DIF.

Finally, any equity attainment projects, and assessment reviews should follow prescribed procedures for identifying DEI issues. Since this was a novel project for program development, specific directions or procedures were not provided, and teams set out by engaging of full reviews with limited guiding information. DIF analyses and substantive reviews of assessment content should be defined and based on best practices. Hayes, Trajkovski, and Demeter (2023) present a seven-step process for identifying and addressing bias in educational assessments. Future DEI assessment review projects should follow this approach, where substantive review of assessment content is evaluated independent of DIF results to provide fair equity review while avoiding confirmation bias.

While the DEI Attainment project was exploratory in nature and open-ended in terms of review processes and standards, it provided Program Development the opportunity to explore different approaches for reviewing course content and assessments through the lens of equity. Future iterations of this work should focus on identifying and implementing best practices to ensure a standard approach to DEI in learning design and development in competency-based courses.

REFERENCES

Demeter, M., Hayes, H., & Trajkovski, G. (2022, Oct. 9.). The Importance of DIF: An important tool for identifying potential bias in Performance Assessment. *2022 Assessment Institute,* Indianapolis, Indiana University, Purdue University. https://assessmentinstitute.iupui.edu/program/program-files/2022/Sunday/04M_demeter.pdf

Hayes, H., Trajkovski, G., & Demeter, M. (2023). Seven steps to identify and address bias in educational assessments. *Evolllution.* https://evolllution.com/programming/teaching-and-learning/7-steps-to-identify-and-address-bias-in-educational-assessments/

Henning, G. & Lundquist, A. (2022, Oct. 11). A framework for applying equity-minded and equity-centered assessment practices [Conference session]. *2022 Assessment Institute,* Indianapolis, IN, United States.

Jiao, H., & Lissitz, R. W. (Eds.). (2017). *Test Fairness in the New Generation of Large? Scale Assessment.* IAP.

Montenegro, E., & Jankowski, N. (2017). *Equity and assessment: Moving towards culturally responsive assessment (Occasional Paper No. 29).* Urbana, IL: University of Illinois and Indiana University, National Institute for Learning Outcomes Assessment (NILOA). https://files.eric.ed.gov/fulltext/ED574461.pdf

Montenegro, E., & Jankowski, N. A. (2020). *A new decade for assessment: Embedding equity into assessment praxis (Occasional Paper No. 42).* Urbana, IL: University of Illinois and Indiana University, National Institute for Learning Outcomes Assessment (NILOA). https://files.eric.ed.gov/fulltext/ED608774.pdf

Sireci, S. G., & Rios, J. A. (2013). Decisions that make a difference in detecting differential item functioning. *Educational Research and Evaluation, 19*(2-3), 2–3, 170–187. doi:10.1080/13803611.2013.767621

Western Governors University. (2022). *Diversity equity and inclusion in learning design.* WGU. https://westerngovernorsuniversity.sharepoint.com/sites/DesignDevDEI/SitePages/Our-Project.aspx

Western Governors University. (2022) *How to DE&I at WGU.* WGU. https://intranet.wgu.edu/diversity_inclusion

Western Governors University Academic Programs. (2019). *Item development handbook.* WGU.

Witham, K., Malcom-Piqueux, L. E., Dowd, A. C., & Bensimon, E. M. (2015). *America's unmet promise: The imperative for equity in higher education.* Association of American Colleges and Universities.

APPENDIX 1

Summary of WGU Item Development Handbook Guidelines

The WGU Development Handbook (2019) is distributed internally as well as with external partners such as subject matter experts and vendors to support the object assessment development process. The Handbook outlines several specific guidelines such as item content and properties, fairness, and format. The following list summarizes the major guidelines for objective item development at WGU:

1. Do not use first (I, me, my) or second (you, yours) person pronouns in questions or scenarios.
2. Do not write negatively phrased questions (cannot use not in a question).
3. Do not use people's names or business names.
4. Try to avoid gendered pronouns (his, her, he, she) whenever possible.
5. Do not use the phrase "of the following" or "above" or "below" in question stems.
6. Do not use "all of the above" or "none of the above" or "A and B are correct."
7. Questions should begin with question words such as which, what, when, where, why, etc.
8. Answer choices should be parallel. There are two types of parallelism: a) all four answers are very similar and b) two pairs of similar answer choices.
9. Teaching text is not allowed: do not supply information that the student should have learned from the LR.
10. Cueing is not allowed: if a word appears in the scenario or question stem and in only one answer choice, it is considered "cueing."
11. Do not use **bold**, *italics*, or "quotation marks" for emphasis.
12. Answer choices should be 100% correct and incorrect. WGU does not allow best answer choice types of questions.
13. WGU does not allow questions such as "Which answer is true" or "Which answer is correct."
14. "Which" is followed by a noun and "what" is followed by a verb, per WGU Style Guide.
15. Numbers less than 10 should be spelled out: i.e., three or seven.
16. Numeric answer choices must be written in ascending order. Other types of answer choices are randomized by the testing system.

APPENDIX 2

Table 6. Assessment-level psychometric benchmarks

Measure	Objective Assessments	Performance Assessments
Pass rate	70 – 95%	50 – 95%
Reliability	≥ .60	≥ .60
Discrimination	≥ .15	≥ .15
AQI	20 - 80	N/A

Table 7. Item-level psychometric benchmarks for objective assessments

Discrimination	Performance Category	P-value
≥ .20	High	.40 - .89
.10 - .19	Medium	.30 - .39 or90 - .95
.01 - .09	Low	.25 - .29 or .96 – 1.0
≤ .00	Poor	≤ .24

Chapter 8
Design, Technology, and Measurement Considerations in Virtual–Reality Assessment

Sean P. Gyll

https://orcid.org/0000-0002-9961-4007
Western Governors University, USA

Karen K. Shader
Western Governors University, USA

Paul Zikas
ORamaVR, Switzerland

George Papagiannakis
University of Crete, Greece

ABSTRACT

Virtual reality (VR) simulations as an assessment tool represent a much-needed effort to move beyond the shortcomings of today's forms-based measures. Within VR, we assess for competency and problem-solving skills versus the content memorization typically supported by multiple-choice assessments. This chapter reviews the development process for the behavioral healthcare coordination VR assessment deployed at Western Governors University. It follows three patients undergoing behavioral health care treatment and highlights essential design, technology, and measurement considerations in developing a VR assessment. For any assessment program, construct validity is the chief validity component. This means that standards-based principles must be maintained to support the inferences drawn from test scores. However, without a framework for developing and maintaining those standards, assessment developers are left to their own devices to determine which practices are most likely to be effective. This chapter provides practical examples to aid assessment professionals in maintaining those standards.

DOI: 10.4018/978-1-6684-7644-4.ch008

INTRODUCTION

In online competency-based higher education (OCBHE), students move through their degree programs one course at a time by demonstrating mastery of various content and professional domains. As students work within an individual domain of knowledge, they are assessed on one or more topics, each consisting of a series of competencies with associated test objectives and performance tasks (Gyll & Ragland, 2018). As the popularity of OCBHE programs continues to grow, their integrity will be scrutinized by students and employers alike, and their credibility will largely depend on the quality of the assessments used (McClarty & Gaertner, 2015).

To meet this demand, institutions of higher learning are beginning to realize the importance of real-world, performance-based measures like those found in Virtual Reality (VR) environments, where demonstrations of competence are crucial to success. Central to the development of VR assessments is the need for high-fidelity demonstrations of learner aptitudes and competencies that include a significant emphasis on cognitive abilities (i.e., knowing what) and the performance of those abilities (i.e., demonstrating how). Assessment fidelity describes the *reality of function* and how closely the environment imitates the real-life counterpart. The most significant advantage of this testing mode is the real-world relevance that can be incorporated into the assessment, and technological innovations continue to expand these opportunities.

Competency-based skills education follows a system of assessing needs, designing processes, developing materials, and evaluating them against specific learning outcomes. Within this context, learning is no longer viewed as transmitting knowledge from instructor to student (e.g., sitting passively, listening to a lecture, taking notes, and applying concepts) but as an active process acquired through various instructional and media types. Compared to traditional instructor-led methods, research shows that competency-based skills are improved when technology integrates learning into the educational experience rather than being delivered in a compartmentalized fashion (Ford & Gopher, 2015; Hoogveld, 2003; Van Merrienboer & Kirschner, 2013; Merrill, 2002). As a result, students' capacity to develop a particular domain's competency and then transfer that information to learning outcomes improves (Gyll & Hayes, in press).

Some have suggested that skills development as a first step to acquiring competency can be better taught with high-fidelity VR simulation because VR allows for a more active and immersive learning experience (Kyaw et al., 2019; Birrenbach et al., 2021). For example, VR is often used in medical education for developing skills of varying complexity, ranging from simple nursing skills to laparoscopic/endoscopic/endovascular skills (Pantelidis et al., 2017; Khan et al., 2019) or complex surgical skills (Hooper et al., 2019; Grantcharov, 2008). Additionally, VR simulation using head-mounted devices (HMDs) offers a multisensory, 3-D, fully immersive experience. Through immersion, sense of presence, and interaction with the virtual environment in a real-time and realistic manner, VR simulation can create emotional experiences that facilitate experiential learning, exceeding other 2-D learning modalities (Babini et al., 2020). However, while these studies have demonstrated the utility of VR simulation as a teaching tool, scant literature exists on its utility as an assessment instrument. Furthermore, fewer studies exist on meaningful development guidelines to aid assessment professionals in the development process.

This chapter's remaining sections review the development process for the Behavioral Healthcare Coordination VR assessment deployed at WGU, College of Health Professions. It follows three patients undergoing behavioral health care treatment and highlights essential design, technology, and measurement considerations in developing a summative VR assessment. For any assessment program, construct validity is the chief validity component. This means that standards-based principles must be maintained throughout the development life cycle to support the inferences drawn from test scores. However, without a framework for developing and maintaining those standards, assessment developers are left to their own devices to determine which practices are most likely to be effective. This chapter provides practical examples to aid assessment professionals in maintaining those standards.

Project Background

In 2020, the College of Health Professions at WGU offered two new innovative skills certificate programs designed to upskill healthcare professionals in Chronic and Behavioral Health Care Coordination. The programs were unique to WGU because students were required to pass a summative scenario-based VR assessment to earn a skills certificate; no other programs at WGU require passing a simulation-based assessment delivered in virtual reality. The programs were used as continuing education, employer-required professional development, or as part of employer onboarding for new employees and others leading care delivery transformation.

The skills certificates offered accessible career pathways for new and existing healthcare professionals in career development, career advancement, and mid-career support. They also expanded access by increasing relevancy in health care because the skills and competencies mapped directly to high-demand jobs. Additionally, the certificates provided a pathway for students into the WGU Bachelor of Science in Health Services Coordination (BSHSC) program for students choosing to continue their education. Program certificates, badges, and a skills transcript were awarded to students completing a certificate program.[1]

During the project's planning phase, WGU carefully selected 3 - 5 independent Subject Matter Experts (SMEs) to help design and build the VR assessment; we refer to these SMEs as *practitioners*. Practitioners were required to hold at least a bachelor's degree in Behavioral Healthcare Coordination (or a related field) with at least five years of relevant work experience. While prior assessment experience was not required, at least one had experience working in the assessment industry. WGU also vetted several potential vendors in a comprehensive Request for Proposal (RFP) process before choosing the perfect technology partner, ORamaVR. Finally, practitioners and ORamaVR worked alongside WGU internal staff on all aspects of the project's planning, designing, and implementation phases.

Simulation Versus Virtual Reality

Different labels, such as a game, case study, or exercise, often describe the "simulation" exam. For this chapter, perhaps the most helpful approach is to describe the "computer simulation," followed by examples of how and why it is used for assessment purposes inside and outside education. First, it is essential to note that a simulated environment differs from a VR one. Simulated experiences can and often do use computer systems, but they do not have to. For example, simulation training is increasingly popular in healthcare education and often relies on specially designed manikins or simulated patients in a clinical setting. On the other hand, VR uses computer systems to generate realistic pseudo-environments that provide users with visual, tactile, and auditory sensations, with the possibility of actual interaction with the virtual environment (Pensieri & Pennacchini, 2014).

In testing and assessment, computer simulations are sometimes called high-fidelity, producing samples of likely performance, as opposed to low-fidelity pencil-and-paper assessments having only signs of possible performance.

Fidelity is broadly classified into low, medium, and high.

- Low: the minimum simulation required for a system to respond to and accept inputs and provide outputs
- Medium: responds automatically to stimuli with limited accuracy
- High: nearly indistinguishable or as close as possible to the actual system

Simulation fidelity describes the reality of function and how closely the simulation imitates the real-life counterpart (Fidelity Implementation Study Group Report, 1999). Computer simulations are now reasonably well established as assessment tools in the certification and educational fields. The technique fits well into educational philosophies that stress the importance of the student as an interactive participant in the learning process. Some practical examples of computer simulations as examinations in the School of Information Technology at WGU include CompTIA's, Amazon's AWS, and Cisco's suite of certification exams.

When training health professionals, both new entrants and those who may be reskilling, an essential measure of competence requires the "application of knowledge." For new professionals learning to work with patients and clients to deliver care, information, support, or guidance, the nuances of effective client engagement and psychomotor skills are considered essential entry-level knowledge, skills, and abilities (KSAs). Listening, incorporating, aligning, deciding, and applying knowledge are aspects of these KSAs and can be measured using high-fidelity computer simulations or direct patient care engagements. Hi-fidelity simulations and direct patient care experiences create "presence," where the assessment is embedded as much as possible in real-time. During these encounters, the student experiences physical reactions, including heightened attention and high levels of presence. This is one reason simulations continue to receive increased attention from healthcare professionals, accreditors, and state agencies as valid measures of competence.

Unlike the simulation, in VR environments, users react to certain "simulated conditions" within the environment (e.g., eNASCAR simulators), but the atmosphere is wholly imaginative and false. This "false" environment is created to appear natural, yet users can distinguish between reality and imagination (Keshav, 2017). There can be no real interaction with a natural environment for it to be virtual reality. For example, an information technology learner demonstrating the functionality of a software application through PowerPoint is neither participating in a simulation nor a virtual one. To be a computer simulation, the relevant functions of the software environment must be presented adequately through the computer equipment; to be a virtual exercise, it would have to be wholly imaginative. Without the reality of function, the activity is no more than an exercise or PowerPoint presentation.

The reality of function includes the acceptance of the relevant duties and responsibilities of the simulation. For example, suppose a simulation is about the work of news editors on social media. The materials provide news items for the students to work on within a social media platform. However, if a teacher tells the class, "Pretend you are news editors on social media and invent your own news items," there would be no reality of function; the participants would be authors and inventors, not editors.

The Student Experience

Assessment of Competencies and Associated Skills

Before taking the summative VR assessment, students in the BHCC program completed *Care for Individuals and Families*. The course content and topics covered five competencies and 11 skills validated in the summative VR assessment (see Appendix A). Western Governors University uses skills to develop the competencies on which its educational model is based. This skills-based approach to designing content establishes the "skill" as the common denominator for employers, job seekers, and educational institutions, allowing them to communicate in a common language.

Learning taxonomies describe different types of learning behaviors. Some taxonomies distinguish different 'levels' of learning, whereas others categorize learning. As a result, learning taxonomies demonstrate the growth of the learner's acquisition of knowledge, skills, and abilities (KSAs) across a pathway. At the highest level, *Competency* is an individual's measurable, assessable capability that integrates knowledge, skills, abilities, and dispositions required to successfully perform tasks at a determined level in a defined setting. *Skill* is a lower-level contextualized statement describing an individual's foundational applied capabilities and behaviors for a given task, occupation, or need.

The Scenario Setting

The goal of the VR assessment was for students to demonstrate competence in the BHCCs' cognitive, psychomotor, and affective domains. The interactions within the VR assessment occurred in a conference room and private office within three different healthcare settings:

1. Scenario A occurred in a long-term care facility.
2. Scenario B occurred in a youth residential treatment center.
3. Scenario C occurred in an outpatient community mental health center.

Each agency employed allied health and ancillary professionals, like case managers, therapists, psychologists, psychiatrists, pharmacists, nurses, medical assistants, care coordinators, and administrative staff.

During the assessment experience, students assumed the care coordinator role (i.e., the Behavioral Health Services Coordinator). Students were instructed to behave professionally and respectfully as though their situation was "real." The student was responsible for "suspending disbelief" and acting as if the virtual environment was the actual environment.

What to Expect

How they did it

*   Students used HTC Vive Focus 3 VR headsets with controllers. The Vive Focus 3 is a stand-alone VR headset delivering best-in-class graphics and ergonomic comfort.

What students saw

1. First, students were introduced to their client's character delivered through an opening monologue by the care coordinator (see Figure 1).

Figure 1. Tyson Canty's opening dialogue

2. Then, students found themselves in the care coordinator's office.

    1. They saw a desktop phone with a virtual display to show who was calling or whom they might call (see Figure 2). On the phone, there was a pick-up and hang-up button (green and red buttons, respectively).

Figure 2. Desktop phone

2. They saw a tablet where they could access client information (see Figure 3). The tablet was mounted to a stationary base and had a touch screen where they could make selections and perform actions throughout the scenario (see Figure 4).

Figure 3. Tablet display

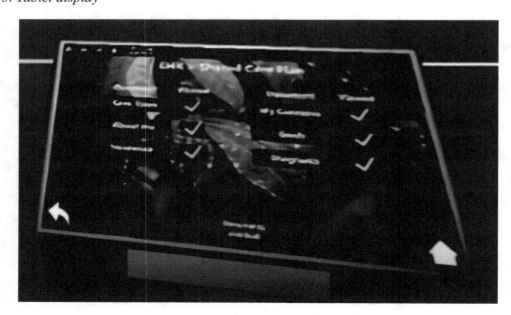

Figure 4. Tablet instructions

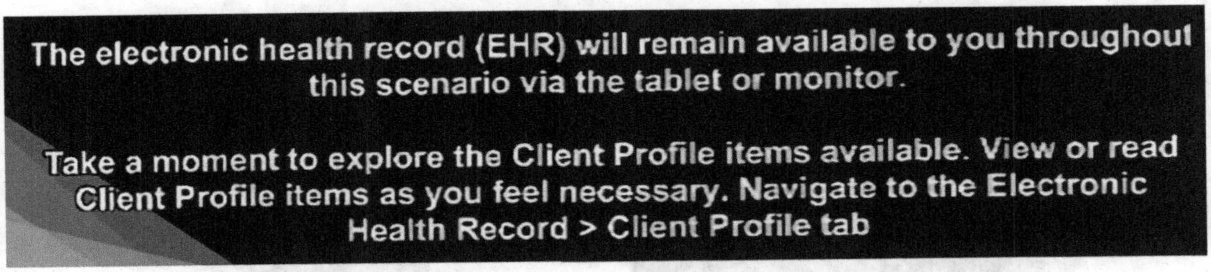

The electronic health record (EHR) will remain available to you throughout this scenario via the tablet or monitor.

Take a moment to explore the Client Profile items available. View or read Client Profile items as you feel necessary. Navigate to the Electronic Health Record > Client Profile tab

3.   They also saw a desktop, keyboard, and mouse in the office with a display screen to complete documentation.

    3.   Next, students were transported to a conference room where client care conferences happened. Again, the client, designated family member, and care coordinator were present.

        1.   The care coordinator and other staff could share a tablet in the room. The tablet remained available throughout the scenario (see Figure 5).

Figure 5. Tyson Canty is sitting with the care coordinator and a family member

2.   A Smart TV was available for video meetings throughout the scenario (see Figure 6).

Figure 6. Smart TV

4. Following interactions in the meeting room, students returned to the care coordinator's office for the remainder of the scenario. The phone and tablet remained available to them during this time.
    What students heard
5. Students heard different characters speaking to them and other characters over phone conversations during the scenarios. Audio displays could be turned on or off at any time during the scenario.
    What students did
6. Performing actions:
    1. Students moved virtually within their office space and conference room.
    2. Students touched buttons on the virtual tablet and phone to:
        -   Respond to emails
        -   Display available resources for the client and family
        -   Select options to complete messages and documentation
        -   Send secure messages to the client or other members of the care team
        -   Provide the client with educational materials like brochures or electronic links
        -   Read and review the client's Electronic Health Record (EHR) and other documents available within the client's medical record
    3. Students touched buttons and icons on the phone in the office space to call other care team members.
7. Responding to questions:
    1. Students were presented with multiple questions while in the virtual environment. They were instructed to read each question carefully before choosing the answer(s) (see Figure 7).

Figure 7. Assessment questions with response options

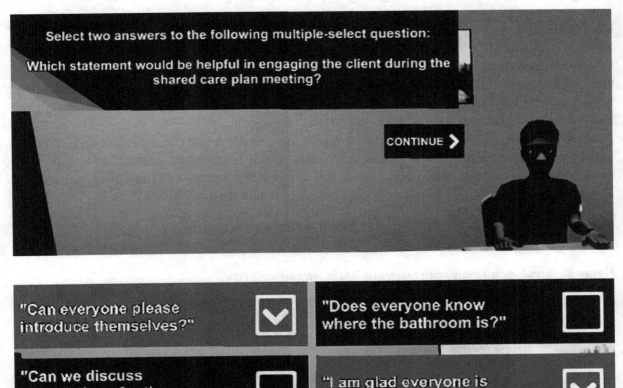

2. Incorrect answers used branching logic to take the student down an errant pathway. However, students could always self-correct and branch back to the correct path depending on subsequent responses. The branching logic impacted students' scores (described later in the *Measurement Considerations* section of this chapter).

DESIGN CONSIDERATIONS

The BHCC scenarios were written and developed to serve as a realistic, content-appropriate, diverse, immersive VR experience. The *scenario-based context-dependent item set* is one of several effective ways to measure complex thinking, such as that required in a VR environment. The term *context-dependent* refers to the idea that while competencies and skills may be similar across job roles (e.g., most require effective communication skills), the scenarios and critical action steps needed to demonstrate those skills differ based on the context of the situation.

Design Consideration 1: Designing the Scenarios

First, SMEs fully understood WGUs definition for each of the competencies and skills related to the BHCC role. Next, SMEs drew from their professional wisdom and personal experiences to craft scenario-based items that effectively measured the associated skill within a particular competency. In doing so, they prepared scenario-based actions that were insightfully grounded in specific content. Finally, they were designed to elicit specific cognitive behavior types, frequently challenging respondents to engage in higher-level cognitive processes above and beyond mere recall.

Each of the three scenarios was designed to take at most 30 minutes to complete, and students could take a break between each scenario. Scenario A consisted of 30 assessment questions and actions, Scenario B consisted of 42 questions and actions, and Scenario C consisted of 17 questions and actions. This allowed for a total of 89 measurement opportunities within the assessment.

Scenario A: Adult Male with Dementia of the Alzheimer's type

Figure 8. David: Adult male with Dementia of the Alzheimer's type

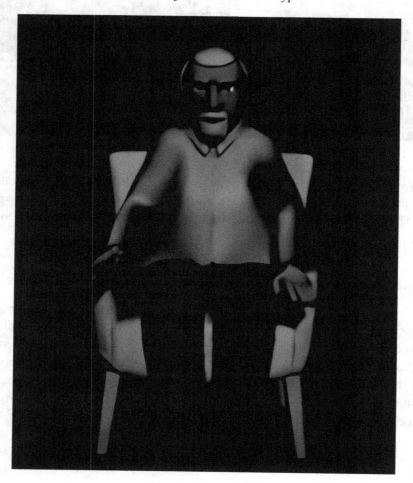

David, the client, was diagnosed with Dementia of the Alzheimer's type at age 57 (see Figure 8). He has received two years of outpatient services as a Long Branch Health Services client. David is currently under the care of Dr. Edward Ruiz for treatment of his condition. David has been prescribed PRN Ativan (2.5 mg) to address agitation and Donepezil (Aricept) 5mg daily to address symptoms of Dementia, including confusion, memory, and awareness. Unfortunately, David's condition is worsening, and it is growing more difficult to manage him at home as he is wandering and increasingly agitated.

Scenario B: Adolescent in Foster Care Diagnosed with ODD, ADHD, and Abuse Trauma

Figure 9. Tyson Canty: Adolescent in foster care

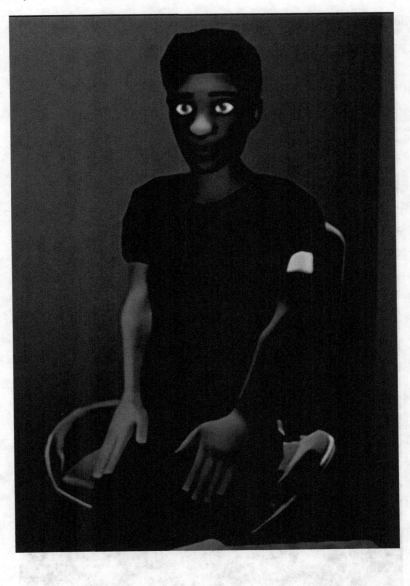

Tyson Canty is a 17-year-old client at the South Bay residential youth treatment center (see Figure 9). Tyson was placed in the center by the state foster care system and has been in their care since he was 12. Tyson will be aging out of care in 90 days and needs assistance in care planning. Tyson had a history of trauma due to physical and sexual abuse and was removed from his mother's care at age 12. Tyson enjoys music and likes writing rap lyrics. He verbalizes his needs and wants to others and advocates for himself. Tyson can resist others' feedback at times but will usually be more receptive when given time to process the information. He displays good social skills when he tries. Tyson takes pride in his appearance and likes to dress well. Tyson is physically healthy and wants to be physically active with basketball and dance activities.

Scenario C: Adult Female with Depression, Anxiety, and Suicidal Ideations

Figure 10. Candace: Adult female with depression, anxiety, and suicidal ideations

Candace is a 36-year-old white female receiving outpatient services at the Springbrook Community Mental Health Center (see Figure 10). Candace has attended weekly outpatient client therapy with her counselor (Sam Holiday, MSW) and monthly medication management meetings with Dr. Ernest Young for the past two years. Candace is diagnosed with Major Depressive Disorder and Generalized Anxiety Disorder. Candace reports experiencing constant sadness and a loss of interest in things that once made her happy. For example, Candace has been an avid swimmer and runner for many years but has lost interest in these activities. In addition, Candace has a history of self-harming behaviors. Candace identifies as a lesbian and is in a long-term relationship. Candace is also a victim of childhood trauma due to sexual abuse.

Design Consideration 2: Keep it Simple

Designing in VR environments relies heavily on using space, objects, and materials. While the temptation is to use all the features that technology offers, best practice design principles always apply, and no one should need an engineering degree to figure things out. When viewed in this context, we have now encountered the fundamental principles of designing for people; provide a good conceptual model and make things visible and easy to use. Individuals form conceptual models through their natural interactions with the world, their experiences, training, and instructions. When designing everyday things, for example, a good conceptual model allows designers to predict the effects of the users' actions on the object. The term *affordance* refers to an object's perceived and actual properties, primarily those fundamental properties that determine an object's use. For example, buttons are for pushing, and levers are for pulling. The same is true when designing in VR environments; the design fails when it needs to be more obvious and straightforward. For example, highlighting the tablet as students hover over it indicates that the Electronic Health Record (EHR) is available to the care coordinator (see Figure 11).

Figure 11. Highlighted HER

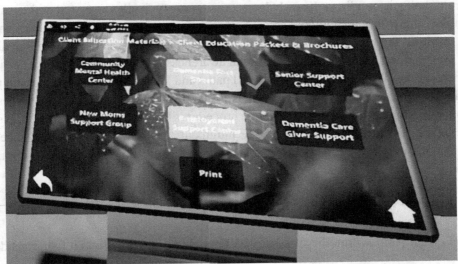

In its simplest form, a device is easy to use when the controls and displays exploit natural mappings. When there is visibility to the set of possible actions, the user anticipates those actions. *Mapping* is a technical term meaning the relationship between two things, in this case, between the controls in the VR space and the object's movements. Natural mappings lead to immediate understanding, just like we encounter daily as we interact in the real world. For example, in a VR environment, to move an object up, move the hand controller up. Likewise, looking away from someone speaking indicates that the person should stop talking. The same is true in VR environments. Therefore, the best user-centered design philosophy is to think from the user's point of view. Assume that every possible mishap will happen and protect against it. For a thoughtful narrative on the *Psychology of Designing Everyday Things*, the interested reader is referred to Norman, 2021.

Design Consideration 3: Developing Errant Paths

Since the early 2000s, there have been attempts to evaluate various aspects of human performance using simulation technology. However, most of these studies focused on the cognitive, perceptual, and motor performance of end-users and paid little attention to simulation fidelity and its relationship to errant paths; that is, the look, feel, and functionality of a computer simulation and how end-users navigate within the simulation environment (Nash, Edwards, Thompson, & Barfield, 2000). Errant paths lead end-users further from a correct response in a computer simulation (Gyll, 2019). There are two types of errant paths: inconclusive and conclusive.

1. Inconclusive (or dead-end) paths allow users to look for or *fish* options but do not provide an opportunity to perform a given task.
2. Conclusive errant paths allow users to navigate options, perform tasks, and see results; however, those results will be incorrect.

Developing errant paths involves understanding navigational awareness and how learners acquire knowledge from their surroundings. Knowledge acquisition is typically measured at the task level (i.e., what the user is doing within a simulated environment) by assessing speed and accuracy in participant response. As a rule of thumb, as knowledge increases, speed and accuracy in responding also increase (Fitts, 1964). One method for assessing navigational awareness is click-stream analysis, which analyzes end-user response patterns from frequently traveled paths and locations to which the participant repeatedly returned. However, since click-stream analysis is an ad-hoc approach that often proves costly and time-consuming, techniques that utilize qualitative procedures like Training Situation Analysis (TSA) or SME judgments are often used. We used the SME judgment approach for this project since it has been proven experientially reliable and time-saving. Those interested in a more thorough description of other methods should refer to Gyll, 2019.

Number of Errant Paths

The number of errant paths within the summative VR assessment was based on four considerations:

1. The level of difficulty of the task
2. The complexity of the functionality required to perform the task

3. The number of steps required to complete the task correctly
4. The complexity of the application itself

The total number of errant paths differed for each scenario. Likewise, the number of inconclusive and conclusive paths within each scenario varied and depended on the type of critical action performed. Sometimes an incorrect response triggered an errant path in the VR simulation, but only sometimes. For example, Scenario A contained five errant paths, Scenario B had four, and Scenario C contained three. Suppose an incorrect response triggered an errant path. In that case, the simulation might have branched the student back to the same question depending on how they performed within the errant path, allowing them to *self-correct* and answer the question again. This self-correcting behavior often occurs in everyday decision-making, especially in a clinical setting after healthcare coordinators have time to consider alternative courses of action. If this was the case, students did not receive the total allowable number of points for their second attempt on the question.

Design Consideration 4: The Uncanny Valley

The Japanese roboticist Masahiro Mori coined the term *Uncanny Valley* (UV) in 1970 (Sudarshan, 2018). As a machine (toy robot or virtual character) acquires more remarkable similarities to a human, it becomes more emotionally appealing to the observer. However, when it becomes disconcertingly close to a human, there is an extreme drop in believability and comfort before finally achieving full humanity and eliciting positive reactions; this is the UV depicted in grayscale in Figure 12 below. The goal of VR design is to avoid the Uncanny Valley.

Figure 12. The uncanny valley

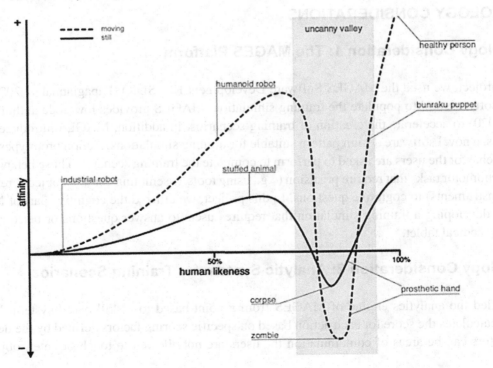

147

Example 1. The Uncanny Valley: Peculiar

"The Polar Express" by Sony Dreamworks was a landmark computer-animation movie that used living characters with full-motion capture techniques for body animations and facial expressions. Oscar-winning actor Tom Hanks represented a human-like virtual character called the Conductor, who was intended to be perceived as a good-humored character and appeal to a younger audience. "Despite these characters' friendly smiles, which appeared on billboard advertisements and a humorous film narrative, attempts to establish a rapport with the audience was lost as soon as most characters moved onscreen. The Conductor's motion was described as puppet-like, and the audience was critical of a lack of human-likeness in his facial expressions that did not match the expressive qualities of his speech. The characters' expressions also appeared out of context with a given situation as he presented an angry expression and a cold personality when interacting with other children characters in the film" (Tinwell, 2014, p. 12).

Example 2. The Uncanny Valley: Exemplar

Pixar's "Up" immediately shattered the stereotype of computer-animated movies being strictly for children. Among other qualities, Up's common acclaim lies in the film's first minutes, showing young Carl Fredricksen's fascination with exploration and his meeting a girl, Ellie, leading into a four-minute montage presenting the pair's shared life, famously named "Married Life." The most noticeable quality of this sequence is its ability to tell a self-contained story that spans nearly 60 years without ever using one line of dialogue or anthropomorphic or realistic computer graphic characters. Instead, it utilizes music and visuals to tell its narrative, almost like a short film in the silent era of animation, but with much more poetry than cartoons of that time were known to have (Taylor, 2014).

TECHNOLOGY CONSIDERATIONS

Technology Consideration 1: The MAGES Platform

For this project, we used the MAGES Software Development Kit (SDK) (Papagiannakis, 2020) as the primary software tool to populate the training simulation; MAGES provides low-code authoring tools (Zikas, 2020) to accelerate the creation of training scenarios. In addition, MAGES introduces Action Prototypes, a novel software design pattern suitable for training simulations. Action prototypes define a specific behavior the users are asked to perform to complete the training scenario. Those behaviors vary from psychomotor tasks that require precision (e.g., using tools, assembling complex objects, removal of medical instruments) to cognitive questions. In this project, we utilized the cognitive part of MAGES, including developing a training simulation that requires users to answer questions or perform simple tasks on a medical tablet.

Technology Consideration 2: Analytic System for Training Scenarios

We modified the analytics engine of MAGES from a point-based to a skill-based system. Natively, MAGES calculates the score for each action based on specific scoring factors defined by the developer. Those factors can be areas of contamination the users are not allowed to touch or enter, objects that should be handled with care, or even wrong decisions made by the user. Typically, each action is given a score out of 100 points depending on which scoring actions they performed.

However, in this case, we followed a different approach. Users were not scored per action; instead, we gave them a total competency score across different skills. For this reason, we modified our analytic system to support this competency-based approach. We grouped actions into skills and defined the minimum requirements to earn competency for the total assessment. At the end of the training scenario, a detailed coaching report was presented to the user, summarizing their scores for each competency.

Technology Consideration 3: From Virtual Reality to Desktop Application

From the beginning of the project, we designed the application to fit well both in VR and desktop environments. Since we used MAGES SDK - a platform-agnostic tool - it was straightforward to export the application to both VR and desktop versions. In addition, we made certain design choices to fit both platforms well, thus avoiding unnecessary discrepancies between the versions. For example, the questions users see can be answered with the VR controllers and the computer mouse. The same applies to the medical tablet, as users can easily navigate the medical records on both platforms.

Additionally, both user interface (UI) platforms were configured in *world space*. In desktop applications, UIs are typically projected in *screen space*, which is more easily accessible. However, this would have created a significant technical debt as the two versions would require different handling interactions. For this reason, all the interfaces were projected in *world space* as 3D objects and were accessed with the computer mouse or the VR controllers.

In the desktop version, users navigated to various points of interest by controlling camera angles, for example, zooming in on the tablet or moving to different characters in the scenario. To accomplish this, we implemented an easy-to-use system with clickable buttons to navigate these various points. The initial solution was done with a free-to-move camera but proved difficult and confusing during beta tests. As a result, we focused on a static camera that utilized a point-and-click approach.

MEASUREMENT CONSIDERATIONS

The VR assessment was different from a typical assessment project at WGU. There were no *items* in the traditional sense, no *forms* to build; there were no items in the bank. In scoring the VR assessment, the number of points possible for each branching scenario (i.e., errant path) varied depending on the number of independent tasks, or critical actions, within the branch. A critical action represented any "measurement opportunity" within the assessment and was akin to a test *item*. For example, a single branching scenario may have contained two or more critical actions within the scenario. For example, a student may be required to respond to a multiple-choice question and spend a minimum amount of time reviewing the Electronic Health Record (EHR) to earn points. Each critical action was then scored against the result of a set of scenarios within the branch.

Measurement Consideration 1: Conducting the Job (Task) Analysis

The purpose of many higher education programs (e.g., credentialing, licensure, certification, selection) is to assure that individuals who practice an occupation or profession have met specific standards (AERA,

2014) by accurately measuring the knowledge, skills, and abilities (KSAs) applied on the job. Meeting or exceeding those standards generally indicates that an individual is qualified to practice a particular occupation or profession. Rationales for maintaining such standards within any assessment program are the following:

1. Assist in identifying individuals with minimum KSA to perform essential job tasks.
2. Assist in maintaining a minimum standard of related skills and competencies over time.
3. Provide decision outcomes – consequential validity - for candidates desiring placement, promotion, and advancement.

To ensure the consequential validity of WGU programs, we engage in JTA studies to empirically document and demonstrate the link between KSAs tested by our assessment products and the activities performed by effective practitioners.

Job (task) analysis is any systematic procedure for collecting and analyzing job-related information to meet a particular purpose (Harvey, 1991):

The collection of data describing (a) observable (or otherwise verifiable) job behaviors performed by workers, including both what is accomplished as well as what knowledge, skills, and abilities are employed to accomplish the results, and (b) verifiable characteristics of the job environment with which workers interact, including physical, attitudinal, social, and informational elements.

Job analysis requires information from knowledgeable individuals, including practitioners, supervisors, managers, educators, and even professional job analysts; a well-conducted JTA helps support program validity by ensuring that critical aspects of the job become the content domain of the assessment.

Task Inventory

The task inventory is the most common method for collecting and analyzing job-related information. A task inventory consists of a list of activities (e.g., topics, domains, competencies, or skills) considered relevant to a profession. First, an initial checklist is developed based on research, direct observation, interviews, job descriptions, and other sources of information. The task statements are then formatted into a questionnaire and rated in terms of specific attributes such as frequency, importance, time spent on a task, or difficulty. Finally, the results are used to identify the KSAs of the job that the test's content and competencies measure.

Scales for Measuring and Describing the JTA

One goal in scaling tasks and KSAs is to arrive at a standard metric – a scale with constant meaning across tasks, people, and positions. Unfortunately, relative scales like "less often than other tasks" generally do not permit inferences across samples of people who may perform different subsets of tasks or across different positions. If possible, rating scales should elicit absolute measurements about tasks or KSAs, e.g., not at all, monthly, weekly, and daily has objective meaning.

Most JTA studies include two or three scales, and the most common rating scales are those that address importance or criticality, difficulty, and time on task:

- Frequency/Performance - How often do you perform this task?
- Importance - How significant is this task in your practice?
- Criticality - What would be the consequences of performing this task incorrectly or not at all?
- Difficulty - How difficult or complex is it to perform or learn this task?

When multiple scales are used, combining various ratings into a single index of overall importance for each task is standard practice. In fact, assessment efforts should focus on tasks that are actually performed, and tasks performed more often or for more significant periods should receive more emphasis on the assessment. An effective assessment must have utility to the essential and frequently performed aspects of the job domain and not support job functions that are unimportant or infrequently performed. Emphasis on such tasks wastes time and resources, as illustrated below in Figure 13. Appendix B shows the steps involved in rating the JTA.

Figure 13. Importance/Frequency analysis

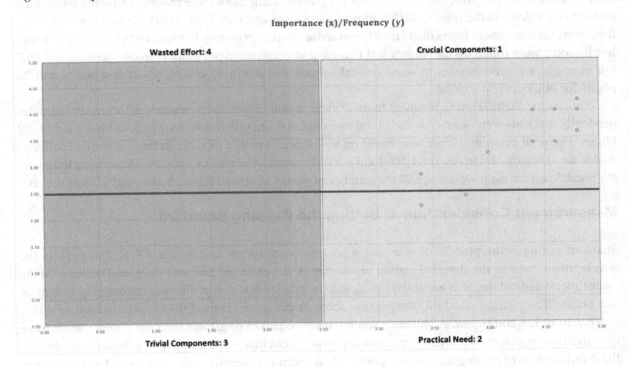

Measurement Consideration 2: Assembling the Test Blueprint

After the job/task analysis, the next step in developing the VR simulation was to create detailed test specifications. Test specifications usually include a test description component and a test blueprint component. The test description specifies aspects of the planned assessment, such as its purpose, the target audience, and the overall length. The test blueprint, sometimes called the table of specifications, lists the major content areas and cognitive levels intended to be included in each assessment form. It also provides for the number of items each assessment form should consist of within these content and cognitive areas.

Measurement Consideration 3: Scoring the Assessment

All critical actions represented a weighted composite, or partial credit score, achieved by awarding different points for correct answers to actions with multiple steps or right answers. The usual motive for partial credit scoring is the hope that it will lead to a more precise estimate of a person's ability than a simple pass/fail score. A desirable quality of measurement scales is variability. If a scale fails to discriminate differences in the underlying trait, its correlations with other measures will be restricted and its utility limited. The total number of possible points varies in polytomous (partial credit) scoring. Each item is scored against the end result of a set of independent tasks within the item, i.e., items are scored using more than two response categories. Polytomously scored items represent a weighted composite (i.e., partial-credit score), achieved by awarding differing point values for correct answers to test items with multiple steps or correct answers. Under the partial credit model, the number of points into which an item is divided and the relative difficulties of these steps can vary from item to item. However, since there were no assessment items in the traditional sense, there was no way to break out scores at the "item" level; scores were rolled up into States and Phases, and each contained more than one "critical action." For example, a correct answer to some critical actions was worth 12 points, whereas it was worth 20 points for other critical actions.

While some States/Phases involved more critical actions than others because all were scored independently, students were scored on their total assessment score rather than on a pass/fail basis per State/Phase. The total examinee score was based on a weighted average of the number of "critical actions" within the assessment. There were 1,500 total possible points. Appendix C displays the scoring template, the breakdown for each scenario, and the number of points allocated for each skill and critical action.

Measurement Consideration 4: Setting the Passing Standard

Standard setting is the process of selecting a passing score for an assessment. Of all the steps in the development process, the standard-setting phase may be the one most like art rather than science. At the same time, statistical methods are always used, and the process is also significantly impacted by judgment and policy. The passing standard (the passing score or cut score) is used to classify students as either competent or not competent. A student's score must be equal to or greater than the passing score to be classified as competent. While many methodologies are in circulation for competency-based assessments, the determination of passing standards is premised on a blend of objective and criterion-related measures. The goal is to ensure that students who graduate from a degree program have met specific standards by accurately measuring the KSAs taught throughout their study. In addition, meeting or exceeding those standards indicates that a student is qualified to practice a particular occupation or profession. Passing standards are typically not shared or made public for test security reasons.

For the BHCC VR assessment, we used a two-stage process developed by WGU psychometricians. It is the same process used for all objective assessments at WGU. In Stage 1, a beta testing event established an initial or preliminary passing score. After that, the focus is on analyzing the statistical quality of the assessment items. Here, the focus was exclusively on a *practitioner* group representing the closest population to WGU students in the BHCC program.

This passing score was temporary and represented an estimate until student performance data could be collected and analyzed.

Next, the Stage 2 passing score was considered the real, permanent, final, or operational passing standard. The Stage 2 score replaced the Stage 1 passing score and represented a more informed standard based on having student data available on which to base the recommendation. The Stage 2 passing score stays in operation until circumstances indicate a revalidation of the passing standard. The setting of the Stage 2 cut score worked as follows:

Judges review the assessment and determine the following information regarding the assessment:

- Lowest acceptable percentage of failing candidates (minimum failure rate)
- Highest acceptable percentage of failing candidates (maximum failure rate)
- Lowest percent correct, which would allow someone to pass (minimum passing score)
- The highest percent correct required for someone to pass (maximum passing score)

The judges' ratings were combined with student data to make a final recommendation. The two-stage process uses as many data points as possible to inform the assessment's most defensible and appropriate passing score, thus ensuring student fairness. The process resulted in a psychometrically defendable score that is fair to students and palatable to the various stakeholder groups. Including empirical data when establishing passing scores follows psychometric best practice and is used nearly universally among testing programs.

Student Feedback

The assessment required students to make decisions and successfully navigate patient engagements in a dynamic, immersive clinical environment. Based on debriefing interviews, students told us they felt wholly immersed and enjoyed the novel, innovative experience. The VR assessment helped them feel like they were taking on the role of a care coordinator. However, using the VR headset seemed to elevate anxiety for some students already anxious about taking a high-stakes assessment. Getting them comfortable and confident is essential long before the assessment starts. For those unable to overcome their anxiety, offering an alternative like the desktop version was necessary.

DISCUSSION

Today, OCBHE programs' criticality in training the next generation's workforce has become a force in education now that employers focus on identifying, recruiting, and retaining employees with transferable skills. Particularly in times of economic challenge, employers need a skilled, adaptable, creative, and equipped workforce that can adapt to the global marketplace. As we work toward the development of alternatives to *practice hours* and challenge and reform outdated norms about *hours being the measure of competency*, new and innovative methods like VR simulations are demonstrating their utility as an alternative approach.

The primary objective of the VR assessment was to serve as a realistic, content-appropriate, and accurate immersive experience for students in the Behavioral Health Care Coordination program at Western Governor's University. The assessment required students to *demonstrate* and *apply* care delivery models to individuals and families through a care plan in various behavioral health care settings. The assessment method employed in the program was an essential factor in the validation process of a student's education. Research shows, for example, that strategies that are more innovative, flexible, and based on learning science practices contribute to higher and more flexible outcomes than traditional methods (Gyll & Hayes, in press). Since the framework and nature of OCBHE, and thus the current method, emphasizes competency in workplace skills and transference of learned competencies to the application of those skills, assessments that employ technology-based methods are particularly conducive to training students to develop KSAs necessary for job success. However, in current affairs, program developers are left to their own devices to determine which practices are most likely to be effective. This chapter provided some real-world examples for maintaining a set of standards when developing VR simulation assessments.

NEXT STEPS AND CONCLUSION

This chapter notes observations and recommendations that might illuminate current affairs and future possibilities. We tried to defer our conclusions until we had completed our chapter, but doubtless, our preformed opinions influenced our illustrative content. While it would be too strong to say that science is uniting a new assessment model, there is convergence in the essential attributes of a successful modality when technology and instructional methods meet. Which begs the question, what's next?

Today's economy values broad knowledge and skills, flexibility, cross-training, multi-tasking, teaming, problem-solving, and project-based work. Learning in an environment that optimizes and aligns explicit and implicit curricula is critical to achieving a new paradigm's desired outcome. Students need not just a degree; they need the ability to apply the knowledge and skills they have built earning that degree. Methods - like VR simulations - that are flexible, variable, and integrated create experiences that bear close proximity to the contexts in which the learning occurred. As a result, students are more engaged in the learning process, more immersed in the content, and better prepared to enter the workforce with the generalizable skills employers expect.

As discussed, much of the focus of conventional assessment methods has been on traditional practices, which are necessary but insufficient to demonstrate skill transfer. At a fundamental level, the term transfer refers to the influence of prior learning on later activity (Holding, 1991). Initial research began in the early 20th century, when Woodrow (1927) claimed, for example, that "improvement resulting from almost any sort of practice yields, as a rule, some transference" (p. 159). He suggested that *any* practice on a given task produces improvement (i.e., positive transfer) in several related functions. While a call to action is probably hyperbole, innovative institutions must position themselves to advance student achievement through – among other things – identifying and assessing high-performing students and their workforce readiness through a variety of learning mechanisms. Rationalization within the market will occur among institutions as they continue exploring enhanced technology solutions' effectiveness in training and graduating high-performing students. For more information about training and transfer, the interested reader is referred to the accompanying chapter, "Training for Better Transfer in an Online Competency-Based Higher Education Program," in this text. Until then, more research is needed!

REFERENCES

Ackerman, P. L., Kyllonen, P. C., & Roberts, R. D. (1999). *Learning and individual differences: Process, trait, and content determinants.* American Psychological Association. doi:10.1037/10315-000

Alexander, P. A., & Murphy, P. K. (1999). Learner profiles: Valuing individual differences within classroom communities. In *Learning and individual differences: Process, trait, and content determinants.* American Psychological Association. doi:10.1037/10315-018

American Educational Research Association, American Psychological Association, & National Council on Measurement in Education (Ed.). (2014). *Standards for educational and psychological testing.* American Educational Research Association.

Babini, M. H., Kulish, V. V., & Namazi, H. (2020). Physiological state and learning ability of students in normal and virtual reality conditions: Complexity-based analysis. *Journal of Medical Internet Research, 22*(6), 6. doi:10.2196/17945 PMID:32478661

Birrenbach, T., Zbinden, J., Papagiannakis, G., Exadaktylos, A. K., Müller, M., Hautz, W. E., & Sauter, T. C. (2021). Effectiveness and utility of virtual reality simulation as an educational tool for safe performance of COVID-19 diagnostics: Prospective, randomized pilot trial. *JMIR Serious Games, 9*(4), 4. doi:10.2196/29586 PMID:34623315

Fidelity Implementation Study Group Report. (1999). Simulation Interoperability Standards Organization. https://www.sisostds.org/ProductsPublications/ReferenceDocum ents.aspx

Fitts, P. M. (1964). Perceptual-motor skill learning. In A. W. Melton (Ed.), *Categories of Human Learning* (pp. 243–285). Academic. doi:10.1016/B978-1-4832-3145-7.50016-9

Ford, R., & Gopher, R. (2015). Competency-based education 101. *Procedia Manufacturing, 3,* 1473–1480. doi:10.1016/j.promfg.2015.07.325

Grantcharov, T. P. (2008). Is virtual reality simulation an effective training method in surgery? *Nature Clinical Practice. Gastroenterology & Hepatology, 5*(5), 5. doi:10.1038/ncpgasthep1101 PMID:18382434

Gyll, S. (2019). *Developing errant paths in a simulation testing environment: A how-to guide for assessment professionals.* Wiley. . doi:10.1002/cbe2.1198

Gyll, S., & Ragland, S. (2018). Improving the validity of objective assessment in higher education: Steps for building a best-in-class competency-based assessment program. *Journal of Competency-Based Education, 3*(1), 1. doi:10.1002/cbe2.1058

Gyll, S. P., & Hayes, H. (2021). Learning and individual differences in skilled competency-based performance: Using a course planning and learning tool as an indicator for student success. *The Journal of Competency-Based Education.* . doi:10.1002/cbe2.1259

Gyll, S. P., & Hayes, H. (2023). (in press). Training for better transfer in an online competency-based higher education program: Using enhanced technology-based instruction to improve assessment outcomes and student learning. *Journal of Applied Testing Technology.*

Harris, D. N., & Sass, T. R. (2008). *Teacher training, teacher quality, and student achievement*. Calder Center. https://www.caldercenter.org/PDF/1001059_Teacher_Training.pdf

Harvey, R. J. (1991). Job analysis. In M. Dunnette & L. Hough (Eds.), *Handbook of industrial and organizational psychology* (2nd ed., Vol. 2, pp. 71–163). Consulting Psychologists Press.

Holding, D. H. (1991). Transfer of training. In J. E. Morrison (Ed.), *Training for Performance: Principles of Applied Human Learning* (pp. 93–126). Wiley.

Hoogveld, A. M. (2003). The teacher as designer of competency-based education. Heerlen: Open University of the Netherlands.

Hooper, J., Tsiridis, E., Feng, J. E., Schwarzkopf, R., Waren, D., & Long, W. J. (2019). Virtual reality simulation facilitates resident training in total hip arthroplasty: A randomized controlled trial. *Arthroplasty, 34*, 10. PMID:31056442

Jonassen, D. H., Tessmer, M., & Hannum, W. H. (1989). Training situation analysis. In *Handbook of Task Analysis Procedures*. Praeger Publishers.

Keshav, V. (2017). *Tech Nanotechnology, Central University of Jharkhand*. Quora. https://www.quora.com/What-is-the-difference-between-virtual-reality-and-simulated-reality

Khan, R., Plahouras, J., Johnston, B. C., Scaffidi, M. A., Grover, S. C., & Walsh, C. M. (2019). Virtual reality simulation training in endoscopy: A Cochrane Review and meta-analysis. *Endoscopy, 51*(07), 653–664. doi:10.1055/a-0894-4400 PMID:31071757

Kyaw, B. M., Saxena, N., Posadzki, P., Vseteckova, J., Nikolaou, C. K., George, P. P., Divakar, U., Masiello, I., Kononowicz, A. A., Zary, N., & Tudor Car, L. (2019). Virtual reality for health professions education: Systematic review and meta-analysis by the Digital Health Education Collaboration. *Journal of Medical Internet Research, 21*(1), 1. doi:10.2196/12959 PMID:30668519

McClarty, K. L., & Gaertner, M. N. (2015). *Measuring Mastery: Best Practices for Assessment in Competency-Based Education*. AE Series on Competency-Based Higher Education.

Merrill, D. (2002). A pebble-in-the-pond model for instructional design. *Performance Improvement, 41*(7), 41–46. doi:10.1002/pfi.4140410709

Mori, M. (1970). The uncanny valley. *Energy*, 33–35.

Nash, E. B., Edwards, G. W., Thompson, J. A., & Barfield, W. (2000). A Review of Presence and Performance in Virtual Environments. *International Journal of Human-Computer Interaction, 12*(1), 1–41. doi:10.1207/S15327590IJHC1201_1

Norman, D. A. (2021). *The design of everyday things*. Basic Books.

Pantelidis, P., Chorti, A., Papagiouvanni, I., Paparoidamis, G., Drosos, C., & Panagiotakopoulos, T. (2017). Virtual and augmented reality in medical education. In Medical and surgical education - past, present, and future (pp. 77–97). IntechOpen.

Papagiannakis, G., Zikas, P., Lydatakis, N., Kateros, S., Kentros, M., Geronikolakis, E., Kamarianakis, M., Kartsonaki, I., & Evangelou, G. (2020). MAGES 3.0: Tying the knot of medical VR. In ACM SIG-GRAPH 2020 Immersive Pavilion (pp. 1-2). ACM.

Pensieri, C., & Pennacchini, M. (2014). Overview: Virtual reality in medicine. *Journal of Virtual Worlds Research*, *7*(1), 1. doi:10.4101/jvwr.v7i1.6364

Penuel, B., & Roschell, J. (1999). *Designing Learning: Cognitive Science Principles for the Innovative Organization* (Tech. No. 10099). . doi:10.13140/RG.2.2.11692.97920

Schumacher, D. J., Englander, R., & Carraccio, C. (2013). Developing the master learner: Applying learning theory to the learner, the teacher, and the learning environment. *Academic Medicine*, *88*(11), 1635–1645. doi:10.1097/ACM.0b013e3182a6e8f8 PMID:24072107

Sudarshan, A. (2018, December 22). 'Half gods' review: The book as machine. *The Hindu*. https://www.thehindu.com/books/half-gods-the-book-as-machine/article25796704.ece

Taylor, B. (2014). How the 'Married Life' Opener Elevates 'Up' to Animation's Greatest Heights. *Rotoscopers*. https://www.rotoscopers.com/2014/05/06/how-the-married-life-opener-elevates-up-to-animations-greatest-heights/

Tinwell, A. (2014). *The Uncanny Valley in Games and Animation*. Taylor & Francis. doi:10.1201/b17830

Van Merrienboer, J. G., & Kirschner, P. (2013). *Ten Steps to Complex Learning*. Routledge.

Woodrow, H. (1927). The effect of type of training upon transference. *Journal of Educational Psychology*, *18*(3), 159–172. doi:10.1037/h0071868

Zikas, P., Kamarianakis, M., Kartsonaki, I., Lydatakis, N., Kateros, S., Kentros, M., Geronikolakis, E., Evangelou, G., Catilo, P. A., & Papagiannakis, G. (2021). Covid-19 VR Strikes Back: Innovative medical VR training. In *ACM SIGGRAPH 2021 Immersive Pavilion (SIGGRAPH' 21)* (p. 202). Association for Computing Machinery. doi:10.1145/3450615.3464546

Zikas, P., Papagiannakis, G., Lydatakis, N., Kateros, S., Ntoa, S., Adami, I., & Stephanidis, C. (2020). Immersive visual scripting based on VR software design patterns for experiential training. *The Visual Computer*, *36*(10-12), 1965–1977. doi:10.100700371-020-01919-0

ENDNOTE

[1]   Note: Separate VR assessments were developed for both programs. This chapter focuses on the Behavioral Health Care Coordination VR assessment.

APPENDIX A: CARE FOR INDIVIDUALS AND FAMILIES COMPETENCIES AND SKILLS

Table 1. Care for individuals and families competencies and skills

Competency Identifier	Competency	Skill	Course Unit
7070.6.1 (Scenario A) (Scenario B)	Competency 1: Models of Care Delivery: The learner applies care delivery models to navigate individuals and families through a care plan in various healthcare settings.	995 Care Delivery Models: The learner collaborates with the interdisciplinary team to determine an appropriate care model. 420 Care Planning: The learner applies comprehensive patient, and family-centered care plans to improve access and health care outcomes. 4034.1 Care Planning: The learner determines if additional resources or potential partners are needed to meet a patient's health needs.	Unit 1
7070.6.2 (Scenario A) (Scenario C)	Competency 2: Helping Individuals and Families Meet Healthcare Goals: The learner implements care plans to support individuals and families in meeting their healthcare goals.	376 Care Planning: The learner applies a comprehensive patient and family-centered care plan. 2213 Care Planning: The learner determines barriers to care and non-compliance. 3852 Care Planning: The learner identifies resources and strategic partners to meet a patient's health care needs.	Unit 2
7070.6.3 (Scenario B)	Competency 3: Prevention Practices: The learner selects prevention practices to educate the individual and family and support their health care goals.	2313 Risk Analysis: The learner determines which prevention practices are most appropriate to implement based on patient risk assessment. 2817 Health Education: The learner educates patients on their condition and treatment plans.	Unit 3
7070.6.4 (Scenario A) (Scenario B) (Scenario C)	Competency 4: Intervention Strategies: The learner applies intervention strategies to meet the health care needs of the individual and family.	564 Health Intervention: The learner applies the appropriate intervention(s) for a patient, given the population the patient belongs to. 3661 Health Intervention: The learner identifies appropriate interventions that promote client-centered care.	Unit 4
7070.6.5 (Scenario A) (Scenario B) (Scenario C)	Competency 5: Shared Decision-Making: The learner executes shared decision-making strategies to support individuals and families in meeting their healthcare goals.	5345 Decision Making: The learner creates models to engage and motivate clients and families toward shared decision-making.	Unit 5

APPENDIX B: JTA STEPS

Process for JTA Ratings

Structuring the JTA is one means by which SMEs facilitate valid assessment development. Therefore, it was expected that basic JTA guidelines and a shared collaboration with other SMEs and WGU facilitators would enhance SME effectiveness in developing the JTA. During the JTA study, SMEs were asked to imagine an individual they would consider competent regarding the definition described in the JTA guidelines and the collection of competencies and skills defined in the JTA Task Inventory. Then, couch the attributes of the individual they have imagined in their experience working with and managing effective healthcare coordinators.

For Each Competency

1.   Assign the percentage of content that the assessment should represent. The total for all *Competencies* must sum to 100%.

   For Each Skill

2.   Rate the level of *Importance* (0-5):
   5.   **Extremely important.** Use this rating for the tasks that are essential for successful job performance. Such a task must be completed and performed correctly to have a satisfactory outcome.
      4.   **Very important.** Use this rating for tasks that are important for the successful completion of the work. These tasks receive higher priority than other tasks but are not the most important tasks.
3.   **Moderately important.** Use this rating for tasks of average importance relative to other tasks but have yet to be given high priority.
      2.   **Some importance.** Use this rating for tasks that have some importance but generally are given low priority.
         1.   **Little importance.** Use this rating for tasks that have very little importance about the successful completion of the job
   0 - Do not perform. Use this rating for tasks you do not perform.
      3.   Rate how *often* an individual would use the skills represented within each competency (0 - 5).
         5.   **More than once a day.** Use this rating for tasks you perform most frequently. On most days, you perform these tasks more than once.
      4.   **Once a day.** Use this rating for tasks you usually perform every day.
         3.   **Once a week.** Use this rating for tasks you perform several times a month, usually weekly but not daily.
   2.   **Once a month.** Use this rating for tasks you usually perform once or at least every other month, but not every week.
   1.   **A few times a year or less.** Use this rating for tasks performed less frequently than every other task. For example, you may perform these tasks a few times a year (up to 6) or even less.
   0 - Do not perform. Use this rating for tasks you do not perform.

APPENDIX C: SCORING TEMPLATE

Figure 14.

Competency	Skill	Scenario A Unique Critical Action Items	Scenario B Unique Critical Action Items	Scenario C Unique Critical Action Items	Total Unique Critical Actions for All Scenarios	Calculated Weighted Percentage (from Blueprint)	Suggested Points Allotment for Skill Based on Weighted Percentage (out of 1500)	Suggested Points Allotment for Each Unique Critical Action Opportunity	Unique Skill Identifier
Competency 1: Models of Care Delivery: The learner applies care delivery models to navigate individuals and families through a care plan in a variety of healthcare settings. Note: This is talking about ACOs, Medical Homes, Care delivery models -Staff models (HMO), ACO, PCMH- Patient Centered Medical Homes (primary Phys supported as lead role providing care), Open systems (PPO), (most care to least care)	995 Care Delivery Models: The learner collaborates with the interdisciplinary team to determine an appropriate care model.	2			2	0.039	59	29	7070.6.1.1.995
	420 Care Planning: The learner applies comprehensive patient and family-centered care plans to improve access and healthcare outcomes.	7			7	0.078	117	17	7070.6.1.2.420
	4034.1 Care Planning: The learner determines if additional resources or potential partners are needed to meet a patient's health needs.	8	5	4	17	0.0878	132	8	7070.6.1.3.4034.1
Competency 2: Helping Individuals and Families Meet Healthcare Goals: The learner implements care plans to support individuals and families in meeting their healthcare goals.	376 Care Planning: The learner applies a comprehensive patient and family-centered care plan.		11		11	0.0732	110	10	7070.6.2.1.376
	2213 Care Planning: The learner determines barriers to care and non-compliance.		11		11	0.0976	146	13	7070.6.2.2.2213
	3852 Care Planning: The learner identifies resources and strategic partners to meet a patient's healthcare needs.		5		5	0.1171	176	35	7070.6.2.3.3852
Competency 3: Prevention Practices: The learner selects prevention practices to educate the individual and family and support their health care goals.	2313 Risk Analysis: The learner determines which prevention practices are most appropriate to implement based on patient risk assessment.			8	8	0.0878	132	16	7070.6.3.1.2313
	2817 Health Education: The learner educates patients on their condition and treatment plans.			3	3	0.1171	176	59	7070.6.3.2.2817
Competency 4: Intervention Strategies: The learner applies intervention strategies to meet the healthcare needs of the individual and family.	564 Health Intervention: The learner applies the appropriate intervention(s) for a patient given the populations the patient belong to.		5		5	0.0878	132	26	7070.6.4.1.564
	3661 Health Intervention: The learner identifies appropriate interventions that promote client-centered care.		4	2	6	0.0976	146	24	7070.6.4.2.3661
Competency 5: Shared Decision-Making: The learner executes shared decision-making strategies to support individuals and families in meeting their healthcare goals.	5345 Decision Making: The learner creates models to engage and motivate clients and families toward shared decision making.	13	1		14	0.1171	176	13	7070.6.5.1.5345
Totals		30	42	17	89	1.00	1500	250	
Ideal Score		401	712	387					

Course Description: Care for Individuals and Families focuses on the education of individuals and families with multifaceted healthcare needs. The course examines how the care coordinator identifies prevention practices and applies intervention strategies created through shared decision making to support individuals and families in meeting the patient's healthcare goals. There are no prerequisites for this course.

Section 3
Technology and Innovation in Education

Chapter 9
Assessing (Educational) Technology:
Separating the Context–Rich Learning Applications From the Mere Spectacle

Zia Nizami
Independent Researcher, USA

Megan Hudgins
Southern Illinois University, Edwardsville, USA

Nate Fisher
University of Idaho, USA

ABSTRACT

The role of technology in education has become salient due to the COVID-19 pandemic. As in-person instruction halted to mitigate the spread of the virus, online classes helped students continue their education. While the benefits of technology in education are clear, is it possible that institutions have gone too far? The dominant forms of new media and technology—radio, television, video cassette recorders, and more recently, the internet—have all been heralded as great boons to pedagogy. Have students and educators benefited from these advances in technology? Why do students from lower socioeconomic groups continue to fail out of the system? Will nascent technologies like virtual and augmented reality change the future of education?

DOI: 10.4018/978-1-6684-7644-4.ch009

INTRODUCTION

The rapid shift to remote and digital learning, triggered by the COVID-19 pandemic, sparked an unprecedented adoption of educational technology. This adoption frenzy, often driven by the necessity to maintain educational continuity, led to a proliferation of video and interactive websites in educational settings. However, the hurried implementation of these technologies has exposed several challenges and has not always translated into meaningful learning experiences. This article delves into the potential pitfalls and prospects of educational technology, with a specific focus on context-rich learning applications and the need to differentiate them from mere spectacles.

The current research highlights the shortcomings in the implementation of video and new media in education. Often, these tools are deployed without a clear understanding of their pedagogical value, resulting in superficial engagement and limited learning gains. This issue is particularly pronounced for students from lower socio-economic backgrounds who are more likely to be exposed to newer technology in the classroom, yet are also more vulnerable to its failures.

A central question this article seeks to address is how to balance the excitement and overpromises of those driving the implementation of technology with the actual learning outcomes. This necessitates a critical examination of the status quo, characterized by an overreliance on PowerPoint presentations and non-engaging lectures, which often result in disinterested and disengaged learners.

A case in point is the high production values of educational content on platforms like MasterClass. While these platforms showcase expertly crafted videos, the learning outcomes may not always match the impressive visuals. The strengths and weaknesses of such content must be carefully assessed to determine the best ways to integrate it into the learning experience.

To create a more immersive and context-rich educational experience, we propose the use of short documentary-style videos where concepts are presented within the framework of a narrative. This approach enables learners to connect abstract ideas with real-world situations, thereby fostering deeper understanding and engagement.

Finally, this article emphasizes the urgent need for more research into creating effective and engaging educational multimedia content. By understanding the intricate relationship between content, context, and learning outcomes, educators and technologists can work together to develop pedagogically sound solutions that truly enhance the educational experience, rather than simply adding visual flair.

This chapter will explore these themes in depth, offering insights and recommendations to guide the development and application of educational technology in a way that prioritizes context-rich learning experiences over mere spectacles.

THE FALLOUT OF PANDEMIC-DRIVEN EDUCATIONAL TECHNOLOGY ADOPTION

The COVID-19 pandemic served as a catalyst for educational institutions to embrace various technologies, including video and interactive websites. As the need for remote learning solutions soared, the swift adoption of these tools inadvertently led to several challenges. This section will explore the fallout of this rapid implementation and the implications for students and educators alike.

Unplanned and Hasty Integration

The urgency to transition to remote learning often resulted in hasty decisions regarding the selection and integration of technology into the educational landscape. Schools and educators scrambled to find digital platforms and tools that could facilitate the continuity of education. Administrations were left with little time to properly train educators on these tools. Consequently, they may have overlooked critical factors such as accessibility, ease of use, and pedagogical alignment.

The unplanned and hurried integration of educational technology led to a range of issues. Firstly, the sheer volume of available tools and resources made it difficult for educators to select the most appropriate solutions for their specific teaching contexts. This often resulted in the adoption of technologies that did not effectively support the desired learning objectives or were poorly suited to the needs of the student population.

Secondly, the rapid transition to remote learning left little time for schools and educators to develop robust strategies for technology integration. As a result, many institutions faced difficulties in ensuring that the implemented tools complemented existing curricula and pedagogical approaches. This lack of coherence led to disjointed learning experiences, with students struggling to make connections between the digital tools and the concepts they were intended to support.

Thirdly, the hasty adoption of technology exposed the need for greater investment in educator training and professional development. Many teachers found themselves overwhelmed by the demands of navigating new digital platforms and adapting their teaching practices to a virtual environment. This often translated into suboptimal learning experiences for students, as educators struggled to capitalize on the potential of the implemented tools.

Digital Divide and Inequitable Access

The pandemic exposed and exacerbated existing disparities in access to technology and digital resources. Students from lower socio-economic backgrounds, in particular, faced greater challenges in accessing remote learning opportunities. Soto-Gomes wrote in EdSurge in 2020 (Soto-Gomes, 2020) that "COVID-19 has exposed the flaws in our ability to deliver remote education in a manner that is equitable, inclusive—and innovative." The digital divide manifested itself in various ways, ranging from a lack of access to essential hardware (e.g., computers and internet-enabled devices) to inadequate internet connectivity and insufficient digital literacy.

In many cases, students from disadvantaged backgrounds were disproportionately affected by the closure of schools and the move to remote learning. These students often relied on the resources and support provided by their educational institutions to access learning opportunities. With the shift to online platforms, they found themselves at a significant disadvantage compared to their more affluent peers, who had ready access to the necessary technology and resources. In some cases, basic requirements such as broadband internet speeds at home were unobtainable.

The digital divide also extended to educators, with many teachers from lower-income schools facing challenges in accessing the training and support needed to effectively navigate the new digital landscape. In some cases, this led to a reliance on lower-quality, free resources that did not offer the same level of pedagogical value as their more expensive counterparts.

These disparities in access to technology and digital resources have implications for the equitable provision of educational opportunities. As schools and educators increasingly rely on technology to facilitate learning, students who are unable to access these resources risk falling further behind their peers. This situation underscores the need for policymakers and educational leaders to address the digital divide and ensure that all students have the opportunity to benefit from the advances in educational technology.

Inadequate Support and Infrastructure

Another fallout of the pandemic-driven adoption of educational technology was the insufficient support and infrastructure provided to schools and educators. The rapid transition to remote learning highlighted the need for robust technical support systems to assist educators in navigating the challenges posed by the new digital landscape.

In many cases, schools found themselves ill-equipped to provide the necessary technical assistance, with existing support staff overwhelmed by the demands of troubleshooting and maintaining newly implemented tools and platforms.

Checklist for Educators Evaluating Resources for Lower Socio-economic Students

- Choose educational technologies that build leadership and teacher capabilities. Any technology or platform that can aid a targeted approach ensures that students at a disadvantage receive appropriate support.
- Implement financial assistance pathways so disadvantaged students can gain access and extra engagement time with tech and multimedia used in the classroom at home.
- Adopt a specialized liaison who can enhance the tech literacy and capability of a student household.

Determine the accessibility of the technology: Check if the technology and multimedia resources are available to students who may not have access to computers or the internet at home. Ensure that all students have equal access to technology resources, such as laptops, tablets, or smartphones.

Evaluate the cost of the technology: Consider the cost of the technology that will be used. If it's expensive, ensure that students who cannot afford it can access the technology via the school or other resources, such as public libraries.

Provide adequate training: Provide sufficient training to students on how to use the technology and multimedia resources. Ensure that students know how to use them to their full potential to benefit their learning.

Consider the language barriers: Ensure that the technology and multimedia resources are available in the students' primary language, if necessary. If not, provide translation services or bilingual support.

Monitor the use of technology: Monitor the use of technology to ensure that students are using it for educational purposes and not for entertainment. Encourage students to use technology to enhance their learning experience.

Promote digital citizenship: Educate students on how to use technology responsibly and ethically. Teach them about cyberbullying, online privacy, and copyright laws.

Evaluate the effectiveness of the technology: Regularly assess the effectiveness of the technology and multimedia resources in enhancing student learning. Use this feedback to make adjustments and improvements as necessary.

Provide additional support: Provide additional support for students who struggle to use technology and multimedia resources. Offer one-on-one support or additional training to help them improve their skills.

Foster a positive attitude towards technology: Foster a positive attitude towards technology and multimedia resources among students. Encourage them to explore and experiment with new tools and resources to enhance their learning experience.

RESEARCH ON THE SHORTCOMINGS OF VIDEO AND NEW MEDIA IN EDUCATION

The widespread use of video and new media in education has not always translated into improved learning outcomes. Brownlee writes in EdSurge, "No longer should we accept that simply delivering curricular materials online constitutes real innovation, nor that the incorporation of instructional videos is a sure-shot method of engaging students." Despite the initial excitement surrounding these tools, research has revealed several limitations in their effectiveness, particularly when not implemented thoughtfully. In an article about how the U.S spends twice as much as predicated on various ed tech solutions, Bart Epstein writes, "if we want to make the most of education technology, we need to understand what works, where, why, and under what circumstances. Context matters." This section will delve into the research highlighting the shortcomings of these technologies and the factors contributing to their suboptimal implementation.

Passive Consumption and Superficial Engagement

One of the most significant challenges associated with the use of video and new media in education is the potential for passive consumption and superficial engagement with the material. Students may be captivated by the presentation but fail to absorb the underlying concepts. This phenomenon can be attributed to several factors, including the lack of interactivity, the absence of opportunities for active learning, and the prioritization of form over substance in the design of educational content.

Research has consistently shown that active learning strategies are more effective in promoting knowledge retention and deep understanding than passive approaches. In the context of video and new media, this necessitates the incorporation of interactive elements that enable students to engage with the content on a deeper level. However, many educational resources prioritize visual appeal and entertainment value over opportunities for active learning, resulting in content that may be engaging but lacks pedagogical substance.

Moreover, the emphasis on visual appeal can also contribute to cognitive overload, a phenomenon where the learner's cognitive resources are overwhelmed by the amount of information being presented. This can lead to reduced comprehension and retention of the material, particularly if the content is not structured in a way that supports the effective processing of information.

Lack of Contextualization and Personalization

Another limitation of video and new media in education is the lack of contextualization and personalization. Many educational resources are designed to be universally applicable, with little consideration for the unique needs, interests, and backgrounds of individual learners. This can result in content that lacks relevance and fails to engage students on a personal level.

Research has shown that learning is most effective when it is grounded in meaningful and authentic contexts. Herrington and Herrington are emphatic about this point when they say,

"The context needs to be all-embracing, to provide the purpose and motivation for learning, and to provide a sustained and complex learning environment that can be explored at length."

This helps learners make connections between abstract concepts and their own experiences, thereby fostering a deeper understanding of the material. Unfortunately, many educational videos and interactive resources fail to provide this contextualization, instead presenting information in a way that is disconnected from the learners' experiences.

Similarly, personalization is an important factor in promoting learner engagement and motivation. This involves tailoring educational content to meet the individual needs and preferences of each student, based on factors such as their prior knowledge, learning goals, and learning styles. However, many video and new media resources lack the adaptability and flexibility required to support personalized learning experiences.

Teacher Training and Technological Literacy

The successful integration of video and new media in education requires teachers to possess the necessary skills and knowledge to harness their potential effectively. However, research has shown that inadequate training and limited technological literacy among educators can hinder the successful implementation of these tools in the classroom.

Many teachers are not adequately prepared to use video and new media effectively, as their pre-service training may not have included instruction on the pedagogical use of these technologies. This gap in training can lead to a lack of confidence and competence in implementing these tools, resulting in suboptimal learning experiences for students.

Furthermore, the rapid pace of technological change means that teachers must continuously update their skills and knowledge to remain current with the latest developments in educational technology. This can be a significant challenge, particularly for educators who may already be stretched thin by the demands of their professional roles.

Assessment and Feedback Challenges

The use of video and new media in education also raises challenges related to assessment and feedback. Traditional assessment methods, such as written exams and quizzes, may not adequately capture the full range of learning outcomes associated with the use of these technologies. Moreover, the asynchronous nature of many video and new media resources can make it difficult for educators to provide timely and meaningful feedback to students.

To address these challenges, educators must develop innovative approaches to assessment that are aligned with the unique affordances of video and new media. This may involve the use of alternative assessment methods, such as project-based assessments, peer evaluations, or self-assessments, which can more effectively measure the diverse learning outcomes associated with these tools. Additionally, the incorporation of interactive elements and opportunities for real-time feedback within the video and new media resources can help address the limitations associated with asynchronous learning.

Ethical and Privacy Concerns

The increasing reliance on video and new media in education also raises ethical and privacy concerns. The collection and use of student data, which is often integral to the functioning of these technologies, can pose risks to student privacy if not managed appropriately. Additionally, issues related to content ownership, copyright, and intellectual property rights can emerge, particularly when educators create or adapt video and new media resources for their teaching.

To mitigate these risks, educational institutions must develop and enforce clear policies and guidelines related to the ethical use of video and new media in the classroom. This includes the development of protocols for data management and privacy protection, as well as guidelines for the creation, adaptation, and sharing of educational content. Educators must also be provided with training and support to help them navigate the ethical and legal complexities associated with the use of these technologies.

Overreliance on Technology

Finally, the widespread adoption of video and new media in education has led to concerns about an overreliance on technology at the expense of traditional teaching methods and face-to-face interactions. While technology undoubtedly offers valuable opportunities for enhancing the learning experience, it should not be viewed as a panacea for all educational challenges.

Research has shown that the most effective learning experiences often involve a blend of technology-enhanced and traditional teaching methods, with educators skillfully combining the two to meet the diverse needs of their students. However, the rapid transition to remote learning during the pandemic may have led some educators to rely too heavily on technology, potentially undermining the quality of the learning experience.

Moving forward, it is crucial for educators to strike a balance between the use of video and new media and the retention of traditional teaching methods that have proven effective over time. This may involve the development of hybrid or blended learning models, which combine the best of both worlds to provide a rich, engaging, and effective educational experience.

The use of video and new media in education offers exciting opportunities for enhancing the learning experience, but it is not without its challenges. To maximize the potential of these technologies, educators must be aware of the pitfalls associated with their implementation and take steps to address them. This includes fostering active learning and deep engagement with the material, providing contextualization and personalization, developing innovative approaches to assessment and feedback, addressing ethical and privacy concerns, and striking a balance between technology-enhanced and traditional teaching methods. By doing so, educators can harness the power of video and new media to create effective, engaging, and meaningful learning experiences for their students.

Checklist for Choosing Context-Rich, Active Learning Video

- **Identify the learning objectives:** Determine the learning objectives of the curriculum and identify the specific concepts that need to be covered through video content.

- **Choose narrative-based videos**: Look for videos that are narrative-based and offer a clear story-line or plot. These videos are more likely to engage students and facilitate better comprehension of the content.
- **Check for relevance:** Ensure that the videos are relevant to the learning objectives and provide context to the concepts being taught. Videos that offer a real-world context or scenario are more likely to be effective in enhancing learning.
- **Assess the quality of the content:** Evaluate the quality of the content of the videos, including the accuracy of the information presented and the credibility of the sources.
- **Consider the production value:** While the quality of the content is essential, also consider the production value of the videos. Videos that are well-produced and visually engaging can help maintain student attention and improve comprehension.
- **Check for accessibility:** Ensure that the videos are accessible to all students, including those with visual or hearing impairments. Look for videos that offer closed captioning or subtitles.
- **Evaluate the length:** Consider the length of the videos and ensure that they are appropriate for the attention span of the target audience. Shorter videos are generally more effective than longer ones.
- **Check for licensing and copyright:** Ensure that the videos are licensed appropriately and that you have permission to use them in the classroom. Respect copyright laws and avoid using videos that infringe on copyright.
- **Preview the videos:** Preview the videos to ensure that they align with the learning objectives, are age-appropriate, and are engaging for students.
- **Evaluate student engagement and comprehension:** After using the videos in the classroom, evaluate student engagement and comprehension to determine their effectiveness. Use this feedback to make adjustments and improvements to the videos or the curriculum as necessary.

Further Readings

These articles provide insights into the effectiveness of using video in the classroom, including its impact on student learning outcomes, engagement, and motivation. They also offer practical advice and guidance for educators on how to effectively integrate video into their teaching practice.

"The Effectiveness of Educational Video: A Meta-Analysis of Research 1970-1989" by R. Clark

"The Role of Video in Language Learning: An Updated Review" by Y. Chen and H. Chen

"Using Video as an Instructional Tool: An Analysis of Practice and Implementation" by S. Huang and S. Liaw

"Effectiveness of Video-Based Instruction in the Classroom: A Meta-Analysis" by Y. Sung and M. Mayer

"The Impact of Video in Education: A Meta-Analysis" by J. Tamim et al.

"The Effectiveness of Videos in the Classroom: A Comparative Analysis" by C. Weber

"Video in the Classroom: Bridging the Gap between Theory and Practice" by M. Devine and L. Hodge

"The Use of Video in the Classroom: A Study of Practices and Effectiveness" by R. Alexander and C. Murphy

"Video-Based Learning in the Classroom: A Review of the Research Literature" by D. Moyer-Packenham and M. Westenskow

"Effective Uses of Video in the Classroom: A Synthesis of Research" by S. Knezek et al.

BALANCING EXCITEMENT AND OVERPROMISES WITH ACTUAL LEARNING OUTCOMES

The rapid adoption of educational technology, fueled by the enthusiasm for its potential, has often led to overpromising and unrealistic expectations of what these tools can achieve. To ensure that the use of technology in education truly supports learning, it is critical to strike a balance between the excitement surrounding these tools and their actual impact on learning outcomes. This section will explore strategies for achieving this balance, focusing on evidence-based practices, thoughtful technology integration, and a commitment to continuous improvement.

Evidence-Based Practices and Informed Decision-Making

One key to balancing the excitement and overpromises of educational technology with actual learning outcomes is to prioritize evidence-based practices and informed decision-making. By grounding decisions related to technology adoption and implementation in empirical research, educators can ensure that their choices are guided by what has been proven to work.

To achieve this, educational institutions should invest in the development of research capacity and the creation of knowledge-sharing networks. This may involve collaborations with external research organizations, the establishment of internal research teams, or the provision of professional development opportunities for educators to develop their research skills. Or as Michael Horn calls them, "autonomous opportunity units"—small teams of educational decision makers responsible for implementing innovations like mastery-based learning and splitting the grading function from the instructional function within education.

Moreover, educators should be encouraged to engage with the research literature and adopt a critical stance when evaluating the claims made by technology providers. This will enable them to make informed decisions about the tools and resources they select, ensuring that these choices are grounded in evidence and aligned with their pedagogical goals.

Thoughtful Technology Integration

Another important aspect of balancing excitement and over promises with actual learning outcomes is thoughtful technology integration. This involves carefully considering the role of technology in the learning process and ensuring that it is used in ways that genuinely support the achievement of learning objectives.

To facilitate thoughtful technology integration, educators should be guided by the following principles:

a) Aligning technology use with pedagogical goals: Before adopting a specific technology, educators should have a clear understanding of the learning objectives they aim to achieve and how the technology can support these objectives. This will ensure that the technology serves a meaningful purpose in the learning process and does not become a distraction or a source of cognitive overload.

b) Prioritizing active learning and deep engagement: To maximize the potential of technology to support learning, educators should prioritize tools and resources that promote active learning and deep engagement with the material. This may involve the incorporation of interactive elements, opportunities for collaboration, and tasks that require students to apply their knowledge in authentic and meaningful contexts.

c) Fostering digital literacy and critical thinking skills: As students navigate the digital landscape, it is crucial for educators to support the development of digital literacy and critical thinking skills. This includes teaching students how to evaluate the credibility and reliability of digital resources, as well as fostering their ability to think critically about the information they encounter.

d) Supporting personalization and differentiation: Technology can play a valuable role in supporting personalized and differentiated learning experiences. Educators should select tools and resources that enable them to tailor their instruction to meet the diverse needs and preferences of their students, ensuring that all learners have the opportunity to achieve their full potential.

Continuous Improvement and Adaptability

Educational technology is a rapidly evolving field, and it is crucial for educators to remain adaptable and open to change. This involves cultivating a culture of continuous improvement, where educators are encouraged to critically evaluate their technology use and make adjustments as needed to better support learning outcomes.

To foster continuous improvement and adaptability, educational institutions should:

a) Encourage reflective practice: Educators should be encouraged to engage in reflective practice, both individually and collaboratively, to identify areas of success and opportunities for growth in their technology use. This may involve regular discussions with colleagues, participation in professional learning communities, or the use of self-assessment tools and frameworks.

b) Provide ongoing professional development: Educational institutions should invest in ongoing professional development opportunities for educators to ensure they remain up-to-date with the latest developments in educational technology and pedagogy. This may include workshops, webinars, or online courses that focus on the effective use of technology in the classroom, as well as the development of new pedagogical approaches that leverage the affordances of these tools.

c) Foster a culture of experimentation and innovation: Encouraging educators to experiment with new technologies and pedagogical approaches can help promote a culture of innovation and continuous improvement. By providing support and opportunities for risk-taking, educational institutions can empower educators to explore new ways of using technology to enhance the learning experience.

d) Establish systems for monitoring and evaluation: To assess the impact of technology use on learning outcomes, educational institutions should establish systems for monitoring and evaluation. This may involve the collection and analysis of data related to student performance, engagement, and satisfaction, as well as the use of feedback from students, parents, and educators to inform decision-making and drive improvements.

Balancing the excitement and overpromises associated with educational technology with actual learning outcomes requires a multifaceted approach. By prioritizing evidence-based practices, thoughtful technology integration, and a commitment to continuous improvement, educators can ensure that the use of technology in education truly supports learning and leads to positive outcomes for students. Ultimately, this involves cultivating a culture of critical reflection, adaptability, and innovation, where educators are empowered to make informed decisions about technology use and continuously strive to enhance the learning experience.

THE POTENTIAL OF CONTEXT-RICH, DOCUMENTARY-STYLE EDUCATIONAL CONTENT

The use of high-quality, context-rich, documentary-style educational content offers a promising avenue for enhancing the learning experience and addressing some of the shortcomings associated with traditional educational videos and new media. By presenting information within the context of a narrative, these resources can help foster deep engagement, promote active learning, and support the development of critical thinking skills. This section will explore the potential of documentary-style educational content, examining its unique strengths and offering recommendations for its effective use in the classroom.

Engaging Learners Through Narrative and Storytelling

One of the key strengths of documentary-style educational content is its ability to engage learners through the power of narrative and storytelling. By situating educational concepts within a broader context, these resources can help learners make connections between abstract ideas and real-world examples, fostering a deeper understanding of the material. Audrey Rule underlines this when she wrote: "learning takes place in meaningful situations that are extensions of the learner's world, and the learner is at the center of instruction."

Research has shown that storytelling is a highly effective means of engaging learners and facilitating the retention of information. Stories capture the imagination, evoke emotions, and provide a memorable framework that can help learners organize and recall information more easily. By presenting educational content within the context of a story, educators can leverage these powerful cognitive effects to enhance the learning experience.

Promoting Active Learning and Critical Thinking

Documentary-style educational content also offers opportunities for promoting active learning and the development of critical thinking skills. By presenting multiple perspectives, encouraging reflection, and providing opportunities for learners to engage with the material in a meaningful way, these resources can help students develop the cognitive skills necessary for success in the 21st century.

For example, documentary-style content may present a complex issue from various viewpoints, encouraging learners to consider different perspectives and weigh the evidence before arriving at their conclusions. Rule puts it this way: "This audience beyond the classroom changes the problem from an 'exercise' to something more important, allowing students to become emotional stakeholders in the problem." This process of evaluation and analysis can help students develop their critical thinking skills and foster a deeper understanding of the material.

Moreover, documentary-style educational content can also promote active learning by encouraging learners to engage with the material beyond passive consumption. This may involve posing questions, encouraging debate, or providing opportunities for learners to apply their knowledge in authentic and meaningful contexts.

Humanizing Complex Concepts and Ideas

Another advantage of documentary-style educational content is its ability to humanize complex concepts and ideas by connecting them to the experiences of real people. This can help learners develop empathy and a deeper understanding of the material, as they are able to see the real-world implications of the concepts they are learning.

For example, a documentary-style video on climate change might showcase the experiences of individuals living in areas affected by extreme weather events or rising sea levels. By highlighting these personal stories, the content can help learners see the human impact of climate change and better understand the urgency of the issue.

Cultivating a Sense of Wonder and Curiosity

Documentary-style educational content can also help cultivate a sense of wonder and curiosity among learners, inspiring them to explore new ideas and seek out additional information. High-quality, visually engaging documentaries can capture the imagination and ignite a passion for learning, particularly when they delve into fascinating or little-known topics.

By fostering this sense of wonder and curiosity, documentary-style educational content can help motivate learners to take ownership of their learning and engage more deeply with the material. This intrinsic motivation is a powerful driver of learning and can lead to improved outcomes for students.

Recommendations for Effective Use of Documentary-Style Educational Content

To maximize the potential of documentary-style educational content, educators should consider the following recommendations:

a)   Select high-quality, accurate, and diverse content: Educators should prioritize documentary-style content that is accurate, well-researched, and diverse in its perspectives. This will ensure that students are exposed to a rich and balanced representation of the material, promoting critical thinking and a deep understanding of the concepts.

b)   Encourage active learning: To promote active learning and deep engagement with documentary-style content, educators should incorporate opportunities for students to interact with the material. This may involve posing thought-provoking questions, facilitating discussions or debates, or assigning tasks that require students to apply their knowledge in authentic contexts.

c)   Scaffold learning: Given the complex nature of some documentary-style content, it is crucial for educators to provide appropriate scaffolding to support student learning. This may involve breaking down complex ideas into smaller, more manageable components or providing additional resources to help students build the necessary background knowledge.

d)   Foster reflection and critical thinking: Encourage students to reflect on the content and engage in critical thinking by asking open-ended questions, challenging assumptions, and promoting the consideration of multiple perspectives. By fostering reflection and critical thinking, educators can help students develop the cognitive skills necessary for success in today's rapidly changing world.

e)   Connect documentary content to the curriculum: To ensure that documentary-style educational content aligns with learning objectives, educators should make explicit connections between the content and the curriculum. This may involve designing lessons or activities that build upon the documentary material and extend students' learning in meaningful ways.

f) Support the development of media literacy skills: As students engage with documentary-style educational content, it is important for educators to support the development of media literacy skills. This includes teaching students how to evaluate the credibility and reliability of sources, recognize bias or misinformation, and critically analyze the content they encounter.

g) Evaluate the impact on learning outcomes: Finally, it is essential for educators to assess the impact of documentary-style educational content on student learning outcomes. This may involve the collection and analysis of data related to student performance, engagement, and satisfaction, as well as the use of feedback from students, parents, and educators to inform decision-making and drive improvements.

Documentary-style educational content offers significant potential for enhancing the learning experience by engaging learners through narrative and storytelling, promoting active learning and critical thinking, humanizing complex concepts, and cultivating a sense of wonder and curiosity. By carefully selecting high-quality content and incorporating strategies for effective use, educators can leverage the power of documentary-style resources to support student learning and achieve positive outcomes.

Further Readings

These articles provide insights into how documentary style video can engage students in learning and promote critical thinking. They also discuss the benefits and challenges of using documentary films in the classroom and provide practical tips for incorporating them into the curriculum.

- "The Power of Documentary: How Documentary Filmmaking Can Help Foster Critical Thinking" by Erik Palmer
- "Why Documentary Filmmaking Works for Education" by Kaytee Reid
- "The Role of Documentary Film in Education" by Olivia Conti
- "Documentary Films in Education: A Review of the Literature" by Monica Revadigar and Elizabeth Dooley
- "Documentary Film and Education: An Assessment of the Field" by Patricia Aufderheide
- "Using Documentary Films to Enhance Teaching and Learning in the Classroom" by Sarah Cooper
- "Documentary Films in the Classroom: A Tool for Teaching Social Justice" by Natasha Tarpley
- "The Use of Documentary Films in the Classroom: Opportunities and Challenges" by Khatereh Kaviani
- "The Effectiveness of Documentary Films in Higher Education: A Review of the Literature" by Michael Milligan and Janice Fournier
- "Documentary Filmmaking as a Learning Tool: A Case Study" by Mandy Rose and Hamish Fyfe

FUTURE DIRECTIONS FOR EDUCATIONAL MULTIMEDIA CONTENT RESEARCH

As the field of educational multimedia content continues to evolve, it is crucial for researchers to explore new avenues and approaches to better understand the most effective ways to design, implement, and evaluate these resources. While pursuing this goal it is useful to keep the designer Don Norman's words in mind: "A brilliant solution to the wrong problem can be worse than no solution at all: solve the correct problem." This section will discuss future directions for research in educational multimedia content, focusing on key areas of investigation, emerging trends, and potential challenges that must be addressed to ensure the continued growth and development of this field.

Understanding the Cognitive Processes Underlying Multimedia Learning

A key area of investigation for future research is the cognitive processes underlying multimedia learning. Richard Mayer suggested the promise of this direction when he wrote: "There is a growing research base showing that students learn more deeply from well-designed multimedia presentations than from traditional verbal-only messages, including improved performance on tests of problem-solving transfer

This involves exploring how different multimedia formats and designs influence the way learners process, organize, and integrate information, ultimately impacting learning outcomes. By developing a deeper understanding of these cognitive processes, researchers can contribute to the design of more effective and engaging multimedia content.

Potential research questions in this area may include:

- How do different multimedia formats (e.g., video, audio, text, interactive elements) interact with and influence cognitive processes such as attention, memory, and comprehension?
- What is the role of individual differences in cognitive abilities and learning styles in multimedia learning, and how can multimedia content be designed to accommodate these differences?
- How do contextual factors, such as the learning environment, social dynamics, and prior knowledge, influence the cognitive processes underlying multimedia learning?

Investigating the Impact of Emerging Technologies on Multimedia Learning

As technology continues to advance, it is essential for researchers to investigate the potential impact of emerging technologies on multimedia learning. This may involve exploring the educational applications of cutting-edge tools such as virtual reality, augmented reality, artificial intelligence, and adaptive learning systems.

Key research questions in this area might include:

- How can emerging technologies be effectively integrated into educational multimedia content to enhance learning outcomes?
- What are the potential benefits and drawbacks of using emerging technologies in multimedia learning, and how can these be balanced to maximize their impact?
- How do emerging technologies interact with existing multimedia formats and designs, and what are the implications for the cognitive processes underlying multimedia learning?

Evaluating the Effectiveness of Multimedia Learning Interventions

As the field of educational multimedia content continues to grow, it is crucial for researchers to evaluate the effectiveness of these interventions in promoting learning outcomes. This involves not only assessing the impact of individual multimedia resources but also examining the broader context in which they are implemented, including the instructional strategies, learning environments, and support systems that accompany them.

Important research questions in this area could include:

- What are the most effective methods for evaluating the impact of multimedia learning interventions on student outcomes, such as knowledge acquisition, skill development, and attitude change?
- How can researchers and educators establish and maintain a culture of evidence-based practice in multimedia learning, ensuring that interventions are grounded in empirical research and continuously refined based on feedback and data?
- How can the effectiveness of multimedia learning interventions be evaluated in diverse educational settings, such as traditional classrooms, online learning environments, and informal learning contexts?

Exploring the Role of Culture, Equity, and Inclusion in Multimedia Learning

As educational multimedia content becomes increasingly prevalent, it is essential for researchers to explore the role of culture, equity, and inclusion in this field. This involves examining how multimedia content can be designed and implemented in ways that promote cultural responsiveness, address the needs of diverse learners, and contribute to the reduction of educational inequities.

Key research questions in this area might include:

- How can educational multimedia content be designed to reflect and respect the diverse cultural backgrounds, perspectives, and experiences of learners?
- What are the most effective strategies for ensuring that multimedia learning interventions are accessible and inclusive for all learners, including those with disabilities or other barriers to participation?
- How can researchers and educators work together to address systemic inequities in access to and participation in multimedia, particularly for students from underrepresented or marginalized communities?

Investigating the Long-Term Impact of Multimedia Learning

While much of the research in educational multimedia content has focused on short-term learning outcomes, it is important for future studies to investigate the long-term impact of these interventions. This may involve exploring how multimedia learning experiences contribute to the development of lifelong learning skills, the retention and transfer of knowledge over time, and the influence of these experiences on learners' educational and career trajectories.

Potential research questions in this area could include:

- How do multimedia learning experiences influence the development of lifelong learning skills, such as critical thinking, problem-solving, and self-regulation?
- What are the factors that contribute to the long-term retention and transfer of knowledge gained through multimedia learning experiences, and how can these be optimized to support durable learning outcomes?
- How do multimedia learning experiences impact learners' educational and career trajectories, and what are the implications for the design and implementation of these interventions?

Addressing Ethical and Privacy Considerations in Multimedia Learning Research

As the field of educational multimedia content continues to evolve, it is essential for researchers to address the ethical and privacy considerations associated with the collection, analysis, and dissemination of data in this context. This may involve examining the potential risks and benefits of data-driven approaches to multimedia learning, as well as developing best practices for protecting the privacy and autonomy of learners.

Important research questions in this area might include:

- What are the ethical considerations associated with the collection, analysis, and dissemination of data in multimedia learning research, and how can these be addressed in the design and conduct of studies?
- How can researchers balance the potential benefits of data-driven approaches to multimedia learning, such as personalization and adaptation, with the need to protect the privacy and autonomy of learners?
- What are the best practices for obtaining informed consent, protecting learner confidentiality, and ensuring the responsible use of data in multimedia learning research?

The future of educational multimedia content research holds significant promise for advancing our understanding of the most effective ways to design, implement, and evaluate these resources. By focusing on key areas of investigation, such as cognitive processes, emerging technologies, evaluation, culture and equity, long-term impact, and ethical considerations, researchers can contribute to the development of innovative, evidence-based multimedia learning experiences that truly support student success. As the field continues to evolve, it is crucial for researchers, educators, and policymakers to work together to harness the potential of multimedia learning and ensure that these interventions are grounded in empirical research, accessible to all learners, and responsive to the diverse needs and contexts of today's rapidly changing world.

REFERENCES

Epstein, B. (2021). *We have no clue how much the US spends on edtech.* Linkedin. https://www.linkedin.com/pulse/we-have-clue-how-much-us-spen ds-edtech-its-least-2x-what-bart-epstein/

Herrington, A. J., & Herrington, J. A. (2007). *What is an authentic learning environment?* University of Wollongong. https://ro.uow.edu.au/edupapers/897

Horn, M. B. (2022). *Reopen to Reinvent:(re) creating School for Every Child.* John Wiley & Sons.

Rule, A. C. (2006). Editorial: The Components of Authentic Learning. *Journal of Authentic Learning, 3*(1), 1–10.

Soto-Gomes. (2020). The challenge of engaging financially stressed students during a pandemic. *EdSurge* https://www.edsurge.com/news/2020-06-09-it-s-as-if-they-just -disappeared-the-challenge-of-engaging-financially-stressed-students-during-a-pandemic

Staton, M. (2022) A Guide to Rethinking Education After Pandemic. *Edsurge.* https://www.edsurge.com/news/2022-09-10-a-guide-to-rethinking-education-after-pandemic

Chapter 10
Web 2.0 Tools Supported Innovative Applications in Science Education Based on the Context-Based Learning Approach

Canan Koçak Altundağ
Hacettepe University, Turkey

Muhammed Yunus Koçer
Hacettepe University, Turkey

ABSTRACT

The research aims to design and develop innovative materials supported by Web 2.0 tools to offer solutions to the problems of science and technology teachers in science education based on a context-based learning approach. For this purpose, the design and development research method were used to test this informative material's design, development, and validity. In the design, students and teachers are considered a common user group. Aside from the literature review, Web 2.0 tool design methods were used in the design process, and the resulting designs were presented. It is considered that innovative materials supported by Web 2.0 tools in science education based on context-based learning practices will enrich science teaching environments and support much more meaningful learning. Innovative technology applications were attempted to be presented to our teachers and students in Science and Technology Teaching using the designs realized within the scope of the research.

DOI: 10.4018/978-1-6684-7644-4.ch010

INTRODUCTION[1]

In the developing world, technology is rapidly changing and developing. Therefore, we need to use technology best in every field of daily life. Today, with the development of technology, our daily lives are affected in every respect. Education is one of the departments that is most affected by technological developments. The more developments in the field of technology increase, the more education is affected by this increase. The technology used in education facilitates comprehension, objectifies many subjects, provides the opportunity to access information quickly, and reduces inequality in education by reaching a broad audience. Due to the conditions of the period in which the students live, it is expected that they have some features such as being able to critically approach the problems around them, perform analysis and synthesis, work together, be open to innovations in the developing world, and think virtually as well as have technology literacy (Altıok, Yükseltürk & Üçgül, 2017).

Teachers and students, who are an element of our education system, are also greatly affected by technological innovations. Teachers must decide which technologies they will use in education, their knowledge skills, and what contribution the technologies will make to learning outcomes and activities (Pamuk, Ülken & Dilek, 2012). One of the technologies that teachers should use in education is Web 2.0. These tools are used in web technologies. They have benefits such as information processing, fast communication, simple access to information, online data preparation, visual richness, and providing access to people of all age groups at a level that they can easily reach (Altun, 2008). Thanks to the benefits and convenience of Web 2.0 tools in education, they positively support every individual in their education. In addition to these, it also offers convenience in getting feedback. Teachers are thought to have to be sufficiently skilled in educational technologies. They have teacher field knowledge to use technology at a level sufficient for educational subjects with developing technology, to have sufficient knowledge on these subjects, to use appropriate methods and techniques appropriate to the subject, and to prepare an effective participation environment in the classroom. (İlhan, 2004). It is also necessary for teachers to update their knowledge about learning approaches to use appropriate methods and techniques in their lessons.

Context-based learning is one of the most up-to-date approaches in education. So, what is "context"? De Jong (2008) answers the question: "Context is a situation that helps students make sense of scientific rules, concepts, and laws." In context-based learning, basic concepts are transferred by associating them with daily life. Creating context between daily life and course content is more complicated than one might think. Because the subjects of chemistry courses are interconnected and have a spiral structure, special care should be taken to prepare the contexts in the chemistry course (Bennett, Grasel, Parchmann, & Waddington, 2005). For this reason, the role of teachers and context-based teaching approaches are crucial to effectively implementing context-based teaching. The research aims to design and develop innovative materials supported by Web 2.0 tools to offer solutions to the problems of science and technology teachers in science education based on the context-based learning approach.

Context-Based Learning in Science Education

Education is a process that aims to change people's behavior in a deliberately desired direction. Planned, programmed, and systematic teaching experiences in schools constitute a large part of the education process (Can, 1998). To adapt to the constantly developing age, countries attach great importance to science education and strive to increase the scope of science education to develop individuals with specific characteristics to put themselves at the forefront of science and technology competition (Ayas, 1995). To adapt to the technologically developing world in the science education process, Turkey keeps up with the competing countries by improving the science education and training process to train people who can use science in every department of daily life. Our national education system has made essential changes in science education programs to not fall behind the competition in the world. The Board of Education and Discipline organized a Science and Technology Course Curriculum for primary and secondary school sciences within the scope of improving the curriculum. In this context, the approaches of the Science Program were examined in detail and prepared by taking the creation of the new program into account. In addition, science education programs in many countries were examined and prepared by considering the conditions in different regions of Turkey (Köseoğlu, 2006).

Science education and training should be considered as a whole. It requires a comprehensive continuum that includes all activities related to in-class and out-of-class learning and teaching. Studies on curriculum development can only prevent problems that arise in symbolizing an excellent example to ensure the continuity of science education and training and improve the Turkish education system. As a result, all problems encountered within science education and teaching continuity affect curriculum elements. The hypothesis inspired that the currently used science curriculum and approaches reveal possible failures in Turkey's failure to achieve the desired results in worldwide comparison exams such as TIMMS and PISA in science education in recent years (Ersoy, 2013).

The context-based learning approach can be defined as adapting students' daily life events to course outcomes (Glynn & Koballa, 2005). The primary purpose of the context-based approach is to present the concepts selected from daily life and to increase the interests and eagerness of the students (Sözbilir, Sadi, Kutu & Yıldırım 2007). Yam (2005) argued that if students can associate a phenomenon and its sub-branches with their daily lives, which include cultures, permanent learning will occur. Thanks to the context-based approach, students learn more efficiently by establishing a relationship between daily life and course content. The results of some international studies point to two main problems. One of these is that as students age, their interest in science courses such as physics, chemistry, and biology decreases (Black & Atkin, 1996; OECD, 2006). The other is that students have low academic success because they have difficulty understanding science lessons (Baumert, Bos, & Lehmann 2000; OECD 2003). One of the most fundamental factors in motivation and student success is the student's interest in the lesson (Krapp, 2002). Due to the low interest in science lessons, today's science literacy education is negatively affected.

The Science and Technology Curriculum aims to train people who analyze and question information, build bridges between daily life and science, and look at the facts through the eyes of scientists (MEB, 2005). Most of the technological tools in the world are developed by interpreting the laws of science. Although science has a close relationship with people's lives, it is known that students in the field of science have a lot of difficulties (Gömleksiz & Bulut, 2007). To prevent this situation, it is stated that the lesson becomes more understandable and remarkable for students when the concepts are associated with daily life (Hoffmann, Haeussler, & Lehrke, 1998). With the development of the science and technology curriculum, the context-based theory is seen as a powerful approach (MEB, 2005). According to Millar and Osborne (1998), the context-based approach aims to raise science-literate individuals who can understand and apply existing knowledge and skills to their lives. It has an essential place because students can relate practice to theory. One of the most important differences between the context-based and other approaches is that the former ensures permanent learning by incorporating theory into science teaching. Therefore, for students to provide valuable and meaningful learning, the science curriculum should be designed according to these features (Reid, 2000).

The Importance of the Context-Based Learning Approach in Science Education

For the science education program to be successful, teachers who oversee education must share their knowledge, skills, and equipment with their students to train science-literate students. If teachers cannot fully grasp the scientific knowledge in the science education program, they cannot be expected to transfer it to students. For science teaching to be carried out in a meaningful way, it is crucial that it be equipped with productive stimuli and that the concepts in the subjects are associated with daily life. Therefore, teachers' adaptation to the context-based approach is significant for actively maintaining the science education curriculum. The attitudes and behaviors of our students toward science are associated with daily life and presented by teachers. The acquisition of meaningful and permanent skills that students will use in their future lives and the teaching process can be achieved if teachers have a favorable view of this approach and include practices in the course content.

Students add meaning to the relationship between science and daily life via activities in the lessons, but they cannot make it useful in their minds. In learning strategies, they use while learning science course topics, their ability to relate the knowledge they have previously learned to daily life is lacking. Students experience difficulties in associating science with daily life and making what they learn useful (Choi & Johnson, 2005). Just as the overall purpose of all teaching approaches, models, methods, and techniques is to ensure that the student is actively learning and useful by increasing the quality of learning, those targeted in the context-based science teaching are the same, but there are some inadequacies in terms of students making use of science and daily life relationship useful.

Students should be made aware of that science knowledge can be used in daily life, in order to prevent the science lesson from being regarded as an abstract and difficult lesson. For example, science can be used to clean a coffee stain that has spilled on garments with detergent, to make the cake rise better, to comprehend how the zeppelins fly, to explain how curly hair is straightened by blowing. Paying attention to the lesson by giving the correct daily life example on the right subject can create the awareness in students that science is everywhere.

If students are asked not only to learn science but also to live it, it is extremely important to correctly determine the perceptions about the relationship between science and daily life. It is possible to say that the association of science and daily life is the starting point of the life-based science approach. Therefore, the relationship between science and daily life can be learned and made useful, only when it is perceived correctly. The more accurate this relationship is perceived by the students, the more meaningful it will be to interpret the relationship between science and daily life and use it in the required environments. Student separating real life and science lessons at school causes students to develop useless information systems related to science (Osborne & Freyberg, 1985). Providing students with useful information that they can use in their daily lives can make them aware of the relationship between science and daily life, and this can cause them to prefer using their science knowledge in interpreting the phenomena they encounter in their daily lives (Busker & Flint, 2022; Georgiou & Sharma, 2012; Kim, Yoon, Ji & Song, 2012).

Educational Technology

Technology has an undeniable importance in people's lives today. In the broadest sense, technology is the functional structure that an individual creates to control all aspects of his life by activating his abilities. In a narrower context, technology is defined as a concept that serves as a transition between science and applications formed by combining all the elements in daily life (Alkan, 1997). When the definitions related to the concept of technology are examined, it can be said that this concept is a general phenomenon and is considered in its physical and cognitive developments (İşman, 2003). In a world where rapid technological developments are recorded, countries have begun to compete to keep up with this situation. It is unavoidable that education plays a key role in keeping up with technology in today's world and rising above a certain level of development. To embody this role, it is necessary to use technological forms in educational studies. Therefore, educational technology is the process of creating, implementing, and shaping learning and teaching mechanisms (Alkan, 1997).

In the beginning, the meaning of technology used in education was separated from the meaning of "instruments used as supportive in education." However, it has since evolved into a process encompassing more than one subject, ranging from technology and human interaction to application technologies. This process, which took place in the theory part of the concept of educational technology, was not at the same level in practice. As Alkan (1997) stated about this issue, those who are interested in this part of the educational technology department, which transforms the knowledge revealed in educational sciences into practice by making it more valuable, do not have sufficient knowledge about the subject, causing the gap between the concept and the practice to become more comprehensive. The people who will apply the educational technology mentioned in the field survey in education and receive feedback are the teachers, who constitute the most crucial part of education. Although educational technologies have advanced in more than one way, the educational element that will reflect and apply this technology to the education process is teachers. Therefore, teachers should use it most effectively by including educational technologies in the process (Yücel, 2006).

The question of how the applications of educational technologies will be administered and which areas they contain is essential in terms of their application. The answer to the question in this context is the National Educational Technology Standards (NETS), which emerged in the United States and spread worldwide and are accepted as a guide for all elements of education regarding the application of educational technologies (Coklar & Odabaşı, 2009). As a result of the inability of all the teachers involved in the education process to benefit enough from educational technology, the need to create unity in educational technology applications has arisen. To meet the conditions of this need, educational technology norms and what kind of knowledge and skills teachers should were determined (Coklar, 2008). Educational technologies help students to develop their ability to perceive and solve problems, increase everyone's level of access to information in education, create opportunities for individual learning, ensure permanent learning, and provide lifelong education opportunities outside of the teaching environment. We must focus on educational technology so future generations can adapt to the developing world.

Web 2.0 Tools

The concept of Web 2.0 is used to describe applications with different features from the first web tools. The idea of forming these tools was put forward as a brainstorming idea during a conference led by Tim O'Reilly (O'Reilly, 2007). Anderson (2007) states that Web 2.0 tools emerged with ideas such as materials produced by people, rapid use and transportation, open-source coding, and participation regardless of time and place. The main purpose of the applications and services created by these tools is to enable individuals to access the tools easily, share the created materials without any restrictions, and make the materials compatible with multimedia options. The contents and information requested to be created in Web 2.0 are shared by the people using these tools. Web 2.0 has some features, such as providing feedback to applications from this content and information, creating links, and annotating them (Caladine, 2008). Thanks to these tools, users can keep up with the age of technology and create Web pages without having too much knowledge. As a result, users who are web literate can create online and offline learning environments in teams. (O'Reilly, 2007; Boulos & Wheelert, 2007; Musser, O'Reilly et.al, 2007; Coleman & Levine, 2008):

Table 1. Comparison of Web 1.0 and 2.0 tools

Web 1.0 Tools	Web 2.0 Tools
Contents are static.	Contents are dynamic.
There are general applications.	There are individual applications.
Messages are sent by e-mail.	Information is transmitted via RSS.
It is not simultaneous.	There can be synchronous and asynchronous interactions.

As a result of the use of Web 2.0 tools, people who use the tools have become internet literate. By using these tools, materials have been made available to everyone thanks to open-source codes, unlike Web 1.0. Thus, the prepared materials can be used continuously, and thus a material archive is created. Thanks to Web 2.0 tools, it has become possible to share materials on the internet and improve these materials. Web 2.0 tools cooperate with constructivist theory and provide opportunities for material production. With these tools, it is possible to create a more meaningful learning environment by preventing differences in individual learning. Thus, constructivist theory becomes prominent as it provides a basis for meaningful learning. By using Web 2.0 applications, teachers and students can reveal information about meaningful learning (Deans, 2009).

Purpose and Significance of The Research

Educators continue their research on using technology effectively to increase the quality of teaching activities with each passing day. The designs made within the scope of this research were carried out to add a new one to the research in the literature. The study aims to design and develop innovative materials supported by Web 2.0 tools to offer solutions to the problems of science and technology teachers in science education based on the context-based learning approach. In this way, it is thought that students' success in science can be increased, their worries about science and technology lessons can be reduced, and the benefits of using technology for educational purposes can be determined. The rapid increase in information, the increase in communication opportunities, and the spread of technology have also changed expectations from education. Educational institutions are now expected to train individuals who can use technology. The education system also expects the same function from teachers. This expectation includes not only teaching the use of technology but also using it in teaching activities. Especially in areas where scientific applications such as science and technology teaching are carried out, technology can enable learning to be more permanent, efficient, and effective.

Technology applications such as Web 2.0 tools can contribute to the efficient execution of science and technology teaching and the full realization of learning. Similar results can be achieved when the context-based learning approach is applied in science and technology teaching. According to the findings obtained from the research results, after the context-based science applications, the positive attitudes of the students towards science lessons increase, and changes can be observed in their perspectives on science lessons. Thanks to the innovative applications designed in the research, it is thought that the positive thoughts of the students that their science and technology knowledge will be advantageous in their daily lives can be increased. As a matter of fact, in a study conducted by Wu (2003), it was revealed that with daily life-based practices in education, students transform their daily life experiences into scientific knowledge, and thus they can make the information more helpful.

Research Question

Can innovative applications supported by Web 2.0 tools based on the context-based learning approach be designed for science and technology teaching?

Sub Questions

1. Which Web 2.0 tools based on the context-based learning approach can be used in science and technology teaching?
2. Innovative applications supported by Web 2.0 tools based on the context-based learning approach in science and technology teaching:
   a. Which grade level are they applicable for?
   b. Which units of the course are they applicable for?
   c. Which subjects are they applicable for?

METHOD

The design of innovative applications supported by Web 2.0 tools based on the context-based learning approach in science and technology teaching has arisen from the necessity of working in the field of legislation related to the subject in the curriculum of secondary schools (MEB, 2018). Innovative designs supported by Web 2.0 tools in science and technology teaching have been attempted to be designed in such a way that they can be used as course material based on the science and technology curriculum determined by the Ministry of National Education. Designs are not limited to science and technology lessons. Applications can also support students in extracurricular science and technology education studies and individual studies.

Design Process

In the data collection process, the studies and applications made so far were examined using the document scanning method and the basic concepts of the science and technology course. As a result of the research, brainstorming and association methods were applied as an intellectual method since there is a product study and, therefore, product design (Onur & Zorlu, 2017). Published studies, articles, master's and doctoral theses published articles on the results of pilot application reports in the field of innovative applications supported by Web 2 tools based on the context-based learning approach in science and technology teaching, MEB reports on the subject, the training set sales sites on the internet, MEB curriculum, and sample activities were examined. First, a roadmap was assigned for product studies on innovative applications supported by Web 2.0 tools based on the context-based learning approach in science and technology teaching. It is known from the very beginning of the process that this map will be open to updating, changing, lengthening, or shortening during the process, as in every design process. Below is Table 2, which summarizes the most recent plan for this roadmap.

Table 2. Implementation plan of Web 2.0 tools

Grade	Unit Name	Activity Name	Objectives and Explanations	Web 2.0 Applications
7th-Grade	Pure Substances and Mixtures	Elements	Students will be able to express the names, symbols, and usage areas of the first 18 elements and common elements (gold, silver, copper, mercury, lead, iron, iodine, platinum) in the periodic system.	Wordwall
7th-Grade	Pure Substances and Mixtures	Compounds	Students will be able to express the formulas, names, and uses of prevalent compounds.	Wordwall
7th-Grade	Household Waste and Recycling	Recycling	Students will be able to distinguish recyclable and non-recyclable materials in household waste. Students will be able to question recycling in terms of the effective use of resources.	Scratch
7th-Grade	Pure Substances and Mixtures	Pure Substances	Students will be able to classify pure substances as elements and compounds and give examples.	Scratch
7th-Grade	Pure Substances and Mixtures	Pure Substances and Mixtures	Students will be able to classify pure substances as elements and compounds and give examples. Students will be able to classify mixtures as homogeneous and heterogeneous and give examples.	Gitmind

FINDINGS

The design of innovative applications supported by Web 2 tools based on the context-based learning approach in science.

1. Innovative applications supported by Web 2 tools based on the context-based learning approach in science and technology teaching should also create different forms and be suitable for new combinations of forms each time.

2. Innovative applications supported by Web 2 tools based on the context-based learning approach in science and technology teaching should be suitable for group or individual work.

3. Innovative applications supported by Web 2 tools based on the context-based learning approach in science and technology teaching should be suitable for arousing curiosity.

4. Innovative applications supported by Web 2 tools in science and technology teaching should provide students with knowledge of some of the subjects covered in the science and technology curriculum.

5. Innovative applications supported by Web 2 tools based on the context-based learning approach in science and technology teaching should be able to be used as course materials in science and technology lessons.

6. Innovative applications supported by Web 2 tools based on the context-based learning approach in science and technology teaching should be suitable for use in the classroom, at home, or both.

7. Innovative applications supported by Web 2 tools based on the context-based learning approach in science and technology teaching should allow students to use them harmoniously.

8. Innovative applications supported by Web 2 tools based on the context-based learning approach should be able to be used repeatedly in science and technology teaching.

DESIGN SUGGESTIONS

Activity 1: Let's Match the Elements

The first of the innovative applications supported by Web 2.0 tools based on the context-based learning approach in science and technology teaching is proposed with the name "Let's Match the Elements," prepared with Wordwall, which can be the course material for the 7th-grade level, Pure Substances and Mixtures Unit (Figures 1 and 2).

Figure 1. Periodic table

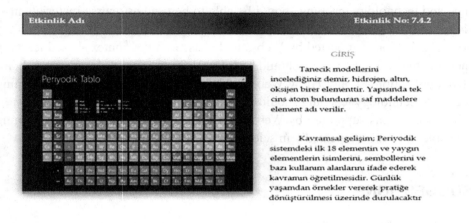

Figure 2. Elements

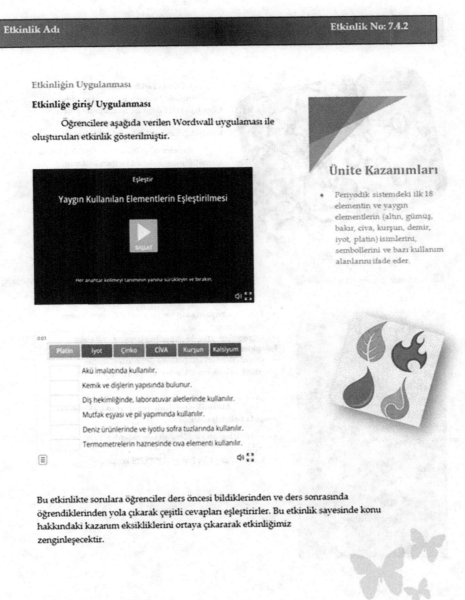

Bu etkinlikte sorulara öğrenciler ders öncesi bildiklerinden ve ders sonrasında öğrendiklerinden yola çıkarak çeşitli cevapları eşleştirirler. Bu etkinlik sayesinde konu hakkındaki kazanım eksikliklerini ortaya çıkararak etkinliğimiz zenginleşecektir.

Activity 2: Let's Match Common Compounds

The second of the innovative applications supported by Web 2 tools based on the context-based learning approach in science and technology teaching is suggested with the name "Let's Match the Compounds," prepared with Wordwall, which can be the course material for the 7th grade, Pure Substances and Mixtures Unit (Figures 3 and 4).

Figure 3. Let's Match Compounds

Etkinlik Adı	Etkinlik No: 7.4.2

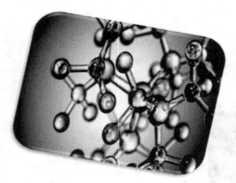

GİRİŞ

En az iki farklı atomun birleştirilmesiyle oluşturulan saf maddelere Bileşik denir. Bileşikler formüllerle gösterilir. Su, tuz, şeker gibi günlük hayatta sıklıkla kullandığımız maddeler bileşikleri oluşturur.

Kavramsal gelişim; Yaygın bileşiklerin formüllerini, isimlerini ve bazı kullanım alanlarını ifade ederek kavramın öğretilmesidir. Günlük yaşamdan örnekler vererek pratiğe dönüştürülmesi üzerinde durulacaktır.

Hedef Kavramlar:

Bileşikler

Materyaller:

Web 2 uygulamalarından wordwall kullanılarak oluşturulmuştur.

Süre: 15 dk.

Etkinlik öncesinde yapılması gerekenler;

- Etkinliğe başlamadan ses ve görüntü sistemlerinin kontrol edilmesi.
- Öğrencilere etkinlikte günlük hayatta kullanılan bileşiklerin hatırlatılması sağlanmalı.
- Öğrencilere etkinliğin süre ile sınırlı olduğu hatırlatılarak süreyi etkili kullanmaları sağlanmalı.

Etkinlik sayesinde cevap aranacak sorular aşağıda belirtilmiştir;

- Günlük hayatta kullanılan bileşiklerden bazıları nelerdir?
- Verilen bileşikler hangi alanlarda kullanılır?

Figure 4. Let's Match Compounds

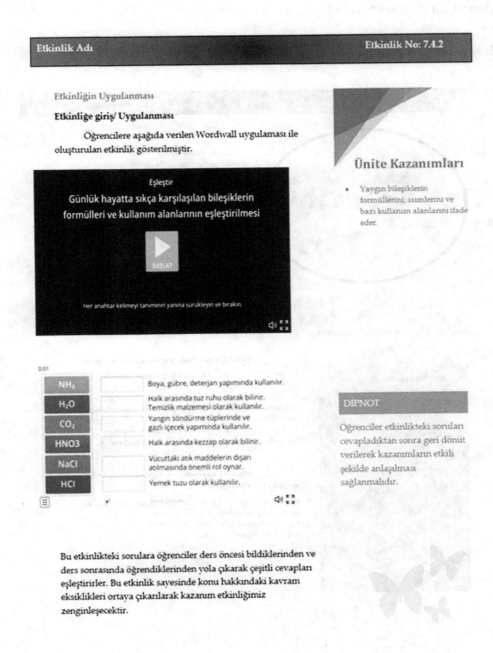

Bu etkinlikteki sorulara öğrenciler ders öncesi bildiklerinden ve ders sonrasında öğrendiklerinden yola çıkarak çeşitli cevapları eşleştirirler. Bu etkinlik sayesinde konu hakkındaki kavram eksiklikleri ortaya çıkarılarak kazanım etkinliğimiz zenginleşecektir.

Activity 3: Which Substances Should Be Recycled?

The third of the innovative applications supported by Web 2.0 tools based on the context-based learning approach in science and technology teaching is suggested with the name "Household Wastes and Recycling," prepared with Scratch, which can be the course material for the 7th-grade level, Pure Substances and Mixtures Unit (Figures 5 and 6).

Figure 5. Household wastes and recycling

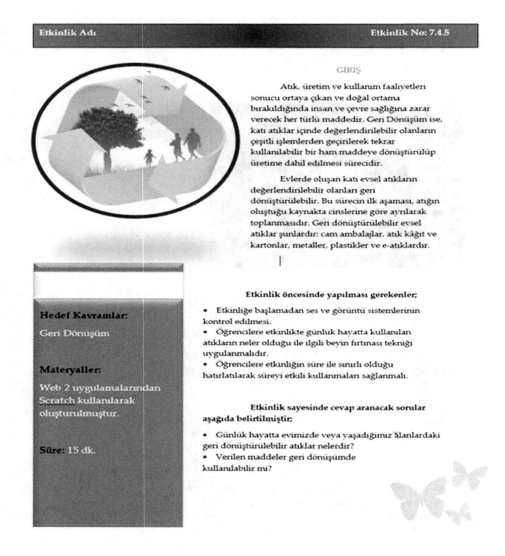

Figure 6. Household wastes and recycling

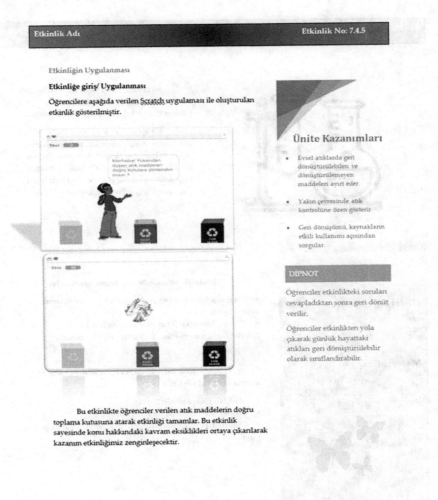

Activity 4: Let's Group the Items

The fourth of the innovative applications supported by Web 2.0 tools based on the context-based learning approach in science and technology teaching is suggested with the name "Pure Substances," prepared with Scratch, which can be a course material for the 7th-grade level, "Pure Substances and Mixtures Unit" (Figures 7 and 8).

Figure 7. Let's Group the Items

Etkinlik Adı	Etkinlik No: 7.4.2 - 7.4.3

GİRİŞ

Aynı cins atom veya moleküllerden oluşan maddelere saf madde denir. Elementler ve bileşikler saf maddelerdir.

Karışım, iki ya da daha fazla maddenin özelliklerini kaybetmeden bir araya gelmesiyle oluşur. Karışımı oluşturan maddeler element ya da bileşik olabilir. Karışımlar görünümlerine göre heterojen ve homojen karışımlar olarak sınıflandırılır.

Hedef Kavramlar:

Saf Madde ve Karışımlar

Materyaller:

Web 2 uygulamalarından Scratch kullanılarak oluşturulmuştur.

Süre: 15 dk.

Etkinlik öncesinde yapılması gerekenler;

- Etkinliğe başlamadan ses ve görüntü sistemlerinin kontrol edilmesi.
- Öğrencilere etkinliğin süre ile sınırlı olduğu hatırlatılarak süreyi etkili kullanmaları sağlanmalı.

Etkinlik sayesinde cevap aranacak sorular aşağıda belirtilmiştir;

- Maddeler kaça ayrılır?
- Elementler ve bileşikler nasıl gösterilir?
- Günlük hayatta kullandığımız maddelerin hangi gruba girer?

Figure 8. Let's Group the Items

Activity 5: Let's Get to Know the Matter

The fifth innovative application supported by Web 2 tools based on the context-based learning approach in science and technology teaching is suggested with the name "Pure Substances," prepared with Gitmind, which can be course material for the 7th-grade level, "Pure Substances and Mixtures Unit" (Figures 9 and 10).

Figure 9. Let's Get to Know the Matter

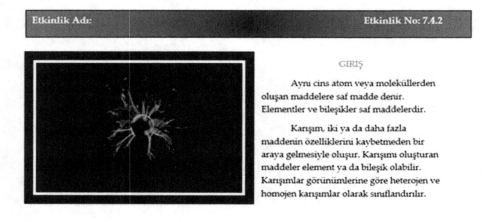

| Etkinlik Adı: | Etkinlik No: 7.4.2 |

GIRIŞ

Ayrı cins atom veya moleküllerden oluşan maddelere saf madde denir. Elementler ve bileşikler saf maddelerdir.

Karışım, iki ya da daha fazla maddenin özelliklerini kaybetmeden bir araya gelmesiyle oluşur. Karışımı oluşturan maddeler element ya da bileşik olabilir. Karışımlar görünümlerine göre heterojen ve homojen karışımlar olarak sınıflandırılır.

Hedef Kavramlar:

Saf Madde ve Karışımlar

Materyaller:

Web 2 uygulamalarından Gitmind kullanılarak oluşturulmuştur.

Süre: 25 dk.

Etkinlik öncesinde yapılması gerekenler;

• Etkinliğe başlamadan ses ve görüntü sistemlerinin kontrol edilmesi.
• Öğrenciler kendi ön bilgilerini öğrenmek için üniteye başlamadan önce yaptırılmalıdır.

Etkinlik sayesinde cevap aranacak sorular aşağıda belirtilmiştir;

• Madde kaça ayrılır?
• Saf ve saf olmayan maddeler nelerdir?
• Homojen karışımlar nelerdir ve kaça ayrılır?
• Heterojen karışımlar nelerdir ve kaça ayrılır?

Figure 10. Let's Get to Know the Matter

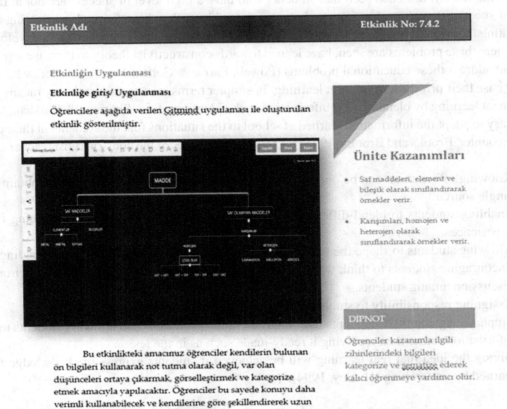

| Etkinlik Adı | Etkinlik No: 7.4.2 |

Etkinliğin Uygulanması

Etkinliğe giriş/ Uygulanması

Öğrencilere aşağıda verilen Çitmind uygulaması ile oluşturulan etkinlik gösterilmiştir.

Ünite Kazanımları

• Saf maddeleri, element ve bileşik olarak sınıflandırarak örnekler verir.

• Karışımları, homojen ve heterojen olarak sınıflandırarak örnekler verir.

DİPNOT

Bu etkinlikteki amacımız öğrenciler kendilerin bulunan ön bilgileri kullanarak not tutma olarak değil, var olan düşünceleri ortaya çıkarmak, görselleştirmek ve kategorize etmek amacıyla yapılacaktır. Öğrenciler bu sayede konuyu daha verimli kullanabilecek ve kendilerine göre şekillendirerek uzun sürede zihinlerde yer etmesi sağlancaktır.

Öğrenciler kazanımla ilgili zihinlerindeki bilgileri kategorize ve sematize ederek kalıcı öğrenmeye yardımcı olur.

CONCLUSION, DISCUSSION, AND RECOMMENDATIONS

Although constructivism is a constantly central concept in the current century, it has become more prominent in the last part of the century. This situation is due to the research on brain structure and functioning in the 1990s. The lack of learning theories has been understood in light of the information obtained, and a new learning theory has been revealed. As a result of this research, constructivist theory became an important concept and enabled educators to work on this subject. Constructivism theory has recently emerged as one of the greatest approaches impacting educational processes as global standards change. Innovative searches in education have emerged to find solutions to problems such as educational quality issues. It has been revealed that students studying in developed countries, especially Germany and the United States of America, have recently fallen behind other developed countries' interpretation, comprehension, and science and math course achievement (Pisa-Schock, 2002).

In some tests, it has been seen that students who have a high level of success are not at the desired level of success in making connections between the subjects they have learned, comparing them, and integrating them into daily life (Yager, 1991). Teachers in many countries, especially in developed countries where these problems are seen, have leaned towards constructivist theory to increase school education and address these educational problems (Powell, Farrar & Cohen, 1985). Teachers who adopt this theory base their priorities on student learning. In simpler terms, constructivist theory means providing permanent learning by blending new information with old information (Sherman & Kurshan, 2005). It is necessary to adapt the information learned at school to the situations that the students in their daily lives may encounter. Brooks and Brooks (1993) list the characteristics of the constructivist teacher as follows:

1. Knowing information can be obtained in a variety of ways, and it should not be obtained from a single source.
2. Enabling students to blend different thoughts with their existing thoughts stemming from their experiences.
3. Allowing students to shape the lesson by removing it from the traditional understanding.
4. Encouraging students to think while preparing in-class questions and creating an environment for discussion among students.
5. Assigning responsibility to students by giving tasks to them
6. Emphasizing cognitive concepts like "analysis" and "synthesis" and allowing students to research information rather than receiving it ready-made such as in the lessons.
7. Giving the idea that real learning will be achieved if students express the knowledge they have learned by researching (Hanley, 1994).

The teacher who transfers the information directly within the scope of education and training and the education solely based on coursebooks has been insufficient in raising students who understand what they read, interpret it, and perpetuate the knowledge they have learned. Therefore, it is necessary to put the teacher in the background and make the learning environment student-centered (Hanley, 1994). From this point of view, theory should be reflected in education with the understanding that "why and how they adopt knowledge" is essential, not that students receive information directly. One of the most crucial conditions put forward by educational theorists in constructivist theory is the information in one's mind. For this reason, teaching theories that give importance to the student's prior knowledge should be used in science teaching. Constructivist theory significantly impacts science education (Yılmaz & Çavaş, 2006).

Using constructivist theory in education is crucial to ensure permanent and meaningful learning in science education. In addition, the constructivist approach has a great place in teaching programs and practices (Terwell, 1999).

Some teaching models have been developed to ensure meaningful learning in science education. Novick and Nussbaum (1981) argued that the science lesson should be given as a three-phase model. In this model, the aim is to investigate scientific concepts and shape these concepts according to the scientific idea. Like Nussbaum and Novick's model, Renner (1982) put forward the idea that the science lesson should be given in three parts. The first stage is where the information will be created. Here, the student is presented with the preliminary information they need to learn. The second part uses terms related to the subject to be learned. In the last part, students associate the information they have just learned with the information they have learned in the past. At this stage, experiments with concepts can be done to strengthen the association. Thus, students can make sense of concepts and events. However, the instructional strategies provided were insufficient in some respects to meet the purpose of science education. As a result, it has been argued that a constructivist approach is necessary for science education.

Today, the opportunities provided by Web 2.0 tools used in education are increasing with the development of technology. This indicates that the interest in and need for Web 2.0 applications are high. This research tried to use the features of innovative materials supported by Web 2 tools, such as facilitating understanding and remembering, providing reinforcement, being exciting and enjoyable, improving experimentation skills, and allowing recognition of the tools and chemical materials to be used during the experiment. The study has great significance for enabling the students, who are the adults of the future, to keep up with the rapidly developing and changing world and to guide them to grow up as well-equipped individuals. The research in science and technology teaching and the design of innovative applications supported by Web 2 tools based on the context-based learning approach emerged from the necessity of working in the field of legislation related to the subject in the curriculum of secondary schools (MEB, 2018). For this reason, the study aims to design and develop innovative materials supported by Web 2.0 tools to offer solutions to the problems of science and technology teachers in science education based on the context-based learning approach. Thus, it was thought that students' science achievements could be increased, their worries about science and technology lessons could be reduced, and the benefits of using technology for educational purposes could be determined.

In the research, care was taken to ensure that innovative applications supported by Web 2 tools, which are based on the context-based learning approach in science and technology teaching, to be suitable: for new combinations each time, for group work or individual work for use in the classroom or at home and for using repeatedly. In the research, the first of the innovative applications supported by Web 2.0 tools based on the context-based learning approach in science and technology teaching was prepared with Wordwall for the 7th-grade level, the Pure Substances and Mixtures Unit. The second innovative application supported by Web 2.0 tools and based on the context-based learning approach in science and technology teaching is proposed with the name "Let's Match the Compounds," prepared with Wordwall, which can be course material for the 7th-grade level, Pure Substances and Mixtures Unit.

The third innovative application supported by Web 2 tools and based on the context-based learning approach in science and technology teaching is proposed with the name "Household Wastes and Recycling," prepared with Scratch, which can be course material for the 7th-grade level, Pure Substances and Mixtures Unit.

The fourth of the innovative applications supported by Web 2 tools and based on the context-based learning approach in science and technology teaching is proposed with the name "Pure Substances," prepared with Scratch, which can be a course material for the 7th-grade level, Pure Substances and Mixtures Unit. The fifth innovative application supported by Web 2 tools and based on the context-based learning approach in science and technology teaching is proposed with the name "Pure Substances," prepared with Gitmind, which can be course material for the 7th-grade level, "Pure Substances and Mixtures Unit." According to Layton (1993), knowledge constructed through activities in science education is similar to technological knowledge (Hill, 1998). From this point of view, it is thought that thanks to innovative applications supported by Web 2 tools in science education based on the context-based learning approach, concrete representations can be reached with technology applications designed for students' abstract information about the course subjects. Science and technology are the branches of science that deal with abstract events, and these concrete representations can help students reduce their mental load. It has been observed in studies that visual representations have great importance in the description of abstract events in learning and teaching (Alkan & Altundağ, 2015; Crawford & Cullin,

2004; Yücel & Koçak, 2010). Kozma and Russell (1997) argued that science is based on representation or symbols by nature, and therefore they emphasized the necessity of using symbols and other forms to create meaning explicitly. Some researchers have stated that three-dimensional visual representations facilitate the understanding of chemical structures and related properties (Urhahne, Nick, & Schanze, 2009). The contribution of technology used in teaching, particularly in chemistry classes, is undeniable in terms of allowing abstract expressions to be animated through visualization (Alkan & Koçak, 2015; Altundağ & Alkan, 2016; Waight, et.al, 2014).

With the introduction of technology into education, not only has the process of structuring and using information changed but so has the process of accessing information. Knowledge use develops when the learner uses the knowledge as much as possible (Klauer, 2001). Hooper and Rieber (1995) proposed a five-factor model for accepting the use of new technologies in education: familiarization, usage, integration, reorientation, and evolution. During the familiarization phase, the teacher learns how to use the new technology. In the usage phase, the teacher starts to use the technology that he has just learned in the classroom, but it is necessary to be understanding as there will be some disruptions during use. In the integration phase, technology now becomes an integral part of the teacher's job, from teaching to classroom management. In the reorientation stage, the teacher manages to use technology effectively as a tool, depending on the function and purpose of the classroom. Finally, thanks to the experience gained during the evolution phase, the teacher can use technology more actively and successfully by shaping it according to the structure of the classroom and the purpose of education and training. Unfortunately, most teachers may not be able to progress to the integration stage. Therefore, recognizing the use of technology in the education of teachers and providing opportunities for using technology is of great importance in modern education.

Integrating advancements in information and communication technologies with educational programs will allow for the creation of a current educational level. Computer technology allows information in the individual's memory to be created graphically and symbolically. Computer technology also provides the opportunity to associate graphics and symbols while creating information, making learning more meaningful on the one hand and helping to prevent information from being forgotten on the other. Due to these features of technology applications, it is recommended that teachers give importance to technology-supported activities. Such applications allow learners to prepare for activities at their own pace. Therefore, technology enhanced courses can boost students' success while increasing their overall satisfaction and confidence (Day & Foley, 2006).

REFERENCES

Alkan, C. (1997). *Eğitim teknolojisi.* (5th Ed.). Ankara: Anı yayıncılık.

Alkan, F. & Altundağ (Koçak), C. (2015). the role of technology in science teaching activities: Web based teaching applications. *Journal for the Education of Gifted Young Scientists*, 3(2),1-7.

Alkan, F., & Koçak, C. (2015). Chemistry laboratory applications supported with simulation original research article. *International Educational Technology Conference, IETC 2014*, Chicago, IL, USA.

Altıok, S., Yükseltürk, E. & Üçgül, M. (2017). Web 2 eğitimine yönelik gerçekleştirilen bilimsel bir etkinliğin değerlendirilmesi: katılımcı görüşleri, *Öğretim Teknolojileri ve Öğretmen Eğitimi Dergisi*, *6*(1), s.1-8.

Altun, A. (2008). Yapılandırmacı öğretim sürecinde viki kullanımı. *In International Educational Technology Conference (IETC)*, Eskişehir, Türkiye.

Altundağ, Koçak C. & Alkan, F. (2016). Volümetrik titrasyonların teknoloji destekli öğretimi. *Cumhuriyet International Journal of Education*, *5*(1), 1–9.

Anderson, P. (2007). What is Web 2.0? ideas, technologies and implications for education, *Bristol: JISC*, *1*(1), 1-64.

Ayas, A. (1995). Lise 1 kimya öğrencilerinin maddenin tanecikli yapısı kavramını anlama seviyelerine ilişkin bir çalışma. II. Ulusal Fen Bilimleri Eğitimi Sempozyumu'nda sunulan bildiri. ODTÜ Eğitim Fakültesi, Ankara.

Ayas, A. (1995). Fen Bilimlerinde Program Geliştirme ve Uygulama Teknikleri Üzerine Bir Çalışma: İki Çağdaş Yaklaşımın Değerlendirilmesi. *Hacettepe Üniversitesi Eğitim Fakültesi Dergisi, 11*, 149–155.

Ayas, A., Çepni, S., Akdeniz, A., Özmen, H., Yiğit, N., & Ayvacı, H. S. (2007). *Kuramdan uygulamaya fen ve teknoloji öğretimi*. PegemA Yayıncılık.

Baumert, J., Bos, W., & Lehmann, R. (2000). *TIMSS/III: Dritte internationale mathematik-und naturwissenschaftsstudie*. Leske & Budrich.

Black, P. & Atkin, J. M. (1996). *Changing the subject: Innovations in science, mathematics and technology educations*. London: Routledge in association with OECD.

Brooks, J., & Brooks, M. (1993). *The case for the constructivist classrooms*, Alexandria, Va: Busker, M., & Flint, A. (2022). Neue Zugänge zu chemischen Reaktionen: Das Basiskonzept des Chemieunterrichts. *Unterricht Chemie, 2022*(190), 2–5.

Caladine, R. (2008). *Enhancing E-learning with media-rich content and interactions. information science publishing*. IGI Global. doi:10.4018/978-1-59904-732-4

Can, G. (1998). Fen Bilgisi öğretiminde ölçme ve değerlendirme. *Fen Bilgisi Öğretimi, 10*.

Choi, H. J., & Johnson, S. D. (2005). The effect of context-based video instruction on learning and motivation in online courses. *American Journal of Distance Education*, *19*(4), 215–227. doi:10.120715389286ajde1904_3

Çoklar, A. N. (2008). *Öğretmen adaylarının eğitim teknolojisi standartları ile ilgili öz yeterliklerinin belirlenmesi*. Doktora Tezi, Anadolu Üniversitesi, Eğitim Bilimleri Enstitüsü.

Çoklar, A. N., & Odabaşı, H. F. (2009). Eğitim teknolojisi standartları açısından öğretmen adaylarının ölçme ve değerlendirme özyeterliklerinin belirlenmesi. *Selçuk Üniversitesi. Ahmet Keleşoğlu Eğitim Fakültesi Dergisi, 27*, 1–16.

Deans, P.C. (2009). *Social software and Web 2.0 technology trends*. New York: Information science reference.

Ersoy, Y. (2013). *Fen ve Teknoloji Öğretim Programındaki Yenilikler-I: Değişikliğin Gerekçesi ve Bileşenlerin Çerçevesi.* [Innovations in science and technology curriculum-1: rationale for change and framework of components].

Georgiou, H., & Sharma, M. D. (2012). University students' understanding of thermal physics in everyday contexts. *International Journal of Science and Mathematics Education, 10*(5).

Glynn, S., & Koballa, T. R. (2005). Contextual teaching and learning. In R. E. Yager (Ed.) Exemplary Science: Best Practices in Professional Development (pp. 75-84). Arlington, VA: NSTA Press.

Gömleksiz, M. N., & Bulut, İ. (2007). Yeni fen ve teknoloji dersi öğretim programının etkililiğinin değerlendirilmesi. *Hacettepe Üniversitesi Eğitim Fakültesi Dergisi, 32,* 76–88.

Hanley, S. (1994). *On constructivism, Maryland collaborative for teacher preparation.* The https://terpconnect.umd.edu/~toh/MCTP/Essays/Constructivism.txt

Hoffmann, L., Hausler, P., & Lehrke, M. (1998). *Die IPN-Interessenstudie physik.* IPN.

İlhan, A. Ç. (2004). 21. yüzyılda öğretmen yeterlikleri. *Bilim ve Aklın Aydınlığında Eğitim Dergisi, 58,* 40–45.

İşman, A. (2003). *Öğretim teknolojileri ve materyal geliştirme.* İstanbul: Değişim yayınları.

Kan, A. (2007). Öğretmen adaylarının eğitme-öğretme öz yetkinliğine yönelik ölçek geliştirme ve eğitme-öğretme öz yetkinlikleri açısından değerlendirilmesi *Mersin Üniversitesi Eğitim Fakültesi Dergisi, 3*(1), 35-50.

Kim, M., Yoon, H., Ji, Y. R., & Song, J. (2012). The dynamics of learning science in everyday contexts: A case study of everyday science class in Korea. *International Journal of Science and Mathematics Education, 10*(1), 71–97. doi:10.100710763-011-9278-z

Köseoğlu, F., Yılmaz, H., Koç, Ş., Güneş, B., Bahar, M., Eryılmaz, A., Ateş, S., & Müyesseroğlu, Z. (2006). *İlköğretim fen ve teknoloji dersi öğretim programı.*

MEB. (2005). *İlköğretim Fen ve Teknoloji Dersi Öğretim Programı.*

Millar, R., Osborne, J., & Nott, S. (1998). Science education for the future. *The School Science Review, 80*(291), 19–24.

Nas, S. E. (2008). *Isının yayılma yolları konusunda 5E modelinin derinleşme aşamasına yönelik olarak geliştirilen materyallerin etkililiğinin değerlendirilmesi.* Yüksek Lisans Tezi, Karadeniz Teknik Üniversitesi, Fen Bilimleri Enstitüsü.

Novick, S., & Nussbaum, J. (1981). Pupils' understanding of the particulate nature of matter: A cross-age study. *Science Education, 65*(2), 187–196. doi:10.1002ce.3730650209

O'Reilly, T. (2007). What is Web2.0? Design patterns and business models for the next generation of software. *Communications & Strategies, 65*(1), 17–37. https://papers.ssrn.com/sol3/Delivery.cfm/SSRN_ID1008839_code2969338.pdf?abstractid=1008839&mirid=1

Osborne, M., & Freyberg, P. (1985). *Learning in science: Implications of children's knowledge.* Heinemann.

Pamuk, S.,Ülken, A. & Dilek, N.Ş. (2012). Öğretmen adaylarinin öğretimde teknoloji kullanim yeter-liliklerinin teknolojik pedagojik içerik bilgisi kuramsal perspektifinden incelenmesi. *Mustafa Kemal Üniversitesi Sosyal Bilimler Enstitüsü Dergisi*, 9 – 17.

Pisa-Schock. (2002). Nach dem pladoyer für eine bildungsreform pisa schock. Hamburg: Hrsg: Peter Müler, Hoffmann und Campe Verlag GmbH.

Powell, A., Farrar, E., & Cohen, D. (1985). *The shopping mall high school: Winners and losers in the educational marketplace*. Houghton Mifflin.

Reid, N. (2000). The presentation of chemistry logically driven or applications-Ied? *Chemistry Education: Research and Practice in Europe*, *1*(3), 381–392.

Renner, J. W. (1982). The power of purpose. *Science Education*, *66*(5), 709–716. doi:10.1002ce.3730660507

Sherman, T. M., & Kurshan, B. L. (2005). Constructing learning: Using technology to support teaching for understanding. *Learning and Leading with Technology*, *32*(5), 10.

Sözbilir, M., Sadi, S., Kutu, H. & Yıldırım, A. (2007*). Kimya eğitiminde içeriğe/bağlama dayalı (context-based) öğretim yaklaşimi ve dünyadaki uygulamaları*, I. Ulusal Kimya Eğitimi Kongresi, 20-22 Haziran 2007.

Terwel, J. (1999). Constructivism and its implications for curriculum theory and practice. *Journal of Curriculum Studies*, *31*(2), 195–199. doi:10.1080/002202799183223

Yager, R. (1991). The constructivist learning model: Towards real reform in science education. *Science Teacher (Normal, Ill.)*, *58*(6), 53–57.

Yam, H. (2005). What is contextual learning and teaching in physics. *Retrieved*, (November), 4.

Yılmaz, H., & Çavaş, P. H. (2006). 4-E Öğrenme döngüsü yönteminin öğrencilerin elektrik konusunu anlamalarina olan etkisi. *Türk Fen Eğitimi Dergisi*, *3*(1), 2–18.

Yücel, A. S. (2006). E-learning approach in teacher training. *Turkish Online Journal of Distance Education*, *7*(4), 123–132.

Yücel, A. S., & Koçak, C. (2010). Evaluation of the basic technology competency of the teacher's candidate according to the various variables. *2nd World Conference on Educational Sciences (WCES-2010)*, İstanbul, Turkey.

KEY TERMS AND DEFINITIONS

Chemical Compound: It is a chemical substance composed of many identical molecules containing atoms from more than one chemical element held together by chemical bonds.

Constructivism: It is a theory in education which posits that individuals or learners do not acquire knowledge and understanding by passively perceiving it within a direct process of knowledge transmission, rather they construct new understandings and knowledge through experience and social discourse, integrating new information with what they already know.

Element: It is a chemical substance that cannot be broken down into other substances.

GitMind: It is a free AI-powered mind mapping & brainstorming app.

Mixture: In chemistry, a mixture is a material made up of two or more different chemical substances which are not chemically bonded.

Pure Substance: In chemistry, it is a single substance made of only one type of particle.

Recycling: It is the process of converting waste materials into new materials and objects.

Scratch: It is a free programming language and online community where you can create your own interactive stories, games, and animations.

Wordwall: A cloze activity where you drag and drop words into blank spaces within a text.

ENDNOTE

[1] Prepared from Hacettepe University Institute of Educational Sciences Graduate Project without Thesis.

Chapter 11
Augmented Reality Enabling Better Education

Ambika N.

ⓘ https://orcid.org/0000-0003-4452-5514

St. Francis College, India

ABSTRACT

Training is a significant part of every medical services framework. Patients should be trained in their arranged methodology. The medical services experts should be prepared for their separate callings. The patient schooling and the preparation of medical care experts are face-to-face, which requires assets and is bound to specific environments. The previous methodology parts the perception plan into four levels. The issue portrayal and deliberation depend on the planned concentrate on approach, which carries us to the main level of the settled model. Diverse works are within the accompanying watchword blends connecting with the study. The framework has various pictures. The patient lies in a warped place, and a revision of their position is done. The gantry moves to its underlying location. The gantry gadget moves back to its unique position. The table dives so the patient can get up and leave the room. VIPER was furnished with sound. The term of the entire data movement was 2:45 min.

INTRODUCTION

A real-time direct or indirect view of a physical, real-world environment that has been enhanced or augmented by adding virtual information generated by computers is called augmented reality (Ambika, 2022) (Carmigniani & Furht, 2011). It combines real and virtual objects, is interactive, and can be registered in three dimensions. Fumio Kishino and Paul Milgram define Milgram's Reality-Virtuality Continuum as a continuum that divides the real and virtual environments, with Augmented Reality (Furht, 2011) being closer to the real world and Augmented Virtuality being closer to a purely virtual environment. Augmented reality makes the user's life easier by bringing virtual information to the user's immediate surroundings and any indirect view of the real-world environment, such as a live video stream. The user's perception of and interaction with the natural world are enhanced by augmented reality. By sensory substitution, it can also use augmented reality to augment or substitute users' missing senses. For instance,

DOI: 10.4018/978-1-6684-7644-4.ch011

it can use audio cues to increase the sight of blind or visually impaired users, and it can use visual cues to augment the hearing of deaf users.

Virtual objects are superimposed on the natural environment in the form of augmented reality, which meets three requirements:

- Run interactively and in real-time.
- Register real and virtual objects with one another.
- Combine real and virtual things in a natural environment.

Augmented reality should accurately align the virtual world with the real one. Virtual reality technology, on the one hand, creates a virtual environment that is presented to our senses so that we feel as though we were there. On the other hand, augmented reality (AR) is the process of incorporating virtual objects into a live, three-dimensional scene. Augment reality systems must estimate the virtual object's position and orientation in real-time to guarantee consistent object overlap. Utilizing markers in the actual location is one of the most common methods for obtaining this estimate. Cameras will identify these markers and compare them to previously established patterns. Fig. 1 is a similar instance using the technology.

Figure 1. AR prototype created with Unity
(Gong, Wang, & Xia, 2022)

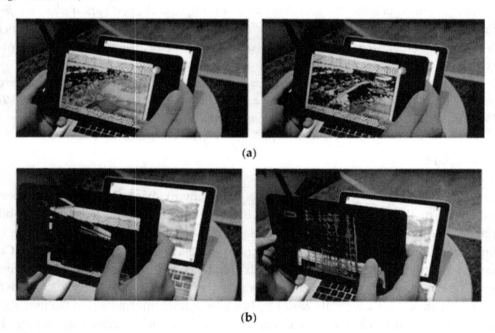

(a)

(b)

Using music experiences and the relationships that develop as a result of them as dynamic forces of change, the therapist in music therapy assists the client in promoting health. It has been defined as a systematic process of intervention. It's possible that just listening to music will automatically change your mood. The listener may immediately be inundated with beautiful ideas when a pleasant memory or association comes to mind. A profound state of relaxation, a peak joyous experience, or a profound comprehension or insight may result. With the individual patient's knowledge and input, the music therapist is responsible for selecting the most suitable music and guiding the patient toward the best possible outcome. Through success-oriented methods, music therapists get people involved in an aesthetic music activity where they add their note or sound, phrase or melody, drum beat, or more sophisticated accompaniment to the musical performance or composition. They take part at whatever level, boosting their self-efficacy and self-esteem. Music therapists are skilled at providing participants with opportunities to improvise, perform, sing, move to, or discuss the music that is particularly meaningful to them or suitable for their specific needs. The suggestion considers music along with augment reality.

One computer for processing, one head-mounted display with a camera, and one electronic keyboard make up the physical setup (Chow, Feng, Amor, & Wünsche, 2013). The user sits in front of the keyboard and wears the head-mounted display. A MIDI interface connects the keyboard to the computer. A USB interface is used to connect the laptop to the head-mounted display. A Trivisio ARvision-3D HMD1 is the head-mounted display we use for this project. The video captured by the cameras in front of the device must be projected onto the display. The system's representation of notes needs to show the key of notice. The music and rhythm games, as well as Karaoke videos, in which text and music are synchronized with visual cues, served as sources of inspiration for the work. Each note is addressed as a line over the comparing key, where the sequence length handles the note's term. In the AR view, the notes move steadily toward the keys. Pressing the appropriate key should occur as soon as the message reaches the keyboard. The key should be released when the note's end comes to the keyboard. A MIDI file that has been saved is used to load the music score and virtual notes. The quality of the user's performance is measured using this MIDI file as a model. The system strictly enforces it uses the timings contained in a MIDI file for each note. C# to create the application. The work used Emgu CV, a .NET wrapper for OpenCV, to take pictures from the camera.

The work (Poupyrev, et al., 2001) is an Augmented Groove, a novel musical instrument that attempts to deviate from conventional methods of performing music, such as using dials, keyboards, or simulated traditional musical controllers. By manipulating simple physical objects, novices can play electronic musical compositions and interactively remix and modulate their elements. During a demonstration at the SIGGRAPH 2000 Emerging Technologies exhibition, it used informal user feedback to gather informal evaluations for Augmented Groove. Visitors could play musical compositions on three records, allowing elements from three tracks to be mixed and modulated simultaneously.

It is a music therapy experiment (Correa, Ficheman, do, & de Deus Lopes, 2009)using an augmented reality musical system. It was developed using augmented reality techniques, making it possible to play games that follow sound and color and create music. The system lets users create melodies, save them, and use them in new music compositions by emulating the sounds of various musical instruments. Color cards with musical symbols allow users to interact with the system. These cards, printed on paper in multiple colors and sizes to replace the keyboard for musical composition, can be positioned following the desired motor exercise. A webcam's image processing allows for the identification of the cards. The system associates a musical instrument's sound and pitch with each printed card symbol. The default instrument is a piano. Users must place one hand in the center of the card without touching it to make a sound. Card obstruction is detected using image processing methods. The music therapist experimented on a child with cerebral palsy following the evaluation.

BACKGROUND

Self-selected music may distract attention and elicit a more robust emotional response regarding the underlying psychological mechanisms. Choosing and listening to the music you like may also help you feel more in control in scary or unfamiliar situations. In these situations, listening to music serves as a distracting stimulus. We are not paying attention to the unpleasant stimulus when we are listening to our favorite music or paying less attention to it. Because we are emotionally engaged while listening to our favorite music, we can move away from the unpleasant stimulus. In addition, listening to self-selected music in a laboratory setting is like bringing a familiar inspiration into an unfamiliar environment, which may also help people feel more in control in unfamiliar situations.

Figure 2. Music-based Interventions in healthcare
(Stegemann, Geretsegger, Phan Quoc, Riedl, & Smetana, 2019)

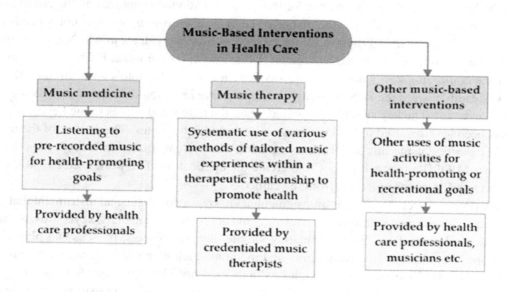

There was a discussion of two projects (MacDonald, 2013) that took a straightforward approach to music therapy. The first, a group improv session with cancer patients, focused on essential aspects of the musical and social environment that can help participants have positive experiences. The improvisatory setting of the sessions was of the utmost significance, which is a crucial point here. The field of improvisation as a whole—and improvised music in particular—receives much attention from academics. Understanding the distinct musical, mental, individual, and social processes through which improvisation takes place in music is a crucial area of interest for music psychology. Musical improvisation offers opportunities for negotiating differences through creative collaboration. It used therapeutic songwriting in the second study, which took place in the context of music therapy. The songwriting process can be creative, collaborative, and expressive, and this project demonstrated a primary method for facilitating participants' positive development.

APPLICATIONS

The combination of technologies that make it possible to mix computer-generated content with a live video display in real-time is referred to as "augmented reality." It interacts not only with a virtual world but also has a degree of interdependence with the natural world and is based on techniques developed in virtual reality. Computer science interface research is where augmented reality technology began. The popular media frequently employ the term "virtual reality" to describe fictitious worlds that exist only in our minds and computers. It improves a user's understanding of and engagement with the real world. The virtual objects display information that the user cannot directly perceive with his senses. A user can use the information provided by the virtual objects to complete real-world tasks.

CHEMISTRY

Figure 3. Augment reality in chemistry
(Keller, Rumann, & Habig, 2021)

Augmented reality apps can use smartphone cameras to transform paper-based, two-dimensional molecular models into three-dimensional ones that users can manipulate. An augmented reality application (Behmke, et al., 2018) that transforms two-dimensional representations of molecular structures into interactive three-dimensional structures is the subject of the work. It will be developed, implemented, and evaluated. One of the many augmented reality platforms that have previously been utilized in educational settings is Aurasma. This platform is free to use for non-commercial purposes, and it offers apps for Android and iOS mobile devices. It has been in operation for some time and provides a reasonable level of stability. A simple web-based authoring environment for creating auras, or augmented reality artifacts, is also provided. There were several steps involved in creating a 3-D molecular aura that a user could manipulate, making a two-dimensional drawing of the molecule. When it pointed the app's camera on the mobile device at this drawing, it eventually served as the trigger for the augmentation. The molecular structure was created as a .mol file. Blender, a free and open-source 3-D creation suite, was used to convert the .mol file into a protein database file into a 3-D molecular structure. The aura was made by linking the 3-D structure file to the 2-D drawing as an overlay in Aurasma Studio.

In addition to designing and developing a set of inquiry-based Augmented Reality learning tools, the study (Cai, Wang, & Chiang, 2014) focused on the composition of substances section of junior high school chemistry classes. It focuses on how augmented reality-based learning tools enhance chemistry instruction. The subject matter of "The composition of substances" was covered in the testing class. Before the design and development of this AR tool, the chemistry teacher was interviewed by the authors. She said that her previous experiences showed that students were not very motivated and did not fully understand the materials in this chapter because the content was dull and abstract. A group of experts in chemistry education, including two junior high school chemistry teachers and three professors who specialize in science education, further examined the quiz, which a junior high school chemistry teacher created. The paper and pencil test has 32 points and 32 effective blanks related to the learning content "the composition of substances." The work created a scenario for inquiry-based group learning in which students were required to explore in groups of three without instruction from their teachers. The activity form helps them learn by giving them operation steps that show them what to do and asking them questions to get them thinking and making connections. The AR software, six markers, and activity form that we created as part of this study make up the set of augmented reality tools. NyARToolkit, Java3D, and Java Media Framework are among the additional packages utilized in the software, which is written in Java.

BIOLOGY

Figure 4. Heart and blood vessels augmented reality (AR) model screenshot
(Petrov & Atanasova, 2020)

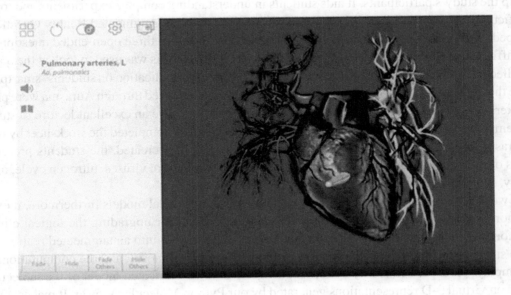

A case study (Petrov & Atanasova, 2020) used this tool to teach STEM (science, technology, engineering, and math) content at a Sofia secondary school. The hardware of the zSpace® system uses a circularly polarized light that enters the eye to switch between the left and right images on the LCD screen, which has 1920 x 1080 pixels. The computer uses the small reflective tabs in the glasses to determine where the wearer is looking. By focusing on the image, this software prevents nausea and headaches. zSpace® combines VR and augmented reality to create lifelike immersive, and interactive experiences. Students can use the system to run experiments, dissect animals and their organs, manipulate compounds and structures in 3D, and save money on expensive lab supplies. High school students were the intended participants, and they were divided into three groups based on their study tracks: humanitarian, STEM, and information technologies. The heart and blood vessels were among the topics covered in the course. Before this study, the students had not used any augmented reality tools.

Mitosis, meiosis, respiration, and their systematic relationships are covered in this educational application for Form 4 Biology Science in Malaysian secondary schools (Weng, Bee, Yew, & Hsia, 2016) that uses Augmented Reality technology. It focuses on the requirements of the students for knowledge regularity. By providing a brief augmented video or 3D storytelling, they create scenarios to explain aerobic and anaerobic respiration to students, such as when these types of respiration will occur in certain circumstances. In addition, ATTech gives students feedback to let them know if they did the exercises right or wrong. The dedicated stereoscopic and photo-realistic views of these lessons make it easier for students to notice, remember, and comprehend concepts in biology. It enables social communication while allowing for personal interaction among students (Given that thinking is epistemic and its organization has individual and social dimensions).

This study (Yapici & Karakoyun, 2021) examined how prospective teachers felt about using Augmented Reality in biology instruction. A case study was the idea behind the study. The 16 future teachers who took Instructional Technologies and Material Design in the third grade in the Biology Teaching Department of a state university's Faculty of Education during the spring term of the 2018–2019 academic year made up the study's participants. It aids students in understanding complex experiments and topics that are difficult to explain and cost a lot of money. Using the "Mobile Augmented Reality Questionnaire" developed by Küçük, Kapakin, and Göktaş, the interview form has three open-ended questions. There are 23 affirmative statements of the Likert type in it. Content analysis was used to look at the qualitative data collected for the study. It installed the Aurasma (HP Reveal) application on students' smartphones to prepare the AR content. Two-layered pictures on the materials arranged through Aurasma were presented as markers. With the help of augmented reality, the researchers gave an excellent lecture to students to help them better understand how to use the program. The students completed the worksheet by watching the Aurasma-created scheme animation. Using the materials they created, the students presented the subjects of their choice. On the muscular system, aerobic respiration, viruses, nitrogen cycle, and heart anatomy, students prepared AG-compatible materials.

The work exhibits the utilization of auto-manufactured substantial models furthermore, it expanded reality for examination and showing in sub-atomic science and for upgrading the logical climate for joint effort and investigation. The physical models are incorporated into an augmented reality environment to simplify the interface between human intent, the physical model, and the computational activity. It employs an expanded reality system that enables an auto-fabricated model of the molecule to be overlaid on virtual 3-D representations generated by our Python Molecular Viewer. It makes it possible to create models with varying degrees of abstraction for various purposes: when large systems and interactions are presented, using representations that focus on molecular shape and incorporating atomic details when necessary to examine function at the nuclear level. The ARToolKit library, developed at the University of Washington, is used to precisely register virtual objects with the real world. Additionally, new components have been designed to export the PMV environment-generated representations in STL or VRML for use in the rapid prototyping machinery. Atomic coordinates are converted into a surface- or feature-based model using a parser. Two technologies for rapid prototyping are used in work. The Z-corp method applies a pigment-binder mixture to powdered gypsum Using ink-jet print heads. After construction, the parts are finished by introducing a strengthening agent into the model. Stratasys employs a fused deposition technique for each layer that involves extruding molten ABS plastic filament.

MATHEMATICS

Figure 5. Convex and concave polyhedra
(Fernández-Enríquez & Delgado-Martín, 2020)

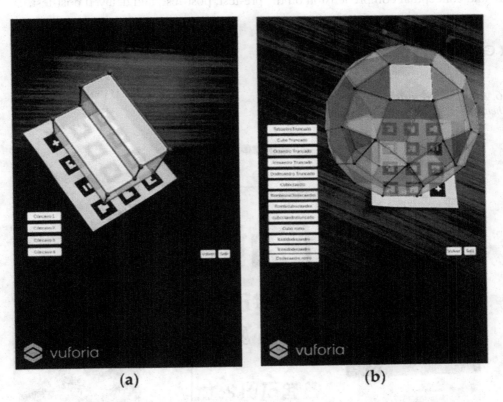

It is a three-point framework (Bujak, et al., 2013). It comprehends augmented reality learning is provided in the recommendation. It asserts both pragmatically and cognitively oriented learning goals. It is supported by physical interaction with objects. As evidenced by their rapid acquisition of eye movement control and hand reaching and grasping, infants begin developing motor skills from birth. On the cognitive level, the study discusses how augmented reality experiences that align information spatially and temporally can help students better understand symbolic concepts by scaffolding the learning process. It argues that augmented reality creates opportunities for collaborative learning around virtual content and in unconventional settings, ultimately facilitating personally meaningful experiences.

The study (Estapa & Nadolny, 2015) looked at student achievement and motivation during an augmented reality mathematics activity at a high school that focused on dimensional analysis. Within a single comprehensive high school in rural Iowa, the gathered data. The same math teacher instructed students in two classes—geometry and algebra—.Sixty-one students from these classes participated in the study, with 56 percent female. Algebra and geometry classes were randomly assigned to treatment groups using a quasi-experimental design. The high school math teacher and the research team created a printed handout with six problems using dimensional analysis to convert units. The high school math teacher chose the specific idea of dimensional analysis because his students didn't understand it in all his classes. The dimensional analysis activity gave you a chance to meet the needs of teachers in several different subject areas. A spring break road trip from Iowa to Cancun, Mexico, served as a common thread through which all of the particular issues were connected. It used the Layar Creator software and a companion mobile application to create the augmented reality environment. Ten questions assessed technical and conceptual comprehension on the pre-test, post-test, and delayed post-test.

TOUR GUIDE

Figure 6. Augmented guide service
(Lin & Chen, 2017)

The Technology Acceptance Model and Uses and Gratifications Theory were also used in this study (Lin & Chen, 2017) to predict users' attitudes toward the AR tour-sharing app's advertised attractions and their intention to use it. It is designed as an augmented reality tour-sharing app that lets users record their visits to each attraction for future reference, provides relevant tour information, and guides users through augmented reality technology. The introduction was printed for the Tour of Hakka Attractions in Thailand to give the tourists pertinent tour information. Users can ask questions by clicking the QAS button. When users tap the play sign, the tour-sharing APP automatically identifies the attraction photos in the introduction, converts the static images into dynamic videos, and begins the video introductions after users initialize the tour-sharing APP on their smartphones. AR guide services give users dynamic warm-ups, let them look through a lot of information about local attractions, and offer guide services.

At the interests, users can record tour videos by double-tapping the play sign. The tour-sharing APP also lets users share videos on social media sites like Facebook after they record videos of the attractions. With the proposed novel random neural networks, a query-answering server is proposed to analyze user queries and classify them into question classes for finding answers. A Chinese knowledge information processing tool and a segmentation mechanism are used to retrieve each word in the query sentence after receiving it. A TF-IDF component is applied to determine the weighting worth of each word in a sentence. The study suggested RNNs with two stages, the training stage, and runtime. Setting the parameters of RNNs, retrieving the vector set of TF-IDF in each sentence in the historical database, and randomly generating m neural network models are the four steps in the training stage. as well as kNN model filtering. Thirty-six users participated in the experiments, and it created thirty-question classes.

The paper (Seo, Kim, & Park, 2010) presents an augmented reality-based on-site tour guide that virtually recreates and visualizes past life at cultural heritage sites. In the local escort, vivified three-dimensional virtual characters are superimposed on the social legacy destinations by outwardly following essential mathematical natives of the destinations like square shapes and assessing camera represents that can be considered a traveler's perspective. There are four parts to the proposed AR tour guide's framework. A camera attached to the augmented reality tour guide takes a snapshot or live video image of the target scenes in the input agent. Using a stylus pen or finger, all required to access a tourist's profile is the selection of graphic user interface menus. A tourist's locations are identified in the context-aware component by comparing snapshot images of wooden tablets to their predefined reference images from a database. After that, they are sent to agents for context and map management. The context management agent organizes contextual information like the tourist's locations, age, and language profiles and links to the information and content of each database that corresponds to them. A tracking module and a rendering module make up the augmentation portion. Without additional sensors (Nagaraj, 2021), the camera pose is estimated by visually tracking the target scenes' simple geometric primitives. In Gyeongbokgung, it put the AR tour guide's prototype through its paces at Gangnyeongjeon and Gyotaejeon. The prototype was used on a laptop with a USB camera (MS LifeCam NX-6000, resolution 640 by 480, 15 frames per second) and an Intel Core2 1.20 GHz processor (LG X-NOTE C1).

INDUSTRIAL MAINTENANCE

Figure 7. Use case setup
(Ortega, et al., 2021)

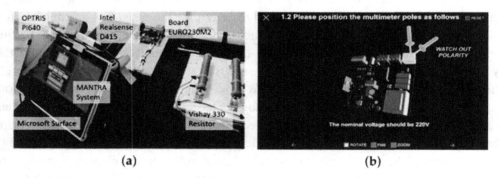

Any three-dimensional object can have virtual information and temperature aligned automatically and immediately by the system (Ortega, et al., 2021). An IRT camera and an RGB-D sensor are used together, resulting in high accuracy and robustness. A posture assessment strategy consolidates a profound learning-based object discovery technique, YOLOV4, along with the layout-based LINEMOD present assessment strategy, as well as a model-based 6DOF posture following method, was created. The 6DOF pose tracking module, the process for incorporating IRT information into the augmented reality system, and the 3D object detection and estimation method. A Microsoft Surface Book 2 and two small cameras make up the AR system known as MANTRA. These are an Optris PI640 thermal imaging camera and an Intel RealSense d415 RGB-D camera with a color resolution of up to 1920 x 1080. A graphical user interface was developed that reads XML files and enables the dynamic loading of maintenance and repair tasks.

BUSINESS

Figure 8. Adapted Milgram's reality–virtuality continuum for the automotive industry
(Boboc, Gîrbacia, & Butilă, 2020)

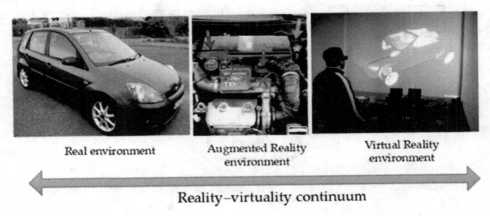

This research (Hagl & Duane, 2020) aims to gain a deeper comprehension of how AR/VR technologies influence the development of new business models in technology companies. It explores the group of information concerning contemporary plan of action development and presents a reasonable structure to direct the exploration. The German business-to-business technology companies that use AR/VR technologies to innovate their business models are the focus of this holistic multiple-case study design. The author developed six criteria for pre-selecting cases. It used thirty-four vital literary phrases in an online case study search, and when it combined them with the terms AR/VR, it produced 68 English and 66 German search strings. In April 2018, a senior AR/VR developer participated in a pre-pilot test. The interviewee picked a VR case carried out on a client in 2017. Visitors to the exposition got a novel experience thanks to the project.

LITERATURE SURVEY

Augment reality is also interesting to clinical care because it gives doctors a view of the patient without requiring invasive procedures. There is a clear need further to investigate the use of augmented reality in healthcare education because medical professionals and students require more situational experiences in clinical care, particularly for patient safety. It gives students a chance to learn more accurately and appeals to various learning styles, giving them a more individualized and exploratory learning experience. Patients' safety is protected if mistakes are made during AR skills training. This section briefs the various contributions towards the domain.

Figure 9. System architecture
(Vidal-Balea, Blanco-Novoa, Fraga-Lamas, & Fernández-Caramés, 2021)

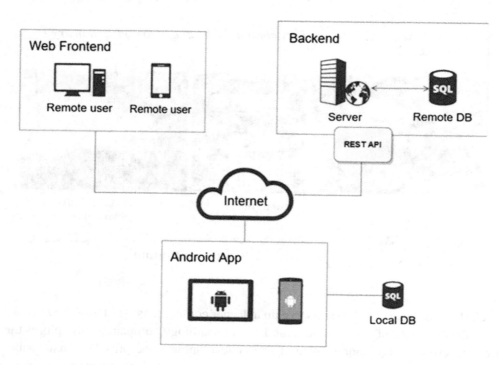

Three parts make up the architecture (Vidal-Balea, Blanco-Novoa, Fraga-Lamas, & Fernández-Caramés, 2021). The backend manages the requests from mobile and web applications through a Representational State Transfer Application Programming Interface. Improving patients' quality of life is always one of the top priorities in a hospital setting. It is essential to reduce anxiety to help children feel more at ease and relaxed during interventions and medical tests that may be performed on them while at the hospital. Less anxious children are more likely to cooperate, have less fear of procedures, require fewer sedatives, and have shorter recovery times. Play activities, such as therapeutic play or play therapy, are frequently used during hospitalization to improve patients' physical and emotional well-being and speed up their recovery. Games are appropriate for pre-operative preparations and invasive procedures because they can lessen the intensity of the negative emotions accompanying children's hospitalizations. The testing group would initially be divided into two subgroups -one person who would use the app daily and another who would not. The plan would be to ask for changes in things like children's behavior, pain level, and mood during their hospital stay in periodic surveys. The experiment's final stage would consist of comparing the results of the two groups and determining whether the proposed application is practical. It would be necessary to carry out surveys before and after children undergo medical tests (To determine whether the mobile application is helpful in such situations). During this evaluation, the application's usability will also be examined, with questions about this topic included in surveys and how children use the application.

The Studierstube system (Kaufmann, 2003) is the foundation of Construct3D. It allows multiple users to share a virtual space by utilizing augmented reality. It makes it possible to combine input from various tracking devices with heterogeneous output devices like personal HMDs, virtual workbenches, and conventional monitors. Each of these devices appears to be an interface to a single distributed system. It uses constructing primitives like points, lines, planes, cubes, spheres, cylinders, and cones as the basic set of functions. The construction functions are intersections, Boolean operations, regular lines and planes, symmetry operations, and taking measurements. Dynamic geometry encourages and supports exploratory behavior. It uses a stylus with six degrees of freedom and direct 3D manipulation, and each construction step is completed. Because AR lets users see their own hands and bodies and the effects of their actions as they work, the construction process involves students physically and more closely resembles handwork than computer work.

A PC gadget (Kamphuis, Barsom,, Schijven, & Christoph, 2014) is required to interface virtual substance to this present reality. It can observe the actual world through this device's window (display). A software application for this device is also required for the virtual components. It becomes visible in this window as an enhancement to reality. The user wears the display on their head, mounted in a helmet or glasses. All augmented reality hardware devices share a processor, camera, GPS, sensors, and compass. Marker-based augmented reality uses images in two or three dimensions, like a QR code or a natural object that the software application can recognize. The augmented virtual content is created and projected onto the identified object by the augmented reality software application when it receives input from the marker or object. The user believes that additional information is present in the environment. Markerless augmented reality uses positional data to locate the user, such as using a compass and a global positioning system to determine orientation or infrared light to produce a silhouette-shaped depth image. In light of this data, the product application can expand the virtual substance on an exact area on or inside the genuine climate, whether or not or not that environment is static.

The project (Martin, Bohuslava, & Igor, 2018) aims to modernize the teaching of industrial auto-mation subjects in specialized laboratories by implementing and utilizing the Industry 4.0 concept. WordPress, an open-source Content Management System with a modular structure that perfectly meets the requirements for such oriented systems, is the foundation for the learning system architecture. A custom data model of the learning component of the entire system enhances the core database of the learning system, which is implemented in a MySql server environment. Expandability of the core of the learning system by user-created javascript or PHP modules, plugins, or snippets makes it possible to create a communication module between the AFB Factory's process level and the core of the learning system. The application web server's request to the PLC web server of a specific workstation results in data sharing from the process level to the AR module. It can use the station AR marker's QR code to identify a particular workstation. On the client side, these data are processed by an application, either in a straightforward graphical form or by altering the properties of virtual scene objects. The selected technical element's and superior unit's technical data are retrieved from the application server's database to supplement the visual portion.

The Tracker image, or live feed camera image, is taken by the camera in this system (Bahuguna, Verma, & Raj, 2018). The Pattern Recognition phase is the next step. In this phase, the tracker image is processed with the assistance of an image processing model to identify the Patten hidden behind the 2D image and link the identified Patten to the appropriate 3D object. Several software packages and hardware are used to create an augmented reality mobile application. The four steps that make up the Android application development process for augmented reality. There are numerous open sources for creating interactive 3D models with visual effects, art, animation, simulation, texture, and raster graphics. An image is tracked reasonably and reasonably compatible with the real and virtual worlds. The vuforia software kit is available for use in creating a tracker image. Every image loaded onto Vuforia's website has its unique pattern. The tool lets you embed a Tracker image and a 3-D model into a Unity package. It is possible to generate an Android file that runs on Android mobile devices running version 4.0 with the assistance of Java and Android Studio.

The Bangor Augmented Reality Education Tool for Anatomy (BARETA) (Thomas, William John, & Delieu, 2010) is a system that combines Rapid Prototyping models with Augmented Reality technology to stimulate both sight and touch in the student. The model was used to manipulate a volume rendering of a human head and was equipped with a miniBIRD sensor so that BARETA could track it. It was possible for the volume rendering to be registered with the model because the dataset used for the volume rendering was the same dataset used to create the model. The entire head was volume rendered rather than just the segmented area. Additionally, it visualized the model's surface model of the ventricles. The surface was rendered in a way that made it look like the ventricles in the volume rendering. The character and volume data assembly made it possible to manipulate both representations with a single transformation. When transformations changed, this also ensured that it kept correct registration. The community underwent two transformations to guarantee that the on-screen rendering and the model registered correctly. The primary change changes the posture of the focal point of the revolution of the gathering. It mirrors the place of the sensor inside the model. It scaled the assembly in the second transformation to match the size of the model displayed on the screen. During volume rendering, it used a piecewise transfer function to keep air from being shown while allowing the organ of interest to be seen. The remaining voxels were made entirely opaque, while all voxels with values less than two were made completely transparent. Utilizing the clipping plane and slab rendering features was the first way it could view the volume, making it possible to see the ventricles. Using a different transfer function that reduced the volume rendering's opacity to the point where the ventricles could be seen while still allowing the volume rendering to be seen as the second method by which it accomplished this.

PREVIOUS WORK

Using a Microsoft HoloLens head-mounted display, the design study describes proofs of concept for two augmented reality (AR) educational tools. VIPER (Raith, Kamp, Stoiber, Jakl, & Wagner, 2022) is an AR prototype aiming to help oncologists and radiographers by providing a reliable source of information and helping cancer patients reduce their anxiety before their first irradiation. The patient waits for a call to enter the irradiation room and places themselves on the treatment table at the beginning of the sequence. Near the irradiation position, the treatment table moves. The patient lies in a crooked part due to the laser's work and the skin markers, and their job is corrected. The irradiation begins after the gantry returns to its initial position. The animation's irradiation duration carefully matched the actual irradiation duration. The gantry device returns to its initial position following the irradiation process, and the table descends to allow the patient to get up and leave the room. VIPER received sound after the modelling and animation were finished.

Figure 10. Sequence of patient information in VIPER
(Raith, Kamp, Stoiber, Jakl, & Wagner, 2022)

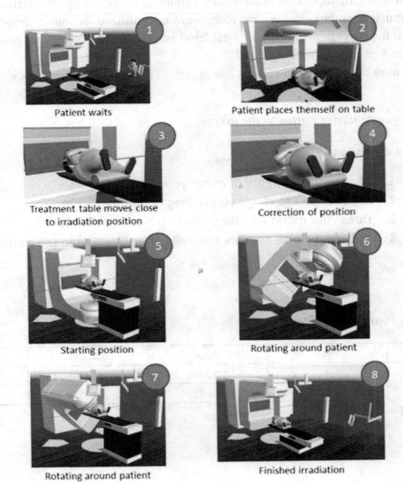

CASE STUDY

VIPER (Raith, Kamp, Stoiber, Jakl, & Wagner, 2022) is an AR prototype aiming to help oncologists and radiographers by providing a reliable source of information and helping cancer patients reduce their anxiety before their first irradiation. The patient waits for a call to enter the irradiation room and places themselves on the treatment table at the beginning of the sequence. Near the irradiation position, the treatment table moves. The patient lies in a crooked part due to the laser's work and the skin markers, and their job is corrected. The irradiation begins after the gantry returns to its initial position. The animation's irradiation duration carefully matched the actual irradiation duration. The gantry device returns to its initial position following the irradiation process, and the table descends to allow the patient to get up and leave the room. VIPER received sound after the modelling and animation were finished.

The use of music therapy for mood and emotion regulation may be beneficial. People with depression and anxiety may benefit from music therapy in reducing their symptoms. Additionally, music therapy aids in everyday life functions. Digital technology has been utilized in treatment and assessment in the clinical practice of music therapy. Computer-assisted charting programs like SCRIBE, AIMSTAR, and EMTEK, which music therapists did not develop, were also utilized by music therapists. To provide better environment for the patients, music is considered as healer. The patients are given music therapy with their favourite's games in the foreground.

1553 samples were collected from various age groups. The following questions were posted.

Figure 11. List of questionaries posted to the users

Questionaries

1. Choose the category of music you like?
2. Choose the age range you belong to?
3. Does your mood elevate when you listen to the music?
4. Will you be able to work normally after listening to the music?

Table 1. Analysis of variance results

Groups	N	Mean	Std. Dev	Std. Error
Types of music chosen	9	172.5556	151.1804	50.3935
Age group	4	388.25	214.8525	107.4262

F-statistic value = 4.41042
P-value = 0.05959

Table 2. ANOVA summary

Source	Degrees of Freedom (DF)	Sum of Squares	Mean squares	F-stat
Between groups	1	128835.8978	128835.8978	
Within groups	11	321328.897	29211.7179	4.4104
Total	12	450164.7948		

Figure 12. One-way ANOVA

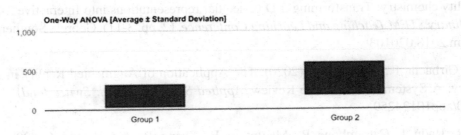

CONCLUSION

Virtual objects are added to the real world through augmented reality, giving the impression that they are in the same space as the real world. It has the potential to facilitate the exploration of the complex interconnections found in real-world information and to provide robust, contextual, and situated learning experiences. Using augmented reality, students can learn new things by interacting with virtual objects that bring data to life. In higher education, augmented reality is used in various fields, including - the sciences of the environment, ecology, language, chemistry, geography, and history.

VIPER is an AR prototype aiming to help oncologists and radiographers by providing a reliable source of information and helping cancer patients reduce their anxiety before their first irradiation. The patient waits for a call to enter the irradiation room and places themselves on the treatment table at the beginning of the sequence. Near the irradiation position, the treatment table moves. The patient lies in a crooked part due to the laser's work and the skin markers, and their job is corrected. The irradiation begins after the gantry returns to its initial position. The animation's irradiation duration carefully matched the actual irradiation duration. The gantry device returns to its initial position following the irradiation process, and the table descends to allow the patient to get up and leave the room. VIPER received sound after the modelling and animation were finished.

The increasing evidence supports music therapy and other music-based interventions in childhood and adolescence. It indicates that treatment is especially effective in enhancing communication, social skills, and quality of life. Music medicine techniques successfully reduce stress, anxiety, and pain. The suggestion adopts music therapy along with augmented games that aims in better elevation of mood of the patient.

REFERENCES

Ambika, N. (2022). An Augmented Edge Architecture for AI-IoT Services Deployment in the Modern Era. In *Handbook of Research on Technical, Privacy, and Security Challenges in a Modern World* (pp. 286–302). IGI Global.

Bahuguna, Y., Verma, A., & Raj, K. (2018). Smart learning based on augmented reality with android platform and its applicability. *3rd International Conference On Internet of Things: Smart Innovation and Usages (IoT-SIU)*. Bhimtal, India. 10.1109/IoT-SIU.2018.8519853

Behmke, D., Kerven, D., Lutz, R., Paredes, J., Pennington, R., Brannock, E., & Stevens, K. (2018). Augmented reality chemistry: Transforming 2-D molecular representations into Interactive 3-D structures. *Interdisciplinary STEM Teaching and Learning Conference*, (2, pp. 3-11). Georgia Southern University. 10.20429tem.2018.020103

Boboc, R., Gîrbacia, F., & Butilă, E. (2020). The Application of Augmented Reality in the Automotive Industry: A Systematic Literature Review. *Applied Sciences (Basel, Switzerland)*, *10*(12), 4259. doi:10.3390/app10124259

Bujak, K. R., Radu, I., Catrambone, R., MacIntyre, B., Zheng, R., & Golubski, G. (2013). A psychological perspective on augmented reality in the mathematics classroom. *Computers & Education*, *68*, 536–544. doi:10.1016/j.compedu.2013.02.017

Cai, S., Wang, X., & Chiang, F. K. (2014). A case study of Augmented Reality simulation system application in a chemistry course. *Computers in Human Behavior*, *37*, 31–40. doi:10.1016/j.chb.2014.04.018

Carmigniani, J., & Furht, B. (2011). Augmented reality: an overview. In Handbook of augmented reality (pp. 3-46). Springer. doi:10.1007/978-1-4614-0064-6_1

Chow, J., Feng, H., Amor, R., & Wünsche, B. C. (2013). Music education using augmented reality with a head mounted display. *Fourteenth Australasian User Interface Conference* (pp. 73-79). Australian Computer Society.

Correa, A. G., & Ficheman, I. K., d. N., & de Deus Lopes, R. (2009). Computer assisted music therapy: A case study of an augmented reality musical system for children with cerebral palsy rehabilitation. *Ninth IEEE International Conference on Advanced Learning Technologies* (pp. 218-22). Riga, Latvia: IEEE. 10.1109/ICALT.2009.111

Estapa, A., & Nadolny, L. (2015). The effect of an augmented reality enhanced mathematics lesson on student achievement and motivation. *Journal of STEM Education: Innovations and Research*, *16*(3), 40–48.

Fernández-Enríquez, R., & Delgado-Martín, L. (2020). Augmented Reality as a Didactic Resource for Teaching Mathematics. *Applied Sciences (Basel, Switzerland)*, *10*(7), 2560. doi:10.3390/app10072560

Furht, B. (2011). Handbook of augmented reality. Springer Science & Business Media. doi:10.1007/978-1-4614-0064-6

Gong, Z., Wang, R., & Xia, G. (2022). Augmented Reality (AR) as a Tool for Engaging Museum Experience: A Case Study on Chinese Art Pieces. *Digital*, *2*(1), 33–45. doi:10.3390/digital2010002

Hagl, R., & Duane, A. (2020). Exploring how augmented reality and virtual reality technologies impact business model innovation in technology companies in Germany. In *Augmented Reality and Virtual Reality* (pp. 75–84). Springer. doi:10.1007/978-3-030-37869-1_7

Kamphuis, C. B. E., Schijven, M., & Christoph, N. (2014). Augmented reality in medical education? *Perspectives on Medical Education*, *3*(4), 300–311. doi:10.1007/S40037-013-0107-7 PMID:24464832

Kaufmann, H. (2003). Collaborative augmented reality in education. *Institute of software technology and interactive systems*, 2-4.

Keller, S., Rumann, S., & Habig, S. (2021). Cognitive Load Implications for Augmented Reality Supported Chemistry Learning. *Information (Basel)*, *12*(3), 96. doi:10.3390/info12030096

Lin, H.-F., & Chen, C.-H. (2017). Combining the Technology Acceptance Model and Uses and Gratifications Theory to examine the usage behavior of an Augmented Reality Tour-sharing Application. *Symmetry*, *9*(7), 113. doi:10.3390ym9070113

MacDonald, R. A. (2013). Music, health, and well-being: A review. *International Journal of Qualitative Studies on Health and Well-being*, *8*(1), 20635. doi:10.3402/qhw.v8i0.20635 PMID:23930991

Martin, J., Bohuslava, J., & Igor, H. (2018). Augmented reality in education 4.0. *13th international scientific and technical conference on computer sciences and information technologies (CSIT)*, *1*, pp. 231-236. Lviv, Ukraine.

Nagaraj, A. (2021). Introduction to Sensors in IoT and Cloud Computing Applications. Bentham Science Publishers.

Ortega, M., Ivorra, E., Juan, A., Venegas, P., Martínez, J., & Alcañiz, M. (2021). MANTRA: An Effective System Based on Augmented Reality and Infrared Thermography for Industrial Maintenance. *Applied Sciences (Basel, Switzerland)*, *11*(1), 385. doi:10.3390/app11010385

Petrov, P., & Atanasova, T. (2020). The Effect of Augmented Reality on Students' Learning Performance in Stem Education. *Information (Basel)*, *11*(4), 209. doi:10.3390/info11040209

Poupyrev, I., Berry, R., Billinghurst, M. K. H., Nakao, K., Baldwin, L., & Kurumisawa, J. (2001). Augmented reality interface for electronic music performance. *9th International Conference on Human-Computer Interaction* (pp. 805-808). New Orleans, USA: Lawrence Erlbaum.

Raith, A., Kamp, C., Stoiber, C., Jakl, A., & Wagner, M. (2022). Augmented Reality in Radiology for Education and Training—A Design Study. *Health Care*, *10*, 672. PMID:35455849

Seo, B. K., Kim, K., & Park, J. I. (2010). Augmented reality-based on-site tour guide: a study in Gyeongbokgung. *Asian Conference on Computer Vision* (pp. 276-285). Springer.

Stegemann, T., Geretsegger, M., Phan Quoc, E., Riedl, H., & Smetana, M. (2019). Music Therapy and Other Music-Based Interventions in Pediatric Health Care: An Overview. *Medicines (Basel, Switzerland)*, *6*(1), 25. doi:10.3390/medicines6010025 PMID:30769834

Thomas, R. G., William John, N., & Delieu, J. M. (2010). Augmented reality for anatomical education. *Journal of Visual Communication in Medicine*, *33*(1), 6–15. doi:10.3109/17453050903557359 PMID:20297908

Vidal-Balea, A., Blanco-Novoa, Ó., Fraga-Lamas, P., & Fernández-Caramés, T. (2021). Developing the Next Generation of Augmented Reality Games for Pediatric Healthcare: An Open-Source Collaborative Framework Based on ARCore for Implementing Teaching, Training and Monitoring Applications. *Sensors (Basel)*, *21*(5), 1865. doi:10.339021051865 PMID:33800070

Viscione, I. (2019). Augmented reality for learning in distance education: The case of e-sports. *Journal of Physical Education and Sport*, *19*, 2047–2050.

Weng, N. G., Bee, O. Y., Yew, L. H., & Hsia, T. E. (2016). An augmented reality system for biology science education in Malaysia. *International Journal of Innovative Computing*, *6*(2), 8–13.

Yapici, I. Ü., & Karakoyun, F. (2021). Using Augmented Reality in Biology Teaching. *Malaysian Online Journal of Educational Technology*, *9*(3), 40–51. doi:10.52380/mojet.2021.9.3.286

Chapter 12

Comparison Analysis of Global Healthcare of virtual reality Systems Market by Geography in Existing Market Scenario

Meeta Singh

https://orcid.org/0000-0003-4175-467X

Manav Rachna International Institute of Research and Studies, India

Poonam Nandal

https://orcid.org/0000-0002-2684-4354

Manav Rachna International Institute of Research and Studies, India

Deepa Bura

Manav Rachna International Institute of Research and Studies, India

ABSTRACT

In the area of virtual reality, there are some critical issues that need to deal with accessing, managing, and sharing the wide amount of information which is increasing day by day. The information produced is not in a form that machines can easily process. So, there is a need to develop and design techniques which can easily process the information and can be embedded with the techniques used for virtual reality. This chapter gives an insight into the various applications of virtual reality, and a comparative analysis of the global healthcare of virtual reality systems market by geography in the existing market scenario.

DOI: 10.4018/978-1-6684-7644-4.ch012

INTRODUCTION

In view of technological expansion, the area of virtual reality is gaining popularity day by day. virtual reality provides simulated environment in which user can behave like an actor. The environment provided by virtual reality helps in interacting with the artificial world which actually does not physically exists in real world.

In technical sense, it can be implemented in the area of cognitive science, robotics, healthcare, psychology, military, gaming, artificial intelligence, etc. The growth of virtual reality is due to the increasing popularity of computer science domain (inherent capacity of computers, ability to perform image processing, ability to create simulated and animated environment) in which there is a need to interact without the intervention of real outside world.

In general, virtual reality does not exist on its own but its foundation is based on Science and Technology in the field of Information and Communication. Its scope is not limited to information and communication however it is extended to number of other applications in various domains. Some of the domains in which virtual reality helps in enhancement of the domain are as follows:

- Digital Model creations in simulated environment using various algorithms. The algorithms applied are analyzed in terms of time and space complexity which helps in the development of the enhanced models.
- Automatic organ creation for human beings with various inability.
- Psychological observations in the behavioural science theory development in virtual simulated environment.
- Designing and development of Ergonomics models having conceptual knowledge that helps in enhancement of techniques used while accessing the virtual simulated environment etc.

In the area of virtual reality, there are some critical issues that need to deal like accessing, managing, sharing, the wide amount of information which is increasing day by day. The information produced is not in the form that can be easily processed by the machines. So, there is a need to develop and design the techniques which can easily process the information and can be embedded with the techniques used for virtual reality.

In fact, the artificial reality is the domain which is the foundation of virtual reality. The dealing of artificial reality with the virtual reality comes into existence when artificial reality deals with data and visualization. The data is the enormous amount of information present for various users. Visualization deals with the use of the data in different context. This is also called contextualization. This helps in displaying data with the context of the information which helps the user in the field of virtual reality. In general, virtual reality enhances the visualization in various domains like cognitive science, neurology, psychology, medical science, robotics, etc.

Virtual reality, mainly supports almost every human activity. In other words, it can be said that virtual reality can be applied to almost all the domains. VR is the foundation of all the domains connected to computer science including animation, entertainment, 3D technology etc.

The thin line that connects virtual reality to the computing domain is also known as Computer Supported Cooperative Work (CSCW). The name comes from the fact that computers have been designed to support all the human activity which are itself inherently cooperative. This idea leads to the origin of new computing domain named as CSCW which mainly deals with the interactions of human with computers which in turn is the core of the virtual reality. The domain CSCW on virtual reality is also categorized on the basis of the type of interaction. To implement virtual reality, the interaction with the system can be contemporal or sequential in terms of time. Also, it can be collocated or distributed in terms of space.

Although, virtual reality applications can be found in every beneficial domain, but its impact on the healthcare has been found tremendously increasing. Like, the implementation of groupware to design a decision support system which helps in finding the health issues related to a patient. In the decision support system, the user (i.e. patient) can input the symptoms in the form of text which is data. This data is further visualized on the basis of the hierarchical structure developed by the implementation of virtual reality while designing the DSS. The DSS in context with virtual reality provides the user the combination of weighted average of all the relationships of the symptoms formed.

In addition to this, virtual reality in CSCW is also applied on the scale related to awareness. The database created for the same should be free from redundancy to have consistent information in the form of text which can be visualized during the phase of visualization of virtual reality implementation.

There are some issues which persist related to the virtual reality in CSCW described as follows:

1. The database creation in the form of such information which is processed easily by the machines using techniques that involves the application of image processing.
2. How much data to be shared and visualized while implementing virtual reality.
3. How many users at time can communicate easily without any interruption on the same interface?
4. How the authorization and authentication be provided to the users depending upon the roles of the system.
5. How to analyze the images produced by the system implement with virtual reality.

However, virtual reality offers various approaches and technologies to deal with the above mentioned issues so that they can be minimized to produce a system which has less complexity and high efficiency. There is one more technique that provides simulated environment and known as augmented reality which connects real world to the 3D objects that allow people to interact with the real world in an interactive way. Augmented reality is becoming a part of daily life. Augmented reality as shown in Figure 1 is useful in so many fields like healthcare, education, rehabilitation, military, navigation, maintenance. Table 1 shows the difference between augmented reality and virtual reality.

Figure 1. Augmented reality

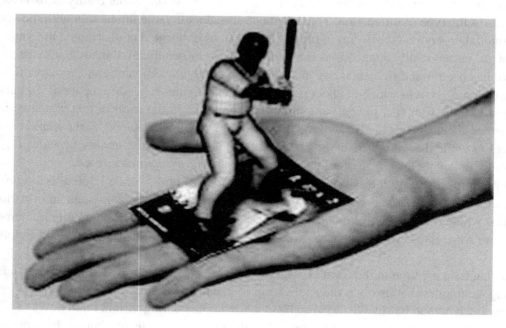

Table 1. Augmented reality vs virtual reality

Augmented Reality (AR)	Virtual Reality (VR)
Connects real world to the imaginary world	Extracts the actual world from the virtual world
A person can feel himself/herself in the world of reality.	A person is away from the world of reality
Use of various devices is needed which helps in displaying the augmented images in reality.	A virtual environment is set up in such a way that any user can found himself/herself to be connected to real world.
Real world controls the user	In virtual reality environment user can feel out of the box and gets controlled by the system.

Purpose

The principle behind virtual reality is to allow user to engross with the 3-D world in the simulated environment which provides the feeling of the real world. There are basically four rudiments which can be used to specify and describe the virtual reality. The first fundamental provides the access to the real world through the simulated environment, wherein the user can perform activities required in its particular application. The second element is the engrossment in the real world with respect to the different levels of the user's belief which can be mental as well as physical perception of the real world. The third rudiment is the sensory response which is fully dependent on the sensory organs of human body. Sensory response can be implemented with the help of integrated hardware and software like hand gloves, head mounted displays etc. Forth element is the interactivity which means the ease of human interaction with the virtual environment.

Similarly, the benefits of virtual reality can be used in the field of healthcare for example, if the patient is suffering from cold shoulder then it allows the patient to practice their prescribed movement exercises in simulated environment.

Simulated environment for surgery, phobia cure, robotic operations & skills education etc are the areas in Healthcare where virtual reality is adopted. Virtual reality provides the secure simulated environment to the practitioners to brush up their existing skills as well as mastering the new technologies without the intervention and any type of risk to the human body.

Background

Ribaupierre et al. (2014) described several teaching models that have been developed using virtual reality. The paper describes several types of simulators available in the market and how the working of these available models can be enhanced to improve accuracy of the model.

Willaert et al. (2012) gave the concept of patient specific virtual reality simulator wherein doctors can practice the operation in simulated environment. 15 several reports were diagnosed using these reports 12 simulators were defined in the field of abdominal surgery, vessel related surgery, bone surgery, nervous system and plastic surgery. Amongst 12 simulators only 1 got commercialized remaining were prototypes.

Giuseppe and Wiederhold (2015) discussed the gaps between virtual reality and real environment. The paper discussed the drawbacks of virtual reality. But with the invention of Oculus designed Gear VR headsets Google Cardboard again a hope was generated for increased accuracy using simulators.

Pensieri and Pennacchini (2014) gave a review article based on 3,443 papers on Pubmed in 2012 and 8,237 papers on Isiknowledge in 2011. Research concluded that none of the papers clearly identified the meaning and uitility of virtual reality in healthcare. Research paper worked on this concept and classified application of virtual reality into four categories to provide a clear understanding of this topic.

Dascal et al. (2017) identified 2,024 citations, studies which were analysed were heterogeneous in nature. Research revealed that virtual reality could be well tolerated by patients and had clinical efficiency.

Khor et al. (2016) differentiated between augmented reality and virtual reality. Specific application is discussed where augmented reality and virtual reality can be applied. Paper discusses various issues faced when using virtual reality and suggests different techniques that can be applied to overcome these drawbacks.

Ferguson et al. (2015) gave a new approach for learning techniques of virtual reality, it provides several techniques which enables the user to learn the virtual reality techniques the way user wants. Paper discusses several possibilities and impacts that these learning techniques have on healthcare. It discuses the existing gap between several applications such as gaming, nursing and education.

Riva et al. (2016) discussed an interesting issue of eating and weight disorders. Paper gave facts of many countries, a large number of people suffer from obesity and other problems because of food eating habits. The paper proposed that a solution can be provided to such problems if virtual and augmented reality could be integrated. Virtual world would be able to meet the expectations of real world. And all the existing gaps could be met if the integration of virtual reality and augmented reality is possible.

Kononowicz et al. (2015) analysed the reason of employment of the term "virtual patient" and so categorized its application in tending education. Research analysed that in total 531 papers were published in the duration 1991 to 2013, out of which 37% papers used virtual reality in their publications.

Rizzo et al. (2016) discussed virtual human agents in simulated environment. These virtual agents can serve as clinical interviewer. It provides an additional advantage in the virtual artificial environment. Virtual agents can help in getting more real environment.

Abari et al. (2016) discussed internet via cable wires limits the mobility of player. This limitation is a disturbance in movement of players hand. Researcher provides novel algorithms to use mmWave technology in wireless manner. This will enable user to avail multi Gbps of data so that effective communication could be maintained between game console and headset. Research concluded that this technology will eliminate any type of limitation of related to movements of hands. However, there was a restriction that waves could be blocked by hands or other body parts. Research also proposed algorithms to overcome this type of limitations.

García-Betances et al. (2015) studied how virtual reality could be used in Alzheimer's disease. It is disease which leads to loss of memory. For dealing with this type of disease the virtual reality process was divided into several categories i.e. analysis of disease, patient mental exercise, caregivers' training. However, the research had limitation that patient could not get full advantage because of level on engrossment. Paper suggested there exists many gaps which is fulfilled will lead to more accurate product. Use of 3D headsets, multiple communication devices and addition of neural response will lead to better products.

Bhagavathula et al. (2018) tried to validate real world scenario with virtual environment. Experiment was conducted on pedestrian, firstly it was evaluated what measures a pedestrian take into account while crossing a road, similarly it was evaluated in simulated environment. Experiment concluded that there was no difference between the two and virtual environment could be used in road safety applications measured.

Rose et al.(2018) analysed virtual reality on rehabilitation systems. Eighteen studies were considered for evaluation purpose. The major parameters taken into account were: the effect of engagement, the association amongst gratification and possible patient devotion to VR therapy, posture steadiness, combined flexibility. Research concluded that all these factors affected performance of virtual reality.

Pillai & Mathew (2019) gave an overview of virtual reality applications. Research stated that virtual reality has gained importance in the field of healthcare as it enables various applications which if done in real world are very expensive. Doctors can gain insight of various treatments and diagnose various disease.

Best (2019) discussed various benefits of virtual reality in healthcare. Paper discussed how doctors can use virtual training for disease diagnosis, training purposes and disease treatment. Various advantages of virtual reality are discussed with case studies.

Definitions Used in Virtual Reality

Virtual reality can be defined as creation of simulated (artificial) environment with the help of automated system which is offered to the user in such a way that it gives the feel of the real world.

Sherman and Craig (2018) defined virtual reality as an environment which does not exist and is not a fact, however it is artificial.

Girvan (2018) separately defined the concept of world and virtual. World means physical universe and virtual means which is not actual, but it can be real. Real in the sense means user is allowed to have the perception of real world.

Cabral et. al (2019) defined virtual reality as an environment that provides 360-degree view and is artificial. This view is of significant use to the users, as it provides an environment which is near to real.

The most significant application that has been designed using virtual reality is head mount display (HMD) which uses the visual ability of the human beings. Head mount display is the combination of basic six fundamental elements. The elements are demonstrate, visual, head tracing, eye tracing and sound. Head mount display is connected to the automated system which is the combination of hardware and software which provides the virtual simulated environment to the user. It is the device that is connected to the head and visuals are offered directly to the eyes of the user so as to provide the visual impact of virtual reality.

Head mount display (HMD) as shown in Figure 2 can be used in many applications like gaming, military, medical, engineering & education.

Figure 2. Head mount set

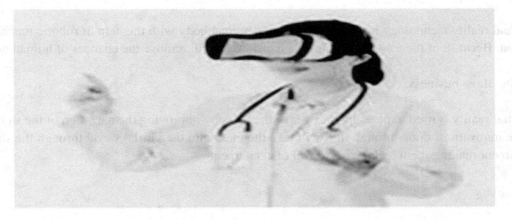

Current Applications of Virtual Reality

In today's era, where there is increase in automation in the domain of computer science there is a need to develop and design the techniques which can enhance the use of machine learning, virtual reality, artificial intelligence, neural networks etc. The technology is growing day by day to minimize the human intervention with the interface used in the field of artificial intelligence to increases the automation. However, the techniques used for artificial intelligence in which virtual reality come under its umbrella can be supervised or unsupervised. In supervised techniques, the automation of the system is done with the involvement of the human intervention whereas, in supervised learning is without the human intervention. The learning techniques used in virtual reality can also be supervised or unsupervised depending upon the demand and requirement of the system. The demand and requirement in terms is of the time and space complexity computed for the developed system. It also includes the use of the already designed techniques which enhance automation of the system by analyzing and visualizing the data for the domain of virtual reality. The applications of virtual reality can be spread over many domains of science and technology. It also includes the domain of mathematics to provide the user the desired output, in terms of the input provided to the system in any field like medical, robotics, cognitive science, brain storming, neuroscience etc.

Nowadays, virtual reality is becoming more and more fascinating and empowering market for different domains. Today's market doesn't consider virtual reality only as just gaming tool but consider it a huge compensation by utilising it.

Virtual reality put great impact on the following applications:

1.   Resolve nervousness problem

Many softwares are designed in virtual reality to resolve the nervousness issues of the human being. Virtual reality headset is used along with eye tracing system which is used to find out various level of nervousness and try to remove the stress level which causes nervousness in human. Virtual reality can also be used to resolve psychological disorders.

2.   Medical operations

Virtual reality technology is used to operate the human body with the help of robotic machine with precision. Because of the robotic machinery precisions, it will remove the chances of human errors.

3.   The Show business

Virtual reality is used to pleasing the eyes of the mass by improving the narration of the storytelling with the innovations done through it. It will take the mass into the virtual world through the simulated environment making them feel the next level of excitement.

4.   Military

Virtual reality is used in the military for providing risk free training by creating a virtual environment which can be dangerous in the real scenario. It can help the military person to train themselves for toughest operation prior to the actual implementation.

5.   3-D to 7-D experiences

Virtual reality is used in movies from 3-D to 7-D experiences which give immense pleasure to the viewer by creating simulated environment replica of the real one.

6.   Training and education

Virtual reality is immensely used in training and education. It is used to handle the dangerous situations with an ease by creating risk free simulated environment without harming any living being.

7.   Exhibitions

Virtual reality is used to project the virtual simulated environment for any exhibition which will give an illusion of the real one and give the feeling to the viewers to be actually present at historic era.

8. Space

Virtual reality is used by space research agencies to create the model of spaceship for making life experience to the viewers. Space research agencies also used virtual reality to train their Astronauts before going to actual mission.

9. Property business

Virtual reality plays an important role in property business. Virtual reality provide the simulated experience to the buyers and developers before the actual implementation.

Beyond the above-mentioned field there are applications specific to the implementation of virtual reality. Some of the applications specific to the healthcare are mentioned below:

1. Virtual reality in Neuropsychology: The applications of virtual reality in medicines helps to provide the demonstrations on numerous medications given based on the desire of the patient. In neuropsychology, the implementation of virtual reality using 3D images and machine learning techniques, the treatment related to various diseases like pain disorders, phobia, brain disorders, simulations of neurons, pain contraction and expansion etc. In addition to the mentioned disease there are furthermore in the integration of virtual reality with neuropsychology in the medical education.

2. Virtual reality in Surgery: The novel technologies like robotics, expert system designing will have tremendous impact in today's era of advancement in health care. The application in surgery can be done by the use of simulators. The simulators helps in embedding the data visualization through image with augmented reality. For the vast and fast development and use of the simulators there is enhancement in the structured courseware, e learning, interactive and automated images etc. The completely and efficiently developed surgical system using virtual reality is done with the help of involvement of knowledge or domain experts in the field of ergonomics, robotics, electromechanical engineering, software engineering psychology, etc. The surgical system developed for the use of the doctors or users is also called medical science simulator in terms of medical education.

3. Virtual reality in Pain Supervision: The augmentation of virtual reality with augment reality is also mainly used for the management of various pain disorders in human being. Specifically, the pain caused to the human due to burn is significant and is critical to be dealt with. The pain due to the burn incidents are very severe and can cause further disorders in human like depression, anxiety, rehabilitation etc. The use of techniques virtual reality often helps in handing with such critical pain disorders and provides the solution to the patients worldwide. Further, it deals with the post burn pain management too.

4. Virtual reality in medical education: The impending of VR tools in medical education is extensively renowned. It has previously seen realistic utilize in an anticipated 20 or further public schools and colleges, and numerous more have been implicated in assessment or examine efforts.

Healthcare Applications of Virtual Reality

Few applications of virtual reality in the field of health care are given below:

1. Medical Education

Virtual reality is used to provide training to the medical practitioners to enhance their skills and ability to diagnose and cure medical problem of their patients. Advance virtual reality products are being developed which provides 360-degree view along with 3-D contents.

It enables the learners to apply their knowledge, gained from the training to provide risk free treatment. Figure 3 gives an application of virtual reality used in medical education and training.

Figure 3. VR in medical education & training

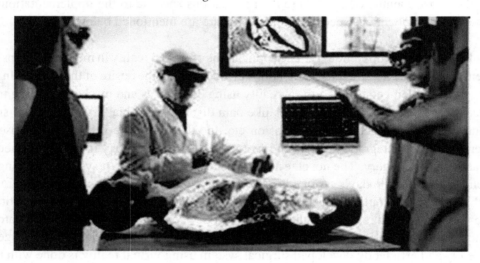

i. Electrocardiography

Electrocardiography is machine that visualizes the heart of human beings. It enables the doctor to study the heart, via the strokes produced by the ECG machine. Using virtual reality, heart can be virtualized in 3D such that doctor can study the heart virtually as stated in Lamounier et al. (2010).

ii. Neurosurgery:

Neurosurgery is a study that deals with brain for e.g. it deals with brain tumours. Virtual reality enables the doctors to create virtual brains to provide the best suitable medical treatment to the patient. Healthcare requires no error in medical diagnosis and healing else it can lead to the risk of patient's life. Virtual reality is gaining popularity in neurosurgery as it will provide risk less treatment to the brain issues of the patients.

iii.   Orthopaedic Surgery

Muscular skeletal surgery comes under Orthopaedic Surgery domain, which is used to replace the bones like knee replacement. Virtual reality allows the doctors to do knee and bone replacement. Orthopaedic surgery has become easier using virtual reality.

iv.   Laparoscopic Surgery

With the growing innovations virtual reality has grown itself in the field of head and neck surgery . Fuchs et al. (1998) present a 3D visualisation virtual system to assist with laparoscopic surgical procedures. This system could help the doctor to visualise a head of the patient in the virtual space so that the doctor can repair the injured part .The provided a deep laparoscopic visualisation in the 3D space.

v.   Ultrasound

Virtual reality visualizes the patient body in 3D and 7D domain. Sato et al. (1998) analysed that ultrasound can also be used to diagnose the womb of the mother to check the functionality of the baby inside the womb. Sauer et al. (2001) developed a system for the visualisation of the ultrasound images via using virtual reality. HMDS is used by the medical practitioners to visualize the human body parts. Breast cancer can also be diagnosed by visualisation of the ultrasound images of breast cancer. The images contain the 3D view of the every part of the tumour before surgery .

2.   Virtual reality in diagnostics

Virtual reality equipments when combined with the existing medical equipments like MRI, CT scan etc. can diagnose the exact problem associated with the patients which leads to a pain less experience.

3.   Psychological sickness healing

Mental sickness can be healed by standard exposure therapy. Due to the advancement in virtual reality, exposure therapy changes to the virtual reality treatments which are best suited in terms of cost, flexibility and risk free solution to heal physiological disorders.

4.   Pain management

Basically distraction techniques are used for the pain treatment. Because of the evolution of virtual reality, some interactive games are introduced which can distract the mind of patient and give relief from the pain. Virtual reality provides many more pain relief management like therapeutic virtual reality for burn victims, limb pain management etc.

5.   Physical strength and healing

There is a major improvement and enhancement in the fitness sector in terms of the exercises done. Fitness sector uses virtual reality in addition to their routine cardio exercises. Because of virtual reality instead of medicines and surgeries patients can be cured with the help of physical therapy.

6.   Virtual reality in surgery

Nowadays, virtual reality has gained recognition in the field of medical surgery. In virtual reality surgery is carried out by a robot under the supervision of a doctor. It leads to reduction in duration and complications related with the surgery. In case of tele-surgery, virtual reality plays most significant role, as the patient who needs to get treated is far away from doctor's location. It also plays vital role in case of dental treatments as it allows to calculate pressure which is required in this treatment. Figure 4 displays surgery using virtual reality.

Figure 4. Virtual reality application in surgery

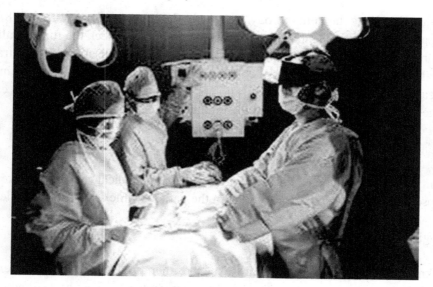

7.   Human simulation techniques

Virtual reality is used for creating the 3-D simulation environment for medical practitioners which enables them to communicate with their patients. Sensors are used to evaluate the expressions of the communicators such as doctors and patients.

8.   Other applications

There are many more application of virtual reality in the healthcare sector like in dental treatment, in nursing care, in robotic surgery, in post traumatic stress disorder, in autism healing, etc.

Market of Healthcare Virtual Reality Systems

In today's world there is an increasing demand of virtual reality in healthcare zone. Medical practitioner requires virtual reality in different medical domains like robotic surgery, phobia treatment; training and education etc. to enhance their ability in the medical domain by taking zero percent risk of the life of their patients. Virtual reality provides the simulated environment which will train the medical practitioner to use life saving techniques which can further be used for helping the human race. Global market demand of virtual reality increases day by day and by the end of year 2020 it will raise up to $3.8 billion as portrayed in Figure 5. Virtual reality can be used to train and help the medical practitioner in lot of different ways like medical education, patient diagnosis and treatment, medical advertisement, medical problem detection and awareness etc.

Figure 5. Revenue share in 2020

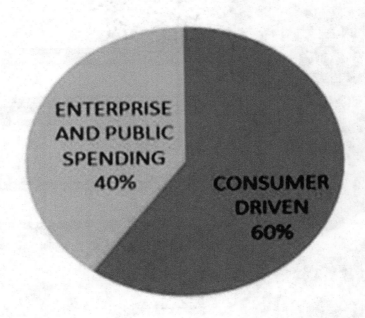

Companies are required to accept virtual reality technolgy as it has no constraint of geography as well as cost. As healthcare industy works in the conventional way but digital advancement revolutionize other industries like trade market, tour market, communication market etc.In heathcare only report maintaing and basic mailing services are digitalized but communication to cure the medical problem in real time between medical practioners with their patient is lagging behind. But with the help of virtual reality this issue can be resolved and provide help to the patients from their doctors in pain free and risk free simulated environment.

Virtual reality have the capabilty to cure psychological disorders, help in medical tratments and surgery etc. Technology used in virtual reality is in position to dislocate $16 billion patients obsevation market. Healthcare industry can dynamically estimate the planning of imapct of their estimation for the investment on patients based on 1.5 million heathcare practioners. Figure 6 shows the market trend key entities.

Figure 6. Market trend entities

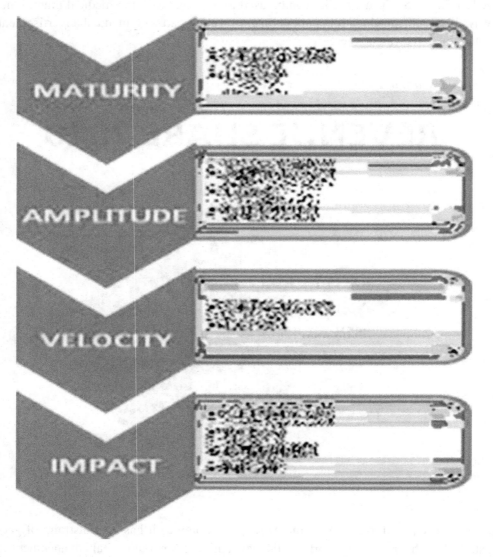

Adoption of virtual reality will increase the revenue generated throughout the years with the increase in the requirement of pain and risk free simulated environment. Figure 7 describes revenue generation in present scenario and prediction of future.

Figure 7. Revenue generation (present scenario to future)

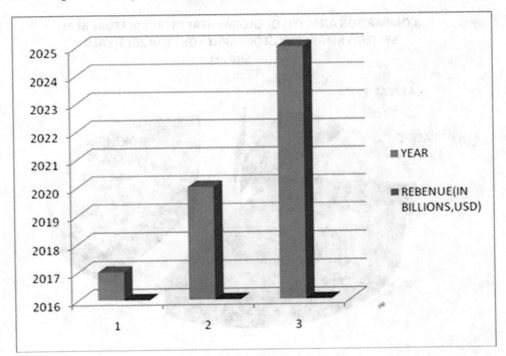

Market evaluation report published on Global healthcare virtual reality systems by SA-BRC (2017) stated that virtual reality market of global healthcare is estimated with lesser rate of percentage of CAGR between 2016 and 2020. This evaluation is based on different parameters like education and development, healing treatments and persistent robotic surgery simulation, captivation healing. Figure 8 and Figure 9 give comparison analysis of Global Healthcare virtual reality Systems for the years 2015 and 2020.

The report also shows the values in percentage for six geographies for the years 2015 and 2020 as shown in the Table 2 and Table 3 is given below:

Table 2. Value share for year 2015

S.No.	GEOGRAPHY	VALUE-% SHARE
1	NORTH AMERICA	41.70%
2	EUROPE	31.30%
3	ASIA PACIFIC	14.70%
4	LATIN AMERICA	6.70%
5	MIDDLE EAST	4.00%
6	AFRICA	1.70%

Figure 8. Comparison analysis of global healthcare virtual reality systems for year 2015

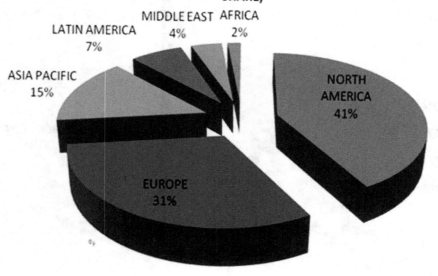

Table 3. Value share for year 2020

S.No.	GEOGRAPHY	VALUE-% SHARE
1	NORTH AMERICA	41.70%
2	EUROPE	31.30%
3	ASIA PACIFIC	15.00%
4	LATIN AMERICA	6.60%
5	MIDDLE EAST	3.90%
6	AFRICA	1.60%

Figure 9. Comparison analysis of global healthcare virtual reality systems for year 2020

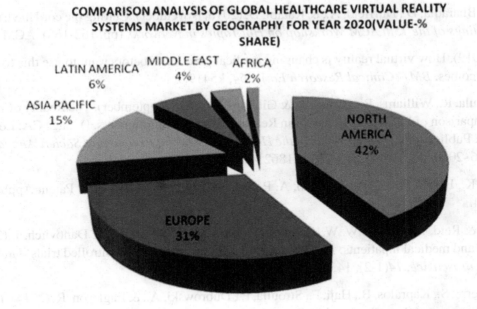

COMPARISON ANALYSIS OF GLOBAL HEALTHCARE VIRTUAL REALITY SYSTEMS MARKET BY GEOGRAPHY FOR YEAR 2020(VALUE-% SHARE)

Areas of Further Research

As stated above, there are many applications of virtual reality used in healthcare sector. Due to the growing need and demand of accuracy and effectiveness of medical treatment virtual reality techniques are required. The prospective of virtual reality is high in healthcare but restricted due to the originality and in genuineness of the technology used.

In future, application areas of virtual reality can be expanded to tourism industry also. virtual reality in tourists can gain insight of the destinations prior to the visit, provides 360^0 view of the sites, hotels. It can be of great benefit as it can help the tourists in making final call of the site to visited or not.

CONCLUSION

In health care, the applications of virtual reality (VR) articulate impending abilities to deal with various domains like psychology, cognitive science, robotics, functional deficiencies and enhancing the learning and training perspective of clinical practitioners. This chapter discussed the purpose, background, definitions used in virtual reality. This chapter also explained the healthcare applications of virtual reality and the technology related with it. This chapter also discussed the current applications of the virtual reality and the areas of further research. It has been concluded from above sections that virtual reality is gaining popularity in terms of market share in every sector. It is not just a gaming experience but it painfree, riskfree environment for training in psychology, cognitive science, robotics, functional deficiencies.

REFERENCES

Abari, O., Bharadia, D., Duffield, A., & Katabi, D. (2016, November). Cutting the cord in virtual reality. In *Proceedings of the 15th ACM Workshop on Hot Topics in Networks* (pp. 162-168). ACM.

Best, J. (2019). How virtual reality is changing medical practice: Doctors want to use this to give better patient outcomes. *BMJ (Clinical Research Ed.)*, *364*, k5419.

Bhagavathula, R., Williams, B., Owens, J., & Gibbons, R. (2018, September). The Reality of virtual reality: A Comparison of Pedestrian Behavior in Real and Virtual Environments. []. Sage CA: Los Angeles, CA: SAGE Publications.]. *Proceedings of the Human Factors and Ergonomics Society Annual Meeting*, *62*(1), 2056–2060. doi:10.1177/1541931218621464

Cabral, B. K., Briggs, F. S., Hsu, J., Pozo, A. P., & Coward, A. H. (2019). U.S. Patent Application No. 10/230,904.

Dascal, J., & Reid, M., IsHak, W. W., Spiegel, B., Recacho, J., Rosen, B., & Danovitch, I. (2017). virtual reality and medical inpatients: A systematic review of randomized, controlled trials. *Innovations in Clinical Neuroscience*, *14*(1-2), 14. PMID:28386517

de Ribaupierre, S., Kapralos, B., Haji, F., Stroulia, E., Dubrowski, A., & Eagleson, R. (2014). Healthcare training enhancement through virtual reality and serious games. In *Virtual, Augmented Reality and Serious Games for Healthcare 1* (pp. 9–27). Springer. doi:10.1007/978-3-642-54816-1_2

Ferguson, C., Davidson, P. M., Scott, P. J., Jackson, D., & Hickman, L. D. (2015). *Augmented reality, virtual reality and gaming: An integral part of nursing*.

Fuchs, H., Livingston, M. A., Raskar, R., Keller, K., Crawford, J. R., Rademacher, P., & Meyer, A. A. (1998, October). Augmented reality visualization for laparoscopic surgery. In *International Conference on Medical Image Computing and Computer-Assisted Intervention* (pp. 934-943). Springer, Berlin, Heidelberg.

García-Betances, R. I., Arredondo Waldmeyer, M. T., Fico, G., & Cabrera-Umpiérrez, M. F. (2015). A succinct overview of virtual reality technology use in Alzheimer's disease. *Frontiers in Aging Neuroscience*, *7*, 80.

Giuseppe, R. I. V. A., & Wiederhold, B. K. (2015). The new dawn of virtual reality in health care: Medical simulation and experiential interface. *Studies in Health Technology and Informatics*, *219*, 3–6. PMID:26799868

Healthcare Virtual Reality & Augmented Reality Systems Market. (2017, March 28). Advertising, Media Consulting, Marketing Research. OpenPR. https://www.openpr.com/news/484319/healthcare-virtual-reality-augmented-reality-systems-market.html

Khor, W. S., Baker, B., Amin, K., Chan, A., Patel, K., & Wong, J. (2016). Augmented and virtual reality in surgery—the digital surgical environment: Applications, limitations and legal pitfalls. *Annals of Translational Medicine*, *4*(23), 454. doi:10.21037/atm.2016.12.23 PMID:28090510

Kononowicz, A. A., Zary, N., Edelbring, S., Corral, J., & Hege, I. (2015). Virtual patients- what are we talking about? A framework to classify the meanings of the term in healthcare education. *BMC Medical Education*, *15*(1), 11. doi:10.118612909-015-0296-3 PMID:25638167

Lamounier, E., Bucioli, A., Cardoso, A., Andrade, A., & Soares, A. (2010, September). On the use of Augmented Reality techniques in learning and interpretation of cardiologic data. In *Annual International Conference of the IEEE* (Vol. 1, pp. 2451-2454). IEEE. 10.1109/IEMBS.2010.5628019

Pensieri, C., & Pennacchini, M. (2014). Overview: virtual reality in medicine. *Journal of Virtual Worlds Research*, *7*(1). Advance online publication. doi:10.4101/jvwr.v7i1.6364

Pillai, A. S., & Mathew, P. S. (2019). Impact of virtual reality in Healthcare: A Review. In Virtual and Augmented Reality in Mental Health Treatment (pp. 17-31). IGI Global. .

Riva, G., Gutiérrez-Maldonado, J., & Wiederhold, B. K. (2016). *Virtual worlds versus real body: virtual reality meets eating and weight disorders.* PMC.

Rizzo, A., Shilling, R., Forbell, E., Scherer, S., Gratch, J., & Morency, L. P. (2016). Autonomous virtual human agents for healthcare information support and clinical interviewing. In Artificial intelligence in behavioral and mental health care (pp. 53-79). Academic Press. .

Rose, T., Nam, C. S., & Chen, K. B. (2018). Immersion of virtual reality for rehabilitation- Review. *Applied Ergonomics*, *69*, 153–161. doi:10.1016/j.apergo.2018.01.009 PMID:29477323

Sato, Y., Nakamoto, M., Tamaki, Y., Sasama, T., Sakita, I., Nakajima, Y., Monden, M., & Tamura, S. (1998). Image guidance of breast cancer surgery using 3 -D ultrasound images and augmented reality visualization. *IEEE Transactions on Medical Imaging*, *17*(5), 681–693. doi:10.1109/42.736019 PMID:9874292

Sauer, F., Khamene, A., Bascle, B., Schinunang, L., Wenzel, F., & Vogt, S. (2001). Augmented reality visualization of ultrasound images: system description, calibration, and features. In *Augmented Reality, 2001. Proceedings. IEEE and ACM International Symposium on* (pp. 30-39). IEEE. 10.1109/ISAR.2001.970513

Sherman, W. R., & Craig, A. B. (2018). *Understanding virtual reality: Interface, application, and design. Morgan Kaufmann.*

Willaert, W. I., Aggarwal, R., Van Herzeele, I., Cheshire, N. J., & Vermassen, F. E. (2012). Recent advancements in medical simulation: Patient-specific virtual reality simulation. *World Journal of Surgery*, *36*(7), 1703–1712. doi:10.100700268-012-1489-0 PMID:22532308

Section 4
Case Studies and Applications of Context–Rich Learning

Chapter 13
Implementing a Comprehensive Leadership Development Program at Byte Brigade:
A Case Study

Jill Walker
Coding Dojo, USA

ABSTRACT

This chapter presents the case study of the leadership development program of a fictitious company Byte Brigade, designed to identify and nurture high-potential employees within the organization. Outlines of the evaluation and assessment methods used to measure the effectiveness of the program, including the use of Kirkpatrick's model and a focus on both qualitative and quantitative metrics are presented, as well as the initial feedback on the program's success and potential impact on the organization's success. The chapter also explores the use of the case study of Byte Brigade's leadership development program in various learning experiences. The case study is used as a tool to help participants understand the importance of leadership development programs, promote diversity and inclusion in leadership, practice effective communication and collaboration, and apply problem-solving skills to real-world situations. It emphasizes the practical nature of using case studies in learning experiences and highlights the potential for participants to apply their learning to their own work contexts.

INTRODUCTION

A case study is a research method that involves an in-depth examination of a particular phenomenon or instance within a real-life context. It typically involves gathering and analyzing a range of data sources, such as interviews, observations, documents, and other artifacts, to understand the complexities and nuances of the case. The purpose of a case study is to provide a detailed and comprehensive understanding of a specific case or phenomenon, often with the aim of generating new insights, theories, or knowledge that can be applied to broader contexts or situations. Case studies are often used in various fields, includ-

DOI: 10.4018/978-1-6684-7644-4.ch013

ing business, social sciences, education, healthcare, and others, as they allow researchers to examine and explore complex real-life situations in a systematic and rigorous manner.

Case studies are invaluable tools used in research, education, and professional development to examine real-world situations and provide insights into how theoretical concepts can be applied to practical problems. They provide a deep and detailed analysis of a particular phenomenon or event and offer an opportunity to explore and understand complex issues in a contextualized and holistic manner. Case studies can help researchers and practitioners identify patterns, trends, and best practices in a particular field or industry, as well as highlight areas where improvements can be made. They also provide an opportunity for critical thinking, problem-solving, and decision-making in a safe and controlled environment, enabling learners to develop their skills and expertise through low-stakes, hands-on experiences.

Byte Brigade is a fictitious company created solely for the purpose of this case study. The chapter is intended to provide an example of a comprehensive Leadership Development Program that can be used as a guide for other organizations seeking to develop their own programs. While the specific details of the program may not be directly applicable to all organizations, the underlying principles and best practices can serve as a valuable resource for companies looking to enhance their leadership development initiatives.

Byte Brigade is a fast-growing software development company that specializes in creating innovative solutions for the transportation industry. The company was founded in 2008 by a group of entrepreneurs who saw an opportunity to provide a better user experience to trucking companies and their customers.

In the early years, Byte Brigade faced many challenges as they worked to establish themselves in a highly competitive market. However, the team's perseverance and commitment to excellence paid off, and the company began to gain traction, attracting a loyal customer base and earning a reputation as an industry leader.

As the company grew, the leadership team recognized the need to invest in their employees' development and growth to continue driving success. They realized that leadership development was key to maintaining the company's competitive edge and ensuring they remained at the forefront of their industry.

Recognizing the importance of effective leadership, the company has implemented a comprehensive Leadership Development Program aimed at identifying and nurturing high-potential employees within the organization.

The Byte Brigade Leadership Development Program is designed to equip participants with the skills and competencies required to excel in leadership roles and contribute to the company's long-term success. The program is based on the belief that effective leadership can be developed through a combination of theoretical knowledge, practical experience, and ongoing support and feedback. It aims to provide participants with the tools and resources they need to become effective leaders, able to navigate complex challenges and lead their teams to success.

This program is unique in its approach, with a strong emphasis on the practical application of leadership principles. Rather than simply providing theoretical knowledge, the program focuses on enabling participants to gain hands-on experience and actively apply their learnings to real-world challenges within the organization. This approach allows participants to develop the critical thinking, problem-solving, and decision-making skills required for effective leadership in a supportive and collaborative environment.

By investing in the development of its employees' leadership capabilities, Byte Brigade is not only positioning itself for long-term success but also demonstrating its commitment to its employees' growth and development. The program's emphasis on practical application ensures that participants are equipped with the skills and competencies required to make meaningful contributions to the organization and grow in their roles over time. This approach also enables Byte Brigade to cultivate a pipeline of strong leaders who can help drive the company's growth and success in the years ahead.

The program represents a significant investment in the company's future success and demonstrates the organization's commitment to developing and supporting its employees. By providing participants with the tools and resources they need to become effective leaders, the program is helping to cultivate a pipeline of strong leaders who can help drive the company's growth and success in the years ahead. The primary objectives of the program are to:

- Identify high-potential employees within the organization and provide them with targeted training and development opportunities to prepare them for leadership roles.
- Develop a comprehensive curriculum that covers essential leadership competencies, including strategic thinking, communication, decision-making, and team building.
- Foster a culture of continuous learning and development within the organization, encouraging participants to actively engage in their personal growth and seek opportunities for professional advancement.
- Create a supportive network of mentors and peers to guide participants throughout their leadership journey, offering guidance, feedback, and encouragement as needed.
- Measure the effectiveness of the program through a combination of qualitative and quantitative metrics, ensuring that the program remains aligned with the organization's strategic objectives and delivers tangible results.

The program has been carefully designed to address the unique needs and challenges of the organization, considering the specific competencies required for success in the software development industry. By investing in the development of its leaders, Byte Brigade aims to create a robust pipeline of talent that is equipped to navigate the complex and ever-changing landscape of the industry, driving innovation, growth, and long-term success for the organization. Through the implementation of this comprehensive program, Byte Brigade demonstrates its commitment to nurturing and empowering its employees, fostering a culture of excellence that will undoubtedly contribute to the organization's continued success in the years to come.

Contributions and Intended Use

This case study of Byte Brigade itself contributes to the body of work on context-rich learning in several ways. It demonstrates the effectiveness of a comprehensive and practical leadership development program that incorporates multiple components and phases. The program has been specifically designed to provide participants with hands-on experience and the opportunity to actively apply their learning to real-world challenges within the organization. This approach is consistent with the principles of context-rich learning, which emphasizes the importance of learning in situ and the transferability of knowledge and skills to real-world contexts.

The case study highlights the value of an integrated approach to leadership development that combines both formal and informal learning activities. In addition to formal training and development sessions, the program also includes coaching and mentoring, job shadowing, and cross-functional projects. These informal learning opportunities provide participants with a more holistic view of the organization and enable them to develop a broader range of skills and competencies.

The case study showcases the importance of ongoing evaluation and assessment in ensuring the success of a leadership development program. The program's evaluation methods, which incorporate both qualitative and quantitative metrics, provide valuable feedback for program improvement and enable participants to track their progress and development over time. This approach aligns with the principles of context-rich learning, which emphasizes the importance of ongoing assessment and feedback to support learning and development.

The study also offers insights into the key components and phases of an effective leadership development program. These include developing a strong theoretical foundation, aligning program goals with organizational objectives, identifying high-potential employees, providing a range of learning opportunities, and incorporating ongoing evaluation and assessment. By highlighting these key components, the case study provides a valuable resource for organizations seeking to develop their own leadership development programs.

The case study offers a practical example of how organizations can apply context-rich learning principles to leadership development. By providing participants with the opportunity to apply their learning to real-world challenges within the organization, the program enables them to develop the skills and competencies required to be effective leaders in complex and dynamic environments. This approach is consistent with the principles of context-rich learning, which emphasizes the importance of learning in context and the transferability of knowledge and skills to real-world situations.

THE CASE STUDY

In today's highly competitive and rapidly evolving business landscape, the role of effective leadership has become increasingly important. Organizations are faced with a myriad of challenges, including globalization, technological advancements, and the need to adapt to a constantly changing environment. Consequently, the ability to develop and maintain a strong leadership pipeline is vital to the long-term success of any organization. Leadership development programs have been recognized as a crucial component in nurturing and preparing future leaders, as they provide opportunities for individuals to acquire the necessary skills, knowledge, and competencies to thrive in their roles and contribute positively to the organization's growth (Barnes & Larcus, 2015; Brue & Brue, 2016).

Leadership Development Programs are essential for any organization that seeks to achieve its goals and objectives. They are designed to enhance the leadership skills of employees at all levels, from entry-level to executives. Such programs help develop a pipeline of leaders who can take on critical roles in the company and ensure its long-term success. Effective leadership is vital for a company's success in today's fast-paced and complex business environment. The success of any organization depends on the quality of its leadership. Investing in Leadership Development Programs is an investment in the company's future. It helps ensure that there are capable leaders in the company who can drive innovation, motivate employees, and make critical decisions in a constantly changing business landscape. These programs also help companies to retain their top talent. Providing employees with opportunities for growth and development helps to boost employee engagement and job satisfaction. It shows that the company values its employees and is committed to their professional development. This, in turn, helps to reduce employee turnover and attract new talent. These programs can help companies to develop a strong organizational culture that aligns with their values and objectives. By investing in the development of their leaders, companies can ensure that their values are shared and that their employees are working towards common goals. This helps to create a sense of purpose and unity in the workplace, which can have a positive impact on the company's bottom line.

The importance of Leadership Development Programs cannot be overstated, as they help organizations to identify high-potential individuals and provide them with targeted training and development opportunities. By investing in the growth and development of their leaders, organizations can enhance employee engagement, improve decision-making, drive innovation, and ultimately, achieve better business outcomes (Cacioppe, 1998; Cohrs et al., 2020). Moreover, effective Leadership Development Programs have been shown to contribute to a positive organizational culture, increased employee satisfaction and loyalty, and the successful implementation of strategic initiatives (deMoville, 2007; Kaplan, 2020).

The purpose of the case study is to provide an overview of the design, implementation, and evaluation of Byte Brigade's Leadership Development Program. The chapter discusses the theoretical foundations and guiding principles of the program, outlines its various components and phases, and describes the timeline, resources, and support required for each component. The chapter also reviews existing research on Leadership Development Programs, their effectiveness, and various approaches, identifies gaps in the literature or areas where Byte Brigade's program may offer unique contributions, and explains the methods used to evaluate the effectiveness of the program. Ultimately, the chapter aims to demonstrate the importance and potential impact of effective Leadership Development Programs in organizations.

LITERATURE REVIEW

Leadership Development Programs: Approaches and Effectiveness

A growing body of research has emerged in recent years, emphasizing the significance of Leadership Development Programs in nurturing and preparing future leaders (Barnes & Larcus, 2015; Brue & Brue, 2016). Leadership Development Programs are designed to equip high-potential employees with the necessary skills, knowledge, and competencies to excel in leadership roles and contribute positively to the organization's growth (Cacioppe, 1998; Cohrs et al., 2020). A review of the existing literature reveals various approaches to leadership development, as well as evidence of their effectiveness.

One popular approach to Leadership Development Programs is based on the principles of positive psychology, which emphasizes the development of strengths and virtues to enhance individual and organizational well-being and performance (Barnes & Larcus, 2015). Positive psychology-based Leadership Development Programs often include elements such as self-awareness, emotional intelligence, resilience, and a focus on personal strengths, which have been shown to contribute to more effective leadership (Brue & Brue, 2016).

Another prevalent approach is the use of experiential learning and immersive experiences in Leadership Development Programs (Cacioppe, 1998; Cohrs et al., 2020). Experiential learning involves engaging participants in hands-on activities and real-world challenges, encouraging them to reflect on their experiences and apply their learnings to their professional contexts. Studies have found that experiential learning in Leadership Development Programs can lead to increased self-awareness, improved decision-making, and enhanced leadership capabilities (Cohrs et al., 2020).

Mentoring and coaching also play a significant role in many Leadership Development Programs, as they provide participants with ongoing guidance, feedback, and support throughout their leadership journey (Sanchez-Nunez et al., 2015). Research indicates that mentoring relationships can contribute to the development of essential leadership competencies, such as strategic thinking, communication, and team building (Sowcik et al., 2018). Furthermore, mentoring has been shown to foster a sense of belonging and support within the organization, which can contribute to increased employee engagement and loyalty (Ruben et al., 2018).

The effectiveness of Leadership Development Programs has been widely studied, with evidence suggesting that well-designed Leadership Development Programs can lead to improved individual and organizational performance (Cacioppe, 1998; Cohrs et al., 2020). In their study, Cohrs et al. (2020) found that participants in a two-day Leadership Development Program exhibited significant improvements in their transformational leadership and communication skills. Similarly, Brue and Brue (2016) reported that participants in a women's Leadership Development Program experienced increased self-confidence, self-awareness, and leadership capabilities as a result of their participation.

Gaps in the Literature and Unique Contributions of Byte Brigade's Program

Despite the extensive research on Leadership Development Programs, certain gaps in the literature remain, offering opportunities for Byte Brigade's program to make unique contributions. For instance, there is limited research on Leadership Development Programs specifically tailored to the software development industry, which presents unique challenges and requirements for effective leadership. Byte Brigade's program, designed with a strong emphasis on the practical application of leadership principles within the context of software development, could provide valuable insights into the specific competencies required for success in this industry.

Existing literature often focuses on traditional, face-to-face Leadership Development Programs, with limited research on the effectiveness of blended or fully online programs (Sowcik et al., 2018). Given the increasing prevalence of remote work and the need for flexible learning options, Byte Brigade's program, which incorporates a combination of in-person and virtual components, can contribute to the understanding of how to design and implement effective Leadership Development Programs in the digital age. Investigating the impact of various delivery methods on participant engagement, learning outcomes, and leadership development could inform future program designs and best practices.

Another gap in the literature pertains to the evaluation of Leadership Development Programs in terms of their long-term impact on organizational performance and success (Making leadership development more effective, 2015). While many studies have examined the immediate outcomes of Leadership Development Programs, such as increased self-awareness or improved leadership skills, less attention has been given to the long-term effects of these programs on the organization as a whole. Byte Brigade's Leadership Development Program, with its focus on the implementation of strategic initiatives and ongoing self-development plans, offers an opportunity to explore the lasting impact of these programs on organizational performance, culture, and employee satisfaction.

Literature reveals a need for a more comprehensive understanding of the factors that contribute to the success of Leadership Development Programs, such as the alignment of the program with the organization's strategic goals, the involvement of senior leadership, and the integration of Leadership Development Programs with other human resource management practices (Dalia Susa Vugec et al., 2020; deMoville, 2007). Byte Brigade's program, which emphasizes the importance of aligning leadership development efforts with the organization's overall strategy and fostering collaboration among various stakeholders, could provide valuable insights into the critical success factors for Leadership Development Programs.

The existing literature on Leadership Development Programs highlights the importance of these initiatives in fostering effective leadership and improving organizational performance. Various approaches to Leadership Development Programs have been studied, including positive psychology-based programs, experiential learning, and mentoring, all of which have demonstrated effectiveness in developing leadership competencies. However, certain gaps in the literature remain, such as the specific needs of the software development industry, the effectiveness of blended or online Leadership Development Programs, and the long-term impact of these programs on organizational success. Byte Brigade's Leadership Development Program, with its unique focus on practical application within the software development context and its blend of in-person and virtual components, offers the potential to contribute valuable insights to the field of leadership development and address some of these gaps in the literature.

PROGRAM DESIGN AND STRUCTURE

The Byte Brigade Leadership Development Program (Leadership Development Program) is designed to address the unique challenges and needs of leaders in the software development industry. Based on a comprehensive review of the literature and informed by best practices in leadership development, the program integrates various theoretical foundations and guiding principles to provide a holistic, multi-dimensional approach to leadership growth and development.

Theoretical Foundation and Guiding Principles

The program is grounded in several key theories and models of leadership development, including positive psychology (Barnes & Larcus, 2015), transformational leadership (Cohrs et al., 2020), and social and emotional intelligence (Sanchez-Nunez et al., 2015). These theoretical frameworks emphasize the importance of cultivating self-awareness, empathy, resilience, and adaptability among leaders, as well as the ability to inspire and engage others in working towards common goals.

Additionally, the program is guided by several key principles, including:

- Alignment with organizational strategy: The Leadership Development Program is designed to ensure that participants' leadership development efforts are closely aligned with Byte Brigade's strategic goals and objectives (Cacioppe, 1998). This is achieved through a focus on practical application and the development of strategic initiatives that support the company's overall vision and direction.
- Blended learning approach: The program incorporates a mix of in-person, virtual, and asynchronous learning opportunities, allowing for greater flexibility and adaptability to participants' needs and preferences (Sowcik et al., 2018).
- Mentorship and support: The Leadership Development Program emphasizes the importance of mentorship and on-going support from senior leaders and HR personnel, fostering a culture of continuous learning and development within the organization (Brue & Brue, 2016).
- Evaluation and feedback: The program includes multiple opportunities for assessment, feedback, and reflection, enabling participants to continuously monitor their progress and make adjustments as needed (Ruben et al., 2018).

Program Components and Phases

The Byte Brigade Leadership Development Program is structured around several key components and phases, each designed to address different aspects of leadership development and build upon the skills and knowledge gained in previous stages. These components and phases include:

- "Lead the Business" (Month 1): This initial phase of the program focuses on building a strong foundation of leadership skills, including self-awareness, emotional intelligence, communication, and decision-making. Participants engage in a 2-day immersive in-person seminar, followed by asynchronous homework assignments, weekly meetings with their mentor, and remote teleconference meetings with the HR Director and other program facilitators.
- "Respect the Business" (Month 2): In this phase, participants delve deeper into the complexities of managing a software development organization, exploring topics such as project management, team dynamics, and stakeholder engagement. Weekly 1-day virtual seminars are held, with a mix of instructor-led and small-group sessions, supplemented by asynchronous homework assignments and biweekly meetings with mentors.
- "Build the Business" (Month 3): This component focuses on strategic thinking and the development of innovative solutions to organizational challenges. Participants continue to engage in weekly 1-day virtual seminars, with a mix of instructor-led and small-group sessions, as well as asynchronous homework assignments and biweekly meetings with their mentor.
- Policies, Procedures, and More (Months 4 and 5): In this phase, participants explore the practical aspects of leading a software development organization, including legal, ethical, and regulatory considerations. Weekly half-day virtual seminars are held, with a mix of instructor-led and small-group sessions, alongside asynchronous homework assignments and biweekly meetings with mentors. During this phase, participants also create a self-development plan and conduct a department or team SWOT analysis, identifying a strategic initiative to implement in their area of responsibility.
- "Empower the Business" (Month 6): This final phase of the program focuses on empowering participants to effectively implement their strategic initiatives and lead change within the organization. Participants engage in a capstone project, applying the knowledge and skills gained throughout the program to address a real-world challenge in their department or team. Weekly half-day virtual seminars are held, with a mix of instructor-led and small-group sessions, alongside asynchronous homework assignments and biweekly meetings with mentors. Additionally, participants present their capstone projects to senior leaders and program facilitators, receiving feedback and guidance to refine their implementation plans.

Timeline, Resources, and Support

The Byte Brigade Leadership Development Program is designed as a 6-month program, with each phase building upon the previous one to provide a comprehensive and immersive learning experience. The program requires a significant investment of time and resources from both participants and the organization, including:

- Time commitment: Participants are expected to dedicate approximately 10-15 hours per week to the program, including attending seminars, completing homework assignments, and engaging in mentorship meetings.
- Financial investment: The organization provides funding for the program, including the cost of seminars, materials, and resources, as well as supporting the time commitment of mentors and program facilitators.
- Mentorship and support: A key component of the program is the ongoing mentorship and support provided by senior leaders and HR personnel. Mentors are selected based on their expertise and experience in the software development industry and their ability to provide guidance and feedback to program participants. Additionally, the HR Director and other program facilitators play a critical role in coordinating program logistics, providing resources and support, and ensuring alignment with organizational goals and objectives.
- Evaluation and feedback: Throughout the program, participants receive regular feedback on their progress and performance from mentors, program facilitators, and their peers. This feedback is used to inform adjustments to the program structure and content, as well as to guide participants in their ongoing development efforts.

The Byte Brigade Leadership Development Program offers a comprehensive and structured approach to cultivating the skills and capabilities needed for effective leadership in the software development industry. Grounded in best practices and informed by a robust review of the literature, the program provides participants with a strong foundation for success, while also contributing to the ongoing growth and development of the organization as a whole.

Evaluation and Assessment

The evaluation and assessment of Byte Brigade's Leadership Development Program are essential components of the program's overall success. To ensure that the program meets its objectives and contributes positively to the organization's growth and development, a comprehensive evaluation framework is employed, incorporating both qualitative and quantitative metrics. This section outlines the methods used to evaluate the program's effectiveness, the metrics employed in the evaluation process, the importance of measuring competence, and the role of self-development plans and department initiatives in the assessment process.

One widely recognized model for evaluating training effectiveness is Kirkpatrick's four-level model, which provides a structured framework for assessing the impact of training programs on different dimensions. Byte Brigade's Leadership Development Program utilizes Kirkpatrick's model to evaluate the program's effectiveness at four levels: reaction, learning, behavior, and results:

- Reaction: The first level of evaluation focuses on the participants' immediate reactions to the program, capturing their perceptions of its relevance, quality, and value. This is typically assessed through post-session surveys, often referred to as 'smile sheets,' which gauge participants' satisfaction with the program's content, delivery, and overall experience. While this level of evaluation provides essential feedback on the program's design and delivery, it is not sufficient to determine the program's overall effectiveness in developing leadership skills.

- Learning: The second level of evaluation measures the extent to which participants have acquired the intended knowledge and skills through the program. This is assessed through various means, such as knowledge checks and quizzes, case study analyses, and reflection exercises. In Byte Brigade's Leadership Development Program, learning is evaluated through assessments conducted at the end of each program component, as well as through the capstone project, where participants apply their newly acquired skills to a real-world challenge in their department or team.

- Behavior: The third level of evaluation focuses on the extent to which participants have applied their new knowledge and skills in their workplace, resulting in changes in their behavior and performance. This level of evaluation is particularly critical for Leadership Development Programs, as the ultimate goal is to enable participants to lead more effectively within the organization. Behavior changes are assessed through various methods, including self-assessments, feedback from supervisors and subordinates, and observations of participants' actions and decision-making. In Byte Brigade's Leadership Development Program, behavior changes are evaluated three and six months after program completion to determine the program's long-term impact on participants' leadership practices.

- Results: The fourth and final level of evaluation examines the program's overall impact on organizational performance, such as improvements in productivity, employee engagement, and profitability. This level of evaluation is the most challenging to measure directly, as it requires isolating the program's specific contributions from other factors that may influence organizational performance. However, by tracking key performance indicators over time and comparing them with industry benchmarks, it is possible to assess the program's overall return on investment.

Qualitative and Quantitative Metrics in the Evaluation Process

In evaluating Byte Brigade's Leadership Development Program, both qualitative and quantitative metrics are employed to provide a comprehensive understanding of the program's effectiveness. Qualitative metrics primarily focus on participants' perceptions and experiences, offering valuable insights into the program's strengths and areas for improvement. Examples of qualitative metrics include participants' satisfaction with program content, delivery, and support, as well as their perceptions of the program's relevance and value.

Quantitative metrics, on the other hand, focus on objectively measurable outcomes and performance indicators. These metrics may include participants' scores on knowledge quizzes and assessments, changes in key performance indicators (such as employee engagement, turnover, and productivity), and the number of successful department initiatives implemented by program participants. By combining both qualitative and quantitative metrics, the evaluation process provides a more robust and nuanced understanding of the program's impact on participants and the organization as a whole.

The Importance of Measuring Competence and the Role of Self-Development Plans and Department Initiatives in the Assessment Process

Measuring competence is a vital aspect of evaluating the effectiveness of Leadership Development Programs. Assessing participants' competence in applying the knowledge, skills, and behaviors acquired during the program helps to determine the program's success in meeting its objectives and its impact on organizational performance. Moreover, measuring competence supports the ongoing development of participants by identifying areas of strength and opportunities for improvement.

Self-development plans play a crucial role in the competence assessment process. These plans allow participants to reflect on their learning journey, set personal development goals, and outline specific actions they will take to achieve these goals. Self-development plans are an essential tool for translating the learning acquired during the program into real-world application, helping participants to continue honing their leadership skills beyond the program's duration.

Department initiatives also play a significant role in the assessment process, serving as a tangible demonstration of participants' competence and the program's impact on the organization. By implementing department initiatives based on their learning from the Leadership Development Program, participants not only contribute to the organization's success but also showcase their ability to apply their new skills in practice. These initiatives provide an opportunity for participants to receive feedback and support from their supervisors and colleagues, further reinforcing their learning and development.

The evaluation and assessment of Byte Brigade's Leadership Development Program are critical components of the program's success. By employing a comprehensive evaluation framework, including Kirkpatrick's four-level model and a combination of qualitative and quantitative metrics, the program's effectiveness can be assessed across multiple dimensions. Measuring participants' competence, supported by self-development plans and department initiatives, ensures that the learning acquired during the program translates into real-world application and contributes to the organization's ongoing growth and development.

RESULTS AND DISCUSSION

The implementation of Byte Brigade's Leadership Development Program (Leadership Development Program) has produced a range of outcomes, both quantitative and qualitative, that provide insights into the program's effectiveness and impact on participants and the organization. In this section, we list the results of the program and their implications for the development of future leadership initiatives:

- Competence Development: The self-development plans and department initiatives undertaken by program participants indicate a substantial improvement in leadership competencies. Participants demonstrated increased confidence in applying their newly acquired knowledge and skills to address organizational challenges and drive strategic initiatives.
- Positive Organizational Outcomes: As a result of the Leadership Development Program, the organization experienced an increase in the successful implementation of strategic plans and improvement in employee satisfaction and loyalty. These outcomes suggest that the program has fostered a culture of effective leadership and contributed to the organization's overall success.
- Evaluation Metrics: The evaluation metrics employed, such as Kirkpatrick's model, revealed positive results across all four levels – reaction, learning, behavior, and results. Participants' reactions to the program were favorable, indicating high engagement and satisfaction. Learning assessments showed a significant increase in knowledge and skill acquisition, while behavior assessments revealed noticeable improvements in participants' leadership behaviors. Finally, the organization experienced positive results linked to the program, such as increased profitability and successful implementation of strategic initiatives.

The results of Byte Brigade's Leadership Development Program demonstrate the effectiveness of the program in enhancing participants' leadership competencies and contributing to the organization's success. The program's design, which integrates theoretical foundations, practical application, and comprehensive evaluation, has played a significant role in producing these positive outcomes.

However, there are several areas for improvement and potential future directions for the program. First, the program may benefit from incorporating additional feedback mechanisms, such as 360-degree assessments, to provide participants with more comprehensive insights into their leadership strengths and areas for growth. This feedback would help participants refine their self-development plans and further enhance their leadership competencies.

The program could be expanded to include a broader range of participants within the organization, such as emerging leaders or employees in non-leadership roles who demonstrate leadership potential. This expansion would help to further develop the organization's leadership pipeline and ensure that future leaders are equipped with the necessary skills to succeed.

The organization should consider conducting longitudinal studies to assess the long-term impact of the Leadership Development Program on participants and the organization. These studies would provide valuable insights into the sustainability of the program's outcomes and inform ongoing program development and refinement.

The results of Byte Brigade's Leadership Development Program demonstrate its effectiveness in developing participants' leadership competencies and contributing to the organization's success. Through continuous evaluation and improvement, the program can continue to provide a robust foundation for the development of current and future leaders within the organization.

USING THE CASE STUDY

The Byte Brigade case study offers a valuable resource for context-rich learning experiences in various fields such as organizational change management, human resources, business strategy, corporate social responsibility, and cross-cultural leadership. It can be used for such learning experiences, including:

- Role-playing: Simulated interactions, decision-making, and problem-solving as different characters in the case study.
- Project-based learning: Developing a leadership program for a fictitious company based on the Byte Brigade case study.
- Group discussions and debates: Engaging in discussions on leadership development, context, self-assessment, and feedback.
- Interactive workshops: Attending workshops on emotional intelligence, communication skills, and strategic thinking.
- Reflective writing: Analyzing and comparing leadership development experiences and identifying areas for improvement.
- Team-based learning: Developing a comprehensive leadership program for a specific organization and presenting it for feedback.
- Coaching and mentoring: Working with a coach or mentor to develop a personalized leadership development plan.

- Online learning modules: Completing online modules on coaching, feedback, goal setting, and performance management.
- Action learning projects: Identifying and solving real-world problems while applying principles learned from the Byte Brigade case study.
- Podcasts and video series: Developing content featuring industry experts and thought leaders sharing insights on leadership development programs and practices.

By utilizing the Byte Brigade case study in a variety of context-rich learning experiences, individuals and organizations can gain a deeper understanding of effective leadership development and gain practical skills and competencies that can contribute to their success.

The learning experience modality can significantly affect the design and implementation of context-rich experiences based on the Byte Brigade case study. For example, if the learning experience is on-ground, participants can engage in field trips to visit Byte Brigade or other similar companies to observe their leadership development programs in action. This may not be possible in an online learning experience, where virtual field trips or case study simulations may be a more suitable option.

Similarly, if the learning experience is online, interactive workshops may need to be modified to suit the online environment. For example, breakout rooms and online discussion forums can be used to facilitate small group discussions and activities. Additionally, reflective writing activities may need to be modified to suit the online environment, such as using online journals or discussion boards to prompt participants to reflect on their experiences.

Technology can be used to enhance context-rich learning experiences using the Byte Brigade case study in several ways. For example:

- Online simulations and virtual reality: Practicing leadership skills in a safe, low stakes, virtual environment using online simulations that mimic real-life scenarios.
- Online collaborative tools: Collaborating on group projects, engaging in debates and discussions, and providing feedback to one another using online tools such as discussion forums, video conferencing, and shared document editing tools.
- Online assessments and self-assessments: Identifying strengths and weaknesses in leadership skills and tracking progress over time using online assessments and self-assessments that provide personalized feedback and recommendations for improvement.
- Gamification: Adding elements of competition, challenge, and rewards to the learning experience through gamification, where participants can earn points, badges, or other incentives for completing certain tasks, demonstrating leadership skills, or participating in group activities.
- Mobile learning: Accessing learning materials, assessments, and resources on-the-go via smartphones or tablets, allowing for context-rich learning experiences anytime, anywhere.

To make these context-rich learning activities low-fi, the following are the formats in which the case study could be used:

- Role-playing exercises: Engage in simulated interactions, decision-making, and problem-solving activities using simple props and costumes.
- Project-based learning: Plan and execute projects using low-tech tools such as whiteboards and sticky notes.

- Group discussions and debates: Engage in discussions and debates in-person or over the phone without the need for video conferencing or other technology.
- Interactive workshops: Attend workshops using basic presentation software or flipcharts and markers.
- Reflective writing: Complete reflective writing exercises using pen and paper or basic word processing software.

By making these context-rich learning activities low-fi, they can be made more accessible to a wider range of learners and can be conducted in various settings, including classrooms, offices, and community centers. Additionally, low-fi activities can be more cost-effective and can reduce the reliance on technology, which can be beneficial for individuals and organizations with limited resources or technological capabilities.

Sample lesson plans are given in the Appendix.

CONCLUSION

The case study of Byte Brigade's Leadership Development Program provides a valuable tool for promoting learning and development in various settings. The program's theoretical foundation and guiding principles, as well as its various components and evaluation methods, offer a framework for developing effective leadership skills and promoting organizational success. The case study's adaptability to different learning experiences, including webinars, action research, and simulation exercises, highlights the practical and actionable nature of using case studies in learning contexts. By engaging in these learning experiences, participants can gain valuable skills and insights that can be applied to their own work contexts, ultimately contributing to the success of their organizations. As such, the Byte Brigade case study represents a valuable resource for educators, trainers, and organizational leaders seeking to enhance leadership development programs and promote organizational success. Areas for investigation of the leadership development program include its long-term impact on organizational success, employee retention, job satisfaction, and evaluation methods. Research can help identify areas for improvement in the evaluation process to better measure effectiveness. Case studies can be studied to identify best practices for incorporating them into various learning experiences.

REFERENCES

Barnes, A. C., & Larcus, J. (2015). Positive Psychology as a Framework for Leadership Development in Recreation and Sport. *New Directions for Student Leadership*, *2015*(147), 77–87. doi:10.1002/yd.20145 PMID:26895016

Brue, K. L., & Brue, S. A. (2016). Experiences and outcomes of a women's Leadership Development Program: A phenomenological investigation. *Journal of Leadership Education*, *15*(3), 75–97. doi:10.12806/V15/I3/R2

Cacioppe, R. (1998). An integrated model and approach for the design of effective Leadership Development Programs. *Leadership and Organization Development Journal*, *19*(1), 44–53. doi:10.1108/01437739810368820

Cohrs, C., Bormann, K. C., Diebig, M., Millhoff, C., Pachocki, K., & Rowold, J. (2020). Transformational leadership and communication: Evaluation of a two-day Leadership Development Program. *Leadership and Organization Development Journal*, *41*(1), 101–117. doi:10.1108/LODJ-02-2019-0097

deMoville, B. (2007). Enterprise Leadership. *Organization Development Journal*, *25*(4), 83–87.

Kaplan, A. S. (2020). Climbing the Ladder to CEO Part II: Leadership and Business Acumen. *Physician Leadership Journal*, *7*(3), 50–52.

Making leadership development more effective: Psychological changes have implications for training programme design. (2015). *Development and Learning in Organizations, 29*(6), 20-22. doi:10.1108/DLO-05-2015-0046

Quinn, F. F. (2018). Human Resource Development, Ethics, and the Social Good. *New Horizons in Adult Education and Human Resource Development*, *30*(2), 52–57. doi:10.1002/nha3.20215

Ruben, B. D., DeLisi, R., & Gigliotti, R. A. (2018). Academic Leadership Development Programs: Conceptual Foundations, Structural and Pedagogical Components, and Operational Considerations. *Journal of Leadership Education*, *17*(3), 241–254. doi:10.12806/V17/I3/A5

Sanchez-Nunez, M. T., Patti, J., & Holzer, A. (2015). Effectiveness of a Leadership Development Program That Incorporates Social and Emotional Intelligence for Aspiring School Leaders. *Journal of Educational Issues*, *1*(1), 64–84. doi:10.5296/jei.v1i1.7443

Sowcik, M., Benge, M., & Niewoehner-Green, J. (2018). A Practical Solution to Developing County Extension Director's Leadership Skills: Exploring the Design, Delivery and Evaluation of an Online Leadership Development Program. *Journal of Agricultural Education*, *59*(3), 139–153. doi:10.5032/jae.2018.03139

Switzer, T. R. (2000). Looking in the mirror: Becoming an effective follower. *Library Mosaics*, *11*(6), 8–10.

Vugec, D. S., Vuksic, V. B., Bach, M. P., Jaklic, J., & Stemberger, M. I. (2020). Business Intelligence and Organizational Performance: The Role of Alignment with Business Process Management. *Business Process Management Journal*, *26*(6), 1709–1730. doi:10.1108/BPMJ-08-2019-0342

Wei, Y. S., O'Neill, H., & Zhou, N. (2020). How Does Perceived Integrity in Leadership Matter to Firms in a Transitional Economy? *Journal of Business Ethics*, *167*(4), 623–641. doi:10.100710551-019-04168-x

APPENDIX: SAMPLE LESSON PLANS

Lesson Plan 1: Enhancing Leadership Skills Through Context-Rich Learning: A Case Study Approach

This lesson plan emphasizes the importance of context-rich learning in leadership development and provides a hands-on approach for applying these principles. Through analysis of the Byte Brigade case study and small group discussions, participants are able to develop a deeper understanding of context-rich learning and its impact on leadership development. The visual representation activity encourages creativity and practical application, allowing participants to identify actionable steps for implementing context-rich learning principles in their own leadership development programs. This professional development course provides a valuable opportunity for managers, executives, and other professionals to enhance their leadership skills through practical, context-rich learning experiences.

Learning Objectives:

- Analyze and evaluate the leadership development program at Byte Brigade as a context-rich learning experience
- Apply context-rich learning principles to the development of leadership skills
- Develop a visual representation of a leadership development program that incorporates context-rich learning principles
- Identify actionable steps for implementing context-rich learning principles in leadership development

Grade Level: Adult learners

Course Type/Description: Professional development course on leadership development through context-rich learning

Target Audience: Managers, executives, and other professionals seeking to enhance their leadership skills

Delivery Outline/Timeline:

- Introduction and overview: 10 minutes
- Reading of case study: 20-30 minutes
- Small group discussions: 30-40 minutes
- Whole group discussion: 20-30 minutes
- Visual representation activity: 20-30 minutes
- Final discussion and conclusion: 10-20 minutes

Duration: 2 hours

Delivery Outline/Timeline:

- Introduce the topic of context-rich learning and its importance for leadership development. Provide a brief overview of Byte Brigade's leadership development program and its goals.

- Distribute the case study and allow participants 20-30 minutes to read it individually.
- Divide participants into small groups and ask them to discuss the following questions:
  - What are the key elements of Byte Brigade's leadership development program?
  - How does the program incorporate context-rich learning principles?
  - What are the strengths and weaknesses of the program?
  - What can we learn from this case study that can be applied to our own leadership development?
- Reconvene the groups and ask them to share their responses with the whole group. Facilitate a discussion to identify common themes and areas of agreement/disagreement.
- Using flipchart paper and markers, ask participants to create a visual representation of a leadership development program that incorporates context-rich learning principles, based on the Byte Brigade case study and their group discussions.
- Allow each group to present their visual representation and explain the rationale behind it.
- Facilitate a final discussion to summarize the key takeaways from the activity and identify actionable steps for implementing context-rich learning principles in leadership development.

Assessment:

- Observe group discussions and evaluate the depth of analysis and critical thinking demonstrated by participants.
- Review the visual representations created by each group and assess their creativity and ability to apply context-rich learning principles.
- Collect the handout with discussion questions and use it to evaluate the level of engagement and participation of each participant.

Lesson Plan 2: Analyzing Byte Brigade's Leadership Development Program

This lesson plan is designed to provide an online leadership course that focuses on analyzing Byte Brigade's leadership development program as a context-rich learning experience and evaluating its effectiveness using Kirkpatrick's model of evaluation. The target audience for this course includes undergraduate and graduate students, as well as working professionals interested in leadership development. The two-week course includes ten daily sessions covering theoretical foundations, program components, evaluation and assessment, and case study analysis. In week two, students will analyze case study sections and present their findings to the class. Additionally, they will evaluate the program's effectiveness using Kirkpatrick's model and develop a self-development plan based on learnings from the case study. The course material includes Byte Brigade's leadership development program case study, Kirkpatrick's model of evaluation, an online discussion forum, and self-development plan templates. Assessment will be based on a group presentation of the case study analysis, evaluation of the leadership development program using Kirkpatrick's model, and a self-development plan.

Grade Level: Undergraduate and graduate

Course Type/Description: Online Leadership Course

Target Audience: Students in leadership courses, working professionals, and anyone interested in leadership development

Duration: Two weeks

Objectives:

- Analyze the theoretical foundation and guiding principles of Byte Brigade's leadership development program
- Evaluate the effectiveness of the program using Kirkpatrick's model
- Develop a self-development plan based on the learnings from the case study

Delivery Outline/Timeline:
Week 1:
Day 1: Introduction to the case study

- Introduce the case study on Byte Brigade's leadership development program
- Discuss the importance of leadership development programs in organizations

Day 2: Theoretical foundation and guiding principles

- Analyze the theoretical foundation and guiding principles of Byte Brigade's leadership development program
- Discuss how the program aligns with the best practices in leadership development

Day 3: Program components and phases

- Identify and discuss the various components and phases of the program, such as "Lead the Business," "Respect the Business," and "Impact the Business"
- Examine how these components contribute to the overall effectiveness of the program

Day 4: Evaluation and assessment

- Introduce Kirkpatrick's model of evaluation and discuss how it is used to evaluate the effectiveness of the program
- Analyze the qualitative and quantitative metrics used in the evaluation process

Day 5: Competence and self-development

- Discuss the importance of measuring competence in leadership development programs
- Analyze the role of self-development plans and department initiatives in the assessment process

Week 2:
Day 6: Case study analysis

- Divide the class into groups and assign each group a section of the case study to analyze
- Instruct the groups to identify the strengths and weaknesses of the leadership development program

Day 7: Group presentations

- Each group will present their analysis of the assigned section to the class
- The class will discuss the common themes and issues that emerged in the presentations

Day 8: Evaluating the effectiveness of the program

- Instruct the students to apply Kirkpatrick's model to evaluate the effectiveness of the program
- Discuss the outcomes of the evaluation and the implications for the organization

Day 9: Developing a self-development plan

- Instruct the students to develop a self-development plan based on the learnings from the case study
- Discuss the importance of aligning personal development goals with organizational goals

Day 10: Conclusion

- Recap the key learnings from the case study and the course
- Discuss how the case study can be applied to other organizations and industries

Assessment:

- Group presentation on the analysis of the assigned section of the case study (30%)
- Evaluation of the leadership development program using Kirkpatrick's model (30%)
- Self-development plan (40%)

Lesson Plan 3: Using the Byte Brigade Case Study to Enhance Social Learning in Leadership Development

This is a lesson plan for a 2-hour social learning event aimed at employees in a company interested in learning about leadership development and innovation. The lesson involves the analysis of the Byte Brigade case study, with participants divided into small groups to analyze and present their findings, followed by group discussions. The lesson plan aims to help participants understand the importance of leadership development programs, identify key points related to innovation and leadership development, apply their learnings to their own roles and responsibilities, and reflect on the importance of leadership development programs in contributing to the success of the organization. No formal assessment is included, with feedback and observation used instead.

Objectives:

- To understand the importance of leadership development programs in achieving organizational success
- To analyze the Byte Brigade case study and identify key points related to innovation and leadership development

- To apply learnings from the case study to participants' own roles and responsibilities within the company
- To reflect on the importance of leadership development programs and how they can contribute to the success of the organization

Delivery Outline/Timeline:
Introduction (10 minutes)

- Start the event by introducing the case study to the participants. Briefly explain the background of Byte Brigade and the leadership development program that the company has implemented.

Case study analysis (30-45 minutes)

- Divide the participants into small groups and assign each group a specific section of the case study to analyze. Ask each group to identify the key points of the section, discuss the relevance of the section to the overall case study, and propose how they would approach the situation if they were part of the Byte Brigade team.

Group discussion (30-45 minutes)

- After each group has completed their analysis, bring everyone back together for a group discussion. Ask each group to present their findings, encourage questions and comments from the other groups, and facilitate a conversation around the key takeaways from the case study.

Application (30 minutes)

- Have participants apply their learnings to their own roles and responsibilities within the company. Encourage them to think about how they can incorporate the principles of the Byte Brigade leadership development program into their own work and how they can contribute to the company's success.

Reflection (10-15 minutes)

- End the event by asking participants to reflect on what they have learned and how they can apply it to their work moving forward. Encourage participants to share their thoughts and ideas with each other and to continue the conversation beyond the event.

Assessment:
Assessment of the social learning event can be done through observation and feedback from participants. Encourage participants to share their thoughts and feedback on the effectiveness of the activity and whether they found it helpful in understanding the importance of leadership development programs.

Lesson Plan 4: Using the Byte Brigade Case Study to Promote Diversity and Inclusion in Leadership - ERG Discussion Plan

This lesson plan is designed for Employee Resource Groups (ERGs) focused on promoting diversity and inclusion in leadership within organizations. The goal of the lesson is to use the Byte Brigade case study to facilitate a discussion on the importance of diversity and inclusion in leadership, explore the ways in which Byte Brigade's leadership development program promotes diversity and inclusion, identify areas for improvement in the group's own organization's leadership development programs with a focus on diversity and inclusion, and brainstorm new ideas and strategies to promote diversity and inclusion in leadership. The lesson can be delivered in a flexible timeline and can be adjusted based on the needs of the group. The delivery outline includes introducing the case study, dividing the group into smaller teams to analyze and discuss specific aspects of the case study, reconvening the group to share findings and insights, brainstorming new ideas and strategies, and concluding the discussion. The assessment of the discussion can be done through observation and feedback from participants.

Objectives:

- To use the Byte Brigade case study to facilitate a discussion on the importance of diversity and inclusion in leadership
- To explore the ways in which Byte Brigade's leadership development program promotes diversity and inclusion
- To identify areas for improvement in the group's own organization's leadership development programs with a focus on diversity and inclusion
- To brainstorm new ideas and strategies to promote diversity and inclusion in leadership

Delivery Outline/Timeline:

- Introduce the case study and explain its relevance to the ERG's focus on diversity and inclusion in leadership
- Divide the group into smaller teams to analyze and discuss specific aspects of the case study
- Reconvene the group to share findings and insights, and to discuss how the case study can inform their own organization's approach to leadership development
- Brainstorm new ideas and strategies to promote diversity and inclusion in leadership
- Conclude the discussion and encourage continued conversation beyond the event

Assessment:

Assessment of the discussion can be done through observation and feedback from participants. Encourage participants to share their thoughts and feedback on the effectiveness of the activity and whether they found it helpful in promoting diversity and inclusion in leadership.

Lesson Plan 5: Developing Effective Leaders Webinar

This webinar will explore Byte Brigade's leadership development program, analyzing its theoretical foundation, guiding principles, and evaluation methods. Participants will gain an understanding of the importance of leadership development programs and will be able to evaluate the effectiveness of Byte Brigade's program using Kirkpatrick's model and other metrics. Additionally, participants will identify gaps in the literature and suggest directions for future research or program development.

Learning Objectives

- Evaluate the effectiveness of Byte Brigade's leadership development program using Kirkpatrick's model and other qualitative and quantitative metrics.
- Analyze the theoretical foundation and guiding principles of Byte Brigade's leadership development program.
- Identify gaps in the literature or areas where Byte Brigade's program may offer unique contributions.
- Suggest directions for future research or program development.
- Develop a comprehensive understanding of the importance of leadership development programs in organizations.

Agenda

I. Introduction (5 min)
    ◦ Welcome and introductions
    ◦ Overview of the webinar and learning objectives
II. Theoretical Foundation of Byte Brigade's Leadership Development Program (15 min)
    ◦ Overview of the theoretical framework and guiding principles of the program
    ◦ Discussion of the program components and phases (e.g., "Lead the Business," "Respect the Business")
III. Evaluation and Assessment (15 min)
    ◦ Explanation of the methods used to evaluate the effectiveness of the program (e.g., Kirkpatrick's model)
    ◦ Description of the qualitative and quantitative metrics used in the evaluation process
    ◦ Discussion of the importance of measuring competence and the role of self-development plans and department initiatives in the assessment process
IV. Case Study Analysis (20 min)
    ◦ Analysis of the case study of Byte Brigade
    ◦ Identification of the program's strengths and weaknesses based on the learning objectives
V. Discussion and Q&A (20 min)
    ◦ Open discussion of the case study and its relevance to participants' experiences
    ◦ Answering of participant questions related to the content covered
VI. Conclusion (5 min)
    ◦ Summary of key points covered in the webinar
    ◦ Suggestions for future research and program development

Materials:

- Case study of Byte Brigade's leadership development program
- Slide deck presentation

- Webinar software

Assessment:

- Participants will be given a short quiz at the end of the webinar to evaluate their understanding of the content covered.
- An evaluation form will be provided to participants to gather feedback on the effectiveness of the webinar and to identify areas for improvement.

Duration: 1.5 hours

Lesson Plan 6: Improving Leadership Development Programs Through Action Research

This is a lesson plan on how to use the Byte Brigade case study to conduct action research aimed at improving leadership development programs. The plan is designed for professionals involved in designing, implementing, and evaluating leadership development programs in organizations. The learning experience includes identifying research questions, conducting research, developing action plans, and evaluating outcomes. The plan consists of several stages, including exploring research questions, conducting research, developing action plans, implementing the action plans, evaluating outcomes, and reflecting on the process. This learning experience can be conducted over several sessions, ranging from several days to several weeks depending on the scope of the research questions and the resources available.

Note: Action research typically involves identifying a problem, developing a plan of action to address the problem, implementing the plan, collecting and analyzing data, reflecting on the results, and making adjustments as needed. The goal of action research is to produce practical knowledge that can be used to improve practice and inform future action.

Learning Objectives:

- Understand the principles of action research and its application to leadership development programs
- Develop research questions that address the challenges facing leadership development programs
- Conduct research using a variety of methods to collect and analyze data
- Develop feasible and practical action plans based on research findings
- Evaluate the outcomes of the action plans and share findings with others
- Reflect on the action research process and its strengths and limitations

Procedure:
Welcome and introductions
Begin by providing a brief overview of the case study and its relevance to the participants' work or interests.

- Explain the purpose and goals of the action research learning experience
- Introduce the case study and its relevance to the participants' work or interests

Explore the Research Questions

- Discuss the importance of developing research questions that address the challenges facing leadership development programs
- Identify a set of research questions that will guide the action research process. These questions should focus on improving the leadership development program at Byte Brigade or a similar organization. Examples of research questions could include:
  - How can the leadership development program be made more effective?
  - What are the key challenges facing leaders at Byte Brigade, and how can the leadership development program address these challenges?
  - How can the leadership development program be adapted to better serve the needs of diverse employees?
- Divide participants into small teams based on the research questions they want to explore

Conduct Research

The teams will conduct research using a variety of methods, such as surveys, interviews, focus groups, and observations. They will analyze the data they collect and use it to identify areas where the leadership development program could be improved.

- Provide instructions and guidance on conducting research using various methods such as surveys, interviews, focus groups, and observations
- Encourage participants to collect and analyze data that will inform the development of feasible and practical action plans

Develop Action Plans

- Based on their research findings, the teams will develop action plans for improving the leadership development program. These plans should be practical and feasible and should take into account the resources and constraints of the organization.
- Based on their research findings, each team will develop feasible and practical action plans that address the challenges facing leadership development programs
- Encourage participants to consider the resources and constraints of their organization when developing their action plans

Implement the Action Plans

The teams will implement their action plans, monitoring their progress and making adjustments as needed. They will collect data on the effectiveness of their interventions and use this information to refine their approach.

- Each team will implement their action plans, monitor progress, and adjust as needed
- Encourage participants to collect data on the effectiveness of their interventions

Evaluate the Outcomes

At the end of the action research process, each team will evaluate the outcomes of their interventions

- Teams will share their findings with the larger group and discuss the implications for the leadership development program at Byte Brigade or a similar organization

Reflect on the Process

- Participants will reflect on the action research process and what they have learned from it
- Encourage participants to discuss the strengths and limitations of action research and consider how they can apply it in their own work

Assessment:

Assessment of the action research learning experience can be done through observation and feedback from participants. Encourage participants to share their thoughts and feedback on the effectiveness of the activity and whether they found it helpful in improving leadership development programs.

Lesson Plan 7: Leading Change Simulation

This simulation exercise is designed to provide participants with a low stake, hands-on experience in leading change within an organization, using the case study of Byte Brigade. Participants will work together in small groups to develop and implement a change initiative within the company, facing the same challenges and opportunities that the characters in the case study did. The exercise will involve several stages, including planning, implementation, and evaluation, with feedback and reflection sessions throughout the process.

Learning Objectives:

- Develop and apply skills in leading organizational change
- Practice effective communication and collaboration skills
- Develop strategic thinking skills
- Apply problem-solving skills to real-world situations
- Gain experience in decision-making and critical thinking

Preparation:

- Participants will be given access to the Byte Brigade case study in advance of the simulation exercise, along with the simulation scenario and instructions.
- Facilitators will review the facilitator guide and prepare for the feedback and reflection sessions.

Activity:
Introduction (10 minutes)

- Facilitator welcomes participants and provides an overview of the simulation exercise

- Participants introduce themselves and share their goals for the exercise (additional time may be needed for larger groups)

Planning Stage (60 minutes)

- Participants work in small groups to develop a change initiative plan based on the Byte Brigade case study, including goals, strategies, timelines, and resources required
- Facilitator provides guidance and support as needed, emphasizing the importance of effective communication and collaboration

Implementation Stage (90 minutes)

- Participants work in their groups to implement their change initiative plan, addressing any challenges or obstacles that arise
- Facilitator provides feedback and support as needed, emphasizing the importance of strategic thinking and problem-solving skills

Evaluation and Reflection (30 minutes)

- Participants evaluate the success of their change initiative plan, using the evaluation forms provided by the facilitator
- Facilitator leads a reflection session, encouraging participants to share their experiences, challenges, and successes
- Participants share their insights and learning points from the simulation exercise

Wrap-up (10 minutes)

- Facilitator summarizes the key takeaways from the simulation exercise
- Participants provide feedback on the exercise and suggest areas for improvement

Assessment:

- Participants will be evaluated based on their contributions to the group, their problem-solving and critical thinking skills, their communication and collaboration skills, and their overall engagement in the simulation exercise.
- The facilitator will provide feedback to each participant based on their performance, using the evaluation forms provided.

Follow-up:

- Participants will be encouraged to apply the insights and skills gained from the simulation exercise to their real-world work situations.
- Facilitators may provide additional resources or follow-up sessions to support ongoing learning and development.

Chapter 14
Training for Better Transfer in an Online Competency–Based Higher Education Program:
Technology's Role in Preparing the Next Generation Workforce

Sean P. Gyll

ⓘ https://orcid.org/0000-0002-9961-4007
Western Governors University, USA

Karen K. Shader
Western Governors University, USA

Paul Zikas
ORamaVR, Switzerland

George Papagiannakis
University of Crete, Greece

ABSTRACT

Virtual reality simulations represent a much-needed effort to move beyond the shortcomings of traditional form-based assessments. Within VR, we assess competency and problem-solving skills versus the content memorization typically supported by conventional measures. This chapter explores an innovative VR simulation recently deployed at Western Governors University. The authors explored the utility of a VR simulation as an assessment tool when students engaged in more inclusive, immersive, and interactive experiences compared to conventional methods. The authors investigated students' summative assessment scores across a 2D (desktop) and 3D VR (headset) version and how additional factors like motion sickness, cognitive workload, and system usability impacted their scores. The results showed that students in the Desktop version outperformed those in the VR version on the summative assessment while feeling equally immersed in the simulation. Implications for future research are discussed, especially for optimizing learning experiences in an online competency-based higher education program.

DOI: 10.4018/978-1-6684-7644-4.ch014

INTRODUCTION

Somewhere at the intersection between competency-based instruction and workforce demand exists an opportunity to apply what we currently know about how students learn to build competency-based credentials supported by practice scholarship. Science supports learning that builds from and inextricably links to the environment, the situations, and the working culture in which students will eventually find themselves (Schumacher, Englander, and Carpaccio, 2013). Within online competency-based higher education (OCBHE), learning is no longer viewed as a process of transmitting knowledge from instructor to student (e.g., sitting passively, listening to a lecture, taking notes, and applying concepts) but as an active process acquired through a variety of instructional and media types. As a result, students' capacity to develop a particular domain's competency and then transfer that knowledge to future job performance improves.

At a fundamental level, the term *transfer* refers to the influence of prior learning on later activity (Holding, 1991). Initial research began in the early 20th century, when Woodrow (1927) claimed, for example, that "improvement resulting from almost any sort of practice yields, as a rule, some transference" (p. 159). He suggested that *any* practice on a given task produces improvement (i.e., positive transfer) in several related functions. Today, OCBHE programs' criticality in training the next generation's workforce has become evident now that employers focus on identifying, recruiting, and retaining employers with transferable skills. Particularly in times of economic challenge, employers need a skilled, adaptable, creative, and equipped workforce for success in the global marketplace.

To meet this demand, institutions of higher learning are beginning to realize the importance of real-world, performance-based measures like virtual reality (VR) simulations, where performance demonstrations are crucial to success. Central to the development of VR simulations is the need for high-fidelity demonstrations of learner aptitudes and competencies that include a significant emphasis on cognitive abilities (i.e., knowing what) and the performance of those abilities (i.e., demonstrating how). The most important advantage of this testing mode is the real-world relevance that can be incorporated into the assessment, and technological innovations continue to expand these opportunities.

This chapter explores some fundamental principles currently being incorporated into the science of teaching at Western Governors University (WGU) and examines their effectiveness in an OCBHE program. These basic principles are summarized below:

- *Skill acquisition is specific to the conditions practiced during training, and many training programs are only effective to the extent that training will transfer to new situations.* Inefficiently developed training programs can interfere with developing flexible solutions to problem-solving. Programs that train students using a variety of technologies must also evaluate students using those technologies if they want to maximize training transfer.
- *Training that promotes attention flexibility improves learning.* Lessons from dual-task studies suggest that compared to learning single tasks alone, when tasks are practiced together, the cognitive system can coordinate task performance and minimize interference, thus, maximizing learning.
- *Learning complex tasks requires variability in training to maximize learning.* The most robust learning is likely to result from a combination of many experiences that allows students to engage in multiple attention processes when planning and executing solutions from memory.

A key element to each of these principles is that reviewing the same materials at different times and using reorganized contexts from other objectives and perspectives is essential for attaining advanced knowledge acquisition goals. The knowledge that will eventually be used in many ways must be represented, organized, and assessed in many ways. The alternative is knowledge only usable in situations where learners acquired the skill.

It is worth noting that less than a decade ago, terms like learning, memory, and cognition were hardly uttered within competency-based circles. Those less versed in learning theory and cognitive science found phrases like *training for better transfer*, *skill acquisition*, and *memory processing components* rather jargon-laced and somewhat confusing in the context of OCBHEs purpose. Moreover, understanding the instructional means involved in online learning was contextually different and unrelated to institutions' primary goal of educating and graduating students. Since then, seminal publications like *Make it Stick* by Brown, Roedigner, and McDaniels (2014) on successful learning science have altered this view. They provided everyday examples with straightforward explanations about why learning science principles work in an asynchronous environment.

This chapter's remaining sections examine some fundamental learning science principles supporting technology-based learning. We were particularly interested in exploring the utility of a VR simulation as an assessment tool when students engage in more inclusive, collective, and interactive experiences compared to conventional methods in the traditional sense. We investigated students' summative assessment scores across a 2D (desktop) and 3D VR (headset) version and how additional factors like motion sickness, cognitive workload, and system usability impacted their scores. Our results showed that students in the *Desktop* version outperformed the *VR* version on the summative assessment while feeling equally *immersed* in the simulation. Finally, implications for future research are discussed, especially for optimizing learning experiences in an OCBHE program.

Project Background

In 2020, the College of Health Professions at WGU offered two new innovative skills certificate programs designed to upskill healthcare professionals in Chronic and Behavioral Health Care Coordination. The programs were unique to WGU because students were required to pass a summative scenario-based VR simulation to earn a skills certificate; no other programs at WGU require passing a simulation-based assessment delivered in virtual reality. The programs were used as continuing education, employer-required professional development, or as part of employer onboarding for new employees and others leading care delivery transformation.

The skills certificates offered accessible career pathways for new and existing healthcare professionals in career development, career advancement, and mid-career support. They also expanded access by increasing relevancy in health care because the skills and competencies mapped directly to high-demand jobs. Additionally, the certificates provided a pathway for students into the WGU Bachelor of Science in Health Services Coordination (BSHSC) program for students choosing to continue their education. Program certificates, badges, and a skills transcript were awarded to students completing a certificate program.

Competency-Based Education

Competency-based credentials have become another way to demonstrate the flexibility and talent required to learn and grow in an evolving labor market. Consider the differences between traditional higher education and OCBHE programs' approach to learning. In the conventional system, students are awarded credit hours per *seat time* of instruction, and the transmission of knowledge is passed from teacher to student through some lecture or discourse (Johnston, 2011). As participants in this system, all students are taught the same materials simultaneously, resulting in inefficient use of students' and teachers' time. Students who need to learn more quickly fail rather than being allowed to succeed at their own pace, leading some to argue that learning in higher education is one of the least sophisticated aspects of the teaching and learning process (James, 2003).

In contrast, OCBHE programs strive to balance various learning approaches requiring students to master critical concepts before graduating. Students learn at their own pace and earn degrees by demonstrating knowledge and skill in required subject areas through carefully designed competency-based assessments (Gyll & Ragland, 2018). As the popularity of OCBHE programs continues to rise, they will be scrutinized by students and employers alike, and their credibility depends mainly on the quality of the assessments being used (McClarty & Gaertner, 2015).

Within OCBHE programs, assessments associated with traditional linear-based methods are no longer a sufficient means of evaluation. Program designers must now develop learning tasks that represent skilled "competency" based performance, especially those designed to transfer to the world of work. Thus, "competent for (doing) what?" is essential to any competence definition. Successful businesses are looking for employees who can adapt to changing needs, juggle multiple responsibilities, and independently make decisions. Competencies can be acquired through experience, from relevant contextual situations, or influenced by training or other external interventions. For OCBHE institutions to confirm that learners have developed the knowledge, skills, abilities, attitudes, and dispositions to demonstrate successful performance on the job, the definition of competence requires shifting from the conceptual paradigm of an evaluative stance to assuming responsibility for measuring future performance. Forces that might aid this conceptual transformation include the growing acceptance of *high-fidelity, performance-based measures*, which are quickly becoming a way of life in many occupations and professions.

Once student competence has been concretely defined in ways that hinge on quantifiable student achievement, it can be measured and operationalized. Put somewhat differently, and despite the current lack of consensus regarding the definition of competence, it is justifiable and productive to furnish an operational, albeit limited and contestable, definition of competence validated via sound design principles and empirical data. In doing so, institutions have a tool that will increase the likelihood that they will successfully graduate competent students of a particular type than they would otherwise be able to do sans the validated assessment.

For this chapter, competence is defined as "an outcome-based approach to education that incorporates modes of instructional delivery and assessment efforts designed to evaluate mastery of learning by students through their demonstration of the knowledge, attitudes, values, skills, and behaviors required for the degree sought" (Gervais, 2016, p. 99). This definition was chosen because it highlights the importance of student *demonstrations* of knowledge, skills, and abilities (KSAs) throughout the learning process. Demonstrating those KSAs within a competency-based framework is the first step toward ensuring the validity of educational programs and the utility of their outcomes. As such, an evaluation of competence should foretell a student's effectiveness in prospective job situations in a manner that will be fully explored throughout the remainder of this chapter.

Designing for Learning

Compared to traditional instructor-led methods, research suggests that competency-based skills are improved when learning is integrated into the educational experience rather than delivered in a compartmentalized fashion (Ford & Gopher, 2015; Hoogveld, 2003; Van Merrienboer & Kirschner, 2013; Merril, 2002). Furthermore, when content and learning strategies meet accepted education standards, technology increases mastery and helps better prepare students (Penuel & Cohen, 1999). While the literature has produced a sizable amount of evidence in this regard, more is needed to be dedicated to learning science, especially as it applies to training for better transfer in an asynchronous environment. The theories mentioned here represent a few early and more recent ones, and their discussion is not meant to be comprehensive. Instead, the intent is to provide an overview of the selected theoretical issues supporting this chapter's purpose.

Skill Acquisition

In general, skill acquisition follows a predictable pattern, which begins with very slow and effortful problem-solving that leads to fast and automatic problem-solving. Fitts (1964), for example, proposed that skill acquisition progresses through three stages. During the early and intermediate stages, problem-solving is slow and effortful as learners acquire general rules about a task. Then, over time, and after repeated practice, problem-solving in the late stage becomes faster and more automatic as they begin to proceduralize prior learning into action. It is at this point that learners become *expert* problem solvers.

Another skill acquisition model, Adaptive Control of Thought (ACT-R), also suggests that cognitive skill acquisition follows a sequence of learning activities that eventually leads to the automization of the skill (Anderson, 1993). In this theory, all knowledge begins in declarative form (i.e., learning what rather than knowing how). During the initial stages, the learner commits to memory a declarative representation of how rules work. Like Fitts's model, the early acquisition of a skill is slow and effortful, as the learner still needs to achieve an efficient means for solving problems. Instead, learners apply declarative rules that help them solve a problem. Then, through repeated practice, the learner develops a procedural understanding of how rules work. This occurs because knowledge for solving problems is read from the declarative and written to procedural memory. At this point, problem-solving becomes very fast, requires little attention, and can be accomplished while the learner is engaged in other mental activities.

These theories promote a general skill acquisition process, from slow and effortful to faster and more routine. As skills become proceduralized, they lend themselves to faster processing, and the learner is more likely to apply that information to solve complex problems. This is important for guiding our understanding of the effectiveness and utility of a VR simulation because assessing for competency in VR may require standardized procedures that gradually introduce users to its functionality while increasing their situational awareness within the environment.

Learning and Transfer: Lessons From Dual-Task Studies

OCBHE aims to develop students' capacity to acquire competency or mastery of a domain and then transfer that knowledge to new conditions (e.g., solving problems on the job). One method for demonstrating transfer was derived from dual-task studies, which suggest that when tasks are practiced together, learners have more opportunities to minimize interference between tasks and interlace them into a single flow of operations (Kramer, Larish, & Strayer, 1995). In a conventional dual-task, learners work simultaneously on two different tasks, for example, working on a math problem while simultaneously working within a spreadsheet. In general, these studies suggest that compared to learning single tasks alone, when they are practiced together, the cognitive system can coordinate task performance and minimize interference between them, thus, maximizing learning.

According to Brown and Carr (1989), three general methods for acquiring dual-task skills are *restructuring*, *intratask automaticity*, and *task-combination strategies*. The latter of these methods, task-combination strategies, considers dual-task learning and decreases in cognitive interference in the changing relations between two tasks (e.g., solving a math problem while entering the formula into a spreadsheet). Although the functions are performed independently, they can be combined into one processing sequence by interlacing their separate components into a single flow of mental operations. This is important within the context of VR because users are often required to combine bits and pieces of information from overlapping information sources and incorporate them into a single problem-solving activity when called upon to apply that information.

Variability Training

Research in variability training also proposes that irregularity during training may improve learning. For instance, Johnston, Strayer, and Vecera (1998) suggest that narrow-minded practice leads to an overspecialized network that performs well under specific conditions but transfers poorly to new environments. Broad-minded networks (i.e., ones trained on various task components), on the other hand, adapt better to new learning patterns under changed conditions. The learning mechanism responsible for the effectiveness of variability training is significant for understanding training in VR because it provides evidence to suggest that flexibility in attention strategies increases performance on different tasks:

"It appears that systematically altering practice to encourage additional, or at least different, information processing activities can degrade performance during practice, but can at the same time have the effect of generating greater performance capabilities in retention on transfer tests" (p. 215).

Although the principles involving dual-task studies and flexibility training differ from the situated learning in VR, the methods responsible for their effectiveness are noteworthy; it suggests that *integration* during the learning process may increase the application of those skills under changed (i.e., transfer) conditions. Support for these techniques rests in the proposition that flexibility within the cognitive system solves the flexibility dilemma (Johnston et al., 1998). Chiefly, that flexibility within training promotes lasting relationships that allow information to be used in many ways during the skill transfer (Spiro, Feltovich, Jacobson, & Coulson, 1991), like in VR environments.

Constructivist Theory of Learning and Instruction

Education research has also looked at the training dilemma in learning. For example, according to the constructivist theory of learning and instruction (also referred to in their article as cognitive flexibility theory), Spiro et al. (1991) propose that:

"The remedy for learning deficiencies related to domain complexity and irregularity requires the inculcation of learning processes that afford greater cognitive flexibility: This includes the ability to represent knowledge from different conceptual and case perspectives and then, when the knowledge must later be used, the ability to construct from those different conceptual and case representations a knowledge ensemble tailored to the needs of the understanding or problem-solving situations at hand" (p. 24).

A key element to this theory is that reviewing the same materials at different times and using reorganized contexts from other objectives and perspectives is essential for attaining advanced knowledge acquisition goals. The knowledge that will eventually be used in many ways must be represented, organized, and used in many ways during training. The alternative is knowledge only usable in situations where learners acquired the skill.

Designing for Learning in VR Environments

Since the development of VR technology, modern VR applications have been transformed into rich learning experiences leading to an increase in published educational applications. In recent years, collaborative VR applications for learning (Greenwald, 2017), studies on the impact of VR in exposure treatment (Bouchard, 2016), as well as surveys for human-social interactions (Pan, 2018) have all shown the potential of VR as a training tool. Additionally, methodologies for designing learning experiences in VR have evolved. For example, one study examined the impact of a VR Head-Mounted Display (HMD) on high school students' science self-efficacy (Huang, 2022). Hamilton (2021) also discussed VR as a pedagogical tool and proposed maintaining an explicit curriculum in VR space. While still in the early phases, these approaches define the steps required to utilize VR as a pedagogical tool while illustrating the steps needed for completing action-based scenarios within a VR environment.

For the rapid creation of training in VR environments, authoring tools accelerate content creation and provide the platform and assets required by the educational curriculum. For this project, we used MAGES SDK (Zikas, 2022). This platform enables rapid prototyping of any VR simulation in a fraction of the time and cost it typically takes to create VR scenarios. Additionally, we extended MAGES's main capabilities to support the cognitive requirements for this project's needs.

Designing for Learning at WGU

At WGU, students learn at their own pace. All course content is organized, so students navigate different competencies and lectures throughout the learning process. While students are paired with a course instructor, they only receive individualized help from their instructor when needed. Instead, students access the content within the learning management system and navigate freely throughout the course with suggested learning pathways. All WGU courses incorporate the following design principles:

- Learning modules are delivered in short blocks, and the content is practiced at a varied pace rather than one skill at a time.
- Formative questions provide prescriptive feedback and allow learners to return to course materials when needed. The formative questions are varied in type (e.g., multiple-choice, multiple-select, fill-in-the-blank, and drag and drop) and also varied in style (e.g., scenarios, reading checks, and "apply what you know" activities). When students grow accustomed to one type of question, they start to digest content with a particular lens toward that question instead of developing a more well-rounded perspective.
- The content is paired with visual anchors throughout the course. For example, especially in digital environments, the images provide visual cues to the content, which helps improve knowledge retrieval.
- Finally, well-produced videos are integrated into the learning experience.

A recent Gyll and Hayes (2023) study supported these principles. Researchers investigated two different technology methods and their effect on learning outcomes: (1) *traditional* online instruction, whereby students accessed the content through a mix of video lectures supplemented with learning resource materials, and (2) *enhanced* online instruction, whereby students accessed the content through a variety of innovative technology types. They demonstrated that the instructional method in an OCBHE program was an essential factor in the learning process of a student's education; methods that were more innovative, flexible, and based on cognitive science contributed to higher and quicker learning rates than more traditional ones.

The VR Assessment Experience

When training healthcare professionals, both new entrants and those who may be reskilling, an essential measure of competence involves meaningful measures of what students know and can do. For example, for new professionals learning to work with patients and clients to deliver care, information, support, or guidance, the nuances of effective client engagement and psychomotor skills are considered essential entry-level skills. Listening, incorporating, aligning, deciding, and applying knowledge are aspects of these KSAs and can be measured using high-fidelity simulations like those in VR environments.

Hi-fidelity simulations create *presence,* where the assessment is embedded as much as possible in real-time. As a result, the student experiences physical reactions, including heightened attention and awareness. Riva (2019) suggested that presence is more robust when interacting with virtual characters and human avatars than in other mediums. This occurs because the brain creates embodied reproductions of its environment to effectively regulate and control movements, understand concepts and emotions, and make predictions. This is one reason VR simulations continue to receive increased attention from healthcare professionals, accreditors, and state agencies as valid measures of competence.

The Scenario Setting

The goal of the VR assessment was for students to demonstrate competence in the healthcare coordinator's cognitive, psychomotor, and affective domains. The interactions within the assessment occurred in a conference room and private office within various healthcare settings. The Chronic Care Coordinator (CCC) assessment happened over a single client-based scenario. It focused on Emil, a 55-year-old male recently diagnosed with type 2 diabetes complicated by a history of dyslexia and rheumatoid arthritis. The Behavioral Healthcare Coordinator (BHCC) assessment took place over three different scenarios:

1. Scenario A occurred in a long-term care facility.
2. Scenario B occurred in a youth residential treatment center.
3. Scenario C occurred in an outpatient community mental health center.

The scenarios utilized allied health and ancillary professionals, like case managers, therapists, psychologists, psychiatrists, pharmacists, nurses, medical assistants, care coordinators, and administrative staff.

During the assessment experience, students assumed the care coordinator role (i.e., the Chronic Care Coordinator or Behavioral Health Care Coordinator). Students were instructed to behave professionally and respectfully as though their situation was "real." The student was responsible for "suspending disbelief" and acting as if the virtual environment was the actual environment.

Theory Meets Practice

Within the VR assessment, assessing for learning is no longer viewed in the traditional sense. There were no *items* in the conventional sense, no *forms* to build; there were no items in the bank. In scoring the VR assessment, the number of points possible for each scenario varied depending on the number of independent tasks or critical actions within the branch. A critical action represented any "measurement opportunity" within the assessment and was akin to a test *item*. For example, a single branching scenario may contain two or more critical actions within the scenario. A student may be required to respond to a multiple-choice question and spend a minimum amount of time reviewing the Electronic Health Record (EHR) to earn points. Each critical action was then scored against the result of a set of scenarios within the branch.

What does this mean for students? Let's consider one. Meet *Janelle*, a student at WGUs Health Professions College. By building a VR assessment with various simulation types, Janelle has multiple opportunities to process and respond to information in new and novel ways. When she engages with her assessment, Janelle finds:

- *Scenario-based branching logic:* Each scenario contains branching logic seated within several errant pathways. Errant paths lead end-users further from a correct response in a computer simulation (Gyll, 2019). There are two types of errant paths: inconclusive and conclusive:

  1. *Inconclusive* (or dead-end) paths allow users to look for or *fish* options but do not provide an opportunity to perform a given task.
  2. *Conclusive* errant paths enable users to navigate options, complete tasks, and see results; however, those results will be incorrect.

Sometimes an incorrect response triggers an errant path, but only occasionally. For example, Scenario A contained five errant paths, Scenario B had four, and Scenario C included three. Suppose an incorrect response triggered an errant path. In that case, the simulation might have branched Janelle back to the same question depending on how she performed within the errant path, allowing her to *self-correct* and answer the question again. If this was the case, she did not receive the total allowable points for her second attempt at the question.

- Distributing the content within her assessment helps Janelle *actively* construct her understanding of the content. Students who participate in active knowledge retrieval can have 6X improvement in outcomes (Dollar & Steif, 2008). This is more than a correlative effect. Frequently testing retrieval is one of the best ways to assess learning and transfer.
- *Varied item types:* Janelle's item types are varied (e.g., multiple-choice, multiple-select, fill-in-the-blank) and also varied in style (e.g., scenarios and "apply what you know" activities). When students grow accustomed to one type of question, they start to digest content with a particular lens toward that question style instead of developing a more well-rounded perspective of the content. These varied item types were also interspersed throughout Janelle's course experience, providing a more exciting and "sticky" learning experience.
- *Chunking:* The content of Janelle's assessment was arranged as distributed scenarios in short blocks, so each took a slightly different amount of time to complete. Each of the three scenarios was designed to take at most 30 minutes to complete, and she could take a break between each scenario. For example, scenario A consisted of 30 assessment questions and actions, Scenario B consisted of 42 questions and actions, and Scenario C consisted of 17 questions and actions. This helped Janelle plan for a steady pace and provided the right-sized blocks to consume in a testing session.
- *Relevance:* To increase Janelle's interest and engagement, well-produced simulation videos integrating real-world experiences were incorporated into the assessment. Short bursts of relevant content helped to maintain attention and motivation.
- *Visual Anchors:* The cognitive system is not built for remembering text. We remember by tagging what we learn to visual imagery. Especially in digital environments, the images provided visual anchors to improve retrieval. Janelle's assessment content was paired with visuals so her brain could tag and connect content.
- *Variable priority:* The assessment content was designed so Janelle could get through some of it quickly, while other sections took much more time. Also known as "interleaving," variable priority means assessing at a varied pace rather than one skill at a time. Think "abc, abc," NOT "aa, bb, cc."

Method

This project aimed to engage students in authentic assessment experiences to test the efficacy of emerging technologies like VR simulations to supplement WGUs assessment practices as a viable alternative to competency-based education. We postulated that we could further advance student learning beyond traditional performance- and linear-based methods by re-creating presence through immersive, simulated assessments. The VR simulation assessment was made available in a 2D (desktop) and 3D (VR headset) version.

Research Questions

1. Do summative 2D (desktop) and VR (3D) assessment scores differ by version?

2. Did the student's cognitive- and task- workload differ by assessment version?
3. Did simulation sickness scores differ by assessment version?
4. Did system usability contribute to student performance on the 2D and VR summative assessments?
5. Does immersion in the 3D version make it more difficult for students to answer questions in the headset?

Participants

Thirty-six students were invited to participate in the research. Students were enrolled in the Chronic Care Coordination (n = 29) and Behavioral Health Care Coordination (n = 7) skills certificate programs during the 2021 and 2022 academic years at WGU. Twelve CCC students and one BHCC student participated in the research. Unfortunately, the BHCC student was excluded from the data analysis, so results are limited to the 12 students in the CCC program. Research participants were awarded a $50 Amazon gift card for their participation.

Apparatus

Students in the *VR* version used HTC Vive Focus 3 VR headsets with controllers. The Vive Focus 3 is a stand-alone VR headset delivering best-in-class graphics and ergonomic comfort. VR and desktop interfaces were projected in world space as 3D objects and accessed with the computer mouse (desktop) or the VR controllers (headset). Students in the *Desktop* version used a Windows PC with an i5-7260 CPU and a GTX1060 GPU. In the *Desktop* version, students navigated to various points of interest by controlling camera angles, for example, zooming in on the tablet or moving to different characters in the scenario. To accomplish this, we implemented an easy-to-use system with clickable buttons to navigate these various points.

Process

Before the Assessment

Before the summative assessment, students in the CCC program completed *Care for Individuals and Families*. The course content and topics covered five competencies and 11 skills validated in the assessment (see Appendix A). Western Governors University uses skills to develop the competencies on which its educational model is based. This skills-based approach to designing content establishes the "skill" as the common denominator for employers, job seekers, and educational institutions, allowing them to communicate in a common language.

Learning taxonomies describe different types of learning behaviors. Some taxonomies distinguish different 'levels' of learning, whereas others categorize learning. As a result, learning taxonomies demonstrate the growth of the learner's acquisition of knowledge, skills, and abilities (KSAs) across a pathway. At the highest level, *Competency* is an individual's measurable, assessable capability that integrates knowledge, skills, abilities, and dispositions required to successfully perform tasks at a determined level in a defined setting. *Skill* is a lower-level contextualized statement describing an individual's foundational applied capabilities and behaviors for a given job, occupation, or need.

During the Assessment: Chronic Care Coordinator Scenario Description

The CCC scenario offered multiple opportunities for care coordination across disciplines, including the care coordinator (and others - primary care provider, nutritionist/dietitian, endocrinologist, diabetic educator, pharmacist), the patient, and the patient's family. The scenario began with an opportunity for the care coordinator to review patient information in the electronic health record (EHR). Next, it built into a conference meeting with the client while ever-increasingly implementing care coordination-specific assessments and interventions. At this point, the care coordinator interacted with members of the interdisciplinary team, and ultimately the care coordinator documented her impressions and care plans.

Specifically, the scenario describes Emil, a 55-year-old Hispanic male with several chronic conditions, including rheumatoid arthritis (RA), dyslexia, and type 2 diabetes. Emil lives alone at home and is employed as a rural mail carrier. He describes work as stressful because he was recently reprimanded for delivering mail to the wrong addresses. He also reports worsening pain and dexterity in his hands due to the RA.

Emil recently visited his primary care provider (PCP) and received a new diagnosis of type 2 diabetes with an HbA1C of 12. The PCP prescribed insulin glargine (ten units daily) and metformin 500 mg (twice daily). In addition, he was asked to keep a daily glucose log and a diary of day-to-day activities and meals. The PCP noted pronounced tension between Emil and his sister, Patricia, regarding how best to manage Emil's medical care. At this point, Patricia is trying to pull back from managing his day-to-day care and is primarily focused on managing his finances. As a result, the PCP referred Emil to the chronic care coordinator.

Emil has had one previous visit with the care coordinator, where he brought his daily glucose, activity, and meal logs to the visit. Unfortunately, he was logging information in the wrong columns and was not tracking the data daily. This issue was addressed at the previous meeting, and the care coordinator arranged for Emil to complete an *electronic* daily activity and glucose log. This has proven successful, and the care team has noticed improved frequency and accuracy of the records.

However, new concerns need to be addressed by the care coordinator and team. For example, Emil is not using his insulin pens appropriately due to dexterity issues; he cannot depress the button when administering the insulin. Additionally, he needs to understand the nutritional guidelines (e.g., he feels that all sugar is bad and should be avoided), and the medical team feels he is at risk for hypoglycemia. Finally, Emil is only willing to administer one injection daily despite having higher insulin requirements because he "does not like the pokes," will not take both long-acting and short-acting insulin, and will not agree to multiple injections for using a glucose correction scale. Therefore, the care coordinator will need to work with the other professionals on the team to establish a plan that provides Emil with prefilled single-dose insulin syringes due to safety-related dexterity and dyslexia concerns.

After the Assessment

Assessments were computer-scored, and students received their results immediately. Students were categorized into one of two groups:

- Competent (pass)
- Approaching competence (fail)

To set the passing score for the assessment, we used a two-stage process developed by WGU psychometricians. It is the same process used for all objective assessments at WGU. Unfortunately, passing standards at WGU are not shared or made public for test security reasons. For a thorough description, please refer to the chapter "Design, Measurement, and Technology Considerations in Virtual-Reality Assessment."

Additionally, students received a coaching report showing their scores for each competency. The coaching report was also made available to their student mentor. We recognized early on that the VR assessment was new, innovative, and prone to planning failures. Likewise, we knew that students were also new to VR and inclined to execution errors. We were all on a steep learning curve, and we prepared for this. Therefore, if a student did not pass after their first attempt, they could retake the assessment (either in VR or on the desktop version) or debrief with a student mentor. Debriefing helped them to "think through" the assessment experience and remediate each skill. It was at the student mentor's discretion whether to award additional points for a particular competency based on the debriefing protocol. The debriefing questions were modeled after the PEARLS Debriefing Framework (Eppich & Cheng, 2015) and included the following questions:

- Provide a summary of the case.
- How are you feeling after completing the simulation?
- What aspects of the simulation do you think went well?
- What are some key takeaways you have from this simulation?
- What would you do differently next time if you were to do the simulation again?

After the debrief, the student's assessment was rescored, and a final pass/fail decision was made.

Variables

Subjective Measures

- *Cognitive workload* was modeled after the NASA Task Load Index (2005): The NASA task load index (TLX) measures subjective mental and physical workload. The TLX rates performance across six dimensions to determine an overall workload rating. We modified the TLX to a 4-point ordinal scale (0 = No effort, 1 = A little effort, 2 = Some effort, and 3 = A lot of effort). Total scores ranged from 0 to 18, with higher scores indicating higher workload levels. The six dimensions were:
  - Mental demand - the amount of thinking, deciding or calculating required to perform the task.
  - Physical demand - the amount and intensity of physical activity required to complete the task.
  - Temporal demand - the amount of time pressure involved in completing the task.
  - Annoyance/frustration - how annoyed/frustrated the participant felt during the task.
  - Stress - how stressed the participant felt during the task.
  - Difficulty - the overall difficulty in completing the task.

- *Simulation sickness* was modeled after the Simulator Sickness Questionnaire (SSQ, 1993): The SSQ measures users' level of simulator sickness in VR research. We used a modified 13-item *SSQ*. Participants rated the severity of each symptom on a 4-point ordinal scale (0 = None, 1 = Slight, 2 = Moderate, and 3 = Severe). Total scores ranged from 0 to 39, with higher scores indicating higher simulation sickness levels. The 13 symptoms were:
  - Fatigue, headache, eyestrain, focus, sweating, nausea, concentration, blurred vision, dizziness (eyes open/closed/vertigo), upset stomach, and burping.
- *System usability* was modeled after the System Usability Scale (SUS, 2006). The SUS is a widely used tool allowing users to evaluate various products and services, including hardware, software, mobile devices, websites, and applications. We used a modified 7-item scale. Participants rated the severity of each symptom on a 3-point ordinal scale (0 = Poor, 1 = Acceptable, 2 = Good). Total scores ranged from 0 to 14, with higher scores indicating higher system usability levels. The seven categories were:
  - Text resolution, image resolution, virtual setting/location, characters/avatars, realistic movement/actions, vocals/speech volume, and pronunciation.
- *Immersion and presence* were measured by asking students to describe their sense of "being" in the office space and working with patients while taking the assessment. Students rated their level of agreement to five questions using a 3-point ordinal scale (0 = Not all, 1 = Somewhat, 2 = A lot). Total scores ranged from 0 - 10, with higher scores indicating higher levels of agreement. The five questions were:
  - The office space feels realistic.
  - The office space seemed like someplace I had visited before.
  - I felt a sense of being in the office space.
  - I thought I was standing in the office space.
  - I felt like I was interacting with an actual patient.

Objective Measures

- *Summative Assessment - VR* (3D) Version
  a. Students were scored on their total assessment score rather than on a pass/fail basis per scenario. The total score was based on a weighted composite of the number of "critical actions" within the assessment. There were 500 total possible points. See Appendix B.
- *Summative Assessment - Desktop* (2D) Version
  a. Scoring in the Desktop version worked the same as in the VR version.

Analysis and Results

Our goal was to test hypotheses related to the effectiveness and utility of VR simulations as a viable alternative to assessment in an OCBHE program. However, the limited number of respondents (n = 12), and thus the small sample size, precluded any statistical inferences from being drawn. Therefore, our results are descriptive and exploratory.

Demographics

There were ten female and two male respondents across five ethnicities (see Appendix C). The majority (50%) were between 35 - 44 years old, and many (42%) held at least a 4-year college degree. All respondents worked in *Health Care and Social Assistance*, and their years of employment varied between 3 - 20. Most (83%) had *No* prior experience with virtual reality simulations or equipment.

Study Variables

The grand mean (M) and standard deviation (SD) values for each study variable are in Table 1. On average, students in the *Desktop* version scored five percentage points higher on the summative assessment (M = 43% correct) than those in the *VR* version (M = 38% correct). In addition, students in the *Desktop* version reported lower *Task Load* and *Simulation Sickness* scores than those in the *VR* version. However, differences in *System Usability* and *Immersion* scores were not notably different between the two versions. It can be reasoned that students in the *Desktop* version not only outperformed students in the *VR* version on the summative assessment but also felt equally *immersed* in the simulation while experiencing similar *quality*.

Table 1. Comparison of Study Variables for VR versus Desktop Versions

Assessment Version	% Correct Score	Task Load	Simulation Sickness	System Usability	Immersion
VR	M = 38%, SD = 10%	M = 11.8, SD = 4.26	M = 6.2, SD = 5.07	M = 8.8, SD = 4.44	M = 4.8, SD = 5.02
Desktop	M = 43%, SD = 8%	M = 7.42, SD = 5.0	M = 3.7, SD = 2.69	M = 7.57, SD = 5.47	M = 5.14, SD = 3.93

DISCUSSION

The focus on ensuring that degrees correlate with careers is a promising development in online competency-based higher education. Nearly every academic discipline and job require some skills transference from college to career. As we work toward the development of alternatives to *practice hours* and challenge and reform outdated norms about *hours being the measure of competency* in higher education, new and innovative methods like VR simulations are demonstrating their effectiveness and utility as a valid measure of competency. In addition, learning theory suggests that programs that practice a blend of assessment approaches may improve training transfer when integrated into the learning experience compared to those learned in the traditional format (Gyll et al., 2023). While it would be too strong to say that science is uniting a new learning theory, there is convergence in the essential attributes of a successful model when technology and instructional methods meet.

Today's economy values broad knowledge and skills, flexibility, cross-training, multi-tasking, teaming, problem-solving, and project-based work. Learning in an environment that optimizes and aligns explicit and implicit curricula is critical to achieving a new paradigm's desired outcome. Janelle does not just need a degree; she needs the ability to apply the knowledge and skills she has built earning that degree. The principles discussed here support learning that is flexible, variable, and integrated, creating learning experiences that bear a close similarity to the contexts in which the learning results will be applied. As a result, students are more engaged in the learning process, more interested in the content, and better prepared to enter the workforce with the generalizable skills employers expect.

Limitations

The apparent quasi-experimental nature of our research is worth noting. Our study included variables that did not use random assignment to create the comparisons from which statistical inferences were gathered. Instead, our comparisons depended on the nonequivalent groups that differed in many ways other than the presence of a treatment whose effects were being compared. Especially in a field setting as complex as higher education, we recognize the inherent threats to valid causal inference that non-random assignment brings to the process. Yet, we must deal with those threats in some meaningful way. After all, designing experimental research in an applied educational setting is seldom done well, as day-to-day operations allow little to *design experiments*. As a result, a convenience sample provided the only means to draw somewhat meaningful conclusions without the afforded capability of manipulating variables in an operational setting.

Additionally, although the sample size was small, it is worth noting that even small samples can be impressive. What makes some research seem important is not their magnitude but rather the studies' methodologies that produced them. Lacking any statistical process control or research design methodology (there were no manipulations of the IV), our findings supported the learning science principles described throughout this chapter.

Stated somewhat differently, researchers adopt a tremendous variety of experimental approaches, including computer simulations, longitudinal studies, psychometric assessments, content analyses, meta-analyses, citation assessments, and biographical data. The research units can be as small as single discoveries and as large as whole generations. The sample sizes can vary from single-case studies to inquiries with thousands of records. Since our research did not employ a strong causal design, I suspect that a future study could be designed to maximize its power and statistical strength with sufficient ingenuity. As Einstein and Infeld (1938) once concurred, in a different context:

"The formulation of a problem is often more essential than its solution, which may be merely a matter of mathematical or experimental skill. To raise new questions, new problems, to regard old problems from a new angle, requires creative imagination and marks real advances in science" (p. 95).

Nevertheless, students in the *Desktop* version outperformed those in the *VR* version on the summative assessment. They also reported lower *Task Load* and *Simulation Sickness* scores than those in the *VR* version while feeling equally *immersed* in the simulation. While we can only speculate, there are perhaps many factors that contributed to lower summative assessment scores in the *VR* version, not just the *VR* experience. Such as donning the headset (compounded BY), working in 3D, (compounded BY) test anxiety, (compounded BY) prior experience with VR, etc.

During debriefing interviews, students told us they felt wholly immersed and enjoyed the novel, innovative experience. The VR assessment helped them feel like they were taking on the role of a care coordinator. However, using the VR headset seemed to elevate anxiety for some students already anxious about taking a high-stakes assessment. Getting them comfortable and confident is essential long before the assessment starts. For those unable to overcome their anxiety, offering an alternative like the desktop version was necessary.

Next Steps

There is little doubt that OCBHE is here to stay; students benefit from more inclusive, collective, and interactive experiences than traditional learning methods. Which begs the question, what's next? As discussed, much of the focus of conventional learning methods has been on traditional practices, which are necessary, but insufficient for learning transfer. As a result, OCBHE must position itself to advance student achievement through – among other things – identifying and assessing high-performing students and their workforce readiness through a variety of mechanisms. Rationalization within the market will occur among institutions as they learn the effectiveness of OCBHE programs and their ability to graduate high-performing students.

VR Training Platforms

In VR training platforms, a new competency-based approach to learning is beginning to emerge using a blend of artificial intelligence and live human interaction. Musion provides an immersive VR training platform for mastering essential skills such as interpersonal communication, leadership, and emotional intelligence. Using trained professionals who orchestrate the interactions between learners and avatar-based characters, Musion simulations achieve the realism needed to deliver measurable, high-impact results.[1]

Learning and Individual Differences

Our human actions (i.e., individual differences) can limit the precision of a training program's effectiveness, despite our best intentions. Research on individual differences can reinforce and complement inquiry into students' unique learning characteristics. Individual differences are the enduring psychological characteristics that distinguish one person from another (Ackerman, Kyllonen, & Roberts, 1999). Some have argued that student achievement is the byproduct of multiple distinguishable causes. Therefore, it refers to effective instructional practices as an entity or personal attribute that holds steady over time and space. However, as Harris and Sass (2008) point out, the "differences between the age, academic level, and needs of students mean that teaching requires different skills and knowledge in a different context. These multiple contexts underscore that effective teaching is not fixed but reflects the particular organizational environment and student needs" (p. 22). Attempts to differentiate students in a nuanced fashion based solely on the broad learning approaches discussed in this chapter are surely misguided, as students enter their degree program with varying degrees of KSAs and differing learning styles.

Among the dominant trends in the educational literature is characterizing those differences in students' knowledge, experiences, and strategic capabilities. By uncovering those characteristics, educators are more likely to orchestrate learning experiences that serve each student's needs. For example, recent research has demonstrated that students' confidence, experience, and knowledge notably affect study behavior and performance outcomes (Gyll & Hayes, 2021) in an OCBHE program. Specifically, students with a higher understanding of the course content (measured a-priori) performed well despite less studying. In addition, students with higher confidence also performed well. Still, students with high experience with the course struggled more with the course material and demonstrated performance decrements on the summative assessment. In other words, individual differences in learning style can indicate the amount of effort required to succeed in an OCBHE course, but more research is needed.

Aptitude-Based Learner Guidance

Aptitude measures - tests assessing the human potential to be successful in specific areas or occupations - can serve as a helpful complement to traditional interest-only measures by connecting students' interests to their abilities and matching them to career possibilities that may have previously gone overlooked as viable choices. Different occupations require different KSAs, and individuals who show strengths in those KSAs are more likely to succeed and persist in a particular field (Krane & Tirre, 2012). Without educators assisting students in understanding what they have the potential to accomplish, many learners, especially the underserved, could be guided away from high-demand, high-wage careers for which they have a high ability. Knowing one's strengths (such as aptitudes) can be a great starting point.

Research studies have questioned whether conventional endorsements of students' interests predict anything useful regarding educational outcomes at all. For example, student *interest* in STEM careers is more strongly predictive of pursuing a STEM degree than academic achievement or ability (Rothstein, 2015). Additionally, we know that the percentage of college students majoring in engineering has grown markedly from 1% in 1970 to 17% today. This figure indicates fewer than two out of every ten engineering majors (Carnevale, Smith, & Gulish, 2018) and those graduating with Bachelor's degrees are female (Burrelli & Woodin, 2008; Yoder, 2014). Unfortunately, higher-education authorities are rarely trained in research-based strategies and typically remain unaware of the aptitude-based learner guidance literature. So, in lieu of meaningful predictors, career guidance counselors who use interest-only measures are left to their own devices to determine which career choices are most likely to be a good fit for students. In other words, a more holistic and accurate career potential assessment is possible when considering both factors.

Individual Learning Style

Finally, it is undoubtedly critical to appreciate that one's learning style is not uniform or unidimensional from an instructional standpoint. Instead, as educators have frequently attested, individuals can - and do - differ, even for the same instructor, same content, or within the same school (Alexander & Murphy, 1999). Given the distinctive nature of individual learning styles, OCBHE institutions should adopt a robust notion of student attributes and holistic and comprehensive views of every student using prescribed methods. In addition to scientifically validated academic planning tools, supplementary techniques and components such as readiness for self-directed learning, confidence and level of experience with course content, interactions with faculty, behavioral archetypes, and the like should be utilized to as great an extent as the faculty deems necessary and practical. Stated somewhat differently, science should not over-emphasize asynchronous learning as a tool but also include individual difference factors when designing better learning systems. Augmented, extended, simulated, virtual, etc., whatever we call it, is a starting point, not a definitive answer.

CONCLUSION

Looking ahead, several issues hinder the market's functioning as it relates to an agreed-upon set of approaches. These include a lack of research in - the topics mentioned above - for adult learners (especially those transitioning into new careers), agreed-upon definitions of what it means to be "competent," inadequate transparency and portability of employer-backed credentials, and a lack of policy support. Although there are many promising examples and much momentum around competency-based learning, the current marketplace is far from flourishing, and more research is required. Whether creating a data-driven, systematic value chain will be left primarily to competency-based institutions or alternative providers remains to be seen.

REFERENCES

Ackerman, P. L., Kyllonen, P. C., & Roberts, R. D. (1999). *Learning and individual differences: Process, trait, and content determinants*. American Psychological Association. doi:10.1037/10315-000

Alexander, P. A., & Murphy, P. K. (1999). Learner profiles: Valuing individual differences within classroom communities. In *Learning and individual differences: Process, trait, and content determinants*. American Psychological Association. doi:10.1037/10315-018

Anderson, J. R. (1993). *Rules of the Mind*. Lawrence Erlbaum Associates.

Bouchard, S., Dumoulin, S., Robillard, G., Guitard, T., Klinger, E., Forget, H., Loranger, C., & Roucaut, F. X. (2016). Virtual reality compared with in vivo exposure in the treatment of social anxiety disorder: A three-arm randomised controlled trial. *The British Journal of Psychiatry*, *12*, 210. PMID:27979818

Brooke, J. (1996). SUS: A quick and dirty usability scale. In P. W. Jordan, B. Thomas, B. A. Weerdmeester, & A. L. McClelland (Eds.), *Usability Evaluation in Industry*. Taylor and Francis.

Brown, P. C., Roediger, H. L. III, & McDaniel, M. A. (2014). *Make it Stick: The Science of Successful Learning*. The Belknap Press of Harvard University Press.

Brown, T. L., & Carr, T. H. (1989). Automaticity in skill acquisition: Mechanisms for reducing interference in concurrent performance. *Journal of Experimental Psychology. Human Perception and Performance*, *15*(4), 686–700. doi:10.1037/0096-1523.15.4.686

Burrelli, J. S., & Woodin, T. S. (2008). *Higher education in science and engineering. In the National Science Board, Science and engineering indicators*. National Science Foundation.

Carnevale, A. P., Smith, N., & Gulish, A. (2018). Women can't win: Despite making educational gains and pursuing high-wage majors, women still earn less than men. Washington, DC: Georgetown University: Center on Education and the Workforce.

Dollár, A., & Steif, P. S. (2008). An interactive, cognitively informed, web-based statistics course. *International Journal of Engineering Education*, *24*, 1229–1241.

Einstein, A., & Infeld, L. (1938). *The Evolution of Physics: The Growth of Ideas from Early Concepts to Relativity and Quanta*. Simon & Shuster.

Eppich, W., & Cheng, A. (2015). Promoting excellence and reflective learning in simulation (PEARLS): Development and rationale for a blended approach to health care simulation debriefing. *Simulation in Healthcare*, *10*(2), 106–115. doi:10.1097/SIH.0000000000000072 PMID:25710312

Fitts, P. M. (1964). In A. W. Melton (Ed.), *Perceptual-motor skill learning. Categories of Human Learning* (pp. 243–285). Academic. doi:10.1016/B978-1-4832-3145-7.50016-9

Ford, R., & Gopher, R. (2015). Competency-based education 101. *Procedia Manufacturing*, *3*, 1473–1480. doi:10.1016/j.promfg.2015.07.325

Gervais, J. (2016). The operational definition of competency-based education. *The Journal of Competency-Based Education*, *1*(2), 98–106. doi:10.1002/cbe2.1011

Greenwald, S., Kulik, A., Kunert, A., Beck, S., Froehlich, B., Cobb, S., Parsons, S., Newbutt, N., Gouveia, C., Cook, C., Snyder, A., Payne, S., Holland, J., Buessing, S., Fields, G., Corning, W., Lee, V., Xia, L., & Maes, P. (2017). *Technology and applications for collaborative learning in virtual reality*. In *CSCL Conference*. CSCL.

Gyll, S., & Ragland, S. (2018). Improving the validity of assessment in higher education: Steps for building a best-In-Class competency-based assessment program. *The Journal of Competency-Based Education*, *3*(1), 1. doi:10.1002/cbe2.1058

Gyll, S. P. (2019). Developing errant paths in a simulation testing environment: A how-to guide for assessment professionals. *The Journal of Competency-Based Education*. . doi:10.1002/cbe2.1198

Gyll, S. P., & Hayes, H. (2021). Learning and individual differences in skilled competency-based performance: Using a course planning and learning tool as an indicator for student success. *The Journal of Competency-Based Education*. . doi:10.1002/cbe2.1259

Gyll, S. P., & Hayes, H. (2023). (in press). Training for better transfer in an online competency-based higher education program: Using enhanced technology-based instruction to improve assessment outcomes and student learning. *Journal of Applied Testing Technology*.

Hamilton, D., McKechnie, J., Edgerton, E., & Wilson, C. (2021). Immersive virtual reality as a pedagogical tool in education: A systematic literature review of quantitative learning outcomes and experimental design. *Journal of Computer Education*, *8*(1), 1–32. doi:10.100740692-020-00169-2

Harris, D. N., & Sass, T. R. (2008). *Teacher training, teacher quality, and student achievement*. Calder Center. https://caldercenter.org/sites/default/files/1001059_Teacher_Training.pdf

Holding, D. H. (1991). Transfer of training. In J. E. Morrison (Ed.), *Training for Performance: Principles of Applied Human Learning* (pp. 93–126). Wiley.

Hoogveld, A. M. (2003). The teacher as designer of competency-based education. Heerlen: Open University of the Netherlands.

Huang, W. (2022). Examining the impact of head-mounted display virtual reality on the science self-efficacy of high schoolers. *Interactive Learning Environments*, *31*(1), 100–112. doi:10.1080/1049482 0.2019.1641525

James, R. (2003). Academic standards and the assessment of student learning. *Tertiary Education and Management, 9*(3), 187–198. doi:10.1080/13583883.2003.9967103

Johnston H. (2011). *Proficiency-based education.* Education Partnership. www.educationpartnerships.org

Johnston, W. A., Strayer, D. L., & Vecera, S. P. (1998). Broad-mindedness and perceptual flexibility: Lessons from dynamic ecosystems. In J. S. Jordan (Ed.), *Systems Theories and A Priori Aspects of Perception* (pp. 87–103). Elsevier Science B. V. doi:10.1016/S0166-4115(98)80019-8

Kennedy, R. S., Lane, N. E., Berbaum, K. S., & Lilienthal, M. G. (1993). Simulator sickness questionnaire: An enhanced method for quantifying simulator sickness. *The International Journal of Aviation Psychology, 3*(3), 3. doi:10.120715327108ijap0303_3

Kramer, A. F., Larish, J. F., & Strayer, D. L. (1995). Training for attentional control in dual-task settings: A comparison of young and old adults. *Journal of Experimental Psychology. Applied, 1*(1), 50–76. doi:10.1037/1076-898X.1.1.50

Krane, N. E. R., & Tirre, W. C. (2012). Ability assessment in career counseling. In S. D. Brown & R. W. Lent (Eds.), *Career development and counseling: Putting theory and research to work* (pp. 330–352). Wiley.

McClarty, K. L., & Gaertner, M. N. (2015). *Measuring Mastery: Best Practices for Assessment in Competency-Based Education.* AE Series on Competency-Based Higher Education.

Merrill, D. (2002). A pebble-in-the-pond model for instructional design. *Performance Improvement, 41*(7), 41–46. doi:10.1002/pfi.4140410709

NASA Task Load Index (2005). *Agency for Healthcare Research and Quality.* Digital Healthcare Research (ahrq.gov).

Pan, X., & Hamilton, A. (2018). Why and how to use virtual reality to study human social interaction: The challenges of exploring a new research landscape. *British Journal of Psychology, 109*(3), 3. doi:10.1111/bjop.12290 PMID:29504117

Penuel, B., & Cohen, A. (1999). *Designing Learning: Cognitive Science Principles for the Innovative Organization* (Tech. No. 10099). Research Gate. . doi:10.13140/RG.2.2.11692.97920

Prentice, D. A., & Miller, D. T. (1992). When small effects are impressive. *Psychological Bulletin, 12*(1), 160–164. doi:10.1037/0033-2909.112.1.160

Riva, G., Brenda, K., Mantovani, W., & Mantovani, F. (2019). Neuroscience of virtual reality: From virtual exposure to embodied medicine. *Cyberpsychology, Behavior, and Social Networking, 22*(1), 82–96. doi:10.1089/cyber.2017.29099.gri PMID:30183347

Rothstein, S. M. (2015). Scaling the number of STEM professionals. In S. T. E. Mconnector (Ed.), *Advancing a jobs-driven economy: Higher education and business partnerships lead the way.* Morgan James Publishing.

Spiro, R. J., Feltovich, P. J., Jacobson, M. J., & Coulson, R. L. (1991). Cognitive flexibility, constructivism, and hypertext: Random access instruction for advanced knowledge acquisition in ill-structured domains. *Educational Technology*, (May), 24–33.

Van Merrienboer, J. G., & Kirschner, P. (2013). *Ten Steps to Complex Learning*. Routledge.

Woodrow, H. (1927). The effect of type of training upon transference. *Journal of Educational Psychology*, *18*(3), 159–172. doi:10.1037/h0071868

Yoder, B. (2014). Engineering by the numbers. *American Society for Engineering Education*. https://www.asee.org/papers-and-publications/publications/collegeprofiles/14EngineeringbytheNumbersPart1.pdf

Zikas, P., Protopsaltis, A., Lydatakis, N., Kentros, M., Geronikolakis, S., Kateros, S., Kamarianakis, M., Evangelou, G., Filippidis, A., Grigoriou, E., Angelis, D., Tamiolakis, M., Dodis, M., Kokiadis, G., Petropoulos, J., Pateraki, M., & Papagiannakis, G. (2022). MAGES 4.0: Accelerating the world's transition to VR training and democratizing the authoring of the medical metaverse. *ORamaVR: Internal Technical Report*.

ENDNOTE

[1]   www.musion.com

APPENDIX A: CARE FOR INDIVIDUAL AND FAMILIES' COMPETENCIES AND SKILLS

Table 2. Care for individuals and families competencies and skills

Competency Identifier	Competency	Skill	Course Unit
7070.6.1 (Scenario A) (Scenario B)	**Competency 1: Models of Care Delivery:** The learner applies care delivery models to navigate individuals and families through a care plan in various healthcare settings.	**995 Care Delivery Models:** The learner collaborates with the interdisciplinary team to determine an appropriate care model.	Unit 1
		420 Care Planning: The learner applies comprehensive patient, and family-centered care plans to improve access and health care outcomes.	
		4034.1 Care Planning: The learner determines if additional resources or potential partners are needed to meet a patient's health needs.	
7070.6.2 (Scenario A) (Scenario C)	**Competency 2: Helping Individuals and Families Meet Healthcare Goals:** The learner implements care plans to support individuals and families in meeting their healthcare goals.	**376 Care Planning:** The learner applies a comprehensive patient and family-centered care plan.	Unit 2
		2213 Care Planning: The learner determines barriers to care and non-compliance.	
		3852 Care Planning: The learner identifies resources and strategic partners to meet a patient's health care needs.	
7070.6.3 (Scenario B)	**Competency 3: Prevention Practices:** The learner selects prevention practices to educate the individual and family and support their health care goals.	**2313 Risk Analysis:** The learner determines which prevention practices are most appropriate to implement based on patient risk assessment.	Unit 3
		2817 Health Education: The learner educates patients on their condition and treatment plans.	
7070.6.4 (Scenario A) (Scenario B) (Scenario C)	**Competency 4: Intervention Strategies:** The learner applies intervention strategies to meet the health care needs of the individual and family.	**564 Health Intervention:** The learner applies the appropriate intervention(s) for a patient, given the population the patient belongs to.	Unit 4
		3661 Health Intervention: The learner identifies appropriate interventions that promote client-centered care.	
7070.6.5 (Scenario A) (Scenario B) (Scenario C)	**Competency 5: Shared Decision-Making:** The learner executes shared decision-making strategies to support individuals and families in meeting their healthcare goals.	**5345 Decision Making:** The learner creates models to engage and motivate clients and families toward shared decision-making.	Unit 5

APPENDIX B: SCORING RUBRIC FOR CHRONIC CARE COORDINATION - EMIL

Figure 1. Scoring rubric for chronic care coordination - Emil

Competency	Skill	Unique Critical Actions	Calculated Weighted Percentage (from Blueprint)	Suggested Points Allotment for Skill · Based on Weighted Percentage (out of 500)	Suggested Points Allotment for Each Unique Critical Action Opportunity
Competency 1: Models of Care Delivery: The learner applies care delivery models to navigate individuals and families through a care plan in a variety of healthcare settings. *Note: This is talking about ACOs, Medical Homes. Care delivery models. Staff models. [HMO], ACO, PCMH- Patient Centered Medical Home. (primary Plus supported at least role providing care), Open systems [EPO]. Direct care to level care)*	**995 Care Delivery Models:** The learner collaborates with the interdisciplinary team to determine an appropriate care model.	4	0.0939	47	12
	420 Care Planning: The learner applies comprehensive patient and family-centered care plans to improve access and healthcare outcomes.	3	0.1379	69	23
	4034.1 Care Planning: The learner determines if additional resources or potential partners are needed to meet a patient's health needs.	4	0.0575	29	7
Competency 2: Helping Individuals and Families Meet Healthcare Goals: The learner implements care plans to support individuals and families in meeting their healthcare goals.	**576 Care Planning:** The learner applies a comprehensive patient and family-centered care plan.	5	0.1226	61	12
	2213 Care Planning: The learner determines barriers to care and non-compliance.	5	0.0926	46	9
	3852 Care Planning: The learner identifies resources and strategic partners to meet a patient's healthcare needs.	3	0.0805	40	13
Competency 3: Prevention Practices: The learner selects prevention practices to educate the individual and family and support their health care goals.	**2313 Risk Analysis:** The learner determines which prevention practices are most appropriate to implement based on patient risk assessment.	3	0.1207	60	20
	2817 Health Education: The learner educates patients on their condition and treatment plans.	2	0.0766	38	19
Competency 4: Intervention Strategies: The learner applies intervention strategies to meet the healthcare needs of the individual and family.	**564 Health Intervention:** The learner applies the appropriate intervention(s) for a patient given the populations the patient belong to.	3	0.0575	29	10
	3661 Health Intervention: The learner identifies appropriate interventions that promote client-centered care.	6	0.067	34	6
Competency 5: Shared Decision-Making: The learner executes shared decision-making strategies to support individuals and families in meeting their healthcare goals.	**5345 Decision Making:** The learner creates models to engage and motivate clients and families toward shared decision making.	3	0.0939	47	16
	Totals	41	1.00	500	147

APPENDIX C: DEMOGRAPHICS

Table 3. Demographics

Gender	N	%
Female	10	83.3%
Male	2	16.7%

Age	N	%
35 to 44	6	50.0%
45 to 54	2	16.7%

Ethnicity	N	%
African American/Non-Latino	4	33.3%
Asian	3	25.0%
Caucasian/Non-Latino	2	16.7%
Latino	2	16.7%
Western European	1	8.3%

Education	N	%
2-year college degree	3	25.0%
4-year college degree	5	41.7%
High school	1	8.3%
Post-graduate degree	2	16.7%
Trade/Tech/Vocational School	1	8.3%

Years	N	%
11 - 15 years	2	16.7%
16 - 20 years	3	25.0%
3 - 5 years	2	16.7%
6 - 10 years	3	25.0%
More than 20 years	2	16.7%

Chapter 15
The Use of Virtual Reality in Education for Sustainable Development

Raziye Sancar
https://orcid.org/0000-0002-2875-9233
Kırşehir Ahi Evran University, Turkey

Deniz Atal
https://orcid.org/0000-0001-8030-9996
Ankara University, Turkey

Hüseyin Ateş
Kırşehir Ahi Evran University, Turkey

ABSTRACT

Environmental sustainability is one of the major global topics of the 21st century. In order to effectively include the concept of sustainability in the topic of environmental education, educators are responsible for incorporating the concept into the existing curriculum. However, it may not always be possible to conduct field studies based on environmental education due to economic, transport, and time constraints, while certain situations and conditions may be particularly difficult to replicate. One recent solution to this problem is the application of Virtual Reality technology, which has been shown in various recent studies. VR is a computer-generated three-dimensional environment that allows the user to perceive content more realistically. In the process of teaching sustainability issues such as climate change, waste management, food consumption, air and water pollution, and deforestation, the present study has revealed that cooperation between different fields of expertise, including science education and computer and instructional technologies, plays an important role.

DOI: 10.4018/978-1-6684-7644-4.ch015

INTRODUCTION

Environmental sustainability is one of the most important global topics of the 21st century (Ahmad et al., 2021; Feroz et al., 2021; Kirikkaleli, & Adebayo, 2021). The increase in industrial production, resource use, and private consumption, particularly after the industrial revolution, is exacerbating the harm done to the environment (Thøgersen, 2009). It is clear that the harmful effects of environmental problems such as global warming, water scarcity, air pollution, soil erosion, depletion of natural resources, deforestation, and loss of biological diversity, are all greatly threatening sustainability (Abd-Elaty et al., 2022; Azadi et al., 2019; Lange & Dewitte, 2019; Ricart et al., 2021). Climate change, which can be defined as "a change in the state of the climate that can be identified by changes in the mean and/or the variability of its properties, and that persists for an extended period, typically decades or longer" (Intergovernmental Panel on Climate Change, Fifth Assessment Report (IPCC, 2021), is perhaps the most significant environmental challenge currently facing all human civilization (Sonnett, 2022). Recent studies clearly demonstrate the negative effects of climate change on human life (e.g., Lacroix et al., 2020; Ngo et al., 2020; Zhang, et al., 2020). For example, IPCC (2021) reports show that increasing annual emissions of $CO2$ have led to widespread and rapid changes in the atmosphere, ocean, cryosphere, and biosphere. More specifically, sea levels increased by 0.20m between 1901 and 2018, while the total anthropogenic global surface temperature increased by an estimated 1.07°C between 1850 and 2019 (IPCC, 2021). Furthermore, The United Nations Environment Program [UNEP] (2007) reports indicate that climate changes observed during the last 50 years have occurred due to human behavior that is threatening both life and the planet (Wynes & Nicholas, 2017). Similarly, recent studies also showed that human beings are a factor in the occurrence of environmental problems (Ateş, 2021; Nielsen et al., 2021; Savari et al., 2021).

Although the changes in the climate due to the harmful behavior of individuals threaten the future of the world, an increasing awareness in society over the last few decades about environmental protection can be seen (Dowd & Burke, 2013). This awareness is apparent in areas such as household recycling (Issock et al., 2021), transport (Zhai, & Wolff, 2021), energy consumption (Zeiske et al., 2021), and food consumption (Ateş, 2020). Examination of the effects of human behavior on the environment is occurring in behavioral sciences such as environmental psychology (Edgerton et al., 2021), organizational psychology (Norton et al., 2015), behavior analysis (Lehman & Geller, 2004), and environmental education (Casas et al., 2021). The latter is the specific focus of this study, and has been defined as follows by UNESCO:

"A process aimed at developing a world population that is aware of and concerned about the total environment and its associated problems, and which has the knowledge, attitudes, motivations, commitments, and skills to work individually and collectively toward solutions to current problems and the prevention of new ones." (UNESCO, 1978, p. 1).

Environmental education has been a topic of research in recent years since it provides a rethinking of the relationship between human and nature and helps social transformation towards sustainability (Colom & Sureda, 1981). Moreover, environmental education can have a positive effect on the behavior of individuals (Ardoin et al., 2020), and so is extremely important to the formation of pro-environmental preferences (Varela-Candamio et al., 2018). It can therefore be said that well-developed environmental education plays an important role in the fostering of environmentally sensitive individuals (Jurin & Fortner, 2002). It is hoped that those who have studied environmental education will develop into conscientious citizens who can weigh various aspects of an environmental problem and make responsible decisions, both as individuals and as members of their communities (Fraser & Jamieson, 2003).

There is no doubt that quality and standards-based environmental education plays an important role in promoting the management of natural resources, the work of planners and managers in the achievement of a better future (Ateş, 2020; Fan et al., 2010), and overall guidance of values and behavior (Varela-Candamio et al., 2018). It is frequently emphasized by researchers in the literature that science education is the most significant research aspect of environmental education (Boyes & Stanisstreet, 2012; Wals et al., 2014) as it provides an understanding of the scientific principles that form the basis of sustainable issues (Littledyke, 2008). Science education also plays an important role in improving positive attitudes towards the environment, increasing environmental awareness (Littledyke et al., 2013) and strengthening the moral obligation to act in an environmentally friendly manner (Ateş, 2020). Furthermore, science education can improve the young generation's connections with environmental issues and so develop their curiosity towards science (Cobern, 2000).

THE TEACHING OF SUSTAINABLE ENVIRONMENTAL EDUCATION

In order to effectively include the concept of sustainability in the topic of environmental education (González-Gaudiano, 2006), educators are responsible for incorporating the concept into the existing curriculum (Spearman & Eckhoff, 2012). There is a growing sense of the importance of teaching environmental education and sustainability, namely that doing so envisages an environmentalist approach to education. This means that environmental education and sustainability becomes a learning style, rather than just a subject of study, and helps in the development of new knowledge, skills and values to achieve a better environment and a higher quality of life (Nagra, 2010). The rationale for teaching sustainability is based on the premise that unless children are able to develop a sense of respect for the natural environment early on, they will never have a positive and proactive attitude to the environment in later life (Wilson, 1994). Taking positive action in regard to existing environmental problems is of great value in encouraging a positive sense of their environment (Nagra, 2010). McNaughton (2004) argues that teaching sustainability topics to students helps in three areas: awareness, knowledge and understanding (1), attitudes and personal lifestyle decisions (2) and the creation of action skills for a better environment (3). Efficient, productive, and attractive instructional material are required for these goals to be achieved.

Previous studies have tested various teaching methods for sustainable environmental education such as projects, simulations, experiments, dramas, debates, laboratory experiments, and technology applications (Koutsoukos et al., 2015; Liu et al., 2021; Maciel et al., 2022; Markaki, 2014; Ozkan, 2021). An example given by McNaughton (2004) found that drama can be a useful tool in teaching sustainability topics effectively. The study also found that drama can help develop students' collaborative and communicational skills, and so allow them to feel empathy with individuals who are facing environmental problems. In a study conducted by Trevors (2007), students were involved in active learning by participating in hands-on activities, and the results of the research revealed that this method increased knowledge and awareness of the environment. Fieldwork has also been found to be another effective method of teaching environmental issues (Stokes et al., 2011). However, it may not always be possible to conduct field research due to economic, transport, and time constraints (Fan et al., 2010), while certain situations and conditions may be particularly difficult to replicate. One recent solution to this problem is the application of Virtual Reality (VR) technology, which has been shown in various recent studies

(Fauville et al., 2021; Scurati et al., 2021; Viveiros et al., 2021) to be an effective method for the teaching of sustainable subjects.

BACKGROUND

Definition of VR

A basic definition of VR is a computer-generated three-dimensional (3D) environment that allows the user to perceive content more realistically (Araiza-Alba et al., 2022). Carrozzino and Bergamasco (2010) defined VR as: "a complex technology which exploits more low-level technologies (such as computer science, 3D graphics, robotics, etc.) to create a digital environment in which users feel completely immersed inside, and which they may interact." As understood from these definitions, this computer-generated world should, with head tracking as a minimum requirement, surround the participant and create a feeling of being part of that environment (Slater, 2018).

The VR environment has two main features, namely 'immersion' and 'presence', that differ from other technologies. Immersion can be defined as the presence of physical actions necessary to perceive and interact with a particular environment (Slater, 2009) and is related to what rendering software and display technology are able to deliver from an objective point of view. Immersion is often shaped by the audio, haptic and visual technologies of the VR systems, and can therefore be seen as the objective level of sensory fidelity (Slater, 2018). Presence, on the other hand, can be defined as an individual and context-dependent user response that is related to the experience of 'being there' (Slater & Wilbur, 1997). Unlike the immersive experience, 'presence' describes possible subjective responses. In other words, an immersive VR system can create different levels of presence for each participant (Diemer et al., 2015; Slater, 2009).

The two terms of 'immersion' and 'presence' are often confused in the literature and are even sometimes used interchangeably as if they have the same meaning. However, Slater's (2009) 'color' analogy helps to clarify the difference. Slater points out that colors are formed by the wavelength of light and therefore can, on one level, be assessed objectively. However, colors that are on different wavelengths can be perceived subjectively. Following this analogy, the phrase 'wavelength distribution' describes 'immersion', while 'color perception' relates to 'presence'. It can therefore be seen that while immersion can be regulated and determined objectively with VR technologies and devices, the sense of presence is shaped by the subjective evaluation of individuals within an environment. Thus, it can be seen that wearing a VR headset (head-mounted display, HMD), looking around, and perhaps even moving the body, is more immersive than just simply staring at a computer screen. On the other hand, participants wearing the same HMD may not perceive and react in the same manner in that VR environment due to differences in perception.

According to Markowitz et al. (2018) the higher the level of immersive presence, the less the sense of it being a mediated experience. However, constantly creating such a high level of immersive presence can be difficult, expensive, and time-consuming, and so various types of VR can be seen in the literature which use a variety of technologies and processes to create different levels of immersion and presence. In an attempt to organize this wide range, the work of Araiza-Alba et al. (2022) expanded the classification of Biocca and Delaney (1995, 59) to divide the VR system into six groups: Windows systems/computer-based VR; mirror systems; vehicle-based systems; cave automatic virtual environments

(CAVE systems); immersive VR including 360 VR videos and fully immersive VR; and augmented reality systems (Araiza-Alba et al., 2022).

According to the classification created by Araiza-Alba et al. (2022), the experiences offered by different VR environments range from passive (i.e., just being able to look around) to a more interactive experience in which the user can navigate freely and fully interact with the VR environment. Each type of VR has differences in the levels of immersion, control, realism, and interactivity, depending on the system and equipment used. Participants can explore, experience, interact and even act while interacting with simulated scenarios at different levels depending on the genre used. For instance, 360-degree, or immersive, VR combines 360-degree videos and VR headsets to create a realistic and responsive environment with less interaction (Kim et al., 2022; Schöne et al., 2021; Snelson & Hsu, 2020). On the other hand, computer-generated 3D VR environments are various fully immersive VR scenarios in which movement, interaction and manipulation are possible through the use of game engines such as Unity or Unreal (Jamei et al., 2017; Velev & Zlateva, 2017). While the levels of interaction and immersion of these technologies vary, creating 360 video VR is faster, cheaper and requires less expertise than creating fully immersive VR.

Such considerations as these need to be borne in mind by researchers and educators when considering the choice and integration of appropriate technologies. The use of VR technology, limited for many years due to high hardware and design costs, is becoming widespread in schools. This has become particularly true with the decrease in technology costs since 2013, the increase in affordable VR-support devices (e.g., Google Cardboard), and the development of web-based VR design environments (Chirico et al., 2021). There are many web-based applications, such as CoSpace Edu and InstaVR, where both teachers and students can design their own VR environment quickly and easily with basic programming knowledge, and then implement the environment with a mobile-based VR headset (Atal et al., 2021). The focus of some researchers has shifted to unlocking the educational potential of this technology (Al-Gindy et al., 2020; Andone & Frydenberg, 2019), and the next section of this work will likewise consider the educational usage and educational value of VR technology.

Educational Uses of VR Technology

The VR environment allows the visualization of three-dimensional virtual objects and abstract concepts. This enables users to experience and interact with different events, as well as making huge saving in time and cost by allowing the instantaneous visiting of places (Chen et al., 2021; Freina & Ott, 2015; Shu et al., 2018). Moreover, dangerous situations can be experienced, and methods for effective management of these situations can be taught safely as many times as required (Araiza-Alba et al., 2022; Makransky et al., 2019). For instance, student teachers can improve their classroom management skills and noticing abilities by practicing in a VR virtual classroom environment (Kosko et al., 2021; Lugrin et al., 2016;). In rehabilitation and health care education, VR can provide practice virtual cases in scenarios such as supporting the disabled, providing basic skills and experience during serious surgery, or in the provision of emotional support (Fang et al., 2014; Jensen & Konradsen, 2018; Parsons & Cobb, 2011). VR can also be used in the training of firefighters by enabling them to virtually experience dangerous fire environments (Cha et al., 2012).

All these experiences can have positive cognitive, effective, and behavioral effects on participants. According to Araiza-Alba et al. (2022), VR can provide meaningful knowledge and support different learning styles in an authentic context since it offers a learning environment that targets different senses.

The creation of a suitable learning environment can make theoretical concepts easier to understand (Hardie et al., 2020). VRs can also change a user's perspective, which can facilitate the cognitive process and encourage inventive thinking (Kim et al., 2022). In addition to cognitive support, some studies focus on the effect of VR technology on areas such as interest, motivation, emotion, and attitude (Filter et al., 2020; Kim et al., 2022; Scurati & Ferrise, 2020). For example, Scurati and Ferrise (2020) suggest utilizing VR for making an emotional connection with the environment and thus instilling a sense of responsibility, while Riva et al. (2007) determine a relationship between presence and emotions. Although it is difficult to observe the behavioral change that occurs through technology, some studies have revealed such changes in individuals with the use of VR. For instance, Hsu et al. (2018) used virtual reality technology to increase behavioral intention towards saving water. The results showed that an immersive VR game caused significant improvements in cognition and enthusiasm. Following the virtual experience, participants' understanding of actual water consumption and their engagement in water conservation was seen to increase.

Sustainable Environmental Education With VR

Changing people's behavior toward the environment is not an easy task as environmental issues are complex and difficult to internalize. According to Schuldt et al. (2016), one reason that many people feel ambivalent or ignorant about an environmental problem, such as climate change, is that they do not actually regularly engage with the problem firsthand. To overcome these limitations, it is suggested that environmental problems are perceived as being more psychological or presented directly to observers as this helps to internalize them. This method encourages users to adopt more pro-environmental behavior (Pearson et al., 2016). In addition, the provision of motivation, information, and awareness, with the help of various technologies, encourage pro-environmental attitudes (Scurati & Ferrise, 2020). There is no doubt that there have been remarkable increases in the use of VR technology in sustainable environmental education issues.

According to some researchers, immersive VR has a similar effect on the brain as real-life experiences. This is felt to be the case because the same brain regions of individuals are activated in both VR and in real-life experiences (Kisker et al., 2021). Providing a more realistic experience within an immersive VR is therefore of great value in encouraging people to participate in environmental issues (Breves & Heber, 2020; Markowitz et al., 2018). Moreover, the design, manipulation, and interaction features offered by VR technology allow various topics in different contexts to be addressed, and so supporting environmental transformation such as changing consumer habits, raising environmental awareness, and promoting behavioral changes. According to Scurati and Ferrise (2020), VR has a huge potential for changing people's behavior and attitude as it enables individuals to be informed through visualizations which can allow them to experience environmental problems. They also suggest that the possible future adverse effects which may occur if behavior is not changed can be effectively demonstrated. Scurati and Ferrise (2020) grouped the potential of the VR experience for sustainable behavior change into five categories: summarizing behavioral outcomes, providing journeys in place and time, creating a figurative and concrete expression, presenting, and considering future resolutions and testing subsequent effects (Scurati & Ferrise, 2020). As for understanding the categories, beyond the informing of people and creating awareness, VR can also be used to compare and evaluate possible solutions, test new designs, and support decision-making processes that consider sustainability criteria. However, there are few studies on the subject since VR technology has only just begun to be used in environmental education.

Furthermore, according to Markowitz et al. (2018), it still remains unclear whether immersive VR can facilitate learning about complex social and environmental issues.

MAIN FOCUS OF THE CHAPTER

A review of research on sustainable environmental education with VR reviewed

The use of virtual reality technology for educational purposes remains a novelty, and so it is no surprise that the use of VR technology is not sufficiently widespread in sustainable environmental education. Consequently, there are few review and research articles of considerable quality in the literature. One located review was conducted by Rambach et al. (2021) and analyzes the publications related to augmented reality (AR), VR, and mixed reality (MR) technologies. The review classified the publications into four main categories: environmental monitoring, ecological awareness, resource efficiency, and environmental education. The category of environment monitoring means that actual environmental processes were recorded or simulated by employing VR, AR, or MR technologies so that they could be observed. Ecological awareness was categorized to gather research focusing on enhancing awareness, perceptions, behaviors, and responses to environmental problems. Resource efficiency is a more technical category than the others because of its focus on mechanical systems to produce renewable energy, while environmental education, or teaching people to better appreciate nature and become more involved in ecological conservation, is directly related to the focus of this chapter.

Figure 1. A framework for the design of VR experiences to support sustainable behaviors
Source: (Scurati et al., 2021)

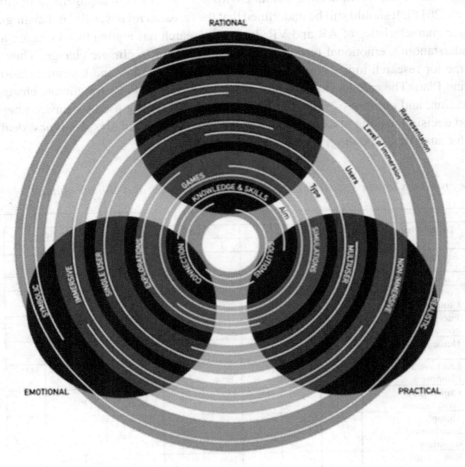

Another literature review which completely focuses on VR technologies was produced by Scurati et al. (2021). This review uses a framework for the direction of the design process of VR experiences in the determination of behavioral changes in sustainable environmental research. In this framework, three spheres are identified in the design of a VR experience for sustainable behavior change (See in Figure 1). These spheres are the emotional sphere, which focuses on emotions related to environmental issues, the rational sphere, which provides information and understanding of sustainability issues and their causes and effects, and the practical sphere, which includes assessment and decision-making for environmental problems. The colored areas in Figure 1 represent the design elements, while the white lines represent categories for each element according to the behavioral spheres. With this model, the aim of the experience (knowledge and skills, solution and connection), the type of the experience (simulations, games, explorations), the number of users (single-user, multi-user), the level of immersion (non-immersive, immersive), and the type of representation (realistic and symbolic), can all be considered in the making of fundamental design decisions (Scurati et al., 2021).

There is increasing interest in VR due to its valuable characteristics such as immersion, and a recent study addresses this issue of immersive virtual environments (IVEs) in engagement in climate change (Queiroz et al., 2018). It should still be underlined that the research reviewed did not distinguish between the immersive characteristics of AR and VR. Instead, research has argued that IVEs are able to affect people's understanding, emotional response, and action related to climate change. They also created another theme for research topics covered by 3 categories: Education and Communication (EdCom), Analytics, and Plan. The category of EdCom relates to the use of IVEs for climate change communication, education, and awareness. 'Plan' concentrates on IVEs being used for environmental or urban planning and decision making at a community or landscape scale. Finally, 'Analytics' deals with IVEs being used for analytics, modeling, and data visualization.

Table 1. The crosstabs for the research conducted related to IVEs and climate change

Topic / Outcomes	EdCom			Plan			Analytics		
	U	E	A	U	E	A	U	E	A
Animals	[19, 20]								
Carbon footprint	[21]						[22]		
Concepts about Climate Change	[23–28]	[29]		[30]					
Energy consumption			[31, 32]				[33, 34]		
Heritage Sites	[35, 36]								
Land use and Urban Planning			[37]	[38–40]	[43]	[38–43]	[44, 45]		[45]
Landscape visualization	[46–48]		[49]	[50–53]		[51, 53]	[47, 54, 55]		
Multiple environmental scenarios	[56, 57]						[58–64]	[60]	
Risk assessment / management		[65]	[65]	[66]			[67–70]		[69, 70]
Sea rise		[71]		[72]		[72]	[73]		

U:Understanding; E: Emotion; A: Action.

Source: (Queiroz et al., 2018)

Table 1 depicts the research conducted on IVEs and climate change in the categories of animals, carbon footprint, energy consumption, and rise in sea levels. Common results of the three-review research clarify the literature topics, subject area and main focus. Results are further provided on personal effects (such as attitude, meaning making, or behavior). The following section summarizes studies on the use and effects of VR technology on sustainable environmental education.

Current Trends in Research on Sustainable Environmental Education With VR

In this section, the studies using VR technologies for sustainable environmental education are classified into three layers (see in Figure 2). The first and the main layer is the subject area, which embodies the content and type of the subjects in the research. The subject area of studies varies from animal life to the effects in a particular region, from climate change to the carbon footprint. The studies demonstrate that using visualized and immersive technologies are valuable in communicating climate change and provide a creative opportunity to professionally handle a global crisis (Sheppard, 2005; Sheppard et al., 2008). It is also made clear that there is a growing interest in environmental ethics. When Liu et al. (2019) implemented VR-based environmental education for three hours a week over 32 weeks, they found that the employment of VR to teach environmental ethics has a noticeable effect. They implied that teachers could integrate VR technologies to broaden students' vision of learning environmental ethics, the contact made with nature, and to better promote the impact of environmental education. The focus of Liu et al. (2019) was to use VR technologies in class teaching practice to help students better explore and experience environmental education.

Figure 2. The classification model for sustainable environmental education with VR

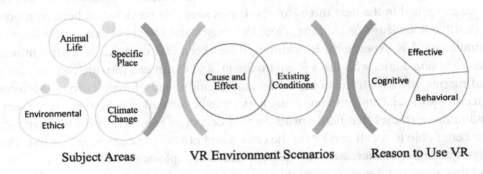

The second layer consists of the design of VR environment scenarios. While reviewing studies on VR in sustainable environmental education, it was discovered that there are two main categories of scenarios: Cause and Effect and Existing Conditions. The first relates to the studies focused on the process effect, an example being scenario design on how people's water consumption habits affect environmental sustainability. The second of these two categories, Existing Conditions, is used to bring together studies that aim to demonstrate all forms of current natural life. For example, a scenario might focus on simulating or demonstrating animal life or ocean wildlife.

The third layer relates to reasons for using VR in sustainable environmental education, and what can be achieved in the studies. These studies are classified into three categories: Cognitive, Effective, and Behavioral. Making a change in people's behavior, providing detailed information on any subject, or raising awareness about the subject are covered by these categories. A study by Chirico et al. (2021) uses immersive VR to show consumption of plastic bottles, both individually and as a community, over different time spans. This study is classified by its subject area, 'Consumption', its type of scenario, 'Cause and Effect', and 'Effective', which relates to the reason for using VR technology. The aim of this study was to influence participants' attention, attitudes, and behavioral intentions toward plastic waste and consumption by testing differentially representative statistical data. In this regard, the study creates three different virtual environments which compare numerical, concrete, and mixed (combining numeric and visual presentation) presentations of plastic consumption. It is assumed that visual presentation of plastic waste leads to deeper cognitive elaboration and a positive attitude toward using, recycling, wasting, and consuming plastic. In the study, participants' emotions, sense of presence, attitudes, and sense of social desirability were all measured. According to the results, while the numerical format was the least effective across all dimensions, the mixed format was seen to be more effective than numerical and concrete representation in terms of being persuasive regards pro-environmental-related attitudes and behavior. This research, which focuses on the effect of design variables, provides more evidence of the power of VRs to encourage environmental behavior.

In research performed by Markowitz et al. (2018), four VR environments were used to facilitate learning or to increase interest in learning about marine science. Of specific focus was perceptions of the consequences of climate change with different participants (high school students, college students, and adults). This study was classified by its subject area in terms of the specific place (the ocean), the type of scenario (existing conditions), and the reason for using VR technology (cognitive and effective). In the study, the current knowledge and learning of students about ocean acidification in immersive VR was initially focused on, while the effects of embodiment, movement, and situated action in a VR environment were examined in the next three studies. It was seen that participants became more interested in gaining positive knowledge or learning about the causes and effects of ocean acidification with the use of an immersive VR experience. In addition, it was seen that complex scientific information can be presented to young adults with the VR environment, and that it can provide concrete insights about oceanic and marine life transformations, ocean acidification, and climate change. Moreover, results showed that complex social and environmental issues can be learned in an immersive VR environment. It was found in these studies that participants formed deeper cognitive relationships with the content, and so were better able to recall and retain the causes and effects of ocean acidification. This increase in knowledge was linked to increased engagement with and exploration of the virtual space. However, it was found that avatars and motion manipulations did not create a difference in the psychological experience of participants.

One other study is classified by its subject area of animal life (wolves), its type of scenario, through the use of existing conditions (with 360-degree videos), and the reason for using VR technology, in both an effective and behavioral manner. VR technologies were used to present the life of wolves to help protect them, as well as the wider ecosystem, while promoting a sustainable environment (Filter et al., 2020). The aim was to provoke emotional responses by enabling the actual sensations of wild animals, such as wolves, to be experienced in the VR environment. It is hoped that this will help reveal the effect of immersive VR on university students' pro-environmental behavior and make learning more effective in the context of sustainable development. The study focused on wolves in their natural habitat and used two different 360-degree YouTube videos. 50 university students were divided into two groups, one watched 360-degree videos with HMD as an immersive VR experience, while the other watched the same videos in a non-immersive format on a computer screen. The participants' attitudes toward wolves, their feeling of presence in the virtual environments, and their retrospective emotions of interest, joy, and fear were measured. The results of the research demonstrated that a high sense of presence (through the use of an immersive head-mounted display), created a subsequently high level of emotional reactions and interest, even with participants who do not normally have a positive attitude towards wolves and the environment. In short, it can be said that 360-degree video-based VR can provide natural experiences that have positive affective learning outcomes.

CONCLUSION

In the process of teaching sustainability issues such as climate change, waste management, food consumption, air and water pollution, and deforestation (Ateş, 2021; Guerrero et al., 2021; Ighalo et al., 2021; Koul et al., 2022; Mujtaba, & Shahzad, 2021; Rani et al., 2022), the present study has revealed that cooperation between different fields of expertise, including science education and computer and instructional technologies, plays an important role. The effects of VR on education for sustainable development was also identified. Earlier studies indicated that teaching environmental issues using VR is effective and crucial to the development of students since it creates an environmental connection, provides knowledge and skills, and tests or offers solutions to environmental problems (Bevan et al., 2019; Liu et al., 2019; Scurati et al., 2021). Some of the studies reviewed employed a framework including rational, emotional and practical dimensions that aided in the categorization of research on sustainable environmental education with VR (e.g., De Medeiros et al., 2018; Tang & Bahmra, 2008; Withanage et al., 2016). Furthermore, some studies developed classification models, including subject area, environment scenarios, and reasons to use VR for sustainable environmental education with VR (e.g., Barbalios et al., 2013; Schott, 2017).

In accordance with the related literature, it is suggested that the classification model for sustainable environmental education with VR includes three layers. The first of these is the subject area, which embodies the content and type of the subjects in the research. The second layer is VR environment scenarios, which consist of Cause and Effect and Existing Conditions. The third layer relates to the reasons for using VR in sustainable environmental education, and what can be achieved in studies divided into Cognitive, Affective, and Behavioral areas. Based on the results of previous research, it can be suggested that this classification makes it easier to determine the availability of material for study, while examination of the scenarios in the studies can reveal the main reason for using VR. It is also suggested that, in addition to work which focuses on experience, activities, and interactions in VR, studies that focus on design dimensions and various technology usage can be conducted. Chirico et al. (2021) emphasize that there are limited studies which focus specifically on design variables that can increase the effectiveness of VR. Therefore, more studies which can focus on message, scenario, and process design in a VR environment is likely to support sustainable behavior. Finally, it is felt that the work done in this study has implications for students, teachers, science educators, VR developers, and policymakers.

REFERENCES

Abd-Elaty, I., Kuriqi, A., & Shahawy, A. E. (2022). Environmental rethinking of wastewater drains to manage environmental pollution and alleviate water scarcity. *Natural Hazards*, *110*(3), 2353–2380. doi:10.100711069-021-05040-w PMID:34602747

Ahmad, M., Muslija, A., & Satrovic, E. (2021). Does economic prosperity lead to environmental sustainability in developing economies? Environmental Kuznets curve theory. *Environmental Science and Pollution Research International*, *28*(18), 22588–22601. doi:10.100711356-020-12276-9 PMID:33420933

Al-Gindy, A., Felix, C., Ahmed, A., Matoug, A., & Alkhidir, M. (2020). Virtual reality: Development of an integrated learning environment for education. *International Journal of Information and Education Technology (IJIET)*, *10*(3), 171–175. doi:10.18178/ijiet.2020.10.3.1358

Andone, D., & Frydenberg, M. (2019). Creating virtual reality in a business and technology educational context. In *Augmented reality and virtual reality* (pp. 147–159). Springer., doi:10.1007/978-3-030-06246-0_11

Araiza-Alba, P., Keane, T., & Kaufman, J. (2022). Are we ready for virtual reality in K–12 classrooms? *Technology, Pedagogy and Education, 31*(4), 1–21. doi:10.1080/1475939X.2022.2033307

Ardoin, N. M., Bowers, A. W., & Gaillard, E. (2020). Environmental education outcomes for conservation: A systematic review. *Biological Conservation, 241,* 108224. doi:10.1016/j.biocon.2019.108224

Atal, D., Sancar, R., Aydın, M., & Aydın, M. (2021). *Web Tabanlı Sanal Gerçeklik Geliştirme Ortamları. (Editörler: B. Akkoyunlu, A. İşman ve H. F. Odabaşı). Eğitim Teknolojileri Okumaları 2021- içinde (ss.* Pegem Akademi.

Ateş, H. (2020). Merging theory of planned behavior and value identity personal norm model to explain pro-environmental behaviors. *Sustainable Production, and Consumption, 24,* 169–180. doi:10.1016/j.spc.2020.07.006

Ateş, H. (2021). Understanding students' and science educators' eco-labeled food purchase behaviors: Extension of the theory of planned behavior with self-identity, personal norm, willingness to pay and eco-label knowledge. *Ecology of Food and Nutrition, 60*(4), 454–472. doi:10.1080/03670244.2020.18 65339 PMID:33405967

Azadi, Y., Yazdanpanah, M., & Mahmoudi, H. (2019). Understanding smallholder farmers' adaptation behaviors through climate change beliefs, risk perception, trust, and psychological distance: Evidence from wheat growers in Iran. *Journal of Environmental Management, 250,* 109456. doi:10.1016/j.jenvman.2019.109456 PMID:31513997

Barbalios, N., Ioannidou, I., Tzionas, P., & Paraskeuopoulos, S. (2013). A model supported interactive virtual environment for natural resource sharing in environmental education. *Computers & Education, 62,* 231–248. doi:10.1016/j.compedu.2012.10.029

Bevan, A., Palmisano, A., Woodbridge, J., Fyfe, R., Roberts, C. N., & Shennan, S. (2019). The changing face of the Mediterranean–Land cover, demography and environmental change: Introduction and overview. *The Holocene, 29*(5), 703–707. doi:10.1177/0959683619826688

Biocca, F., & Delaney, B. (1995). Immersive virtual reality technology. *Communication in the age of virtual reality, 15*(32), 10-5555.

Boyes, E., & Stanisstreet, M. (2012). Environmental education for behaviour change: Which actions should be targeted? *International Journal of Science Education, 34*(10), 1591–1614. doi:10.1080/095 00693.2011.584079

Breves, P., & Heber, V. (2020). Into the wild: The effects of 360 immersive nature videos on feelings of commitment to the environment. *Environmental Communication, 14*(3), 332–346. doi:10.1080/175 24032.2019.1665566

Carrozzino, M., & Bergamasco, M. (2010). Beyond virtual museums: Experiencing immersive virtual reality in real museums. *Journal of Cultural Heritage, 11*(4), 452–458. doi:10.1016/j.culher.2010.04.001

Casas, E. V. Jr, Pormon, M. M., Manus, J. J., & Lejano, R. P. (2021). Relationality and resilience: Environmental education in a time of pandemic and climate crisis. *The Journal of Environmental Education*, *52*(5), 314–324. doi:10.1080/00958964.2021.1981205

Cha, M., Han, S., Lee, J., & Choi, B. (2012). A virtual reality based fire training simulator integrated with fire dynamics data. *Fire Safety Journal*, *50*, 12–24. doi:10.1016/j.firesaf.2012.01.004

Chen, C. H., Hung, H. T., & Yeh, H. C. (2021). Virtual reality in problem-based learning contexts: Effects on the problem-solving performance, vocabulary acquisition and motivation of English language learners. *Journal of Computer Assisted Learning*, *37*(3), 851–860. doi:10.1111/jcal.12528

Chirico, A., Scurati, G. W., Maffi, C., Huang, S., Graziosi, S., Ferrise, F., & Gaggioli, A. (2021). Designing virtual environments for attitudes and behavioral change in plastic consumption: A comparison between concrete and numerical information. *Virtual Reality (Waltham Cross)*, *25*(1), 107–121. doi:10.100710055-020-00442-w

Cobern, W. W. (2000). Worldview theory and science education research. In *Everyday Thoughts about Nature* (pp. 6–12). Springer. doi:10.1007/978-94-011-4171-0_2

Colom, A., & Sureda, J. (1981). *Hacia una teoría del medio educativo*. Ediciones ICE, Universidad de Palma de Mallorca.

De Medeiros, J. F., Da Rocha, C. G., & Ribeiro, J. L. D. (2018). Design for sustainable behavior (DfSB): Analysis of existing frameworks of behavior change strategies, experts' assessment and proposal for a decision support diagram. *Journal of Cleaner Production*, *188*, 402–415. doi:10.1016/j.jclepro.2018.03.272

Diemer, J., Alpers, G. W., Peperkorn, H. M., Shiban, Y., & Mühlberger, A. (2015). The impact of perception and presence on emotional reactions: A review of research in virtual reality. *Frontiers in Psychology*, *26*(6), 1–9. doi:10.3389/fpsyg.2015.00026 PMID:25688218

Dowd, K., & Burke, K. J. (2013). The influence of ethical values and food choice motivations on intentions to purchase sustainably sourced foods. *Appetite*, *69*, 137–144. doi:10.1016/j.appet.2013.05.024 PMID:23770118

Edgerton, E., Romice, O., & Spencer, C. (2021). *Environmental psychology: Putting research into practice*. Cambridge Scholars Publishing.

European Environment Agency. (2013, February 28). Final energy consumption by sector [Data file]. Retrieved April 18, 2023, from https://www.eea.europa.eu/data-and-maps/indicators/final-energy-consumption-by-sector-5/assessment

Fan, S., Zhang, Y., Fan, J., He, Z., & Chen, Y. (2010, April). The application of virtual reality in environmental education: model design and course construction. In *2010 International Conference on Biomedical Engineering and Computer Science* (pp. 1-4). IEEE. 10.1109/ICBECS.2010.5462324

Fang, T. Y., Wang, P. C., Liu, C. H., Su, M. C., & Yeh, S. C. (2014). Evaluation of a haptics-based virtual reality temporal bone simulator for anatomy and surgery training. *Computer Methods and Programs in Biomedicine*, *113*(2), 674–681. doi:10.1016/j.cmpb.2013.11.005 PMID:24280627

Fauville, G., Queiroz, A. C., Hambrick, L., Brown, B. A., & Bailenson, J. N. (2021). Participatory research on using virtual reality to teach ocean acidification: A study in the marine education community. *Environmental Education Research*, 27(2), 254–278. doi:10.1080/13504622.2020.1803797

Feroz, A. K., Zo, H., & Chiravuri, A. (2021). Digital transformation and environmental sustainability: A review and research agenda. *Sustainability*, 13(3), 1530. doi:10.3390u13031530

Filter, E., Eckes, A., Fiebelkorn, F., & Büssing, A. G. (2020). Virtual reality nature experiences involving wolves on YouTube: Presence, emotions, and attitudes in immersive and nonimmersive settings. *Sustainability*, 12(9), 3823. doi:10.3390u12093823

Fraser, R., & Jamieson, G. (2003). Community environmental education: Challenges within the biosphere reserve concept. *Prospects*, 33(3), 293–302. doi:10.1023/A:1025531610879

Freina, L., & Ott, M. (2015). A literature review on immersive virtual reality in education: State of the art and perspectives. In *Proceedings of eLearning and software for education (eLSE)*, Bucharest.

González-Gaudiano, E. J. (2006). Environmental education: A field in tension or in transition? *Environmental Education Research*, 12(3-4), 291–300. doi:10.1080/13504620600799042

Guerrero, A. M., Jones, N. A., Ross, H., Virah-Sawmy, M., & Biggs, D. (2021). What influences and inhibits reduction of deforestation in the soy supply chain? A mental model perspective. *Environmental Science & Policy*, 115, 125–132. doi:10.1016/j.envsci.2020.10.016

Hardie, P., Darley, A., Carroll, L., Redmond, C., Campbell, A., & Jarvis, S. (2020). Nursing & Midwifery students' experience of immersive virtual reality storytelling: An evaluative study. *BMC Nursing*, 19(1), 1–12. doi:10.118612912-020-00471-5 PMID:32821245

Hsu, W. C., Tseng, C. M., & Kang, S. C. (2018). Using exaggerated feedback in a virtual reality environment to enhance behavior intention of water-conservation. *Journal of Educational Technology & Society*, 21(4), 187–203. https://www.jstor.org/stable/10.2307/26511548

Ighalo, J. O., Adeniyi, A. G., Adeniran, J. A., & Ogunniyi, S. (2021). A systematic literature analysis of the nature and regional distribution of water pollution sources in Nigeria. *Journal of Cleaner Production*, 283, 124566. doi:10.1016/j.jclepro.2020.124566

IPCC. (2021). [The Physical Science Basis Working Group I Contribution to the Sixth Assessment Report of the Intergovernmental Panel on Climate Change. Singer]. *Climatic Change*, 2021.

Issock, P. B. I., Mpinganjira, M., & Roberts-Lombard, M. (2021). Trying to recycle domestic waste and feelings of guilt: A moderated mediation model applied to South African households. *Sustainable Production and Consumption*, 27, 1286–1296. doi:10.1016/j.spc.2021.03.003

Jamei, E., Mortimer, M., Seyedmahmoudian, M., Horan, B., & Stojcevski, A. (2017). Investigating the role of virtual reality in planning for sustainable smart cities. *Sustainability*, 9(11), 1–16. doi:10.3390u9112006

Jensen, L., & Konradsen, F. (2018). A review of the use of virtual reality head-mounted displays in education and training. *Education and Information Technologies*, 23(4), 1515–1529. doi:10.100710639-017-9676-0

Jurin, R. R., & Fortner, R. W. (2002). Symbolic beliefs as barriers to responsible environmental behavior. *Environmental Education Research*, 8(4), 373–394. doi:10.1080/1350462022000026791

Kim, J., Kim, K., & Kim, W. (2022). Impact of Immersive Virtual Reality Content Using 360-degree Videos in Undergraduate Education. *IEEE Transactions on Learning Technologies*, 15(1), 137–149. doi:10.1109/TLT.2022.3157250

Kirikkaleli, D., & Adebayo, T. S. (2021). Do renewable energy consumption and financial development matter for environmental sustainability? New global evidence. *Sustainable Development*, 29(4), 583–594. doi:10.1002d.2159

Kisker, J., Gruber, T., & Schöne, B. (2021). Behavioral realism and lifelike psychophysiological responses in virtual reality by the example of a height exposure. *Psychological Research*, 85(1), 68–81. doi:10.100700426-019-01244-9 PMID:31520144

Kosko, K. W., Ferdig, R. E., & Zolfaghari, M. (2021). Preservice teachers' professional noticing when viewing standard and 360 video. *Journal of Teacher Education*, 72(3), 284–297. doi:10.1177/0022487120939544

Koul, B., Yakoob, M., & Shah, M. P. (2022). Agricultural waste management strategies for environmental sustainability. *Environmental Research*, 206, 112285. doi:10.1016/j.envres.2021.112285 PMID:34710442

Koutsoukos, M., Fragoulis, I., & Valkanos, E. (2015). Connection of Environmental Education with Application of Experiential Teaching Methods: A Case Study from Greece. *International Education Studies*, 8(4), 23–28. doi:10.5539/ies.v8n4p23

Lacroix, K., Gifford, R., & Rush, J. (2020). Climate change beliefs shape the interpretation of forest fire events. *Climatic Change*, 159(1), 103–120. doi:10.100710584-019-02584-6

Lange, F., & Dewitte, S. (2019). Measuring pro-environmental behavior: Review and recommendations. *Journal of Environmental Psychology*, 63, 92–100. doi:10.1016/j.jenvp.2019.04.009

Lehman, P. K., & Geller, E. S. (2004). Behavior analysis and environmental protection: Accomplishments and potential for more. *Behavior and Social Issues*, 13(1), 13–33. doi:10.5210/bsi.v13i1.33

Littledyke, M. (2008). Science education for environmental awareness: Approaches to integrating cognitive and affective domains. *Environmental Education Research*, 14(1), 1–17. doi:10.1080/13504620701843301

Littledyke, M., Lakin, L., & Ross, K. (2013). *Science knowledge and the environment: A guide for students and teachers in primary education*. Routledge. doi:10.4324/9781315068589

Liu, C., Zowghi, D., Kearney, M., & Bano, M. (2021). Inquiry-based mobile learning in secondary school science education: A systematic review. *Journal of Computer Assisted Learning*, 37(1), 1–23. doi:10.1111/jcal.12505

Liu, Q., Cheng, Z., & Chen, M. (2019). Effects of environmental education on environmental ethics and literacy based on virtual reality technology. *The Electronic Library*, 37(5), 860–877. doi:10.1108/EL-12-2018-0250

Lugrin, J. L., Latoschik, M. E., Habel, M., Roth, D., Seufert, C., & Grafe, S. (2016). Breaking bad behaviors: A new tool for learning classroom management using virtual reality. *Frontiers in ICT (Lausanne, Switzerland)*, *26*(3), 1–21. doi:10.3389/fict.2016.00026

Maciel, K. F. K., Fuentes-Guevara, M. D., da Silva Gonçalves, C., Mendes, P. M., de Souza, E. G., & Corrêa, L. B. (2022). Mobile mandala garden as a tool of environmental education in an early childhood school in Southern Brazil. *Journal of Cleaner Production*, *331*, 129913. doi:10.1016/j.jclepro.2021.129913

Makransky, G., Terkildsen, T. S., & Mayer, R. E. (2019). Adding immersive virtual reality to a science lab simulation causes more presence but less learning. *Learning and Instruction*, *60*, 225–236. doi:10.1016/j.learninstruc.2017.12.007

Markaki, V. (2014). Environmental Education through Inquiry and Technology. *Science Education International*, *25*(1), 86–92.

Markowitz, D. M., Laha, R., Perone, B. P., Pea, R. D., & Bailenson, J. N. (2018). Immersive virtual reality field trips facilitate learning about climate change. *Frontiers in Psychology*, *9*, 2364. doi:10.3389/fpsyg.2018.02364 PMID:30555387

McNaughton, M. J. (2004). Educational drama in the teaching of education for sustainability. *Environmental Education Research*, *10*(2), 139–155. doi:10.1080/13504620242000198140

Mujtaba, G., & Shahzad, S. J. H. (2021). Air pollutants, economic growth and public health: Implications for sustainable development in OECD countries. *Environmental Science and Pollution Research International*, *28*(10), 12686–12698. doi:10.100711356-020-11212-1 PMID:33085009

Nagra, V. (2010). Environmental education awareness among school teachers. *The Environmentalist*, *30*(2), 153–162. doi:10.100710669-010-9257-x

Ngo, C. C., Poortvliet, P. M., & Feindt, P. H. (2020). Drivers of flood and climate change risk perceptions and intention to adapt: An explorative survey in coastal and delta Vietnam. *Journal of Risk Research*, *23*(4), 424–446. doi:10.1080/13669877.2019.1591484

Nielsen, K. S., Cologna, V., Lange, F., Brick, C., & Stern, P. C. (2021). The case for impact-focused environmental psychology. *Journal of Environmental Psychology*, *74*. doi:10.31234/osf.io/w39c5

Norton, T. A., Parker, S. L., Zacher, H., & Ashkanasy, N. M. (2015). Employee green behavior: A theoretical framework, multilevel review, and future research agenda. *Organization & Environment*, *28*(1), 103–125. doi:10.1177/1086026615575773

Ozkan, B. (2021). The Effect of Drama-Based Activities on Environmental Sustainability Behaviors of 60-72 Months-Old Children. *International Online Journal of Education & Teaching*, *8*(3), 1486–1496.

Parsons, S., & Cobb, S. (2011). State-of-the-art of virtual reality technologies for children on the autism pectrum. *European Journal of Special Needs Education*, *26*(3), 355–366. doi:10.1080/08856257.201 1.593831

Pearson, A. R., Schuldt, J. P., & Romero-Canyas, R. (2016). Social climate science. *Perspectives on Psychological Science*, *11*(5), 632–650. doi:10.1177/1745691616639726 PMID:27694459

Queiroz, A. C. M., Kamarainen, A. M., Preston, N. D., & da Silva Leme, M. I. (2018). Immersive virtual environments and climate change engagement. *iLRN 2018 Montana*, 153. doi:10.3217/978-3-85125-609-3-27

Rambach, J., Lilligreen, G., Schäfer, A., Bankanal, R., Wiebel, A., & Stricker, D. (2021, July). A survey on applications of augmented, mixed, and virtual reality for nature and the environment. In *International Conference on Human-Computer Interaction* (pp. 653-675). Springer, Cham. 10.1007/978-3-030-77599-5_45

Rani, S., Kumar, R., & Maharana, P. (2022). Climate Change, Its Impacts, and Sustainability Issues in the Indian Himalaya: An Introduction. In *Climate Change* (pp. 1–27). Springer. doi:10.1007/978-3-030-92782-0_1

Ricart, S., Villar-Navascués, R. A., Hernández-Hernández, M., Rico-Amorós, A. M., Olcina-Cantos, J., & Moltó-Mantero, E. (2021). Extending natural limits to address water scarcity? The role of non-conventional water fluxes in climate change adaptation capacity: A review. *Sustainability*, *13*(5), 2473. doi:10.3390u13052473

Riva, G., Mantovani, F., Capideville, C. S., Preziosa, A., Morganti, F., Villani, D., Gaggioli, A., Botella, C., & Alcañiz, M. (2007). Affective interactions using virtual reality: The link between presence and emotions. *Cyberpsychology & Behavior*, *10*(1), 45–56. doi:10.1089/cpb.2006.9993 PMID:17305448

Savari, M., Zhoolideh, M., & Khosravipour, B. (2021). Explaining pro-environmental behavior of farmers: A case of rural Iran. *Current Psychology (New Brunswick, N.J.)*, 1–19. doi:10.100712144-021-02093-9

Schöne, B., Kisker, J., Sylvester, R. S., Radtke, E. L., & Gruber, T. (2021). Library for universal virtual reality experiments (luVRe): A standardized immersive 3D/360 picture and video database for VR-based research. *Current Psychology (New Brunswick, N.J.)*, 1–19. doi:10.100712144-021-01841-1

Schott, C. (2017). Virtual fieldtrips and climate change education for tourism students. *Journal of Hospitality, Leisure, Sport and Tourism Education*, *21*, 13–22. doi:10.1016/j.jhlste.2017.05.002

Schuldt, J. P., Mccomas, K. A., & Byrne, S. E. (2016). Communicating about ocean health: Theoretical and practical considerations. *Philosophical Transactions of the Royal Society of London. Series B, Biological Sciences*, *371*(1689), 1–9. doi:10.1098/rstb.2015.0214 PMID:26880833

Scurati, G. W., Bertoni, M., Graziosi, S., & Ferrise, F. (2021). Exploring the use of virtual reality to support environmentally sustainable behavior: A framework to design experiences. *Sustainability*, *13*(2), 943. doi:10.3390u13020943

Scurati, G. W., & Ferrise, F. (2020). Looking into a future which hopefully will not become reality: How computer graphics can impact our behavior—A study of the potential of VR. *IEEE Computer Graphics and Applications*, *40*(5), 82–88. doi:10.1109/MCG.2020.3004276 PMID:32833623

Sheppard, S. R. (2005). Landscape visualisation and climate change: The potential for influencing perceptions and behaviour. *Environmental Science & Policy*, *8*(6), 637–654. doi:10.1016/j.envsci.2005.08.002

Sheppard, S. R., Shaw, A., Flanders, D., & Burch, S. (2008). Can visualization save the world? Lessons for landscape architects from visualizing local climate change. *Digital Design in Landscape Architecture*, 29-31.

Shu, Y., Huang, Y. Z., Chang, S. H., & Chen, M. Y. (2018). Do virtual reality head-mounted displays make a difference? A comparison of presence and self-efficacy between head-mounted displays and desktop computer-facilitated virtual environments. *Virtual Reality (Waltham Cross)*, 1–10. doi:10.100710055-018-0376-x

Slater, M. (2009). Place illusion and plausibility can lead to realistic behavior in immersive virtual environments. *Philosophical Transactions of the Royal Society of London. Series B, Biological Sciences*, *364*(1535), 3549–3557. doi:10.1098/rstb.2009.0138 PMID:19884149

Slater, M. (2018). Immersion and the illusion of presence in virtual reality. *British Journal of Psychology*, *109*(3), 431–433. doi:10.1111/bjop.12305 PMID:29781508

Slater, M., & Wilbur, S. (1997). A framework for immersive virtual environments (FIVE): Speculations on the role of presence in virtual environments. *Presence (Cambridge, Mass.)*, *6*(6), 603–616. doi:10.1162/pres.1997.6.6.603

Snelson, C., & Hsu, Y. C. (2020). Educational 360-degree videos in virtual reality: A scoping review of the emerging research. *TechTrends*, *64*(3), 404–412. doi:10.100711528-019-00474-3

Sonnett, J. (2022). Climate change risks and global warming dangers: A field analysis of online US news media. *Environmental Sociology*, *8*(1), 41–51. doi:10.1080/23251042.2021.1960098

Spearman, M., & Eckhoff, A. (2012). Teaching young learners about sustainability. *Childhood Education*, *88*(6), 354–359. doi:10.1080/00094056.2012.741476

Stokes, A., Magnier, K., & Weaver, R. (2011). What is the use of fieldwork? Conceptions of students and staff in geography and geology. *Journal of Geography in Higher Education*, *35*(01), 121–141. doi:10.1080/03098265.2010.487203

Tang, T., & Bhamra, T. A. (2008). Changing energy consumption behaviour through sustainable product design. *In: International design conference – design 2008*. Dubrovnik, Croatia.

Thøgersen, J. (2009). The motivational roots of norms for environmentally responsible behavior. *Basic and Applied Social Psychology*, *31*(4), 348–362. doi:10.1080/01973530903317144

Trevors, J. T. (2007). Environmental education. *Water, Air, and Soil Pollution*, *180*(1). doi:10.1023/A:1023647520796

Tukker, A., & Jansen, B. (2006). Environmental impacts of products: A detailed review of studies. *Journal of Industrial Ecology*, *10*(3), 159–182. doi:10.1162/jiec.2006.10.3.159

UNESCO. (1978). *Intergovernmental conference on environmental education: Tbilisi (USSR), 14-26 October 1977. Final Report*. Paris: UNESCO.

United Nations Environment Program [UNEP] (2007). *UNEP 2007 annual report*. UNEP. https://wedocs.unep.org/handle/20.500.11822/7647

Varela-Candamio, L., Novo-Corti, I., & García-Álvarez, M. T. (2018). The importance of environmental education in the determinants of green behavior: A meta-analysis approach. *Journal of Cleaner Production, 170*, 1565–1578. doi:10.1016/j.jclepro.2017.09.214

Velev, D., & Zlateva, P. (2017). Virtual reality challenges education and training. International. *Compass (Eltham), 3*(1), 33–37. doi:10.18178/ijlt.3.1.33-37

Viveiros, L. C., Pereira, A. I., Peroni, J. V., Fachada, I., & Gonçalves, E. (2021). Natureza virtual: Enhancing ecosystem awareness by using virtual reality in educational tourism. In *Augmented Reality and Virtual Reality* (pp. 291–302). Springer., doi:10.1007/978-3-030-68086-2_22

Wals, A. E., Brody, M., Dillon, J., & Stevenson, R. B. (2014). Convergence between science and environmental education. *Science, 344*(6184), 583–584. doi:10.1126cience.1250515 PMID:24812386

Wilson, R. A. (1994). At the early childhood level. *Day Care and Early Education, 22*(2), 23–25. doi:10.1007/BF02361329

Withanage, C., Hölttä-Otto, K., Otto, K., & Wood, K. (2016). Design for sustainable use of appliances: A framework based on user behavior observations. *Journal of Mechanical Design, 138*(10), 101102. doi:10.1115/1.4034084

World Health Organization. (2021). *Ageing*. https://www.who.int/health-topics/ageing#tab=tab_1

Wynes, S., & Nicholas, K. A. (2017). The climate mitigation gap: Education and government recommendations miss the most effective individual actions. *Environmental Research Letters, 12*(7), 074024. doi:10.1088/1748-9326/aa7541

Zeiske, N., Venhoeven, L., Steg, L., & van der Werff, E. (2021). The normative route to a sustainable future: Examining children's environmental values, identity, and personal norms to conserve energy. *Environment and Behavior, 53*(10), 1118–1139. doi:10.1177/0013916520950266

Zhai, M., & Wolff, H. (2021). Air pollution and urban road transport: Evidence from the world's largest low-emission zone in London. *Environmental Economics and Policy Studies, 23*(4), 721–748. doi:10.100710018-021-00307-9

Zhang, L., Ruiz-Menjivar, J., Luo, B., Liang, Z., & Swisher, M. E. (2020). Predicting climate change mitigation and adaptation behaviors in agricultural production: A comparison of the theory of planned behavior and the Value-Belief-Norm Theory. *Journal of Environmental Psychology, 68*, 101408. doi:10.1016/j.jenvp.2020.101408

Zhang, X., Luo, L., & Skitmore, M. (2015). Household carbon emission research: An analytical review of measurement, influencing factors and mitigation prospects. *Journal of Cleaner Production, 103*, 873–883. doi:10.1016/j.jclepro.2015.04.024

KEY TERMS AND DEFINITIONS

Climate change: Climate change is the long-term alteration in Earth's climate and weather patterns, primarily due to human activities such as the burning of fossil fuels, deforestation, and other industrial processes.

Environmental Education: Environmental Education is the process of teaching individuals and communities about the natural world, environmental issues, and sustainable practices.

Environmental Sustainability: Environmental sustainability refers to the responsible use and management of natural resources and ecosystems to meet the needs of the present generation without compromising the ability of future generations to meet their own needs.

Immersion: Immersion, in the context of virtual reality and other digital media, refers to the sensation of being fully absorbed or engaged in a simulated environment or experience.

Presence: Presence, often used in relation to virtual reality, is the psychological state of feeling as though one is physically located within a simulated environment.

Science Education: Science Education is the field dedicated to teaching and learning scientific concepts, principles, and methodologies.

Virtual Reality: Virtual Reality is a computer-generated simulation of a three-dimensional environment or scenario that users can interact with and explore using specialized equipment such as headsets, gloves, or controllers.

Compilation of References

Abari, O., Bharadia, D., Duffield, A., & Katabi, D. (2016, November). Cutting the cord in virtual reality. In *Proceedings of the 15th ACM Workshop on Hot Topics in Networks* (pp. 162-168). ACM.

Abd-Elaty, I., Kuriqi, A., & Shahawy, A. E. (2022). Environmental rethinking of wastewater drains to manage environmental pollution and alleviate water scarcity. *Natural Hazards*, *110*(3), 2353–2380. doi:10.100711069-021-05040-w PMID:34602747

Ackerman, P. L., Kyllonen, P. C., & Roberts, R. D. (1999). *Learning and individual differences: Process, trait, and content determinants*. American Psychological Association. doi:10.1037/10315-000

Adler-Kassner, L., Majewski, J., & Koshnick, D. (2012). The value of troublesome knowledge: Transfer and threshold concepts in writing and history. *Composition Forum, 26.* https://www.compositionforum.com/issue/26/troublesome-knowledge-threshold.php

Adler-Kassner, L. (2015). *Naming what we know: Threshold concepts of writing studies*. Utah State University Press.

Ahmad, M., Muslija, A., & Satrovic, E. (2021). Does economic prosperity lead to environmental sustainability in developing economies? Environmental Kuznets curve theory. *Environmental Science and Pollution Research International*, *28*(18), 22588–22601. doi:10.100711356-020-12276-9 PMID:33420933

Alexander, P. A., & Murphy, P. K. (1999). Learner profiles: Valuing individual differences within classroom communities. In *Learning and individual differences: Process, trait, and content determinants*. American Psychological Association. doi:10.1037/10315-018

Al-Gindy, A., Felix, C., Ahmed, A., Matoug, A., & Alkhidir, M. (2020). Virtual reality: Development of an integrated learning environment for education. *International Journal of Information and Education Technology (IJIET)*, *10*(3), 171–175. doi:10.18178/ijiet.2020.10.3.1358

Alkan, C. (1997). *Eğitim teknolojisi*. (5th Ed.). Ankara: Anı yayıncılık.

Alkan, F. & Altundağ (Koçak), C. (2015). the role of technology in science teaching activities: Web based teaching applications. *Journal for the Education of Gifted Young Scientists*, 3(2),1-7.

Alkan, F., & Koçak, C. (2015). Chemistry laboratory applications supported with simulation original research article. *International Educational Technology Conference, IETC 2014*, Chicago, IL, USA.

Altıok, S., Yükseltürk, E. & Üçgül, M. (2017). Web 2 eğitimine yönelik gerçekleştirilen bilimsel bir etkinliğin değerlendirilmesi: katılımcı görüşleri, *Öğretim Teknolojileri ve Öğretmen Eğitimi Dergisi*, 6(1), s.1-8.

Altun, A. (2008). Yapılandırmacı öğretim sürecinde viki kullanımı. *In International Educational Technology Conference (IETC)*, Eskişehir, Türkiye.

Altundağ, Koçak C. & Alkan, F. (2016). Volümetrik titrasyonların teknoloji destekli öğretimi. *Cumhuriyet International Journal of Education, 5*(1), 1–9.

Ambika, N. (2022). An Augmented Edge Architecture for AI-IoT Services Deployment in the Modern Era. In *Handbook of Research on Technical, Privacy, and Security Challenges in a Modern World* (pp. 286–302). IGI Global.

American Educational Research Association, American Psychological Association, & National Council on Measurement in Education (Ed.). (2014). *Standards for educational and psychological testing*. American Educational Research Association.

American Educational Research Association, American Psychological Association, & National Council on Measurement in Education. (2014). *Standards for Educational and Psychological Testing*. American Educational Research Association.

Anderson, P. (2007). What is Web 2.0? ideas, technologies and implications for education, *Bristol: JISC, 1*(1), 1-64.

Anderson, J. R. (1993). *Rules of the Mind*. Lawrence Erlbaum Associates.

Andone, D., & Frydenberg, M. (2019). Creating virtual reality in a business and technology educational context. In *Augmented reality and virtual reality* (pp. 147–159). Springer., doi:10.1007/978-3-030-06246-0_11

Araiza-Alba, P., Keane, T., & Kaufman, J. (2022). Are we ready for virtual reality in K–12 classrooms? *Technology, Pedagogy and Education, 31*(4), 1–21. doi:10.1080/1475939X.2022.2033307

Ardoin, N. M., Bowers, A. W., & Gaillard, E. (2020). Environmental education outcomes for conservation: A systematic review. *Biological Conservation, 241*, 108224. doi:10.1016/j.biocon.2019.108224

Aristotle. Ross, W. D. 1., & Brown, L. (2009). The Nicomachean ethics. Oxford; New York, Oxford University Press.

Atalay Kabasakal, K., Arsan, N., Gök, B., & Kelecioğlu, H. (2014). Comparing performances (Type I error and Power) of IRT likelihood ratio SIBTEST and Mantel-Haenszel methods in the determination of differential item functioning. *Educational Sciences: Theory and Practice, 14*(6), 2186–2193.

Atal, D., Sancar, R., Aydın, M., & Aydın, M. (2021). *Web Tabanlı Sanal Gerçeklik Geliştirme Ortamları. (Editörler: B. Akkoyunlu, A. İşman ve H. F. Odabaşı). Eğitim Teknolojileri Okumaları 2021- içinde (ss. Pegem Akademi.

Ateş, H. (2020). Merging theory of planned behavior and value identity personal norm model to explain pro-environmental behaviors. *Sustainable Production, and Consumption, 24*, 169–180. doi:10.1016/j.spc.2020.07.006

Ateş, H. (2021). Understanding students' and science educators' eco-labeled food purchase behaviors: Extension of the theory of planned behavior with self-identity, personal norm, willingness to pay and eco-label knowledge. *Ecology of Food and Nutrition, 60*(4), 454–472. doi:10.1080/03670244.2020.1865339 PMID:33405967

Ayas, A. (1995). Lise 1 kimya öğrencilerinin maddenin tanecikli yapısı kavramını anlama seviyelerine ilişkin bir çalışma. II. Ulusal Fen Bilimleri Eğitimi Sempozyumu'nda sunulan bildiri. ODTÜ Eğitim Fakültesi, Ankara.

Ayas, A. (1995). Fen Bilimlerinde Program Geliştirme ve Uygulama Teknikleri Üzerine Bir Çalışma: İki Çağdaş Yaklaşımın Değerlendirilmesi. *Hacettepe Üniversitesi Eğitim Fakültesi Dergisi, 11*, 149–155.

Ayas, A., Çepni, S., Akdeniz, A., Özmen, H., Yiğit, N., & Ayvacı, H. S. (2007). *Kuramdan uygulamaya fen ve teknoloji öğretimi*. PegemA Yayıncılık.

Azadi, Y., Yazdanpanah, M., & Mahmoudi, H. (2019). Understanding smallholder farmers' adaptation behaviors through climate change beliefs, risk perception, trust, and psychological distance: Evidence from wheat growers in Iran. *Journal of Environmental Management, 250*, 109456. doi:10.1016/j.jenvman.2019.109456 PMID:31513997

Babini, M. H., Kulish, V. V., & Namazi, H. (2020). Physiological state and learning ability of students in normal and virtual reality conditions: Complexity-based analysis. *Journal of Medical Internet Research*, *22*(6), 6. doi:10.2196/17945 PMID:32478661

Bahuguna, Y., Verma, A., & Raj, K. (2018). Smart learning based on augmented reality with android platform and its applicability. *3rd International Conference On Internet of Things: Smart Innovation and Usages (IoT-SIU)*. Bhimtal, India. 10.1109/IoT-SIU.2018.8519853

Bamberger, M., & Segone, M. (n.d.). *How to design and manage equity-focused evaluations*. UNICEF.https://evalpartners.org/sites/default/files/EWP5_Equity_foc used_evaluations.pdf

Bank of America. (2023). *About*. Bank of America. https://about.bankofamerica.com/en/making-an-impact/museums-on-us-partners.

Barbalios, N., Ioannidou, I., Tzionas, P., & Paraskeuopoulos, S. (2013). A model supported interactive virtual environment for natural resource sharing in environmental education. *Computers & Education*, *62*, 231–248. doi:10.1016/j.compedu.2012.10.029

Barnes, A. C., & Larcus, J. (2015). Positive Psychology as a Framework for Leadership Development in Recreation and Sport. *New Directions for Student Leadership*, *2015*(147), 77–87. doi:10.1002/yd.20145 PMID:26895016

Barrett, L. F. (2020). *Seven and a half lessons about the brain*. Houghton Mifflin.

Bartholomae, D. (1980). The study of error. *College Composition and Communication*, *31*(3), 254–269. doi:10.2307/356486

Baumert, J., Bos, W., & Lehmann, R. (2000). *TIMSS/III: Dritte internationale mathematik-und naturwissenschaftsstudie*. Leske & Budrich.

Beaufort, A. (2007). *College writing and beyond*. Utah State University Press.

Beaufort, A. (2007). *College writing and beyond: A new framework for university writing instruction*. Utah State University Press.

Behmke, D., Kerven, D., Lutz, R., Paredes, J., Pennington, R., Brannock, E., & Stevens, K. (2018). Augmented reality chemistry: Transforming 2-D molecular representations into Interactive 3-D structures. *Interdisciplinary STEM Teaching and Learning Conference*, (2, pp. 3-11). Georgia Southern University. 10.20429tem.2018.020103

Bennett, R. E. (2009). A Critical Look at the Meaning and Basis of Formative Assessment. Educational Testing Service., ETS RM-09-06.

Benyamin, C. (2022). Montessori: An effective learning approach or a matter of faith? *The Perspective*. https://www.theperspective.com/amp/debates/1321/montessori-universally-effective-learning-approach-simple-matter-faith.html

Best, J. (2019). How virtual reality is changing medical practice: Doctors want to use this to give better patient outcomes. *BMJ (Clinical Research Ed.)*, *364*, k5419.

Bevan, A., Palmisano, A., Woodbridge, J., Fyfe, R., Roberts, C. N., & Shennan, S. (2019). The changing face of the Mediterranean–Land cover, demography and environmental change: Introduction and overview. *The Holocene*, *29*(5), 703–707. doi:10.1177/0959683619826688

Bhagavathula, R., Williams, B., Owens, J., & Gibbons, R. (2018, September). The Reality of virtual reality: A Comparison of Pedestrian Behavior in Real and Virtual Environments. []. Sage CA: Los Angeles, CA: SAGE Publications.]. *Proceedings of the Human Factors and Ergonomics Society Annual Meeting*, *62*(1), 2056–2060. doi:10.1177/1541931218621464

Biocca, F., & Delaney, B. (1995). Immersive virtual reality technology. *Communication in the age of virtual reality,* *15*(32), 10-5555.

Birrenbach, T., Zbinden, J., Papagiannakis, G., Exadaktylos, A. K., Müller, M., Hautz, W. E., & Sauter, T. C. (2021). Effectiveness and utility of virtual reality simulation as an educational tool for safe performance of COVID-19 diagnostics: Prospective, randomized pilot trial. *JMIR Serious Games, 9*(4), 4. doi:10.2196/29586 PMID:34623315

Blaauw-Hara, M. (2014). Transfer theory, threshold concepts, and first-year composition: Connecting writing courses to the rest of college. *Teaching English in the Two-Year College, 41*(4), 354–365.

Black, P. & Atkin, J. M. (1996). *Changing the subject: Innovations in science, mathematics and technology educations.* London: Routledge in association with OECD.

Bloom, B. (1956). *Taxonomy of Educational Objectives.* Longmans.

Bobier, J. F., Merey, T., Robnett, S., Grebe, M., Feng, J., Rehberg, B., & Hazan, J. (2022). *The Corporate Hitchhiker's guide to the metaverse.* Boston Consulting Group.

Boboc, R., Gîrbacia, F., & Butilă, E. (2020). The Application of Augmented Reality in the Automotive Industry: A Systematic Literature Review. *Applied Sciences (Basel, Switzerland), 10*(12), 4259. doi:10.3390/app10124259

Bouchard, S., Dumoulin, S., Robillard, G., Guitard, T., Klinger, E., Forget, H., Loranger, C., & Roucaut, F. X. (2016). Virtual reality compared with in vivo exposure in the treatment of social anxiety disorder: A three-arm randomised controlled trial. *The British Journal of Psychiatry, 12,* 210. PMID:27979818

Bowen, W. G., Chingos, M. M., & McPherson, M. S. (2009). *Crossing the finish line: Completing college at America's public universities.* Princeton University Press. doi:10.1515/9781400831463

Boyes, E., & Stanisstreet, M. (2012). Environmental education for behaviour change: Which actions should be targeted? *International Journal of Science Education, 34*(10), 1591–1614. doi:10.1080/09500693.2011.584079

Braun, J. & Trajkovski, (2023). *Designing Context Rich Learning.* IGI Global. https://www.igi-global.com/book/designing-context-rich-learning-extending/309084

Brearey, O. (2015). Understanding the relationship between first- and second-semester college writing courses. *Teaching English in the Two-Year College, 42*(3), 244–263.

Bresciani Ludvik, M. J. (2019). *Outcomes-Based Program Review: Closing Achievement Gaps In- and Outside the Classroom with Alignment to Predictive Analytics and Performance Metrics.* Stylus Publishing, LLC: Sterling.

Breves, P., & Heber, V. (2020). Into the wild: The effects of 360 immersive nature videos on feelings of commitment to the environment. *Environmental Communication, 14*(3), 332–346. doi:10.1080/17524032.2019.1665566

Brint, S., & Karabel, J. (1989). *The Diverted Dream, Community Colleges and the Promise of Educational Opportunity in America, 1900-1985.* Oxford University Press. doi:10.1093/oso/9780195048155.001.0001

Brooke, J. (1996). SUS: A quick and dirty usability scale. In P. W. Jordan, B. Thomas, B. A. Weerdmeester, & A. L. McClelland (Eds.), *Usability Evaluation in Industry.* Taylor and Francis.

Brooks, J., & Brooks, M. (1993). *The case for the constructivist classrooms,* Alexandria, Va: Busker, M., & Flint, A. (2022). Neue Zugänge zu chemischen Reaktionen: Das Basiskonzept des Chemieunterrichts. *Unterricht Chemie, 2022*(190), 2–5.

Brown, P. C., Roediger, H. L. III, & McDaniel, M. A. (2014). *Make it stick: The science of successful learning.* Harvard University Press.

Brown, P. C., Roediger, H. L. III, & McDaniel, M. A. (2014). *Make it Stick: The Science of Successful Learning*. The Belknap Press of Harvard University Press.

Brown, T. L., & Carr, T. H. (1989). Automaticity in skill acquisition: Mechanisms for reducing interference in concurrent performance. *Journal of Experimental Psychology. Human Perception and Performance*, 15(4), 686–700. doi:10.1037/0096-1523.15.4.686

Brue, K. L., & Brue, S. A. (2016). Experiences and outcomes of a women's Leadership Development Program: A phenomenological investigation. *Journal of Leadership Education*, 15(3), 75–97. doi:10.12806/V15/I3/R2

Bujak, K. R., Radu, I., Catrambone, R., MacIntyre, B., Zheng, R., & Golubski, G. (2013). A psychological perspective on augmented reality in the mathematics classroom. *Computers & Education*, 68, 536–544. doi:10.1016/j.compedu.2013.02.017

Burrelli, J. S., & Woodin, T. S. (2008). *Higher education in science and engineering. In the National Science Board, Science and engineering indicators*. National Science Foundation.

Cabral, B. K., Briggs, F. S., Hsu, J., Pozo, A. P., & Coward, A. H. (2019). U.S. Patent Application No. 10/230,904.

Cacioppe, R. (1998). An integrated model and approach for the design of effective Leadership Development Programs. *Leadership and Organization Development Journal*, 19(1), 44–53. doi:10.1108/01437739810368820

Cai, S., Wang, X., & Chiang, F. K. (2014). A case study of Augmented Reality simulation system application in a chemistry course. *Computers in Human Behavior*, 37, 31–40. doi:10.1016/j.chb.2014.04.018

Caladine, R. (2008). *Enhancing E-learning with media-rich content and interactions. information science publishing*. IGI Global. doi:10.4018/978-1-59904-732-4

Camilli, G., & Shepard, L. A. (1994). *Methods for Identifying Biased Test Items*. Sage.

Camilli, G., & Smith, J. K. (1990). Comparison of the Mantel-Haenszel Test with a randomized and jackknife test for detecting biased items. *Journal of Educational and Behavioral Statistics*, 15(1), 53–67. Advance online publication. doi:10.3102/10769986015001053

Can, G. (1998). Fen Bilgisi öğretiminde ölçme ve değerlendirme. *Fen Bilgisi Öğretimi*, 10.

Carmigniani, J., & Furht, B. (2011). Augmented reality: an overview. In Handbook of augmented reality (pp. 3-46). Springer. doi:10.1007/978-1-4614-0064-6_1

Carnevale, A. P., Smith, N., & Gulish, A. (2018). Women can't win: Despite making educational gains and pursuing high-wage majors, women still earn less than men. Washington, DC: Georgetown University: Center on Education and the Workforce.

Carrozzino, M., & Bergamasco, M. (2010). Beyond virtual museums: Experiencing immersive virtual reality in real museums. *Journal of Cultural Heritage*, 11(4), 452–458. doi:10.1016/j.culher.2010.04.001

Casas, E. V. Jr, Pormon, M. M., Manus, J. J., & Lejano, R. P. (2021). Relationality and resilience: Environmental education in a time of pandemic and climate crisis. *The Journal of Environmental Education*, 52(5), 314–324. doi:10.1080/00958964.2021.1981205

Cha, M., Han, S., Lee, J., & Choi, B. (2012). A virtual reality based fire training simulator integrated with fire dynamics data. *Fire Safety Journal*, 50, 12–24. doi:10.1016/j.firesaf.2012.01.004

Chen, M. Y., Liu, Y., & Zumbo, B. D. (2018). Testing for Differential Item Functioning in Performance Assessments [Conference presentation]. *11th conference of The International Test Commission*, Montréal, Canada.

Chen, C. H., Hung, H. T., & Yeh, H. C. (2021). Virtual reality in problem-based learning contexts: Effects on the problem-solving performance, vocabulary acquisition and motivation of English language learners. *Journal of Computer Assisted Learning*, *37*(3), 851–860. doi:10.1111/jcal.12528

Cheryan, S., Master, A., & Meltzoff, A. (2022). There Are Too Few Women in Computer Science and Engineering. *Scientific American*, (July), 27.

Chirico, A., Scurati, G. W., Maffi, C., Huang, S., Graziosi, S., Ferrise, F., & Gaggioli, A. (2021). Designing virtual environments for attitudes and behavioral change in plastic consumption: A comparison between concrete and numerical information. *Virtual Reality (Waltham Cross)*, *25*(1), 107–121. doi:10.100710055-020-00442-w

Choi, H. J., & Johnson, S. D. (2005). The effect of context-based video instruction on learning and motivation in online courses. *American Journal of Distance Education*, *19*(4), 215–227. doi:10.120715389286ajde1904_3

Chow, J., Feng, H., Amor, R., & Wünsche, B. C. (2013). Music education using augmented reality with a head mounted display. *Fourteenth Australasian User Interface Conference* (pp. 73-79). Australian Computer Society.

Cobern, W. W. (2000). Worldview theory and science education research. In *Everyday Thoughts about Nature* (pp. 6–12). Springer. doi:10.1007/978-94-011-4171-0_2

Cohrs, C., Bormann, K. C., Diebig, M., Millhoff, C., Pachocki, K., & Rowold, J. (2020). Transformational leadership and communication: Evaluation of a two-day Leadership Development Program. *Leadership and Organization Development Journal*, *41*(1), 101–117. doi:10.1108/LODJ-02-2019-0097

Çoklar, A. N. (2008). *Öğretmen adaylarının eğitim teknolojisi standartları ile ilgili öz yeterliklerinin belirlenmesi*. Doktora Tezi, Anadolu Üniversitesi, Eğitim Bilimleri Enstitüsü.

Çoklar, A. N., & Odabaşı, H. F. (2009). Eğitim teknolojisi standartları açısından öğretmen adaylarının ölçme ve değerlendirme özyeterliklerinin belirlenmesi. *Selçuk Üniversitesi. Ahmet Keleşoğlu Eğitim Fakültesi Dergisi*, *27*, 1–16.

Colom, A., & Sureda, J. (1981). *Hacia una teoría del medio educativo*. Ediciones ICE, Universidad de Palma de Mallorca.

Correa, A. G., & Ficheman, I. K., d. N., & de Deus Lopes, R. (2009). Computer assisted music therapy: A case study of an augmented reality musical system for children with cerebral palsy rehabilitation. *Ninth IEEE International Conference on Advanced Learning Technologies* (pp. 218-22). Riga, Latvia: IEEE. 10.1109/ICALT.2009.111

Costa, R. (2019, April 4). Information architecture: A UX designer's guide. *Justinmind*. https://www.justinmind.com/blog/information-architecture-ux-guide/

Cotner, S., Jeno, L. M., Walker, J. D., Jordensen, C., & Vandvick, V. (2020). Gender gaps in the performance of Norwegian biology students: The roles of test anxiety and science confidence. *International Journal of STEM Education*, *7*(1), 55. doi:10.118640594-020-00252-1

Daemmrich, I. (2007). Novices encounter a novice literature: Introducing digital literature in a first-year college writing class. *Teaching English in the Two-Year College*, *34*(4), 420–433.

Darling-Hammond, L. (2004). The color line in American education: Race, resources, and student achievement. *Du Bois Review*, *1*(2), 213–246. doi:10.1017/S1742058X0404202X

Darling-Hammond, L. (2017). *Developing and Measuring Higher Order Skills: Models for State Performance Assessment Systems*. Council of Chief State School Officers.

Dascal, J., & Reid, M., IsHak, W. W., Spiegel, B., Recacho, J., Rosen, B., & Danovitch, I. (2017). virtual reality and medical inpatients: A systematic review of randomized, controlled trials. *Innovations in Clinical Neuroscience, 14*(1-2), 14. PMID:28386517

De Medeiros, J. F., Da Rocha, C. G., & Ribeiro, J. L. D. (2018). Design for sustainable behavior (DfSB): Analysis of existing frameworks of behavior change strategies, experts' assessment and proposal for a decision support diagram. *Journal of Cleaner Production, 188*, 402–415. doi:10.1016/j.jclepro.2018.03.272

de Ribaupierre, S., Kapralos, B., Haji, F., Stroulia, E., Dubrowski, A., & Eagleson, R. (2014). Healthcare training enhancement through virtual reality and serious games. In *Virtual, Augmented Reality and Serious Games for Healthcare 1* (pp. 9–27). Springer. doi:10.1007/978-3-642-54816-1_2

Deans, P.C. (2009). *Social software and Web 2.0 technology trends*. New York: Information science reference.

Debord, G. (2012). *Society of the Spectacle*. Bread and Circuses Publishing.

DeMars, C. (2010). *Item Response Theory: Understanding Statistics Measurement*. Oxford University Press. doi:10.1093/acprof:oso/9780195377033.001.0001

Demeter, M., Hayes, H., & Trajkovski, G. (2022, Oct. 9.). The Importance of DIF: An important tool for identifying potential bias in Performance Assessment. *2022 Assessment Institute,* Indianapolis, Indiana University, Purdue University. https://assessmentinstitute.iupui.edu/program/program-files/2022/Sunday/04M_demeter.pdf

deMoville, B. (2007). Enterprise Leadership. *Organization Development Journal, 25*(4), 83–87.

Dewey, J. (1934). *Art as experience*. GP Putnam's Sons.

Diaz, E., Brooks, G., & Johanson, G. (2021). Detecting differential item functioning: Item Response Theory Methods versus the Mantel-Haenszel Procedure. *International Journal of Assessment Tools in Education, 8*(2), 376–393. doi:10.21449/ijate.730141

Diemer, J., Alpers, G. W., Peperkorn, H. M., Shiban, Y., & Mühlberger, A. (2015). The impact of perception and presence on emotional reactions: A review of research in virtual reality. *Frontiers in Psychology, 26*(6), 1–9. doi:10.3389/fpsyg.2015.00026 PMID:25688218

Dollár, A., & Steif, P. S. (2008). An interactive, cognitively informed, web-based statistics course. *International Journal of Engineering Education, 24*, 1229–1241.

Donham, C., Pohan, C., Menke, E., & Kranzfelder, P. (2022). Increasing student engagement through course attributes, community, and classroom technology: Lessons from the pandemic. *Journal of Microbiology & Biology Education, 23*(1), e00268-21. doi:10.1128/jmbe.00268-21 PMID:35496700

Dorans, N. J., & Holland, P. W. (1993). DIF detection and description: Mantel Haenszel and standardization. In P. W. Holland & H. Wainer (Eds.), *Differential Item Functioning* (pp. 35–66). Lawrence Erlbaum Inc.

Dougherty, K. J. (1995). *The contradictory college: The conflicting origins, impacts, and future of the community college*. SUNY Press.

Dowd, K., & Burke, K. J. (2013). The influence of ethical values and food choice motivations on intentions to purchase sustainably sourced foods. *Appetite, 69*, 137–144. doi:10.1016/j.appet.2013.05.024 PMID:23770118

Downs, D., & Wardle, E. (2007). Teaching about writing, righting misconceptions: (Re)envisioning 'first year composition' as 'introduction to writing studies. *College Composition Composition and Communication, 58*(4), 552–584.

Edgerton, E., Romice, O., & Spencer, C. (2021). *Environmental psychology: Putting research into practice.* Cambridge Scholars Publishing.

Eggers, D. (2009). *Dave Eggers TED prize 4 minute talk.* [Video]. TED. https://youtu.be/l3QbzvT6vko

Eide, B. L., & Eide, F. F. (2011). *The Dyslexic Advantage: Unlocking the Hidden Potential of the Dyslexic Brain.* Hudson Street Press.

Einstein, A., & Infeld, L. (1938). *The Evolution of Physics: The Growth of Ideas from Early Concepts to Relativity and Quanta.* Simon & Shuster.

Embretson, S. E. (1983). Construct validity: Construct representation versus nomothetic span. *Psychological Bulletin, 93*(1), 179–197. doi:10.1037/0033-2909.93.1.179

Embretson, S. E., & Reise, S. P. (2000). *Item Response Theory for Psychologists.* Lawrence Erlbaum Associates Publishers.

Eppich, W., & Cheng, A. (2015). Promoting excellence and reflective learning in simulation (PEARLS): Development and rationale for a blended approach to health care simulation debriefing. *Simulation in Healthcare, 10*(2), 106–115. doi:10.1097/SIH.0000000000000072 PMID:25710312

Epstein, B. (2021). *We have no clue how much the US spends on edtech.* Linkedin. https://www.linkedin.com/pulse/we-have-clue-how-much-us-spends-edtech-its-least-2x-what-bart-epstein/

Ersoy, Y. (2013). *Fen ve Teknoloji Öğretim Programındaki Yenilikler-I: Değişikliğin Gerekçesi ve Bileşenlerin Çerçevesi.* [Innovations in science and technology curriculum-1: rationale for change and framework of components].

Estapa, A., & Nadolny, L. (2015). The effect of an augmented reality enhanced mathematics lesson on student achievement and motivation. *Journal of STEM Education: Innovations and Research, 16*(3), 40–48.

European Environment Agency. (2013, February 28). Final energy consumption by sector [Data file]. Retrieved April 18, 2023, from https://www.eea.europa.eu/data-and-maps/indicators/final-energy-consumption-by-sector-5/assessment

Fang, T. Y., Wang, P. C., Liu, C. H., Su, M. C., & Yeh, S. C. (2014). Evaluation of a haptics-based virtual reality temporal bone simulator for anatomy and surgery training. *Computer Methods and Programs in Biomedicine, 113*(2), 674–681. doi:10.1016/j.cmpb.2013.11.005 PMID:24280627

Fan, S., Zhang, Y., Fan, J., He, Z., & Chen, Y. (2010, April). The application of virtual reality in environmental education: model design and course construction. In *2010 International Conference on Biomedical Engineering and Computer Science* (pp. 1-4). IEEE. 10.1109/ICBECS.2010.5462324

Faulkner-Bond, M., & Soland (2020). Comparability when assessing English learner students. In A. Berman, E. Haertel, & J. Pellegrino (Eds.) *Comparability issues in large-scale assessment* (pp. 149-175). National Academy of Education Press.

Fauville, G., Queiroz, A. C., Hambrick, L., Brown, B. A., & Bailenson, J. N. (2021). Participatory research on using virtual reality to teach ocean acidification: A study in the marine education community. *Environmental Education Research, 27*(2), 254–278. doi:10.1080/13504622.2020.1803797

Ferguson, C., Davidson, P. M., Scott, P. J., Jackson, D., & Hickman, L. D. (2015). *Augmented reality, virtual reality and gaming: An integral part of nursing.*

Fernández-Enríquez, R., & Delgado-Martín, L. (2020). Augmented Reality as a Didactic Resource for Teaching Mathematics. *Applied Sciences (Basel, Switzerland), 10*(7), 2560. doi:10.3390/app10072560

Feroz, A. K., Zo, H., & Chiravuri, A. (2021). Digital transformation and environmental sustainability: A review and research agenda. *Sustainability*, *13*(3), 1530. doi:10.3390u13031530

Fidalgo, A. M., Ferreres, D., & Muniz, J. (2004). Liberal and conservative differential item functioning detection using Mantel-Haenszel and SIBTEST: Implications for Type I and Type II error rates. *Journal of Experimental Education*, *73*(1), 23–39. doi:10.3200/JEXE.71.1.23-40

Fidelity Implementation Study Group Report . (1999). Simulation Interoperability Standards Organization. https://www.sisostds.org/ProductsPublications/ReferenceDocuments.aspx

Filter, E., Eckes, A., Fiebelkorn, F., & Büssing, A. G. (2020). Virtual reality nature experiences involving wolves on YouTube: Presence, emotions, and attitudes in immersive and nonimmersive settings. *Sustainability*, *12*(9), 3823. doi:10.3390u12093823

Fitts, P. M. (1964). Perceptual-motor skill learning. In A. W. Melton (Ed.), *Categories of Human Learning* (pp. 243–285). Academic. doi:10.1016/B978-1-4832-3145-7.50016-9

Ford, R., & Gopher, R. (2015). Competency-based education 101. *Procedia Manufacturing*, *3*, 1473–1480. doi:10.1016/j.promfg.2015.07.325

Fraser, R., & Jamieson, G. (2003). Community environmental education: Challenges within the biosphere reserve concept. *Prospects*, *33*(3), 293–302. doi:10.1023/A:1025531610879

Freina, L., & Ott, M. (2015). A literature review on immersive virtual reality in education: State of the art and perspectives. In *Proceedings of eLearning and software for education (eLSE)*, Bucharest.

Freire, P. (2020). *Pedagogy of the oppressed*. UCSC. https://envs.ucsc.edu/internships/internship-readings/freire-pedagogy-of-the-oppressed.pdf

Freire, P. (1986). *Pedagogy of the Oppressed*. Continuum.

Fuchs, H., Livingston, M. A., Raskar, R., Keller, K., Crawford, J. R., Rademacher, P., & Meyer, A. A. (1998, October). Augmented reality visualization for laparoscopic surgery. In *International Conference on Medical Image Computing and Computer-Assisted Intervention* (pp. 934-943). Springer, Berlin, Heidelberg.

Furht, B. (2011). Handbook of augmented reality. Springer Science & Business Media. doi:10.1007/978-1-4614-0064-6

Gagne, R. M. (1970). *The conditions of learning*. Holt, Rinehart and Winston.

Gallardo, K. (2020). Competency-based assessment and the use of performance-based evaluation rubrics in higher education: Challenges toward the next decade. *Problems of Higher Education in the 21st Century, 78*, 1, 61-79.

García-Betances, R. I., Arredondo Waldmeyer, M. T., Fico, G., & Cabrera-Umpiérrez, M. F. (2015). A succinct overview of virtual reality technology use in Alzheimer's disease. *Frontiers in Aging Neuroscience*, *7*, 80.

George, D. (1999). *Kitchen cooks, plate twirlers, & troubadours*. Boyton/Cook.

Georgiou, H., & Sharma, M. D. (2012). University students' understanding of thermal physics in everyday contexts. *International Journal of Science and Mathematics Education, 10*(5).

Gervais, J. (2016). The operational definition of competency-based education. *The Journal of Competency-Based Education*, *1*(2), 98–106. doi:10.1002/cbe2.1011

Gilligan, C. (2014). Moral injury and the ethic of care: Reframing the conversation about differences. *Journal of Social Philosophy*, *45*(1), 89–106. doi:10.1111/josp.12050

Giuseppe, R. I. V. A., & Wiederhold, B. K. (2015). The new dawn of virtual reality in health care: Medical simulation and experiential interface. *Studies in Health Technology and Informatics*, *219*, 3–6. PMID:26799868

Gleason, B. (2006). Reasoning the need: Graduate education and basic writing. *Journal of Basic Writing*, *25*(2), 49–75. doi:10.37514/JBW-J.2006.25.2.04

Glynn, S., & Koballa, T. R. (2005). Contextual teaching and learning. In R. E. Yager (Ed.) Exemplary Science: Best Practices in Professional Development (pp. 75-84). Arlington, VA: NSTA Press.

Goldblatt, E. (2007). *Because they live here: Sponsoring literacy beyond the college curriculum.* Hampton Press.

Gómez-Benito, J., Hildago, M. D., & Padilla, J. L. (2009). Efficacy of effect size measures in logistic regression: An application for detecting DIF. *Methodology*, *5*(1), 18–25. doi:10.1027/1614-2241.5.1.18

Gömleksiz, M. N., & Bulut, İ. (2007). Yeni fen ve teknoloji dersi öğretim programının etkililiğinin değerlendirilmesi. *Hacettepe Üniversitesi Eğitim Fakültesi Dergisi*, *32*, 76–88.

Gong, Z., Wang, R., & Xia, G. (2022). Augmented Reality (AR) as a Tool for Engaging Museum Experience: A Case Study on Chinese Art Pieces. *Digital*, *2*(1), 33–45. doi:10.3390/digital2010002

González-Gaudiano, E. J. (2006). Environmental education: A field in tension or in transition? *Environmental Education Research*, *12*(3-4), 291–300. doi:10.1080/13504620600799042

Graham, S. (2019). Changing how writing is taught. *Review of Research in Education*, *43*(1), 277–303. doi:10.3102/0091732X18821125

Grantcharov, T. P. (2008). Is virtual reality simulation an effective training method in surgery? *Nature Clinical Practice. Gastroenterology & Hepatology*, *5*(5), 5. doi:10.1038/ncpgasthep1101 PMID:18382434

Greengard, S. (2018). *Virtual Reality.* The MIT Press.

Greenwald, S., Kulik, A., Kunert, A., Beck, S., Froehlich, B., Cobb, S., Parsons, S., Newbutt, N., Gouveia, C., Cook, C., Snyder, A., Payne, S., Holland, J., Buessing, S., Fields, G., Corning, W., Lee, V., Xia, L., & Maes, P. (2017). *Technology and applications for collaborative learning in virtual reality.* In *CSCL Conference.* CSCL.

Guerrero, A. M., Jones, N. A., Ross, H., Virah-Sawmy, M., & Biggs, D. (2021). What influences and inhibits reduction of deforestation in the soy supply chain? A mental model perspective. *Environmental Science & Policy*, *115*, 125–132. doi:10.1016/j.envsci.2020.10.016

Guilera, G., Gómez-Benito, J., Hildago, M. D., & Sánchez-Meca, J. (2013). *Type I error and statistical power of the Mantel-Haenszel procedure for detecting DIF: A meta-analysis.* American Psychological Association. doi:10.1037/a0034306

Gully, B. (2012). Feedback on developmental students' first drafts. *Journal of Developmental Education*, *36*(1), 17–36.

Gyll, S. (2019). *Developing errant paths in a simulation testing environment: A how-to guide for assessment professionals.* Wiley. . doi:10.1002/cbe2.1198

Gyll, S. P., & Hayes, H. (2021). Learning and individual differences in skilled competency-based performance: Using a course planning and learning tool as an indicator for student success. *The Journal of Competency-Based Education.* . doi:10.1002/cbe2.1259

Gyll, S. P., & Hayes, H. (2023). (in press). Training for better transfer in an online competency-based higher education program: Using enhanced technology-based instruction to improve assessment outcomes and student learning. *Journal of Applied Testing Technology.*

Gyll, S., & Ragland, S. (2018). Improving the validity of objective assessment in higher education: Steps for building a best-in-class competency-based assessment program. *Journal of Competency-Based Education, 3*(1), 1. doi:10.1002/cbe2.1058

Hagl, R., & Duane, A. (2020). Exploring how augmented reality and virtual reality technologies impact business model innovation in technology companies in Germany. In *Augmented Reality and Virtual Reality* (pp. 75–84). Springer. doi:10.1007/978-3-030-37869-1_7

Halberstam, J. (2011). *The queer art of failure.* Duke University Press.

Hambleton, R. K., & Jones, R. W. (1994). Item parameter estimation errors and their influence on test information functions. *Applied Measurement in Education, 7*(3), 171–186. doi:10.120715324818ame0703_1

Hambleton, R. K., & Murphy, E. (1992). A psychometric perspective on authentic measurement. *Applied Measurement in Education, 5*(1), 1–16. doi:10.120715324818ame0501_1

Hambleton, R. K., Swaminathan, H., & Rogers, H. J. (1991). *Fundamentals of Item Response Theory.* Sage Publications, Inc.

Hamilton, D., McKechnie, J., Edgerton, E., & Wilson, C. (2021). Immersive virtual reality as a pedagogical tool in education: A systematic literature review of quantitative learning outcomes and experimental design. *Journal of Computer Education, 8*(1), 1–32. doi:10.100740692-020-00169-2

Hancock, G. R. (1994). Cognitive complexity and the comparability of multiple-choice and constructed-response test formats. *Journal of Experimental Education, 62*(2), 143–158. doi:10.1080/00220973.1994.9943836

Hanley, S. (1994). *On constructivism, Maryland collaborative for teacher preparation.* The https://terpconnect.umd.edu/~toh/MCTP/Essays/Constructivism.txt

Hanushek, E. A. (1971). Teacher characteristics and gains in student achievement: Estimation using micro-data. *The American Economic Review, 61*(2), 280–288.

Hardie, P., Darley, A., Carroll, L., Redmond, C., Campbell, A., & Jarvis, S. (2020). Nursing & Midwifery students' experience of immersive virtual reality storytelling: An evaluative study. *BMC Nursing, 19*(1), 1–12. doi:10.118612912-020-00471-5 PMID:32821245

Harley, A. (2017). *Ideation for Everyday Design Challenges.* Nielsen Norman Group. https://www.nngroup.com/articles/ux-ideation/

Harris, D. N., & Sass, T. R. (2008). *Teacher training, teacher quality, and student achievement.* Calder Center. https://caldercenter.org/sites/default/files/1001059_Teacher_Training.pdf

Harris, D. N., & Sass, T. R. (2008). *Teacher training, teacher quality, and student achievement.* Calder Center. https://www.caldercenter.org/PDF/1001059_Teacher_Training.pdf

Harvey, R. J. (1991). Job analysis. In M. Dunnette & L. Hough (Eds.), *Handbook of industrial and organizational psychology* (2nd ed., Vol. 2, pp. 71–163). Consulting Psychologists Press.

Hassel, H., & Baird Giordano, J. (2009). Transfer institutions, transfer of knowledge: The development of rhetorical adaptability and underprepared writers. *Teaching English in the Two-Year College, 37*(1), 24–40.

Hayes, H., & Embretson, S. E. (2012). Psychological measurement: Scaling and analysis. In H. Cooper, M. N. Coutanche, McMullen, L. M., & A. T. Panter (Eds.) APA Handbook of Research Methods in Psychology: Volume 1. Foundations, Planning, Measures, and Psychometrics. American Psychological Association.

Hayes, H., Gyll, S. P., Ragland, S., & Meyers, J. L. (2022). High-Stakes Assessments in Online Competency-Based Higher Education: The Assessment Development Cycle. In Handbook of Research on Future of Work and Education: Implications for Curriculum Delivery and Work Design (p. 230-252). IGI Global.

Hayes, H., Trajkovski, G., & Demeter, M. (2023). Seven steps to identify and address bias in educational assessments. *Evolllution.* https://evolllution.com/programming/teaching-and-learning/7-steps-to-identify-and-address-bias-in-educational-assessment s/

Healthcare Virtual Reality & Augmented Reality Systems Market. (2017, March 28). Advertising, Media Consulting, Marketing Research. OpenPR. https://www.openpr.com/news/484319/healthcare-virtual-reality-augmented-reality-systems-market.html

Henning, G. & Lundquist, A. (2022, Oct. 11). A framework for applying equity-minded and equity-centered assessment practices [Conference session]. *2022 Assessment Institute,* Indianapolis, IN, United States.

Herrington, A. J., & Herrington, J. A. (2007). *What is an authentic learning environment?* University of Wollongong. https://ro.uow.edu.au/edupapers/897

Hoffmann, L., Hausler, P., & Lehrke, M. (1998). *Die IPN-Interessenstudie physik.* IPN.

Holding, D. H. (1991). Transfer of training. In J. E. Morrison (Ed.), *Training for Performance: Principles of Applied Human Learning* (pp. 93–126). Wiley.

Holladay, M. (2018, November 16). The eight principles of information architecture. *Medium.* https://medium.com/@hollabit/the-eight-principles-of-information-architecture-6feff11f907a

Holland, P. W., & Thayer, D. T. (1988). Differential item performance and the Mantel-Haenszel procedure. In H. Wainer & H. I. Braun (Eds.), *Test Validity* (pp. 129–145). Lawrence Erlbaum, Inc.

Hoogveld, A. M. (2003). The teacher as designer of competency-based education. Heerlen: Open University of the Netherlands.

Hooper, J., Tsiridis, E., Feng, J. E., Schwarzkopf, R., Waren, D., & Long, W. J. (2019). Virtual reality simulation facilitates resident training in total hip arthroplasty: A randomized controlled trial. *Arthroplasty, 34,* 10. PMID:31056442

Horner, B., & Lu, M. Z. (1999). *Representing the "other": Basic writers and the teaching of basic writing.* NCTE.

Horn, M. B. (2022). *Reopen to Reinvent:(re) creating School for Every Child.* John Wiley & Sons.

Howell Raines, Helon. (1990). Is there a writing program in this college? Six-hundred and thirty-six two-year schools respond. *College Composition and Communication 42*(2), 151-165.

Hsu, W. C., Tseng, C. M., & Kang, S. C. (2018). Using exaggerated feedback in a virtual reality environment to enhance behavior intention of water-conservation. *Journal of Educational Technology & Society*, *21*(4), 187–203. https://www.jstor.org/stable/10.2307/26511548

Huang, W. (2022). Examining the impact of head-mounted display virtual reality on the science self- efficacy of high schoolers. *Interactive Learning Environments*, *31*(1), 100–112. doi:10.1080/10494820.2019.1641525

Ighalo, J. O., Adeniyi, A. G., Adeniran, J. A., & Ogunniyi, S. (2021). A systematic literature analysis of the nature and regional distribution of water pollution sources in Nigeria. *Journal of Cleaner Production, 283,* 124566. doi:10.1016/j.jclepro.2020.124566

İlhan, A. Ç. (2004). 21. yüzyılda öğretmen yeterlikleri. *Bilim ve Aklın Aydınlığında Eğitim Dergisi, 58,* 40–45.

IPCC. (2021). [The Physical Science Basis Working Group I Contribution to the Sixth Assessment Report of the Intergovernmental Panel on Climate Change. Singer]. *Climatic Change,* 2021.

Isaacson, W. (2011). *Steve Jobs.* Simon & Schuster.

İşman, A. (2003). *Öğretim teknolojileri ve materyal geliştirme.* İstanbul: Değişim yayınları.

Issock, P. B. I., Mpinganjira, M., & Roberts-Lombard, M. (2021). Trying to recycle domestic waste and feelings of guilt: A moderated mediation model applied to South African households. *Sustainable Production and Consumption, 27,* 1286–1296. doi:10.1016/j.spc.2021.03.003

Jamei, E., Mortimer, M., Seyedmahmoudian, M., Horan, B., & Stojcevski, A. (2017). Investigating the role of virtual reality in planning for sustainable smart cities. *Sustainability, 9*(11), 1–16. doi:10.3390u9112006

James, R. (2003). Academic standards and the assessment of student learning. *Tertiary Education and Management, 9*(3), 187–198. doi:10.1080/13583883.2003.9967103

Janangelo, J., & Klausman, J. (2012). Rendering the idea of a writing program: A look at six two-year colleges. *Teaching English in the Two-Year College, 40*(2), 131–144.

Jencks, C., & Phillips, M. (Eds.). (2011). *The Black-White Test Score Gap.* Brookings Institution Press.

Jensen, L., & Konradsen, F. (2018). A review of the use of virtual reality head-mounted displays in education and training. *Education and Information Technologies, 23*(4), 1515–1529. doi:10.100710639-017-9676-0

Jiao, H., & Lissitz, R. W. (Eds.). (2017). *Test Fairness in the New Generation of Large? Scale Assessment.* IAP.

Jodoin, M. G., & Gierl, M. J. (2001). Evaluating power and Type I error rates using an effect size with the logistic regression procedure for DIF. *Applied Measurement in Education, 14,* 329–349. doi:10.1207/S15324818AME1404_2

JohnstonH. (2011). *Proficiency-based education.* Education Partnership. www.educationpartnerships.org

Johnston, W. A., Strayer, D. L., & Vecera, S. P. (1998). Broad-mindedness and perceptual flexibility: Lessons from dynamic ecosystems. In J. S. Jordan (Ed.), *Systems Theories and A Priori Aspects of Perception* (pp. 87–103). Elsevier Science B. V. doi:10.1016/S0166-4115(98)80019-8

Jonassen, D. H., Tessmer, M., & Hannum, W. H. (1989). Training situation analysis. In *Handbook of Task Analysis Procedures.* Praeger Publishers.

Jones, J. (2022, June 3). Foundry Art Centre's Block Party Steamrolls its Way into St. Charles. *Riverfront Times.*

Jurin, R. R., & Fortner, R. W. (2002). Symbolic beliefs as barriers to responsible environmental behavior. *Environmental Education Research, 8*(4), 373–394. doi:10.1080/1350462022000026791

Kamphuis, C. B. E., Schijven, M., & Christoph, N. (2014). Augmented reality in medical education? *Perspectives on Medical Education, 3*(4), 300–311. doi:10.1007/S40037-013-0107-7 PMID:24464832

Kan, A. (2007). Öğretmen adaylarının eğitme-öğretme öz yetkinliğine yönelik ölçek geliştirme ve eğitme-öğretme öz yetkinlikleri açısından değerlendirilmesi *Mersin Üniversitesi Eğitim Fakültesi Dergisi, 3*(1), 35-50.

Kane, L. (2019, June 30). *The attention economy*. Nielsen Norman Group. https://www.nngroup.com/articles/attention-economy/

Kanner, L. (1943). Autistic disturbances of affective contact. *Nervous Child: Journal of Psychopathology, Psychotherapy, Mental Hygiene, and Guidance of the Child*, 2, 217–250.

Kaplan, A. S. (2020). Climbing the Ladder to CEO Part II: Leadership and Business Acumen. *Physician Leadership Journal*, 7(3), 50–52.

Kaufmann, H. (2003). Collaborative augmented reality in education. *Institute of software technology and interactive systems*, 2-4.

Kaufman, S. B. (Ed.). (2018). *Twice exceptional: supporting and educating bright and creative students with learning difficulties*. Oxford University Press. doi:10.1093/oso/9780190645472.001.0001

Keats, J. (2023). *Ode on a Grecian urn*. Poetry Foundation. https://www.poetryfoundation.org/poems/44477/ode-on-a-grecian-urn

Keller, S., Rumann, S., & Habig, S. (2021). Cognitive Load Implications for Augmented Reality Supported Chemistry Learning. *Information (Basel)*, 12(3), 96. doi:10.3390/info12030096

Kennedy, R. S., Lane, N. E., Berbaum, K. S., & Lilienthal, M. G. (1993). Simulator sickness questionnaire: An enhanced method for quantifying simulator sickness. *The International Journal of Aviation Psychology*, 3(3), 3. doi:10.120715327108ijap0303_3

Keshav, V. (2017). *Tech Nanotechnology, Central University of Jharkhand*. Quora. https://www.quora.com/What-is-the-difference-between-virtual-reality-and-simulated-reality

Khan, R., Plahouras, J., Johnston, B. C., Scaffidi, M. A., Grover, S. C., & Walsh, C. M. (2019). Virtual reality simulation training in endoscopy: A Cochrane Review and meta-analysis. *Endoscopy*, 51(07), 653–664. doi:10.1055/a-0894-4400 PMID:31071757

Khor, W. S., Baker, B., Amin, K., Chan, A., Patel, K., & Wong, J. (2016). Augmented and virtual reality in surgery—the digital surgical environment: Applications, limitations and legal pitfalls. *Annals of Translational Medicine*, 4(23), 454. doi:10.21037/atm.2016.12.23 PMID:28090510

Kim, J., Kim, K., & Kim, W. (2022). Impact of Immersive Virtual Reality Content Using 360-degree Videos in Undergraduate Education. *IEEE Transactions on Learning Technologies*, 15(1), 137–149. doi:10.1109/TLT.2022.3157250

Kim, M., Yoon, H., Ji, Y. R., & Song, J. (2012). The dynamics of learning science in everyday contexts: A case study of everyday science class in Korea. *International Journal of Science and Mathematics Education*, 10(1), 71–97. doi:10.100710763-011-9278-z

Kim, S.-H., & Cohen, A. S. (1995). A comparison of Lord's chi-square, Raju's area measures, and the likelihood ratio test on detection of differential item functioning. *Applied Measurement in Education*, 8(4), 291–312. doi:10.120715324818ame0804_2

Kirikkaleli, D., & Adebayo, T. S. (2021). Do renewable energy consumption and financial development matter for environmental sustainability? New global evidence. *Sustainable Development*, 29(4), 583–594. doi:10.1002d.2159

Kisker, J., Gruber, T., & Schöne, B. (2021). Behavioral realism and lifelike psychophysiological responses in virtual reality by the example of a height exposure. *Psychological Research*, 85(1), 68–81. doi:10.100700426-019-01244-9 PMID:31520144

Klausman, J. (2008). Mapping the terrain: The two-year college writing program administrator. *Teaching English in the Two-Year College, 35*(3), 238–251.

Klausman, J. (2013). Toward a definition of a writing program at a two-year college: You say you want a revolution? *Teaching English in the Two-Year College, 40*(3), 257–273.

Kline, R. B. (2010). *Principles and practice of structural equation modeling* (3rd ed.). Guilford.

Kononowicz, A. A., Zary, N., Edelbring, S., Corral, J., & Hege, I. (2015). Virtual patients- what are we talking about? A framework to classify the meanings of the term in healthcare education. *BMC Medical Education, 15*(1), 11. doi:10.118612909-015-0296-3 PMID:25638167

Köseoğlu, F., Yılmaz, H., Koç, Ş., Güneş, B., Bahar, M., Eryılmaz, A., Ateş, S., & Müyesseroğlu, Z. (2006). *İlköğretim fen ve teknoloji dersi öğretim programı.*

Kosko, K. W., Ferdig, R. E., & Zolfaghari, M. (2021). Preservice teachers' professional noticing when viewing standard and 360 video. *Journal of Teacher Education, 72*(3), 284–297. doi:10.1177/0022487120939544

Koul, B., Yakoob, M., & Shah, M. P. (2022). Agricultural waste management strategies for environmental sustainability. *Environmental Research, 206*, 112285. doi:10.1016/j.envres.2021.112285 PMID:34710442

Koutsoukos, M., Fragoulis, I., & Valkanos, E. (2015). Connection of Environmental Education with Application of Experiential Teaching Methods: A Case Study from Greece. *International Education Studies, 8*(4), 23–28. doi:10.5539/ies.v8n4p23

Kramer, A. F., Larish, J. F., & Strayer, D. L. (1995). Training for attentional control in dual-task settings: A comparison of young and old adults. *Journal of Experimental Psychology. Applied, 1*(1), 50–76. doi:10.1037/1076-898X.1.1.50

Krane, N. E. R., & Tirre, W. C. (2012). Ability assessment in career counseling. In S. D. Brown & R. W. Lent (Eds.), *Career development and counseling: Putting theory and research to work* (pp. 330–352). Wiley.

Kuang, C., & Fabricant, R. (2019). *User friendly: How the hidden rules of design are changing the way we live, work & play.* Random House.

Kuby, C. R., & Gutshall Rucker, T. L. (2015, May). Everyone has a Neil: Possibilities of literacy desiring in Writers' Studio. *Language Arts, 92*(5), 314–327.

Kuhlman, B. B. personal communication, October 13, 2019

Kyaw, B. M., Saxena, N., Posadzki, P., Vseteckova, J., Nikolaou, C. K., George, P. P., Divakar, U., Masiello, I., Kononowicz, A. A., Zary, N., & Tudor Car, L. (2019). Virtual reality for health professions education: Systematic review and meta-analysis by the Digital Health Education Collaboration. *Journal of Medical Internet Research, 21*(1), 1. doi:10.2196/12959 PMID:30668519

Lacroix, K., Gifford, R., & Rush, J. (2020). Climate change beliefs shape the interpretation of forest fire events. *Climatic Change, 159*(1), 103–120. doi:10.100710584-019-02584-6

Lamounier, E., Bucioli, A., Cardoso, A., Andrade, A., & Soares, A. (2010, September). On the use of Augmented Reality techniques in learning and interpretation of cardiologic data. In *Annual International Conference of the IEEE* (Vol. 1, pp. 2451-2454). IEEE. 10.1109/IEMBS.2010.5628019

Lange, F., & Dewitte, S. (2019). Measuring pro-environmental behavior: Review and recommendations. *Journal of Environmental Psychology, 63*, 92–100. doi:10.1016/j.jenvp.2019.04.009

Lankford, H., Loeb, S., & Wyckoff, J. (2002). Teacher sorting and the plight of urban schools: A descriptive analysis. *Educational Evaluation and Policy Analysis, 24*(1), 37–62. doi:10.3102/01623737024001037

Lee, M. (2009). Rhetorical roulette: Does writing-faculty overload disable effective response to student writing? *Teaching English in the Two-Year College, 37*(2), 165–177.

Lehman, P. K., & Geller, E. S. (2004). Behavior analysis and environmental protection: Accomplishments and potential for more. *Behavior and Social Issues, 13*(1), 13–33. doi:10.5210/bsi.v13i1.33

Lerman, L. (1993). Toward a process for critical response. *High Performance, 16*(4), 46–49.

Liedtka, J., Salzman, R., & Azer, D. (2017). *Design Thinking for the Greater Good.* Columbia Business School Publishing. doi:10.7312/lied17952

Lin, H.-F., & Chen, C.-H. (2017). Combining the Technology Acceptance Model and Uses and Gratifications Theory to examine the usage behavior of an Augmented Reality Tour-sharing Application. *Symmetry, 9*(7), 113. doi:10.3390ym9070113

Littledyke, M. (2008). Science education for environmental awareness: Approaches to integrating cognitive and affective domains. *Environmental Education Research, 14*(1), 1–17. doi:10.1080/13504620701843301

Littledyke, M., Lakin, L., & Ross, K. (2013). *Science knowledge and the environment: A guide for students and teachers in primary education.* Routledge. doi:10.4324/9781315068589

Liu, C., Zowghi, D., Kearney, M., & Bano, M. (2021). Inquiry-based mobile learning in secondary school science education: A systematic review. *Journal of Computer Assisted Learning, 37*(1), 1–23. doi:10.1111/jcal.12505

Liu, Q., Cheng, Z., & Chen, M. (2019). Effects of environmental education on environmental ethics and literacy based on virtual reality technology. *The Electronic Library, 37*(5), 860–877. doi:10.1108/EL-12-2018-0250

Locke, A. (1928, November). Art or Propaganda? In *Harlem: A Forum of Negro Life, 1*(1), 1–2. https://www.vonsteuben.org/ourpages/auto/2015/5/8/45168339/lockeartorpropaganda.pdf

Lord, F. M., & Novick, M. R. (1968). *Statistical Theories of Mental Test Scores.* Addison-Wesley.

Lugrin, J. L., Latoschik, M. E., Habel, M., Roth, D., Seufert, C., & Grafe, S. (2016). Breaking bad behaviors: A new tool for learning classroom management using virtual reality. *Frontiers in ICT (Lausanne, Switzerland), 26*(3), 1–21. doi:10.3389/fict.2016.00026

M, R. (2018, March 19). *Psychology + design: Gestalt principles you can use as design solutions.* UX Collective. https://uxdesign.cc/psychology-design-4-gestalt-principles-to-use-as-your-next-design-solution-fcdec423a6bf

MacDonald, R. A. (2013). Music, health, and well-being: A review. *International Journal of Qualitative Studies on Health and Well-being, 8*(1), 20635. doi:10.3402/qhw.v8i0.20635 PMID:23930991

Maciel, K. F. K., Fuentes-Guevara, M. D., da Silva Gonçalves, C., Mendes, P. M., de Souza, E. G., & Corrêa, L. B. (2022). Mobile mandala garden as a tool of environmental education in an early childhood school in Southern Brazil. *Journal of Cleaner Production, 331*, 129913. doi:10.1016/j.jclepro.2021.129913

Making leadership development more effective: Psychological changes have implications for training programme design. (2015). *Development and Learning in Organizations, 29*(6), 20-22. doi:10.1108/DLO-05-2015-0046

Makransky, G., Terkildsen, T. S., & Mayer, R. E. (2019). Adding immersive virtual reality to a science lab simulation causes more presence but less learning. *Learning and Instruction, 60*, 225–236. doi:10.1016/j.learninstruc.2017.12.007

Malenczyk, R. (2013). *A rhetoric for writing program administrators*. Parlor Press.

Markaki, V. (2014). Environmental Education through Inquiry and Technology. *Science Education International*, 25(1), 86–92.

Markowitz, D. M., Laha, R., Perone, B. P., Pea, R. D., & Bailenson, J. N. (2018). Immersive virtual reality field trips facilitate learning about climate change. *Frontiers in Psychology*, 9, 2364. doi:10.3389/fpsyg.2018.02364 PMID:30555387

Martin, J., Bohuslava, J., & Igor, H. (2018). Augmented reality in education 4.0. *13th international scientific and technical conference on computer sciences and information technologies (CSIT)*, 1, pp. 231-236. Lviv, Ukraine.

Mastro, M. (2022, May 11th). Meet the six local art businesses that call St. Charles' Foundry Arts Centre home. *St. Louis Magazine*.

McClarty, K. L., & Gaertner, M. N. (2015). *Measuring Mastery: Best Practices for Assessment in Competency-Based Education*. AE Series on Competency-Based Higher Education.

McNaughton, M. J. (2004). Educational drama in the teaching of education for sustainability. *Environmental Education Research*, 10(2), 139–155. doi:10.1080/13504620242000198140

MEB. (2005). *İlköğretim Fen ve Teknoloji Dersi Öğretim Programı*.

Melguizo, T., Kienzl, G. S., & Alfonso, M. (2011). Comparing the educational attainment of community college transfer students and four-year college rising juniors using propensity score matching methods. *The Journal of Higher Education*, 82(3), 265–291. doi:10.1353/jhe.2011.0013

Merrill, D. (2002). A pebble-in-the-pond model for instructional design. *Performance Improvement*, 41(7), 41–46. doi:10.1002/pfi.4140410709

Messick, S. (1989). Validity. In R. Linn (Ed.), *Educational Measurement* (3rd ed., pp. 13–100). American Council on Education.

Michaud, M. (2011). The "reverse commute": Adult students and the transition from professional to academic literacy. *Teaching English in the Two-Year College*, 38(3), 244–260.

Millar, R., Osborne, J., & Nott, S. (1998). Science education for the future. *The School Science Review*, 80(291), 19–24.

Modello, B. A history of museums, 'The memory of mankind'. NPR. (2008, November 24). Kratz, S., & Merritt, E. (2011). Museums and the future of education. *On the Horizon*.

Montenegro, E., & Jankowski, N. (2017). *Equity and assessment: Moving towards culturally responsive assessment (Occasional Paper No. 29)*. Urbana, IL: University of Illinois and Indiana University, National Institute for Learning Outcomes Assessment (NILOA). https://files.eric.ed.gov/fulltext/ED574461.pdf

Montenegro, E., & Jankowski, N. A. (2020). *A new decade for assessment: Embedding equity into assessment praxis (Occasional Paper No. 42)*. Urbana, IL: University of Illinois and Indiana University, National Institute for Learning Outcomes Assessment (NILOA). https://files.eric.ed.gov/fulltext/ED608774.pdf

Montessori, M. & George, A. (2012). *The Montessori Method: Scientific Pedagogy as applied to child education in 'the children's houses' with additions and revisions by the author*. Project Gutenberg. https://archive.org/details/TheMontessoriMeathod/mode/2up?q=%22Let+us+consider+the+attitude+of+the+teacher+in+the+light+of+another+example.%22

Montessori, M. (2004). *The discovery of the child*. Aakar books.

Moran, K. (2019, December 1). *Usability testing 101*. Nielsen Norman Group. https://www.nngroup.com/articles/usability-testing-101/

Mori, M. (1970). The uncanny valley. *Energy*, 33–35.

Mujtaba, G., & Shahzad, S. J. H. (2021). Air pollutants, economic growth and public health: Implications for sustainable development in OECD countries. *Environmental Science and Pollution Research International, 28*(10), 12686–12698. doi:10.100711356-020-11212-1 PMID:33085009

Muniz, J., Hambleton, R. K., & Xing, D. (2001). Small sample studies to detect flaws in item translations. *International Journal of Testing, 1*(2), 115–135. doi:10.1207/S15327574IJT0102_2

Myers, D. G. (2006). *The Elephants Teach: Creative Writing since 1880*. University of Chicago Press. https://eric.ed.gov/?id=ED525636

Nagaraj, A. (2021). Introduction to Sensors in IoT and Cloud Computing Applications. Bentham Science Publishers.

Nagra, V. (2010). Environmental education awareness among school teachers. *The Environmentalist, 30*(2), 153–162. doi:10.100710669-010-9257-x

NASA Task Load Index (2005). *Agency for Healthcare Research and Quality*. Digital Healthcare Research (ahrq.gov).

Nash, E. B., Edwards, G. W., Thompson, J. A., & Barfield, W. (2000). A Review of Presence and Performance in Virtual Environments. *International Journal of Human-Computer Interaction, 12*(1), 1–41. doi:10.1207/S15327590IJHC1201_1

Nas, S. E. (2008). *Isının yayılma yolları konusunda 5E modelinin derinleşme aşamasına yönelik olarak geliştirilen materyallerin etkililiğinin değerlendirilmesi*. Yüksek Lisans Tezi, Karadeniz Teknik Üniversitesi, Fen Bilimleri Enstitüsü.

New London Group. (1996, Spring). *Harvard Educational Review, 66*(1).

Ngo, C. C., Poortvliet, P. M., & Feindt, P. H. (2020). Drivers of flood and climate change risk perceptions and intention to adapt: An explorative survey in coastal and delta Vietnam. *Journal of Risk Research, 23*(4), 424–446. doi:10.1080/13669877.2019.1591484

Nielsen, K. S., Cologna, V., Lange, F., Brick, C., & Stern, P. C. (2021). The case for impact-focused environmental psychology. *Journal of Environmental Psychology, 74*. doi:10.31234/osf.io/w39c5

Nist, E. A., & Raines, H. H. (1995). Two-year colleges: Explaining and claiming our majority. In *Resituating writing: Constructing and administrating writing programs*. Boynton/Cook.

Norman, D. A. (1988). *The design of everyday things*. Basic books.

Norton, T. A., Parker, S. L., Zacher, H., & Ashkanasy, N. M. (2015). Employee green behavior: A theoretical framework, multilevel review, and future research agenda. *Organization & Environment, 28*(1), 103–125. doi:10.1177/1086026615575773

Novick, S., & Nussbaum, J. (1981). Pupils' understanding of the particulate nature of matter: A cross-age study. *Science Education, 65*(2), 187–196. doi:10.1002ce.3730650209

O'Reilly, T. (2007). What is Web2.0? Design patterns and business models for the next generation of software. *Communications & Strategies, 65*(1), 17–37. https://papers.ssrn.com/sol3/Delivery.cfm/SSRN_ID1008839_code2969338.pdf?abstractid=1008839&mirid=1

Oozeerally, S., Ramma, Y., & Bholoa, A. (2020). *Science Education in Theory and Practice: An Introductory Guide to Learning Theory*, 323-342. Multiliteracies—New London Group.

Ortega, M., Ivorra, E., Juan, A., Venegas, P., Martínez, J., & Alcañiz, M. (2021). MANTRA: An Effective System Based on Augmented Reality and Infrared Thermography for Industrial Maintenance. *Applied Sciences (Basel, Switzerland)*, *11*(1), 385. doi:10.3390/app11010385

Osborne, M., & Freyberg, P. (1985). *Learning in science: Implications of children's knowledge*. Heinemann.

Ostman, H. (2013). *Writing program administration and the two-year college*. Parlor Press.

Ozkan, B. (2021). The Effect of Drama-Based Activities on Environmental Sustainability Behaviors of 60-72 Months-Old Children. *International Online Journal of Education & Teaching*, *8*(3), 1486–1496.

Padmanabha, C. H. (2021). Assessment for Learning, Assessment of Learning, Assessment as Learning: A Conceptual Framework. *i-manager's. Journal of Educational Psychology*, *14*(4), 14–21. doi:10.26634/jpsy.14.4.17681

Paek, I., & Guo, H. (2011). Accuracy of DIF estimates and power in unbalanced designs using the Mantel-Haenszel DIF detection procedure. *Applied Psychological Measurement*, *35*(7), 518–535. doi:10.1177/0146621611420559

Pae, T.-I., & Park, G.-P. (2016). Examining the relationship between differential item functioning and differential test functioning. *Language Testing*, *23*(4), 475–496. doi:10.1191/0265532206lt338oa

Pamuk, S.,Ülken, A. & Dilek, N.Ş. (2012). Öğretmen adaylarinin öğretimde teknoloji kullanim yeterliliklerinin teknolojik pedagojik içerik bilgisi kuramsal perspektifinden incelenmesi. *Mustafa Kemal Üniversitesi Sosyal Bilimler Enstitüsü Dergisi*, 9 – 17.

Pantelidis, P., Chorti, A., Papagiouvanni, I., Paparoidamis, G., Drosos, C., & Panagiotakopaulos, T. (2017). Virtual and augmented reality in medical education. In Medical and surgical education - past, present, and future (pp. 77–97). IntechOpen.

Pan, X., & Hamilton, A. (2018). Why and how to use virtual reality to study human social interaction: The challenges of exploring a new research landscape. *British Journal of Psychology*, *109*(3), 3. doi:10.1111/bjop.12290 PMID:29504117

Papagiannakis, G., Zikas, P., Lydatakis, N., Kateros, S., Kentros, M., Geronikolakis, E., Kamarianakis, M., Kartsonaki, I., & Evangelou, G. (2020). MAGES 3.0: Tying the knot of medical VR. In ACM SIGGRAPH 2020 Immersive Pavilion (pp. 1-2). ACM.

Parsons, S., & Cobb, S. (2011). State-of-the-art of virtual reality technologies for children on the autism pectrum. *European Journal of Special Needs Education*, *26*(3), 355–366. doi:10.1080/08856257.2011.593831

Pearson, A. R., Schuldt, J. P., & Romero-Canyas, R. (2016). Social climate science. *Perspectives on Psychological Science*, *11*(5), 632–650. doi:10.1177/1745691616639726 PMID:27694459

Penfield, R. D., & Lam, T. C. M. (2000). Assessment differential item functioning in performance assessment: Review and recommendations. *Educational Measurement: Issues and Practice*, *19*(3), 3, 5–15. doi:10.1111/j.1745-3992.2000.tb00033.x

Pensieri, C., & Pennacchini, M. (2014). Overview: Virtual reality in medicine. *Journal of Virtual Worlds Research*, *7*(1), 1. doi:10.4101/jvwr.v7i1.6364

Penuel, B., & Roschell, J. (1999). *Designing Learning: Cognitive Science Principles for the Innovative Organization* (Tech. No. 10099). . doi:10.13140/RG.2.2.11692.97920

Peske, H. G., & Haycock, K. (2006). *Teaching inequality: How poor and minority students are short-changed on teacher quality: A report and recommendations by the Education Trust*. Education Trust.

Petrov, P., & Atanasova, T. (2020). The Effect of Augmented Reality on Students' Learning Performance in Stem Education. *Information (Basel)*, *11*(4), 209. doi:10.3390/info11040209

Pillai, A. S., & Mathew, P. S. (2019). Impact of virtual reality in Healthcare: A Review. In Virtual and Augmented Reality in Mental Health Treatment (pp. 17-31). IGI Global. .

Pisa-Schock. (2002). Nach dem pladoyer für eine bildungsreform pisa schock. Hamburg: Hrsg: Peter Müler, Hoffmann und Campe Verlag GmbH.

Poupyrev, I., Berry, R., Billinghurst, M. K. H., Nakao, K., Baldwin, L., & Kurumisawa, J. (2001). Augmented reality interface for electronic music performance. *9th International Conference on Human-Computer Interaction* (pp. 805-808). New Orleans, USA: Lawrence Erlbaum.

Powell, A., Farrar, E., & Cohen, D. (1985). *The shopping mall high school: Winners and losers in the educational marketplace*. Houghton Mifflin.

Prentice, D. A., & Miller, D. T. (1992). When small effects are impressive. *Psychological Bulletin*, *12*(1), 160–164. doi:10.1037/0033-2909.112.1.160

Queiroz, A. C. M., Kamarainen, A. M., Preston, N. D., & da Silva Leme, M. I. (2018). Immersive virtual environments and climate change engagement. *iLRN 2018 Montana*, 153. doi:10.3217/978-3-85125-609-3-27

Quinn, F. F. (2018). Human Resource Development, Ethics, and the Social Good. *New Horizons in Adult Education and Human Resource Development*, *30*(2), 52–57. doi:10.1002/nha3.20215

Raith, A., Kamp, C., Stoiber, C., Jakl, A., & Wagner, M. (2022). Augmented Reality in Radiology for Education and Training—A Design Study. *Health Care*, *10*, 672. PMID:35455849

Raju, N. S., Drasgow, F., & Slinde, J. A. (1993). An empirical comparison of the area methods, Lord's chi-square test, and the Mantel-Haenszel technique for assessing differential item functioning. *Educational and Psychological Measurement*, *53*(2), 301–314. doi:10.1177/0013164493053002001

Raju, N., & Ellis, B. (2002). Differential item and test functioning. In F. Drasgow & N. Schmitt (Eds.), *Measuring and analyzing behavior in organizations* (pp. 156–188). Jossey-Bass.

Rambach, J., Lilligreen, G., Schäfer, A., Bankanal, R., Wiebel, A., & Stricker, D. (2021, July). A survey on applications of augmented, mixed, and virtual reality for nature and the environment. In *International Conference on Human-Computer Interaction* (pp. 653-675). Springer, Cham. 10.1007/978-3-030-77599-5_45

Randall, J., & Paek, P. (2022, March 21-23). *Taking the BS out of Bias & Sensitivity* [Conference presentation]. ATP Innovations in Testing 2022, Orlando, FL, United States.

Rani, S., Kumar, R., & Maharana, P. (2022). Climate Change, Its Impacts, and Sustainability Issues in the Indian Himalaya: An Introduction. In *Climate Change* (pp. 1–27). Springer. doi:10.1007/978-3-030-92782-0_1

Reid, N. (2000). The presentation of chemistry logically driven or applications-led? *Chemistry Education: Research and Practice in Europe*, *1*(3), 381–392.

Relles, S., & Tierney, G. (2013). Understanding the writing habits of tomorrow's students: Technology and college readiness. *The Journal of Higher Education*, *84*(4), 477–505.

Renner, J. W. (1982). The power of purpose. *Science Education*, *66*(5), 709–716. doi:10.1002ce.3730660507

Ricart, S., Villar-Navascués, R. A., Hernández-Hernández, M., Rico-Amorós, A. M., Olcina-Cantos, J., & Moltó-Mantero, E. (2021). Extending natural limits to address water scarcity? The role of non-conventional water fluxes in climate change adaptation capacity: A review. *Sustainability*, *13*(5), 2473. doi:10.3390u13052473

Riva, G., Gutiérrez-Maldonado, J., & Wiederhold, B. K. (2016). *Virtual worlds versus real body: virtual reality meets eating and weight disorders*. PMC.

Riva, G., Brenda, K., Mantovani, W., & Mantovani, F. (2019). Neuroscience of virtual reality: From virtual exposure to embodied medicine. *Cyberpsychology, Behavior, and Social Networking*, *22*(1), 82–96. doi:10.1089/cyber.2017.29099. gri PMID:30183347

Riva, G., Mantovani, F., Capideville, C. S., Preziosa, A., Morganti, F., Villani, D., Gaggioli, A., Botella, C., & Alcañiz, M. (2007). Affective interactions using virtual reality: The link between presence and emotions. *Cyberpsychology & Behavior*, *10*(1), 45–56. doi:10.1089/cpb.2006.9993 PMID:17305448

Rizzo, A., Shilling, R., Forbell, E., Scherer, S., Gratch, J., & Morency, L. P. (2016). Autonomous virtual human agents for healthcare information support and clinical interviewing. In Artificial intelligence in behavioral and mental health care (pp. 53-79). Academic Press. .

Roksa, J., & Carlos Calcagno, J. (2010). Catching up in community colleges: Academic preparation and transfer to four-year institutions. *Teachers College Record*, *112*(1), 261–288. doi:10.1177/016146811011200103

Rose, M. (1983). Remedial writing courses: A critique and a proposal. *College English*, *45*(2), 109–128. doi:10.2307/377219

Rose, M. (1990). *Lives on the Boundary*. Penguin Books.

Rose, S. K., & Weiser, I. (1999). *The writing program administrator as researcher*. Boynton/Cook.

Rose, S. K., & Weiser, I. (2002). *The writing program administrator as theorist*. Boynton/Cook.

Rose, T., Nam, C. S., & Chen, K. B. (2018). Immersion of virtual reality for rehabilitation- Review. *Applied Ergonomics*, *69*, 153–161. doi:10.1016/j.apergo.2018.01.009 PMID:29477323

Rossett, A. (1995). Needs assessment. *Instructional technology: Past, present, and future*, 183-196.

Rothstein, S. M. (2015). Scaling the number of STEM professionals. In S. T. E. Mconnector (Ed.), *Advancing a jobs-driven economy: Higher education and business partnerships lead the way*. Morgan James Publishing.

Rousseau, J. J. (2009). *Discourse on the Arts and Sciences*. University of Adelaide Library. https://www.academia.edu/download/61519660/5018_Rousseau_Discourse_on_the_Arts_and_Sciences20191215-95479-hstkne.pdf

Roussos, L. A., & Stout, W. F. (1996). Simulation studies of the effects of small sample size and studied item parameters on SIBTEST and Mantel-Haenszel Type I error performance. *Journal of Educational Measurement*, *33*(2), 215–230. doi:10.1111/j.1745-3984.1996.tb00490.x

Ruben, B. D., DeLisi, R., & Gigliotti, R. A. (2018). Academic Leadership Development Programs: Conceptual Foundations, Structural and Pedagogical Components, and Operational Considerations. *Journal of Leadership Education*, *17*(3), 241–254. doi:10.12806/V17/I3/A5

Rubin, B. D. (2016). *Excellence in Higher Education Guide: A Framework for the Design, Assessment, and Continuing Improvement of Institutions, Departments, and Programs* (8th ed.). Stylus Publishing.

Rule, A. C. (2006). *The components of authentic learning*. Digital Library. https://digitallibrary.oswego.edu/SUOS000026/00001

Rule, A. C. (2006). Editorial: The Components of Authentic Learning. *Journal of Authentic Learning, 3*(1), 1–10.

Sanchez-Nunez, M. T., Patti, J., & Holzer, A. (2015). Effectiveness of a Leadership Development Program That Incorporates Social and Emotional Intelligence for Aspiring School Leaders. *Journal of Educational Issues, 1*(1), 64–84. doi:10.5296/jei.v1i1.7443

Sapio, D. (2020, March 2). *10 principles for ethical UX designs.* UX Collective.https://uxdesign.cc/10-principles-for-ethical-ux-designs-21f af5ab243d

Sato, Y., Nakamoto, M., Tamaki, Y., Sasama, T., Sakita, I., Nakajima, Y., Monden, M., & Tamura, S. (1998). Image guidance of breast cancer surgery using 3 -D ultrasound images and augmented reality visualization. *IEEE Transactions on Medical Imaging, 17*(5), 681–693. doi:10.1109/42.736019 PMID:9874292

Sauer, F., Khamene, A., Bascle, B., Schinunang, L., Wenzel, F., & Vogt, S. (2001). Augmented reality visualization of ultrasound images: system description, calibration, and features. In *Augmented Reality, 2001. Proceedings. IEEE and ACM International Symposium on* (pp. 30-39). IEEE. 10.1109/ISAR.2001.970513

Savari, M., Zhoolideh, M., & Khosravipour, B. (2021). Explaining pro-environmental behavior of farmers: A case of rural Iran. *Current Psychology (New Brunswick, N.J.),* 1–19. doi:10.100712144-021-02093-9

Schöne, B., Kisker, J., Sylvester, R. S., Radtke, E. L., & Gruber, T. (2021). Library for universal virtual reality experiments (luVRe): A standardized immersive 3D/360 picture and video database for VR-based research. *Current Psychology (New Brunswick, N.J.),* 1–19. doi:10.100712144-021-01841-1

Schott, C. (2017). Virtual fieldtrips and climate change education for tourism students. *Journal of Hospitality, Leisure, Sport and Tourism Education, 21,* 13–22. doi:10.1016/j.jhlste.2017.05.002

Schuldt, J. P., Mccomas, K. A., & Byrne, S. E. (2016). Communicating about ocean health: Theoretical and practical considerations. *Philosophical Transactions of the Royal Society of London. Series B, Biological Sciences, 371*(1689), 1–9. doi:10.1098/rstb.2015.0214 PMID:26880833

Schumacher, D. J., Englander, R., & Carraccio, C. (2013). Developing the master learner: Applying learning theory to the learner, the teacher, and the learning environment. *Academic Medicine, 88*(11), 1635–1645. doi:10.1097/ACM.0b013e3182a6e8f8 PMID:24072107

Scurati, G. W., Bertoni, M., Graziosi, S., & Ferrise, F. (2021). Exploring the use of virtual reality to support environmentally sustainable behavior: A framework to design experiences. *Sustainability, 13*(2), 943. doi:10.3390u13020943

Scurati, G. W., & Ferrise, F. (2020). Looking into a future which hopefully will not become reality: How computer graphics can impact our behavior—A study of the potential of VR. *IEEE Computer Graphics and Applications, 40*(5), 82–88. doi:10.1109/MCG.2020.3004276 PMID:32833623

Seo, B. K., Kim, K., & Park, J. I. (2010). Augmented reality-based on-site tour guide: a study in Gyeongbokgung. *Asian Conference on Computer Vision* (pp. 276-285). Springer.

Shafer, G. (2007). Dialects, gender, and the writing class. *Teaching English in the Two-Year College, 35*(2), 169–178.

Shaughnessy, M. P. (1977). *Errors and expectations: A guide for the teacher of basic writing.* Oxford University Press.

Shealy, R., & Stout, W. (1993). A model-based standardization approach that separate true bias/DIF form group ability differences and detects test bias/DTF as well as item bias/DIF. *Psychometrika, 58*(2), 159–194. doi:10.1007/BF02294572

Sheppard, B. (2018). *The Business Value of Design*. McKinsey & Company. https://www.mckinsey.com/capabilities/mckinsey-design/our-insights/the-business-value-of-design

Sheppard, S. R., Shaw, A., Flanders, D., & Burch, S. (2008). Can visualization save the world? Lessons for landscape architects from visualizing local climate change. *Digital Design in Landscape Architecture*, 29-31.

Sheppard, S. R. (2005). Landscape visualisation and climate change: The potential for influencing perceptions and behaviour. *Environmental Science & Policy*, 8(6), 637–654. doi:10.1016/j.envsci.2005.08.002

Sherman, W. R., & Craig, A. B. (2018). *Understanding virtual reality: Interface, application, and design. Morgan Kaufmann.*

Sherman, T. M., & Kurshan, B. L. (2005). Constructing learning: Using technology to support teaching for understanding. *Learning and Leading with Technology*, 32(5), 10.

Shu, Y., Huang, Y. Z., Chang, S. H., & Chen, M. Y. (2018). Do virtual reality head-mounted displays make a difference? A comparison of presence and self-efficacy between head-mounted displays and desktop computer-facilitated virtual environments. *Virtual Reality (Waltham Cross)*, 1–10. doi:10.100710055-018-0376-x

Sireci, S. G. (2020). Standardization and UNDERSTANDardization in Education Assessment. *Educational Measurement: Issues and Practice*, 39(3), 100–105. doi:10.1111/emip.12377

Sireci, S. G., Banda, E., & Wells, C. S. (2018). Promoting valid assessment of students with disabilities and English learners. In S. N. Elliott, R. J. Kettler, P. A. Beddow, & A. Kurz (Eds.), *Handbook of Accessible Instruction and Testing Practices: Issues, Innovations, and Application* (pp. 231–246). Sage. doi:10.1007/978-3-319-71126-3_15

Sireci, S. G., & O'Riordan, M. (2020). Comparability issues in assessing individuals with disabilities. In A. Berman, E. Haertel, & J. Pellegrino (Eds.), *Comparability issues in large-scale assessment* (pp. 177–204). National Academy of Education Press.

Sireci, S. G., & Rios, J. A. (2013). Decisions that make a difference in detecting differential item functioning. *Educational Research and Evaluation*, 19(2-3), 2–3, 170–187. doi:10.1080/13803611.2013.767621

Slater, M. (2009). Place illusion and plausibility can lead to realistic behavior in immersive virtual environments. *Philosophical Transactions of the Royal Society of London. Series B, Biological Sciences*, 364(1535), 3549–3557. doi:10.1098/rstb.2009.0138 PMID:19884149

Slater, M. (2018). Immersion and the illusion of presence in virtual reality. *British Journal of Psychology*, 109(3), 431–433. doi:10.1111/bjop.12305 PMID:29781508

Slater, M., & Wilbur, S. (1997). A framework for immersive virtual environments (FIVE): Speculations on the role of presence in virtual environments. *Presence (Cambridge, Mass.)*, 6(6), 603–616. doi:10.1162/pres.1997.6.6.603

Slocum-Gori, S. L., & Zumbo, B. D. (2011). Assessing the unidimensionality of psychological scales: Using multiple criteria from factor analysis. *Social Indicators Research*, 102(3), 443–461. doi:10.100711205-010-9682-8

Snelson, C., & Hsu, Y. C. (2020). Educational 360-degree videos in virtual reality: A scoping review of the emerging research. *TechTrends*, 64(3), 404–412. doi:10.100711528-019-00474-3

Sonnett, J. (2022). Climate change risks and global warming dangers: A field analysis of online US news media. *Environmental Sociology*, 8(1), 41–51. doi:10.1080/23251042.2021.1960098

Soto-Gomes. (2020). The challenge of engaging financially stressed students during a pandemic. *EdSurge* https://www.edsurge.com/news/2020-06-09-it-s-as-if-they-just-disappeared-the-challenge-of-engaging-financially-stressed-students-during-a-pandemic

Sowcik, M., Benge, M., & Niewoehner-Green, J. (2018). A Practical Solution to Developing County Extension Director's Leadership Skills: Exploring the Design, Delivery and Evaluation of an Online Leadership Development Program. *Journal of Agricultural Education, 59*(3), 139–153. doi:10.5032/jae.2018.03139

Sözbilir, M., Sadi, S., Kutu, H. & Yıldırım, A. (2007). *Kimya eğitiminde içeriğe/bağlama dayalı (context-based) öğretim yaklaşimi ve dünyadaki uygulamaları*, I. Ulusal Kimya Eğitimi Kongresi, 20-22 Haziran 2007.

Spearman, M., & Eckhoff, A. (2012). Teaching young learners about sustainability. *Childhood Education, 88*(6), 354–359. doi:10.1080/00094056.2012.741476

Spiro, R. J., Feltovich, P. J., Jacobson, M. J., & Coulson, R. L. (1991). Cognitive flexibility, constructivism, and hypertext: Random access instruction for advanced knowledge acquisition in ill-structured domains. *Educational Technology*, (May), 24–33.

Staton, M. (2022) A Guide to Rethinking Education After Pandemic. *Edsurge*. https://www.edsurge.com/news/2022-09-10-a-guide-to-rethinking-education-after-pandemic

Stegemann, T., Geretsegger, M., Phan Quoc, E., Riedl, H., & Smetana, M. (2019). Music Therapy and Other Music-Based Interventions in Pediatric Health Care: An Overview. *Medicines (Basel, Switzerland), 6*(1), 25. doi:10.3390/medicines6010025 PMID:30769834

Stokes, A., Magnier, K., & Weaver, R. (2011). What is the use of fieldwork? Conceptions of students and staff in geography and geology. *Journal of Geography in Higher Education, 35*(01), 121–141. doi:10.1080/03098265.2010.487203

Struyven, K., Dochy, F., Janssens, S., Schelfhout, W., & Gielen, S. (2006). The overall effects of end-of-course assessment on student performance: A comparison between multiple-choice testing, peer assessments, case-based assessment, and portfolio assessment. *Studies in Educational Evaluation, 32*(3), 202–222. doi:10.1016/j.stueduc.2006.08.002

Sudarshan, A. (2018, December 22). 'Half gods' review: The book as machine. *The Hindu*. https://www.thehindu.com/books/half-gods-the-book-as-machine/article25796704.ece

Sullivan, P., & Nielson, D. (2013). "Ability to benefit": Making forward-looking decisions about our most underprepared students. *College English, 75*(3), 319–343.

Swaminathan, H., & Rogers, H. J. (1990). Detecting differential item functioning using logistic regression procedures. *Journal of Educational Measurement, 27*(4), 361–370. doi:10.1111/j.1745-3984.1990.tb00754.x

Switzer, T. R. (2000). Looking in the mirror: Becoming an effective follower. *Library Mosaics, 11*(6), 8–10.

Tang, T., & Bhamra, T. A. (2008). Changing energy consumption behaviour through sustainable product design. *In: International design conference – design 2008*. Dubrovnik, Croatia.

Taylor, B. (2014). How the 'Married Life' Opener Elevates 'Up' to Animation's Greatest Heights. *Rotoscopers*. https://www.rotoscopers.com/2014/05/06/how-the-married-life-opener-elevates-up-to-animations-greatest-heights/

Taylor, T. (2009). Writing program administration at the two-year college: Ghosts in the machine. *WPA. Writing Program Administration, 32*(3), 120–139.

Terwel, J. (1999). Constructivism and its implications for curriculum theory and practice. *Journal of Curriculum Studies, 31*(2), 195–199. doi:10.1080/002202799183223

Thissen, D., Steinberg, L., & Wainer, H. (1993). Detection of differential item functioning using the parameters of item response models. In P. Holland & Wainer (Eds.), Differential Item Functioning (pp. 67-113). Hillsdale, NJ: Lawrence Erlbaum Associates.

Thøgersen, J. (2009). The motivational roots of norms for environmentally responsible behavior. *Basic and Applied Social Psychology, 31*(4), 348–362. doi:10.1080/01973530903317144

Thomas, R. G., William John, N., & Delieu, J. M. (2010). Augmented reality for anatomical education. *Journal of Visual Communication in Medicine, 33*(1), 6–15. doi:10.3109/17453050903557359 PMID:20297908

Tinberg, H. B. (1997). *Border talk: Writing and knowing in the two-year college.* National Council of Teachers of English.

Tinwell, A. (2014). *The Uncanny Valley in Games and Animation.* Taylor & Francis. doi:10.1201/b17830

Trail, B. A. (2022). *Twice-Exceptional Gifted Children: Understanding, Teaching, and Counseling Gifted Students* (2nd ed.). Routledge., doi:10.4324/9781003261216

Tran, L. U. (2007). Teaching science in museums: The pedagogy and goals of museum educators. *Science education, 91*(2), 278–297. doi:10.1002ce.20193

Trevors, J. T. (2007). Environmental education. *Water, Air, and Soil Pollution, 180*(1). doi:10.1023/A:1023647520796

Tubik. (2017, May 25). *Information architecture. Basics for designers.* UX Planet. https://uxplanet.org/information-architecture-basics-for-designers-b5d43df62e20

Tukker, A., & Jansen, B. (2006). Environmental impacts of products: A detailed review of studies. *Journal of Industrial Ecology, 10*(3), 159–182. doi:10.1162/jiec.2006.10.3.159

UNESCO. (1978). *Intergovernmental conference on environmental education: Tbilisi (USSR), 14-26 October 1977. Final Report.* Paris: UNESCO.

United Nations Environment Program [UNEP] (2007). *UNEP 2007 annual report.* UNEP. https://wedocs.unep.org/handle/20.500.11822/7647

Vaidya, M. (2020, September 5). *Accessibility: Guidelines for information architecture, UX design, and visual design.* IBM Design.https://medium.com/design-ibm/accessibility-guidelines-for-information-architecture-ux-design-and-visual-design-5ae33ed1d52d

Van Merrienboer, J. G., & Kirschner, P. (2013). *Ten Steps to Complex Learning.* Routledge.

Varela-Candamio, L., Novo-Corti, I., & García-Álvarez, M. T. (2018). The importance of environmental education in the determinants of green behavior: A meta-analysis approach. *Journal of Cleaner Production, 170,* 1565–1578. doi:10.1016/j.jclepro.2017.09.214

Velev, D., & Zlateva, P. (2017). Virtual reality challenges education and training. International. *Compass (Eltham), 3*(1), 33–37. doi:10.18178/ijlt.3.1.33-37

Vidal-Balea, A., Blanco-Novoa, Ó., Fraga-Lamas, P., & Fernández-Caramés, T. (2021). Developing the Next Generation of Augmented Reality Games for Pediatric Healthcare: An Open-Source Collaborative Framework Based on ARCore for Implementing Teaching, Training and Monitoring Applications. *Sensors (Basel)*, *21*(5), 1865. doi:10.339021051865 PMID:33800070

Viscione, I. (2019). Augmented reality for learning in distance education: The case of e-sports. *Journal of Physical Education and Sport*, *19*, 2047–2050.

Viveiros, L. C., Pereira, A. I., Peroni, J. V., Fachada, I., & Gonçalves, E. (2021). Natureza virtual: Enhancing ecosystem awareness by using virtual reality in educational tourism. In *Augmented Reality and Virtual Reality* (pp. 291–302). Springer., doi:10.1007/978-3-030-68086-2_22

Vugec, D. S., Vuksic, V. B., Bach, M. P., Jaklic, J., & Stemberger, M. I. (2020). Business Intelligence and Organizational Performance: The Role of Alignment with Business Process Management. *Business Process Management Journal*, *26*(6), 1709–1730. doi:10.1108/BPMJ-08-2019-0342

Waldron, C. (2020). Design Products for the End User, Not the Stakeholders. *Medium*. uxdesign.cc/design-products-for-the-end-user-not-the-stakeholders-6171695b6c78.

Wals, A. E., Brody, M., Dillon, J., & Stevenson, R. B. (2014). Convergence between science and environmental education. *Science*, *344*(6184), 583–584. doi:10.1126cience.1250515 PMID:24812386

Wardle, E. (2009). "Mutt genres" and the goal of FYC: Can we help students write the genres of the university? *College Composition and Communication*, *60*(4), 765–789.

Wardle, E., & Downs, D. (2007). Teaching about writing, righting misconceptions: (Re)envisioning "first-year composition" as "introduction to writing studies.". *College Composition and Communication*, *58*(4), 552–584.

Wardle, E., & Downs, D. (2014). *Writing about writing: A college reader*. Bedford/St. Martin's.

Webb-Sunderhaus, S., & Amidon, S. (2011). "The *kairotic* moment: Pragmatic revision of basic writing instruction at Indiana University-Purdue University Fort Wayne." *Composition Forum 23*, https://www.compositionforum.com/issue/23/ipfw-revision.php

Weil, S. (1951). *Waiting for God*. Fontana Books.

Weisberger, R. (2005). Community colleges and class: A short history. *Teaching English in the Two-Year College*, *33*(2), 127–141.

Wei, Y. S., O'Neill, H., & Zhou, N. (2020). How Does Perceived Integrity in Leadership Matter to Firms in a Transitional Economy? *Journal of Business Ethics*, *167*(4), 623–641. doi:10.100710551-019-04168-x

Weng, N. G., Bee, O. Y., Yew, L. H., & Hsia, T. E. (2016). An augmented reality system for biology science education in Malaysia. *International Journal of Innovative Computing*, *6*(2), 8–13.

Western Governors University Academic Programs. (2019). *Item development handbook*. WGU.

Western Governors University. (2022) *How to DE&I at WGU*. WGU. https://intranet.wgu.edu/diversity_inclusion

Western Governors University. (2022). *Diversity equity and inclusion in learning design*. WGU. https://westerngovernorsuniversity.sharepoint.com/sites/DesignDevDEI/SitePages/Our-Project.aspx

Whitehead, A. N. (1929). *The aims of education & other essays*. Macmillan.

Wiberg, M. (2009). Differential item functioning in mastery tests: A comparison of three methods using real data. *International Journal of Testing, 9*(1), 41–59. doi:10.1080/15305050902733455

Wilens, T. E., & Spencer, T. J. (2010, September). Understanding attention-deficit/hyperactivity disorder from childhood to adulthood. *Postgraduate Medicine, 122*(5), 97–109. https://doi.com/10.3810/pgm.2010.09.2206. doi:10.3810/pgm.2010.09.2206 PMID:20861593

Willaert, W. I., Aggarwal, R., Van Herzeele, I., Cheshire, N. J., & Vermassen, F. E. (2012). Recent advancements in medical simulation: Patient-specific virtual reality simulation. *World Journal of Surgery, 36*(7), 1703–1712. doi:10.100700268-012-1489-0 PMID:22532308

William, D. (2011). Assessment for learning? [PDF in files]. *Studies in Educational Evaluation, 37*(1), 3–14. doi:10.1016/j.stueduc.2011.03.001 PMID:22114905

Wilson, R. A. (1994). At the early childhood level. *Day Care and Early Education, 22*(2), 23–25. doi:10.1007/BF02361329

Winebrenner, S. (2018). How we can recognize and teach twice- or multi-exceptional students. In Oxford Scholarship Online. doi:10.1093/oso/9780190645472.003.0007

Witham, K., Malcom-Piqueux, L. E., Dowd, A. C., & Bensimon, E. M. (2015). *America's unmet promise: The imperative for equity in higher education.* Association of American Colleges and Universities.

Withanage, C., Höltta-Otto, K., Otto, K., & Wood, K. (2016). Design for sustainable use of appliances: A framework based on user behavior observations. *Journal of Mechanical Design, 138*(10), 101102. doi:10.1115/1.4034084

Wolf, M., & Bowers, P. (1999). The double-deficit hypothesis for the developmental dyslexia. *Journal of Educational Psychology, 91*(3), 415–438. doi:10.1037/0022-0663.91.3.415

Woodrow, H. (1927). The effect of type of training upon transference. *Journal of Educational Psychology, 18*(3), 159–172. doi:10.1037/h0071868

World Health Organization. (2021). *Ageing.* https://www.who.int/health-topics/ageing#tab=tab_1

Wynes, S., & Nicholas, K. A. (2017). The climate mitigation gap: Education and government recommendations miss the most effective individual actions. *Environmental Research Letters, 12*(7), 074024. doi:10.1088/1748-9326/aa7541

Yablonski, J. (2020). *Laws of UX: Using psychology to design better products & services.* O'Reilly Media.

Yager, R. (1991). The constructivist learning model: Towards real reform in science education. *Science Teacher (Normal, Ill.), 58*(6), 53–57.

Yam, H. (2005). What is contextual learning and teaching in physics. *Retrieved,* (November), 4.

Yancey, K., Robertson, L., & Taczak, K. (2014). *Writing across contexts: Transfer, composition, and sites of writing.* Utah State University Press. doi:10.2307/j.ctt6wrr95

Yapici, I. Ü., & Karakoyun, F. (2021). Using Augmented Reality in Biology Teaching. *Malaysian Online Journal of Educational Technology, 9*(3), 40–51. doi:10.52380/mojet.2021.9.3.286

Yates, D., & Boddison, A. (2020). *The School Handbook for Dual and Multiple Exceptionality: High Learning Potential with Special Educational Needs or Disabilities.* Routledge. doi:10.4324/9780429352041

Yeşim, Ö., & Baştuğ, Ö. (2016). A comparison of four differential item functioning procedures in the presence of multidimensionality. *Educational Research Review, 11*(13), 1251–1261.

Yılmaz, H., & Çavaş, P. H. (2006). 4-E Öğrenme döngüsü yönteminin öğrencilerin elektrik konusunu anlamalarina olan etkisi. *Türk Fen Eğitimi Dergisi*, *3*(1), 2–18.

Yoder, B. (2014). Engineering by the numbers. *American Society for Engineering Education*. https://www.asee.org/papers-and-publications/publications/collegeprofiles/14EngineeringbytheNumbersPart1.pdf

Yücel, A. S. (2006). E-learning approach in teacher training. *Turkish Online Journal of Distance Education*, *7*(4), 123–132.

Yücel, A. S., & Koçak, C. (2010). Evaluation of the basic technology competency of the teacher's candidate according to the various variables. *2nd World Conference on Educational Sciences (WCES-2010)*, İstanbul, Turkey.

Zeiske, N., Venhoeven, L., Steg, L., & van der Werff, E. (2021). The normative route to a sustainable future: Examining children's environmental values, identity, and personal norms to conserve energy. *Environment and Behavior*, *53*(10), 1118–1139. doi:10.1177/0013916520950266

Zhai, M., & Wolff, H. (2021). Air pollution and urban road transport: Evidence from the world's largest low-emission zone in London. *Environmental Economics and Policy Studies*, *23*(4), 721–748. doi:10.100710018-021-00307-9

Zhang, L., Ruiz-Menjivar, J., Luo, B., Liang, Z., & Swisher, M. E. (2020). Predicting climate change mitigation and adaptation behaviors in agricultural production: A comparison of the theory of planned behavior and the Value-Belief-Norm Theory. *Journal of Environmental Psychology*, *68*, 101408. doi:10.1016/j.jenvp.2020.101408

Zhang, X., Luo, L., & Skitmore, M. (2015). Household carbon emission research: An analytical review of measurement, influencing factors and mitigation prospects. *Journal of Cleaner Production*, *103*, 873–883. doi:10.1016/j.jclepro.2015.04.024

Zikas, P., Protopsaltis, A., Lydatakis, N., Kentros, M., Geronikolakis, S., Kateros, S., Kamarianakis, M., Evangelou, G., Filippidis, A., Grigoriou, E., Angelis, D., Tamiolakis, M., Dodis, M., Kokiadis, G., Petropoulos, J., Pateraki, M., & Papagiannakis, G. (2022). MAGES 4.0: Accelerating the world's transition to VR training and democratizing the authoring of the medical metaverse. *ORamaVR: Internal Technical Report*.

Zikas, P., Kamarianakis, M., Kartsonaki, I., Lydatakis, N., Kateros, S., Kentros, M., Geronikolakis, E., Evangelou, G., Catilo, P. A., & Papagiannakis, G. (2021). Covid-19 VR Strikes Back: Innovative medical VR training. In *ACM SIGGRAPH 2021 Immersive Pavilion (SIGGRAPH' 21)* (p. 202). Association for Computing Machinery. doi:10.1145/3450615.3464546

Zikas, P., Papagiannakis, G., Lydatakis, N., Kateros, S., Ntoa, S., Adami, I., & Stephanidis, C. (2020). Immersive visual scripting based on VR software design patterns for experiential training. *The Visual Computer*, *36*(10-12), 1965–1977. doi:10.100700371-020-01919-0

Zlatkin-Troitschanskaia, O., & Pant, H. A. (2016). Measurement advances and challenges in competency assessment in higher education. *Journal of Educational Measurement*, *53*(3), 253–264. doi:10.1111/jedm.12118

Zumbo, B. D. (1999). A Handbook on the Theory and Methods of Differential Item Functioning (DIF): Logistic Regression Modeling as a Unitary Framework for Binary and Likert-Type (Ordinal) Item Scores. Ottawa, Canada: Directorate of Human Resources Research and Evaluation, Department of National Defense.

Zwick, R. (2012). *A review of ETS differential item functioning assessment procedures: Flagging rules, minimum sample size requirements, and criterion refinement*. Educational Testing Service.

Zwick, R., Donoghue, J. R., & Grima, A. (1993). Assessing differential item functioning in performance tests. *ETS Research Report Series*, *1993*(1), i-42. doi:10.1002/j.2333-8504.1993.tb01525.x

About the Contributors

Jason Braun has written for, reported for, or been featured in The Nashville City Paper, Jane Friedman's blog, The Evergreen Review, The Riverfront Times, The Chronicle of Higher Education, 88.1 KDHX, and elsewhere. When he's not writing, he's teaching English or doing instructional design. He has a master's degree in English and in Educational Technology.(485ec432-8438-4e60-bd2e-99fbbe34d387)

Goran Trajkovski, Ph.D. is a lifelong learner with a passion for innovation in higher education and technology. With over 30 years of experience in leadership roles at institutions such as Western Governors University, Visa Inc., and Marian University, Dr. Trajkovski has designed and launched numerous academic products in the computing and business disciplines for institutions across the United States. With interests spanning from data-driven decision-making to curriculum and customer learning experience design and development, Dr. Trajkovski has published over 300 works, including research papers and books, on topics such as diversity in IT education, cognitive and developmental robotics, and learning analytics. Numerous professional organizations have recognized his contributions. He remains committed to helping students and colleagues succeed in their academic and professional pursuits. (30b67d48-2735-4c8c-aa22-ffb8157073b3)

Adam al-Sirgany is an Egyptian-American literary, musical, and visual artist, born and raised in the Driftless Midwest. His work has appeared in diverse venues—from Journeys Shoes advertisements to various international literary magazines, to advocacy publications for the National Coalition for the Homeless. He serves as an Acquisitions and Developmental Editor for Santa Fe Writers Project, an Associate Poetry Editor of the Fairy Tale Review, and the Executive Director of the Iowa-based literary arts and education 501(c)(3) organization 1-Week Critique (1WC): 1weekcritique.com. Follow Adam at adamalsirgany.com.(604cdf4c-4cc5-46b7-b342-0db68e5f26a6)

Canan Koçak Altundağ is currently an Associate Professor in the Department of Mathematics and Science Education at Hacettepe University, Ankara, Turkey. Dr. Altundağ received B.Sc., M.Sc., and Ph.D. degree from the Faculty of Education at Hacettepe Univer-sity. Her research interests include daily life chemistry, context based learning and chemistry education. She has teaching experience of more than 10 years in the area of chemistry education. Dr. Altundağ published a number of papers in preferred Journals and participated in a range of conferences.(ca677b70-d1c7-43a2-af3e-6fe1e16df822)

Deniz Atal has a Ph.D. degree in the educational technology research area. Dr. Atal is a research assistant in the Faculty of Education Science at Ankara University, Turkey. Dr. Atal was a visiting scholar at Texas State University, USA in 2018 and at Leiden University in the Netherlands in 2022 to conduct research about professional identity, and virtual reality technology in teacher education. Her current research interests are teacher education, professional development, teacher identity, ICT education, and virtual reality in teacher education. She has published several articles and book chapters on these topics in both national and international refereed journals. Also, she has conducted a national project on virtual reality technology to enhance preservice teachers' digital teaching competency.(d42772bf-4c7b-4758-b132-869117b75d09)

Hüseyin Ateş is a researcher working in the department of science education at Kırşehir Ahi Evran University. He received his Ph.D. in elementary education from Middle East Technical University. His work spans the fields of science education, teacher education, environmental education, education for sustainable development, and educational technology. He is interested in investigating to what extent psychological factors influence teachers' behaviors with regard to the technology-enhanced teaching process, pro-environmental behaviors, and healthy eating. He is also interested in review studies. (94bf1c19-26e9-4c3f-b71f-5a3fead23045)

Deepa Bura received her Bachelor of Engineering in Information Technology in 2002 from Vaish College of Engineering affiliated to Maharishi Dayanand University Rohtak, and Master of Technology in Information Technology in 2009 from University School of Information Technology affiliated to Guru Gobind Singh Indraprastha University, Delhi. She has completed her Ph.D Thesis in 2018 from Uttarakhand Technical University in the field of Software Engineering. She has 20 years of teaching experience. Presently she is working as Professor in Department of Computer Science and Engineering at Faculty of Engineering and Technology, Manav Rachna International University, Faridabad. Her area of interest includes Data Mining, Software Engineering, Cloud Computing, Soft Computing.(f5ded56f-0570-4fa2-90ae-8120947b1752)

Poonam Chahal received her Bachelor of Engineering in Information Technology in 2005 from Institute of Technology and Management affiliated to Maharishi Dayanand University Rohtak, and Master of Technology in Computer Science and Engineering in 2009 from Career Institute of Technology and Management affiliated to Maharishi Dayanand University, Rohtak. She completed her Ph.D in 2017 from YMCA University of Science and Technology in the field of Natural Language Processing. She has 17 years of teaching experience. Presently she is working as Professor in Department of Computer Science and Engineering at Faculty of Engineering and Technology, Manav Rachna International Institute of Research and Studies, Faridabad. She has published more than 40 research papers in reputed International and National Journals and Conferences. Her area of interest includes Information Retrieval, Semantic Web, Artificial Intelligence, Natural Language Processing, Soft Computing, Compiler Design. (50c01288-d699-4c98-9844-30ef27d1dc83)

Marylee Demeter received her Ed.M. in Educational Measurement, Statistics, and Program Evaluation, and MA in Educational Psychology from the Graduate School of Education at Rutgers University. She formerly served in roles as Coordinator for Student Affairs Assessment at Rutgers, Director of Assessment for Cumberland County College, and Chair of the Professional Development Committee for the Student Affairs Assessment Leaders, where she collaboratively developed the MOOC "Developing and Leading Assessment in Student Affairs." She currently serves as a Senior Assessment Developer at

Western Governors University and writes and presents widely on issues of competency-based assessment, assessment development and improvement, evidence-based best practices, and diversity, equity, and inclusion.(7545e721-a90a-445c-8af3-0af76138329d)

Nate Fisher is a cross-genre writer and journalist from Pinckneyville, Illinois. He holds an MFA in Creative Writing from the University of Idaho, where he specialized in poetry and hybrid genre work. He currently works as an education advisor and chief storyteller for Journey12, a St. Louis-based educational initiative whose goal is to tell the stories of rural Illinois high school students through a combination of digital, print, and audio-visual publications.(b15f64a2-024d-4da7-9d87-16b4ec5beebb)

Sean Gyll is a professional psychometrician and educator serving the secondary and post-secondary education markets. His primary focus is helping organizations establish strategic assessment-related partnerships with entities concerned with educational and workplace readiness. His emphasis is on the assessment value chain and its impact on learning outcomes. Sean received his Ph.D. in educational psychology and cognition and student learning from the University of Utah, where he researched cognitive skills acquisition, undetected errors in skilled cognitive performance, and priming processes in memory. He is especially interested in understanding the mental response process engaged in different types of assessments, cognitive diagnostic modeling, innovative forms, and methods of assessments, especially for social-emotional intelligence, and how all of these topics may be helpful for online, competency-based higher educational assessment.(7c728104-f136-46de-9882-0baf5465ba36)

Heather Hayes, PhD, is a psychometrician for the Colleges of Information Technology and Business at Western Governors University. She has been involved in the construction and validation of both cognitive ability and personality assessments for over 20 years. Her work has included the use of personality tests for selection testing in organizations, certification testing with the Veteran's Benefit Association. Her research centers on the use of cognitive theory and Item Response Theory to aid in the construct validation of test scores as well as to improve the test experience itself through computer adaptive testing and automatic item generation.(db3a4109-dc03-41ac-8392-76ffc1cc1396)

Megan Hudgins is an Ad Operations Project Manager and trainer with an MA in Creative Writing (SIUE) and a background in multimedia digital production. She is the author of Two of Cups Press's inaugural poetry chapbook contest winner, CRIXA (2014). She lives in St. Louis, MO, where she makes ceramic and textile art in her spare time.(97690e0a-f092-4c54-8576-563a0fe7c5f3)

Muhammed Koçer graduated from Uludağ University, Department of Science Teaching, and completed his master's degree in Technology and Environment in Chemistry Education at Hacettepe University. He currently works as a science teacher at a state school in Şanlıurfa.(4256ebb8-291b-4699-ab1c-f99264c55284)

Jessica Mannisi is a St. Louis-based curator, arts consultant, and art historian with over 15 years of experience in the museum and gallery field. She's devoted to supporting regional arts, and has worked closely with award-winning artists and organizations to elevate the local arts community. She has led the art and exhibitions programming at the Foundry Art Centre since 2020. A jack-of-all-trades in galleries and museums, her primary roles are curator of the Foundry's 3600sqft Main Galleries of rotating exhibitions and organizer of the Foundry's large-scale art events and programs, including the annual Block Party, the Grand Hall Mural Project, and the Foundry's First Friday Series. After earning her graduate degree in Museum Studies from Southern Illinois University-Edwardsville, Jessica was the assistant curator/registrar of the William and Florence Schmidt Art Center at Southwestern Illinois College in Belleville, Illinois. She followed this 8-year tenure as the assistant curator of visual art for the Angad Arts Hotel in St. Louis' Grand Center, curating the permanent collection and the Hotel's inaugural exhibition year. Prior to joining the Foundry Art Centre, Jessica was an independent consultant and the curatorial director of Houska Gallery in the Central West End, St. Louis.(c5d6b5e0-b223-470d-bb5e-32a7c00946fa)

Lucas Marshall holds an M.A. in English and a Certificate in Teaching Writing from Western Illinois University, where he taught developmental writing and College Composition I for two years. He currently serves as Content & SEO Manager at Milwaukee Tool, where he raises awareness and education about the company's SaaS product, ONE-KEY™. His work has appeared in IoT for All and Construction Executive, among others. He credits his success in web writing to learning and teaching WAW firsthand. He is also a community college graduate.(de1adc20-76b3-4186-826b-4bf7c5548eb4)

Ambika N. is a MCA, MPhil, Ph.D. in computer science. She completed her Ph.D. from Bharathiar university in the year 2015. She has 16 years of teaching experience and presently working for St.Francis College, Bangalore. She has guided BCA, MCA and M.Tech students in their projects. Her expertise includes wireless sensor network, Internet of things, cybersecurity. She gives guest lectures in her expertise. She is a reviewer of books, conferences (national/international), encyclopaedia and journals. She is advisory committee member of some conferences. She has many publications in National & international conferences, international books, national and international journals and encyclopaedias. She has some patent publications (National) in computer science division.(13da00e9-363a-47b0-a5da-4d1372d92596)

Zia Nizami is a visual journalist with a twenty-year history of shooting, editing, and producing award-winning photography and videography at the Belleville News-Democrat, ESPN, The Washington Post, and many more. In addition to current independent films in production, he frequently works creating and editing instructional films for universities.(c77ff319-7d43-4d2e-a6bd-017b96629c0c)

George Papagiannakis is a computer scientist specialized in computer graphics systems, extended reality algorithms and geometric algebra computational models. He is currently Professor of Computer Graphics at the Computer Science department of the University of Crete, Greece, associated faculty member at FORTH-ICS with the Human Computer Interaction Lab and visiting professor at the University of Geneva, Switzerland. His research interests are centered in the field of high-fidelity interactive computer graphics systems for human computer interaction, featuring embodied presence, psychomotor learning and gamification with simulated virtual humans in extended reality based on geometric algebra computational models. He is co-founder and CEO of ORamaVR, a Swiss deep-technology spatial computing medical VR startup, with the mission to accelerate world's transition to medical virtual reality training. He is the author of a Springer-Nature book on Mixed Reality and Gamification which achieved more than 77.000 downloads so far, reaching the top 25% most downloaded eBooks on Springer-Nature. He is a board member of the Computer Graphics Society (CGS) and member of the IEEE, ACM, Eurographics and SIGGRAPH professional societies. He is associate editor of the Springer Visual Computer Journal, research topic lead editor of the Frontiers in Virtual Reality Journal and evaluator/reviewer for the European Commission and several National Research Funding agencies worldwide.(44be25fc-5e57-47e0-a4bc-9997b06e552f)

David Rawson has had short stories, poems, and reviews published in various journals such as The Monarch Review, Monkeybicycle, Prick of the Spindle, and Spork. He was nominated for a Pushcart for a poem which appeared in Mixed Fruit. His journalism has appeared in the Johnston City Herald and the Carterville Courier in Southern Illinois.(0bbdee7d-8175-48d2-b480-8763d0ec9756)

Raziye Sancar received her Ph.D. in Educational Technology from Ankara University in 2019. She was engaged as a research assistant by Krşehir Ahi Evran University in 2013 and has spent the last five years working as a research assistant at the Faculty of Educational Science at Ankara University. She currently works for Krşehir Ahi Evran University's Distance Education Center. Her area of interest is the integration of technology into teacher education and professional development, including the use of digital videos, virtual reality, and other tools. She also frequently lectures and publishes on topics related to online learning.(bce30443-e352-4f81-9a34-379d2e9dd2ae)

Karen Shader is a progressive education leader, specialist in identifying needs, establishing vision, developing plans, leading initiatives, maximizing learning, and achieving results. Karen was awarded a BA in sociology from Loyola University, New Orleans and a PhD in Instructional Systems Design from Florida State University. Karen is committed developing education programs to address social issues as well as advance skills of students who desire to develop and/or advance their careers. Working with teams to develop an engaging programs that use innovative approaches and technologies is core to her work. Karen has worked in leadership roles to support healthcare education at University of Alabama at Birmingham, Academic Medical Center, Troy University, University of Tennessee Health Science Center. She currently works at Western Governors University, Leavitt School of Health.(72860f3b-3edd-43d4-ba85-c3f9ecf4466c)

Meeta Singh received her Master of Technology in Information Technology from Guru Gobind Singh Indraprastha University, New Delhi, in 2007. She completed her Ph.D. (Computer Science and Engineering) from Bhagwant University, Ajmer, in 2015 in the field of Mobile Adhoc Networks. She has 18 years of teaching experience. Presently she is working as an Assistant Professor in the Department of Computer Science and Engineering at the Faculty of Engineering and Technology, Manav Rachna International University, Faridabad. Her area of interest includes cloud computing, wireless ad-hoc network, and computer architecture.(2da4b91e-0456-4e01-934e-293e1d1b3320)

Travis Smith is a Senior Learning Experience Designer at Western Governors University. He has over ten years of experience as an educator in higher learning. Travis has a Master's degree in Instructional Technology and Learning Sciences from Utah State University. He lives in Portland, Oregon, with his partner and child.(f0d01451-460c-428e-826e-d73cfe6c1006)

Goran Trajkovski, Ph.D. is a lifelong learner with a passion for innovation in higher education and technology. With over 30 years of experience in leadership roles at institutions such as Western Governors University, Visa Inc., and Marian University, Dr. Trajkovski has designed and launched numerous academic products in the computing and business disciplines for institutions across the United States. With interests spanning from data-driven decision-making to curriculum and customer learning experience design and development, Dr. Trajkovski has published over 300 works, including research papers and books, on topics such as diversity in IT education, cognitive and developmental robotics, and learning analytics. Numerous professional organizations have recognized his contributions. He remains committed to helping students and colleagues succeed in their academic and professional pursuits.(0540e487-74a1-4283-a7ac-7f1882324610)

Jill Walker, MSML, M.Ed. is an experienced instructional designer and learning experience advocate with a passion for creating effective and engaging learning products, services, and interventions. She has a proven track record of planning, managing, and delivering training through various modalities, including virtual and in-person classrooms and online asynchronous and synchronous learning. She applies solid andragogical principles and instructional design standards to the courseware and assessments she creates, and is recognized as a mentor and leader within her teams. She is committed to student success and is a collaborative team player, serving as an advocate for learning and change management in curriculum development and project planning.(7384c53d-7c6a-409c-9e3e-4f1be713280d)

Paul Zikas is a software engineer with 7+ years of experience in AR/VR industry and academia. He earned his BSc, and MSc in Computer Science from the University of Crete specializing in computer graphics. Currently he is developing his PhD research topics at the Computer Science Department of the University of Geneva, Switzerland. As an enthusiast in Computer Graphics and Game Programming, he designed various Mixed Reality applications for educational and entertainment purposes in mobile and desktop platforms. He is deeply experienced with VR/AR custom/industrial game engines with an excellent computer graphics knowledge. He started working at ORamaVR from its establishment as a software engineer, lead developer and now the VP of engineering. In ORamaVR he is responsible for the training scenegraph, the Unity MAGES SDK and coordinating as well as developing the VR customization modules. He developed and maintained the authoring tools to create low-code VR training scenarios based on proprietary software design patterns. His visual scripting module has revolutionized the production of VR training simulations, providing a sophisticated tool to drastically speed up the content creation.(68a4716b-af8b-4f06-b86f-b253c7b216ff)s

Index

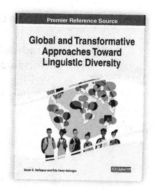

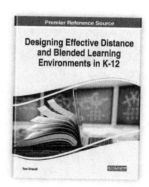

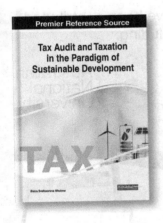

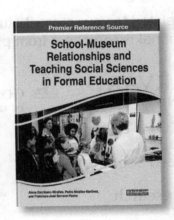
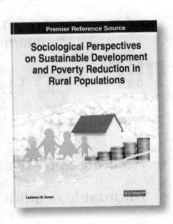

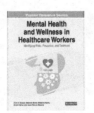

Printed in the United States
by Baker & Taylor Publisher Services